Late Prehistoric Hunter-Gatherers and Farmers of the Jornada Mogollon

Late Prehistoric Hunter-Gatherers and Farmers of the Jornada Mogollon

EDITED BY

Thomas R. Rocek and Nancy A. Kenmotsu

UNIVERSITY PRESS OF COLORADO
Denver

© 2018 by University Press of Colorado

Published by University Press of Colorado
1624 Market Street, Suite 226
PMB 39883
Denver, Colorado 80202-1559

First paperback edition 2023

ASSOCIATION of UNIVERSITY PRESSES   The University Press of Colorado is a proud member of the Association of University Presses.

The University Press of Colorado is a cooperative publishing enterprise supported, in part, by Adams State University, Colorado State University, Fort Lewis College, Metropolitan State University of Denver, University of Alaska Fairbanks, University of Colorado, University of Northern Colorado, University of Wyoming, Utah State University, and Western Colorado University.

ISBN: 978-1-60732-794-3 (cloth)
ISBN: 978-1-64642-378-1(paperback)
ISBN: 978-1-60732-795-0 (ebook)
DOI: https://doi.org/10.5876/9781607327950

Library of Congress Cataloging-in-Publication Data

Names: Rocek, Thomas R., editor. | Kenmotsu, Nancy Adele, editor.
Title: Late prehistoric hunter-gatherers and farmers of the Jornada Mogollon / edited by Thomas R. Rocek and Nancy A. Kenmotsu.
Description: Boulder : University Press of Colorado, [2018] | Includes bibliographical references and index.
Identifiers: LCCN 2018034570| ISBN 9781607327943 (cloth) | ISBN 9781646423781 (paperback) | ISBN 9781607327950 (ebook)
Subjects: LCSH: Mogollon culture. | Mogollon Indians—Antiquities. | Mogollon

Indians—Agriculture. | Agriculture, Prehistoric—Southwest, New. | Excavations (Archaeology)—Southwest, New. | Hunting and gathering societies—Southwest, New. | Indians of North America—Southwest, New—Antiquities. | Southwest, New—Antiquities.
Classification: LCC E99.M76 L28 2018 | DDC 979/.01—dc23
LC record available at https://lccn.loc.gov/2018034570

The publication of this book is supported in part by the Arizona Archaeological and Historical Society and the Center for Material Culture Studies at the University of Delaware.

Cover illustrations of petroglyphs at Three Rivers Petroglyph National Site, South of Carrizozo, New Mexico, © Joseph Sohm/Shutterstock

To Jane Holden Kelley (1928–2016),
pioneer and mentor in the Jornada and far beyond.

Contents

PART I: DIVERSITY AND CHANGE IN THE
JORNADA MOGOLLON

PART II: FARMING THE JORNADA LOWLANDS

Figures

MYLES R. MILLER, NANCY A. KENMOTSU, AND THOMAS R. ROCEK

The reissue of this volume in paperback affords us the opportunity to consider the latest developments in research in and around the Jornada Mogollon region. In the conclusion to the introductory chapter, we noted that "The last several decades have brought great progress" in Jornada research. The half decade since we wrote these words demonstrates that progress has not stopped and has brought continued and exciting new research as well as publications reporting on research from the preceding decades in multiple parts of the region. We cannot cover *all* this material here but highlight *some* of the prominent results as well as list some of the sources that those interested in recent developments in the Jornada would do well to consult. Major work has continued, particularly in the Western Jornada Lowlands (e.g., Foster and Bradley 2021; Kurota and Dello-Russo 2020; Kurota, Rodgers, et al. 2019; Kurota, Solfisburg, et al. 2019, Miller and Graves 2023, Miller, Loendorf, and Willis, et al. 2019; Miller, Willis et al. 2019; Walker and Berryman 2022) and the New Mexico portion of Jornada's Eastern Extension (e.g., Castañeda and Willis 2021, Clark and Speth 2022; Frederick 2021; Loendorf et al. 2019; Miller et al. 2021a, 2021b; Miller, Loendorf, Graves et al. 2019; Railey 2023). Some important work also adds insights regarding developments on the edges of the Sierra Blanca/ Capitan/Sacramento Highlands (e.g., Greenwald 2018, 2019; Neely and Greenwald 2019; Railey in prep.). Additional sources of Jornada research are less easily characterized geographically (e.g., Greenwald and Hewitt 2019; Greenwald et al. 2020; Kurota et al. 2022; Seltzer-Rogers 2022; Wiseman 2019). While this is by no means a complete or even systematic list, in the text that follows we briefly comment on notable features of a selected few of these recent works.

Two particularly important syntheses for researchers are the summary report of work at the Merchant site (LA 43414) and the recent summary of the "Roswell Oasis." The Merchant site is located in the far southeastern corner of New Mexico, a region explored in chapters 8, 9, 12, 13, and 14 (Miller et al. 2021a). This research, like much of the recent work in the Eastern Extension area, was funded by the Carlsbad Field Office of the Bureau of Land Management through the Permian Basin Programmatic Agreement that is mentioned in chapter 2. The Merchant site dates to a poorly understood period in far southeastern New Mexico known as the Ochoa phase (AD 1300–1450). The work consisted of two fieldwork seasons. The initial fieldwork (Miller et al. 2016; included in the first issue of this book) was mostly remedial, designed to evaluate the condition and data potential of the site. The subsequent 2019 field season explored several unresolved issues. The architecture and construction details of the rooms and roomblocks were clarified through exposure of an intact section of contiguous jacal rooms, and additional excavations were conducted in midden deposits surrounding the roomblocks. Excavations confirmed that the pueblo settlement is extensive, consisting of at least 60 rooms and a kiva. Other excavations in the suspected gridded agricultural fields located north of the roomblock confirmed that the patterned distributions of caliche were the remnants of gridded fields. Analysis of the lithic and ceramic assemblages revealed unexpected patterns of resource procurement, production, and distribution, including the identification of large quantities of chipped stone material obtained from sources in central Texas and the Texas Panhandle. By contrast, virtually all the pottery at the site, Ochoa Indented Corrugated ware, appears to have been made and used locally rather than traded with other communities. Statistical modeling and analysis of radiocarbon dates established that the settlement dates to the 1300s.

The cumulative and combined results of the two seasons of excavations at Merchant present a fascinating test case for the study of migration, social interaction, and how new social identities are formed. Additional research on other Ochoa phase sites in southeastern New Mexico and on regional geomorphology, also funded by the Permian Basin Programmatic Agreement (Frederick 2021; Miller et al. 2021a, 2021b), have helped to put the Merchant site in its larger context and, Castañeda and Willis (2021) have examined ground bedrock depressions around Merchant and Custer Mountain (LA 121668), another village site the same region. The manner in which the Plains hunters and pueblo agriculturalists interacted—whether symbiotically through exchange, by merging and creating new expressions of ethnicity and identity, or through conflict and warfare—is an important and fascinating topic of investigation for the history of the Southwest and Plains and for broader anthropological topics as well. Of further significance, such events took place on the Southern Plains as early as the fourteenth century.

The second major publication adds to the literature on substantial pueblo occupations in the Roswell Oasis, an area briefly mentioned in this volume, particularly in chapters 1 and 2. Near Roswell, a series of major aggregated sites, including surface pueblos that resemble sites of the El Paso phase in the Western Jornada Lowlands as well as the Lincoln phase in the Highlands to the west of Roswell, developed in a rapid sequence during the mid-thirteenth to mid-fifteenth century of the current era. Clark and Speth (2022) provide a welcome update on research at the two substantial surface pueblos excavated there, showing diverse architectural patterns (starting with sunken floored architecture, similar to slightly earlier aggregated non-pueblo sites in the area, followed by more surface architecture). The pueblo occupation sequence began with the Henderson site (LA 1549) and continued to Bloom Mound (LA 2528). Henderson and possibly Bloom have distinct early and later temporal components, with the final occupation at Bloom Mound culminating in violence, as indicated by unburied and burned human remains. While Henderson had been previously noted for its substantial size (ca. 70 or possibly more rooms), Bloom proved larger than originally thought; despite heavy looting and damage, enough material remained to show that it included at least 20–25 rooms as well as a large central subterranean chamber. Both Henderson and Bloom show strong indications of substantial maize consumption. Bison, probably from seasonal hunting on the Plains to the east, was also abundant at Henderson, especially from its later occupation. Subsequently, bison hunting dropped dramatically in the Bloom Mound occupation. Virtually all ceramics at both sites appear to have been imported, primarily from the distant Western Jornada Lowlands but also from the Sierra Blanca Highlands to the west. However, a small proportion of longer-distance trade ceramics at the two sites increased through the sequence. Even as the evidence of bison hunting dropped at Bloom, there is strong evidence of a ceramics trade relationship that may suggest that residents there developed a role as go-betweens in the trade between the Plains to the east and the Pueblo communities further west. The second half of the volume documents the skeletal remains and particularly evidence of violence at Bloom, suggesting that the Plains exchange system that had streamed through

Henderson Pueblo and intensified during the occupation of Bloom Mound ultimately culminated in warfare, followed by the destruction and abandonment of the village occupations in the Roswell Oasis.

Aside from these pueblo excavations in the Eastern Extension of southeastern New Mexico, additional reports of El Paso–phase pueblo and more ephemeral Doña Ana–phase sites from the Western Jornada Lowlands have become available. William Walker has completed several seasons of New Mexico State University field school excavations at Cottonwood Spring Pueblo in the southern San Andres Mountains near Las Cruces (Walker and Berryman 2022). Multiple rooms have been excavated at two settlement areas, revealing new information on technologies, architecture, and ritual termination practices. Analyses of the excavation data are ongoing, and several master's theses have been completed on selected materials from the site.

A bit farther to the southwest in the Mesilla Valley of the Western Jornada Lowlands, Foster and Bradley (2021) synthesize the results of excavations carried out in 1981 at La Cabraña (LA 1671) in the riverine zone of the Rio Grande. This compact mid-fourteenth-century El Paso–phase linear roomblock pueblo consisted of 10 rooms, of which one is larger and presumed to be communal in function and another is of somewhat ambiguous size and function. Riverine resources including fish are notable, along with the agricultural base of maize, beans, and squash that are typical for the El Paso phase away from the rivers. The site's occupation was probably relatively brief, and the floors appear to have been cleaned prior to abandonment. Foster and Bradley (2021) discuss the possibility of ritual burning (and offerings) as a termination ceremony of the site and its communal room (as Miller and Graves 2009 have argued for Madera Quemada and a number of other El Paso–phase sites), offering guarded support to the possibility.

The social and ritual organization of Jornada pueblos has been a subject of interest for several decades. Miller (2019) explores the ways in which individual households of Jornada pueblos combined to form larger cooperative social formations and how such formations were actualized and maintained through communal and collective action. Evidence of suprahousehold collective practices and labor organization is revealed through dedicatory deposits of marine shell in communal rooms and the use of wood obtained from distant, high-elevation forests for roof supports and construction beams. Ultimately, the symbolic act of ritual termination of the roomblock served to terminate such social arrangements.

Elsewhere in the Western Jornada Lowlands, on the other side of the San Andreas Mountains to the east, Kurota and Dello-Russo (2020) surveyed and mapped the Lake Lucero site (LA 21162) and Huntington Pueblo (LA 14820) near Lake Lucero in and adjoining the White Sands Missile Range. These sites are relatively expansive locations, with occupation dating primarily to the Doña Ana and early El Paso phases, with indications of earlier use as well. Architectural remains are fragmentary, though heavy erosion and human-caused disturbance constrain preservation of the evidence, multiple midden areas and numerous burials, particularly at the former site, point to substantial use of the area. A variety of roasting features and the limited architectural remains suggest repeated seasonal use rather than full-blown village settlements, at least for part of the occupation. A notable aspect of the sites is an abundance of Mimbres ceramics (see also Kurota, Rogers, and Sternberg 2019), linking the occupants of these sites to peoples to the west of the Jornada. Perhaps not coincidental are suggestions of salt procurement from Lake Lucero and associated trails, both historically and in the past (see chapter 6).

In addition, Kurota, Solfisburg, and Dello-Russo (2019) report on surveys and test excavations at five villages on White Sands Missile Range. Multiple studies of a wide range of material culture were performed, including geochemical sourcing of turquoise, obsidian, and ceramics. Analysis of a sample of El Paso Polychrome sherds identified possible cacao residues, and copper artifacts were found during metal-detecting surveys (see also Kurota et al. 2018). The cumulative results of the excavations and material culture analyses provide new insights into the social and economic relationships of El Paso–phase pueblo settlements in the Western Lowlands. Kurota, Sternberg et al. (2020) provide an overview of the El Paso–phase occupation of the area, with consideration of regional exchange patterns of the southern Tularosa Basin, and argue for an extensive trade system during what they suggest was an economic boom into the fifteenth century AD. An additional outcome of this work by Kurota and others is a refinement in the chronological sequence of El Paso Polychrome, the dominant decorated ware of the El Paso phase that was widely traded across much of the Jornada region (Kurota et al. 2022).

Farther southeast in the Western Jornada Lowlands, a fortuitous combination of the results from a rock-art recording and remote-sensing project completed in 2019 on the Fort Bliss Military Reservation (Loendorf et al. 2019; Miller, Willis, et al. 2019) has expanded the understanding of trails in the Western Jornada Lowlands that were reviewed in chapter 6. In that chapter, it was noted that Darling's Type III trails (trails leading to and from ritual sites or sacred landscape features) surely must have existed in the Jornada, but evidence of such trails had yet to be detected. Since publication of the volume, a large 70–100–room plaza-oriented pueblo known as Plowed Field Pueblo was identified during a geophysical remote-sensing and aerial multispectral-imaging project. The shrine cave known as Sacramento Shelter was documented during a separate rock-art project. Examining transect recording unit (TRU; see chapter 6) data from earlier surveys, researchers discovered that a previously recorded trail leads directly from the Plowed Field Pueblo for a distance of 7 km to the base of the escarpment below the shrine cave. The trail is the first archaeologically defined processional pathway between a major settlement and sacred landscape feature in the Jornada region (Miller, Loendorf, Willis, et al. 2019).

The processional trail and shrine cave, as well as other shrines and rock-art localities, all reflect broader engagements with sacred landscapes surrounding Jornada Pithouse and Pueblo-period communities. Two forthcoming publications examine the ways in which past communities engaged with landscapes of meaning and the cosmovisions embedded in those landscapes that invoked memories of ancestral origins and sense of place. Miller (2023a) examines the recursive relationships between communal spaces in Jornada villages and the constructed and natural features of surrounding landscapes and concludes that social production, power negotiations, and religious rites performed within the confines of communal spaces were inherently connected with those performed at landscape features outside the walls of kivas, communal rooms, and pueblo plazas. These relationships with landscape features are also manifested through the bundled associations of fossils, crystals, cave speleothem, and other items usually found in ritual depositional contexts in pithouses and pueblo roomblocks (Miller 2023b). These materials, acquired from rock formations exposed in mountains, caves, cliffs, and canyons surrounding settlements, represent "pieces of places" (Bradley 2000:88)—the material metaphors and symbolic representations of sacred places and cosmovisions embedded in, and reflected by, those landscapes.

Among recent contributions to the Early Formative and late Archaic periods in the Western Jornada Lowlands, Kurota, Rogers, et al. (2020) summarize results from several projects in the Tularosa Basin in and south of the White Sands Missile Range and White Sands National Monument (now National Park). Consistent with the observations in chapters 1 and 5, they report continuity of hunter-gatherer subsistence and settlement patterns into the Formative Mesilla phase, a pattern contrasting this lowland area with the evidence from the Sierra Blanca/Capitan/Sacramento Highlands.

Much of the research on nonvillage sites in the New Mexico's portion of Jornada's Eastern Extension has been supported by the Permian Basin Programmatic Agreement and the Carlsbad Field Office of the Bureau of

Land Management. Most of this work lies in the lowland areas, but some of it extends onto the eastern edge of the adjacent Sierra Blanca/Capitan/ Sacramento Highlands to the west. Miller, Loendorf, Graves, and Willis (2019) documented and analyzed 21 rock-art sites in the Guadalupe Mountains and Azotea Mesa region near Carlsbad, New Mexico, referred to as the Mountain Slope subdivision of the Eastern Extension of the Jornada in chapter 13. A total of 168 rock-art panels with 1,045 individual elements were drawn, photographed, and described. Plasma oxidation radiocarbon dating indicates that these pictographs and petroglyphs were drawn over a span of 4,000 years. The artistic and symbolic content of the panels include abstract paintings, zigzag elements, and polychrome paintings dating to the Archaic period; possible representational images and masks from the Formative/Ceramic period; and dynamic scenes of Indigenous individuals dating to the 1800s. Several of the Indigenous panels show rare scenes of conflict between groups.

Beyond the rock art itself, the research examined evidence of past human interaction with the landscapes of southeastern New Mexico and showed that the rock-art panels were surrounded by shrine features, cairns, rock walls, house structures, and agave baking pits such as those discussed in chapter 12. Most of the rock art is associated with distinctive natural features such as caves, rockshelters, cliffs, and boulder outcrops. The documentation of plant communities in the vicinity of rock-art panels identified several plant species known for their psychotropic and entheogenic qualities. When considered together, the rock art, shrines, plant communities, striking vistas, and dynamic settings provide profound insights into the ways in which the past inhabitants of the canyons and mountains of the Guadalupe Mountains engaged with the natural and spiritual worlds.

Additional studies of art and sacred sites in the Eastern Extension were carried out in consultation with the Mescalero Apache Tribe and reported by Railey (2023). The effort investigated 19 sites and two isolated artifact finds that were considered of possible cultural and ancestral importance to the Mescalero Apache Tribe. Sites included in this project had either one or both of the following: (1) tipi ring(s) or other stone-ring features, and (2) metal projectile points. Although tipi rings in the Southwest are generally thought to date from very Late Prehistoric and (especially) post-Formative times, these features are notoriously difficult to date and this project did not provide any chronometric determinations associated with them. Thus, it remains an open question as to how far back in time tipi rings extend in the Jornada region. Sites with metal artifacts from the project reported by Railey (2023) include both previously collected and newly discovered arrow points, along with several scraps cut from cans that appear to be tinkler preforms. At one site, LA 109599, a flushloop bell and a blue glass "Russian" bead were found very close to two low stone mounds that may be Apache burial cairns. These various historical features and artifacts most likely date to the nineteenth century.

One notable *prehistoric* site, LA 38326, encompasses what was apparently a sustained settlement on a high bluff edge overlooking the Pecos River valley (Railey 2023). The remains of this settlement include several stacked-stone features, both rings and cairns, along with an associated sheet midden of dark, ashy soil and high artifact density. The stone rings may mark individual wicki-ups, and the cairns are perhaps shrines and/or burial features. There are also numerous bedrock mortars at the site. Diagnostic artifacts suggest the settlement was occupied during the Maljamar phase (AD 1100–1300; see figure 1.3), and radiocarbon dates partially support this affiliation. This is an unusual site for the Carlsbad region, and it adds a new wrinkle to our understanding of late prehistory in the Eastern Extension of the Jornada Mogollon region. In some ways LA 38326 is similar to sites of the Cielo Complex, far to the south in the Big Bend area of Texas and adjacent northeastern Chihuahua and northwestern Coahuila to the south.

Murrell et al. (2018) describe the results of a project examining a sample of small sites on the Southwest Pecos Slopes (the southern part of the Mountain Slope region defined in chapter 13) in the Eastern Extension area. These sites range from the Middle Archaic into the Protohistoric, with the biggest numbers falling in the Late Formative and in the transition between the Late Archaic and the start of the Formative. Murrell et al. define a typology of feature types such as roasting pits, earth ovens, ring middens, and other thermal features (see chapter 12). By far the most common features are roasting pits. Based on their contents, sites are also classified typologically; most are identified as logistical sites, but some (almost all Formative) are identified as residences. Using an array of GIS analyses, Murrell et al. consider patterning of site types across the slope area and examine changes in settlement patterns through time.

Miller and Graves (2023) expand on the analysis of hot rock cooking to consider such features in context across the broad Jornada Mogollon region of New Mexico and into the Eastern Extension of west Texas. Building upon the studies of earth ovens and agave baking presented in chapter 12, they examine the relationship between labor and ritual in the construction and use of plant-baking pits. They consider the 7,000-year-long record of agave and succulent baking in these areas from a historical perspective, beginning with the communal feasting pits of the Middle Archaic period, during which the subsistence and social components of agave baking were first established, and proceeding through the communal baking pits located within the plazas of pueblo communities centuries later. In their study, the interplay of intensification, labor, political economies, and ritual is examined within the theoretical context of path dependence. The study again confirms that plant-baking facilities should be explicitly considered in studies of long-term social and economic change.

Turning to the area abutting the western edge of the Sierra Blanca/Capitan/Sacramento Highlands (at the interface between the areas considered in chapter 3 to the west and chapters 5 and 7 to the east), the Jornada Research Institute's Creekside Village project is proving to be one the more significant projects of recent times, with profound implications for agriculture and social organization during the early centuries of the Formative period (Greenwald 2018, 2019; Neely and Greenwald 2019). Located within the Western Jornada Lowlands on the terraces above the Rio Tularosa as it flows from the Sacramento Mountains, the site consists of an extensive pithouse village associated with agricultural canals, terraces, and fields. Of particular significance is the presence of a Great Kiva measuring 12.4 m in diameter. Radiocarbon dates place the construction and use of the kiva quite early in the Formative, at sometime between AD 660 and 840. The number and range of features at the site—including the large number of pithouses, the presence of intensive hydrological and agricultural features, and a Great Kiva—establishes that the nature of social and ritual organization in the Mesilla phase was of much greater complexity than previously understood. Several additional Great Kivas are found in nearby sites up the Tularosa valley in the mountain foothills. These sites raise intriguing questions about the origin and developmental trajectory of agricultural pithouse communities overlapping in time in the Sierra Blanca/Capitan/Sacramento Highlands to the east (see chapters 2, 5, and 7).

On the northern end of the Jornada region, in the northern Sierra Blanca/Capitan/Sacramento Highlands, Railey (in prep.) describes eight sites along US Highway 54, south of Corona, New Mexico. The most notable site is LA 131144, which covers a large area and which hosted multicomponent occupations. Preliminary observations of the extensive scatter (almost exclusively brown wares) and arrow points (both early and late forms) suggest a Formative date. Surface scraping identified numerous features, including two shallow, conjoined pit structures, one roughly D-shaped, and storage pits, including two bell-shaped ones. Chronometric dates are not yet available, but materials from the pit structures—including a complete lack of decorated or textured ceramics and an early-style arrow point—suggest they may date prior to the Corona phase (i.e., before AD 1100). The final results of this project will help flesh out the picture of Formative-period developments in this poorly known part of the Jornada region.

Finally, several more broadly or disparately aimed studies have appeared. Notable is the synthetic publication of the late Regge Wiseman's (2019) view on diversity within what is lumped into the Jornada Mogollon. Miller and Graves (2019) review the typological and chronometric data compiled on 12,110 projectile points from the Jornada region. They summarize the inherent problems of using extraregional typologies to classify projectile points. Using a subset of points associated with radiocarbon dates, they provide refined age ranges for the production and use of certain forms, although the end dates for many points are complicated by widespread patterns of scavenging and recycling. The radiocarbon records of the Western and Eastern Jornada regions are summarized by Miller (2023c), and the Jornada radiocarbon database was included in the overall North American Radiocarbon Database described by Kelly and others (2022). Additionally, two notable publication series, the proceedings volumes of the biennial Jornada Conference (Seltzer-Rogers 2022), and of the Tularosa Basin Conference (Greenwald and Hewitt 2019; Greenwald et al. 2020), continue to add to the regional literature. In short, research in the Jornada continues to be active and exciting, although our previous observation on gaps and broad areas begging for research remains true as well!

SELECTED REFERENCES

Bradley, Richard. 2000. *An Archaeology of Natural Places*. London: Routledge.

Castañeda, Amanda M., and Mark Willis. 2021. *Investigating Morphological Variation of Ground Stone Bedrock Features at LA 43414 and LA 121668 on the Mescalero Plain, Southeastern New Mexico*. Carlsbad, NM: Carlsbad Field Office, Bureau of Land Management and Versar, Inc. https://doi.org/10.48512/XCV8466180.

Clark, Jamie, L., and John D. Speth. 2022. *Living and Dying on the Periphery: The Archaeology and Human Remains from Two 13th–15th Century AD Villages in Southeastern New Mexico*. Salt Lake City: University of Utah Press.

Foster, Michael S., and Ronna Jane Bradley. 2021. *Mata's La Cabraña: A Jornada Mogollon Pueblo on the Rio Grande of South-Central New Mexico*. Albuquerque: Maxwell Museum Technical Series 39, Maxwell Museum of Anthropology.

Frederick, Charles. 2021. *Geomorphological and Geoarchaeological Investigations on the Mescalero Plain*. Carlsbad, NM: Carlsbad Field Office, Bureau of Land Management and Versar, Inc. https://doi.org/10.48512/XCV8466182.

Greenwald, David H. 2018. *Reconsidering the Mesilla Phase in the Tularosa Basin: Changing Viewpoints on Subsistence Strategies, Socio-political Organization, and*

Residence Patterns based on Preliminary Studies at Creekside Village. Jornada
Research Publications No. 3. Tularosa, NM: Jornada Research Institute.

Greenwald, David H. 2019. "Ongoing Research at Creekside Village: Addressing
Early Village Organization in the Tularosa Basin." In *Reflections of the Past and
Recent Discoveries: Proceedings of the 3rd and 4th Tularosa Basin Conferences*, ed.
David H. Greenwald and Nancy J. Hewitt, 33–34. Jornada Research Publications
No. 4. Tularosa, NM: Jornada Research Institute.

Greenwald, David H., and Nancy J. Hewitt, eds. 2019. *Reflections of the Past and
Recent Discoveries: Proceedings of the 3rd and 4th Tularosa Basin Conferences.* Jornada
Research Publications No. 4. Tularosa, NM: Jornada Research Institute, Tularosa.

Greenwald, David H., Nancy J. Hewitt, and Alexander Kurota, eds. 2020. *Preserving,
Interpreting, and Reconstructing History through Archival Studies, Landscape Archae-
ology and Field Research: Proceedings of the 2019 Tularosa Basin Conferences.* Jornada
Research Publications No. 5. Tularosa, NM: Jornada Research Institute.

Kelly, Robert L., Madeline E. Mackie, Erick Robinson, Jack Meyer, Michael Berry,
Matthew Boulanger, Brian F. Codding, Jacob Freeman, Carey James Garland,
Joseph Gingerich, Robert Hard, James Haug, Andrew Martindale, Scott Meeks,
Myles Miller, Shane Miller, Timothy Perttula, Jim A. Railey, Ken Reid, Ian Schar-
lotta, Jerry Spangler, David Hurst Thomas, Victor Thompson, and Andrew White.
2022. "A New Radiocarbon Database for the Lower 48 States." *American Antiquity*
87(3):581–590.

Kurota, Alexander, and Robert Dello-Russo, comp. 2020. *Survey of Lake Lucero Site
(LA 21162) and Huntington Pueblo (La 14820), Doña Ana County, New Mexico.*
Albuquerque: Office of Contract Archaeology.

Kurota, Alexander, Thatcher Rogers, and Evan S. Sternberg. 2019. "Evidence for
Possible Mimbres Migration into the Jornada: Introducing the Eastern Mimbres
San Andres Aspect" In *Collected Papers from the 20th Biennial Mogollon Archaeology
Conference*, ed. Lonnie C. Ludeman, 135–157. Las Cruces, NM: Friends of Mogol-
lon Archaeology.

Kurota, Alexander, Thatcher Rogers, Evan Sternberg, Robin M. Cordero, Evan
Kay, Scott Alan Gunn, Pamela McBride, William Godby, and David Bust. 2020.
"Research Update on Archaic and Mesilla Phase Occupations in the Tularosa
Basin of South-Central New Mexico." In *The Archaic in New Mexico*, ed. Cherie K.
Walth, 81–107. Albuquerque: New Mexico Archaeological Council.

Kurota, Alexander, Thatcher A. Seltzer-Rogers, and Lora Jackson Legare. 2022. "An
Investigation of Diachronic Trends in El Paso Polychrome Painted Designs of the
Jornada Mogollon." *Kiva* 88(3):291–326.

Kurota, Alexander, Christian Solfisburg, and Robert Dello-Russo. 2019. *Archaeology
of White Sands Missile Range: Archaeological Identification and Protection of Five Sites*

along Tank Trails, Dona Ana County, New Mexico. WSMR Report No. 952. White Sands Missile Range, NM: Conservation Branch, Environmental Division.

Kurota, Alexander, Evan Sternberg, Thatcher A. Rogers, and Robert Dello-Russo. 2020. "New Trends in El Paso Phase Jornada Mogollon Occupations in the Southern Tularosa Basin, New Mexico." In *A Lifelong Journey: Papers in Honor of Michael P. Marshall*, ed. Emily J. Brown, Matthew J. Barbour, and Genevieve N. Head, 129–162. Albuquerque: Papers of the Archaeological Society of New Mexico 46, Archaeological Society of New Mexico.

Kurota, Alexander, Timothy J. Ward, Thatcher Rogers, Anna Wilson, Zahra Faizi, Andrew Hollenshead, Jacob Niehaus, and Shivangi Patel. 2018. "First Evidence of the Use of Cacao at Two Jornada Mogollon Pueblos in the Southern Tularosa Basin, New Mexico." *Pottery Southwest* 34(3–4):24–26.

Loendorf, Lawrence L., Miller, Myles R., Mark Willis, Katherine Jones, and Tim Graves. 2019. *Rock Art at Five Localities in the Southern Sacramento Mountains, Organ Mountains, and Hueco Mountains of Fort Bliss*. Fort Bliss Cultural Resources Report No. 17–15. Fort Bliss, TX: Environmental Division, Fort Bliss Garrison Command.

Miller, Myles R. 2019. "Integrating Households and Communities at Jornada Mogollon Pueblos: Architecture, Landscapes, and Ritual." In *Communities and Households in the Greater Southwest: New Perspectives and Case Studies*, ed. Robert J. Stokes, 229–253. Boulder: University Press of Colorado.

Miller, Myles R. 2023a (in press). "Beyond the Communal Structure: Political Engagements with the Landscapes of Southern and Southeastern New Mexico." In *Structure and Meaning of Mogollon Communal Spaces and Places in the Greater American Southwest*, ed. Robert J. Stokes, Katherine A. Dungan, and Jakob W. Sedig. Salt Lake City: University of Utah Press.

Miller, Myles R. 2023b (in press). "Bringing the Landscape Home: The Materiality of Placemaking and Pilgrimage in Jornada and Mimbres Mogollon Settlement." In *Sacred Southwestern Landscapes: Archaeologies of Religious Ecology*, ed. Aaron Wright. Salt Lake City: University of Utah Press.

Miller, Myles R. 2023c. "Chronometric Data Synthesis and the Late Holocene Archaeological Record of Southern New Mexico and Western Trans-Pecos Texas." In *Pushing Boundaries in Southwestern Archaeology: Chronometry, Collections, and Contexts*, edited by Stephen E. Nash and Erin L. Baxter, 74–93. Denver: University Press of Colorado.

Miller, Myles R., and Tim B. Graves. 2009. *Madera Quemada Pueblo: Archaeological Investigations at a Fourteenth Century Jornada Mogollon Pueblo*. Historic and Natural Resources Report No. 03-12. Fort Bliss, TX: Fort Bliss Garrison Command, Directorate of Public Works, Environmental Division.

Miller, Myles R., and Tim B. Graves. 2019. "Chronological Trends among Jornada Projectile Points." In *Recent Research in Jornada Mogollon Archaeology: Proceedings from the 20th Jornada Mogollon Conference*, ed. G. O. Maloof, 205–260. El Paso: El Paso Museum of Archaeology.

Miller, Myles R., and Tim B. Graves. 2023 (in press). "Labor, Ritual, and Path Dependence: The Social Dimensions of Earth Oven Use in Southern New Mexico and West Texas." In *Earth Ovens and Desert Lifeways: 10,000 Years of Indigenous Cooking in the Arid Landscapes of North America*, ed. C. Koenig and M. R. Miller. Salt Lake City: University of Utah Press.

Miller, Myles R., Tim B. Graves, Charles Frederick, Amanda Castañeda Mark Willis, John D. Speth, J. Phil Dering, Susan J. Smith, Crystal Dozier, John G. Jones, Jeremy Loven, Genevieve Woodhead, Jeff Ferguson, and Mary Ownby. 2021a. *Ochoa Phase Investigations on the Mescalero Plain*. Carlsbad, NM: Bureau of Land Management, Carlsbad Field Office. https://doi.org/10.48512/XCV8466186.

Miller, Myles R., Tim B. Graves, Charles Frederick, Mark Willis, John D. Speth, J. Phil Dering, Susan J. Smith, Crystal Dozier, John G. Jones, Jeremy Loven, Genevieve Woodhead, Jeff Ferguson, and Mary Ownby. 2021b. *Pueblo on the Plains: The Second Season of Investigations at the Merchant Site in Southeastern New Mexico*. 2 vols. Carlsbad, NM: Bureau of Land Management. https://doi.org/10.48512/xcv8466184.

Miller, Myles R, Tim B. Graves, and Robert H. Leslie. 2016. *The Merchant Site: A Late Prehistoric Ochoa Phase Settlement in Southeastern New Mexico*. Prepared for the Bureau of Land Management, Carlsbad Field Office. Versar Cultural Resources Report No. 836EP. El Paso: Versar.

Miller, Myles R., Lawrence L. Loendorf, Tim Graves, and Mark Willis. 2019. *Landscapes of Stone and Paint: Documentation and Analysis of 21 Rock Art Sites in Southeastern New Mexico*. Carlsbad, NM: Bureau of Land Management, Carlsbad Field Office.

Miller, Myles R., Lawrence L. Loendorf, Mark Willis, Chet Walker, and Tim Graves. 2019. "Remote Sensing, Shrine Caves, and Pilgrimage Trails in the Tularosa Basin of Southern New Mexico." Paper presented at the 21st Biennial Jornada Mogollon Conference, El Paso Museum of Archaeology, El Paso.

Miller, Myles R., Mark Willis, Chet Walker, Tim Graves, and David Rachal. 2019. *Searching for Pueblos among the Dunefields: Remote Sensing Investigations at Four Pueblo Settlements on Fort Bliss Military Reservation*. Fort Bliss Cultural Resources Report No. 17–27, Environmental Division. Fort Bliss, TX: Fort Bliss Garrison Command.

Murrell, Monica L., Phillip O. Leckman, and Michael R. O'Connell. 2018. *Camping and Hot-Rock Cooking: Hunter-Gatherer Land Use in the Southwest Pecos Slopes.*

Technical Report 18-21. Statistical Research Incorporated, Albuquerque, New Mexico. https://doi.org/10.6067/XCV8448050.

Neely, James A., and David Greenwald. 2019. "Prehistoric Water Resource Adaptations in the American Southwest: Case Studies from Tularosa, New Mexico and Safford, Arizona." In *Reflections of the Past and Recent Discoveries: Proceedings of the 3rd and 4th Tularosa Basin Conferences*, ed. David H. Greenwald and Nancy J. Hewitt, pp. 55–78. Jornada Research Publications No. 4. Tularosa, NM: Jornada Research Institute, Tularosa.

Railey, Jim A., ed. 2023 *Archaeological Investigation and Evaluation of Potential Mescalero Apache Traditional Cultural Properties with the Bureau of Land Management, Carlsbad Field Office, Eddy County, New Mexico*. Submitted to the Bureau of Land Management, Carlsbad Field Office. Albuquerque: SWCA Environmental Consultants.

Railey, Jim A., ed. In prep. *Archaeological Testing and Data Recovery at Eight Sites along U.S. Highway 54, Mileposts 151.6 to 163.7, Lincoln County, New Mexico*. Submitted to the New Mexico Department of Transportation. Albuquerque: SWCA Environmental Consultants.

Seltzer-Rogers, Thatcher A., ed. 2022. *Ongoing Research in Jornada Mogollon Archaeology: Proceedings of the 21st Jornada Mogollon Conference*. El Paso, TX: El Paso Museum of Archaeology.

Walker, William H., and Judy Berryman. 2022. "Ritual Closure: Rites de Passage and Apotropaic Magic in an Animate World." *Journal of Archaeological Method and Theory* https://doi.org/10.1007/s10816-022-09565-7.

Wiseman, Regge N. 2019. *Pruning the Jornada Branch Mogollon: Changing Perspectives on the Prehistory of Southeastern New Mexico*. Albuquerque, NM: Secord Books.

This volume began as a symposium at the 75th annual meeting of the Society for American Archaeology titled "Diversity on the Edge of the Southwest: Late Hunter-Gatherers and Farmers of the Jornada Mogollon." The discussion during and after that symposium convinced us that a great deal about the archaeology of this region in the southeastern part of the US Southwest and the northern edge of Mexico deserves broader attention. The area is often seen as geographically marginal and of limited research interest. The substantial increase in Jornada data and syntheses in recent decades, particularly resulting from Cultural Resource Management projects, and the great environmental and cultural diversity of the area both receive little exposure to those not working in the Jornada itself. This volume is intended as a step towards rectifying this situation.

Since the original symposium, we have consolidated and deleted some material, updated and added other material to broaden regional and topical coverage, and the authors have worked to make it as up to date as possible. While it remains incomplete in its coverage, the volume aims to present a broad overview and a series of specific studies of many portions of the Jornada region and of the major issues being addressed in Jornada research.

The editors are very grateful for the hard work of the authors; some went to great lengths to help fill gaps that reviewers or the editors noted in early drafts. We are very grateful to the tremendous help (and patience) of Jessica d'Arbonne of the University Press of Colorado. The volume has also benefited tremendously from the comments of two anonymous reviewers. We would also like to thank the Arizona Archaeological and Historical Society as well as the Center for Material Culture Studies at the University of Delaware for their generous support of this volume.

This work is dedicated to Jane Holden Kelley, whose long and incredibly productive career included a broad range of fieldwork, from pioneering archaeological research in the Jornada and northern Mexico through ethnographic research. Her career also included important theoretical writing and, of course, teaching. She was a remarkable mentor, not merely to her own students but to many others, including welcoming and introducing one of us (Rocek) into her Jornada research area decades ago. She continued to guide and help Jornada researchers (along with many others), even arranging for some of the participants to join this volume just a few years before her death. She is greatly missed, but the impact of her many significant contributions will be felt for years to come.

Late Prehistoric Hunter-Gatherers and Farmers of the Jornada Mogollon

PART I
Diversity and Change in the Jornada Mogollon

1

This volume presents core issues and recent advances in the archaeology of the Jornada branch of the Mogollon culture located in south-central and southeastern New Mexico, western Texas, and northern Chihuahua, Mexico (figure 1.1). This region is an ecological and cultural border of the US Southwest. It is an area whose archaeological record displays periods of markedly "Southwestern" puebloan cultural patterns at certain times and places, but also shows substantial interaction and shared cultural patterns with peoples bordering the Southwest on the Southern Plains to the east and in the area of modern northern Mexico to the south. The "Jornada" concept most unambiguously applies to the Formative (starting in the early centuries of the current era), when pottery and housing styles highlight inter-regional variation in the Southwest, and this period is the focus of this volume. However, some chapters consider the broader developmental context and cover periods extending from the Late Archaic through the end of the Formative. Combined, the chapters address topics of interest beyond the Jornada and the American Southwest, such as mobility, forager adaptations, the transition to farming, responses to environmental challenges, and patterns of social interaction.

The significance of the Jornada area has been recognized since at least the 1930s and its formal status as a named culture "branch" dates to the 1940s (Lehmer 1948), but parts of the area have remained understudied and underreported beyond the limited distribution

Diversity and Change in a "Marginal" Region and Environment

Thomas R. Rocek and Nancy A. Kenmotsu

DOI: 10.5876/9781607327950.c001

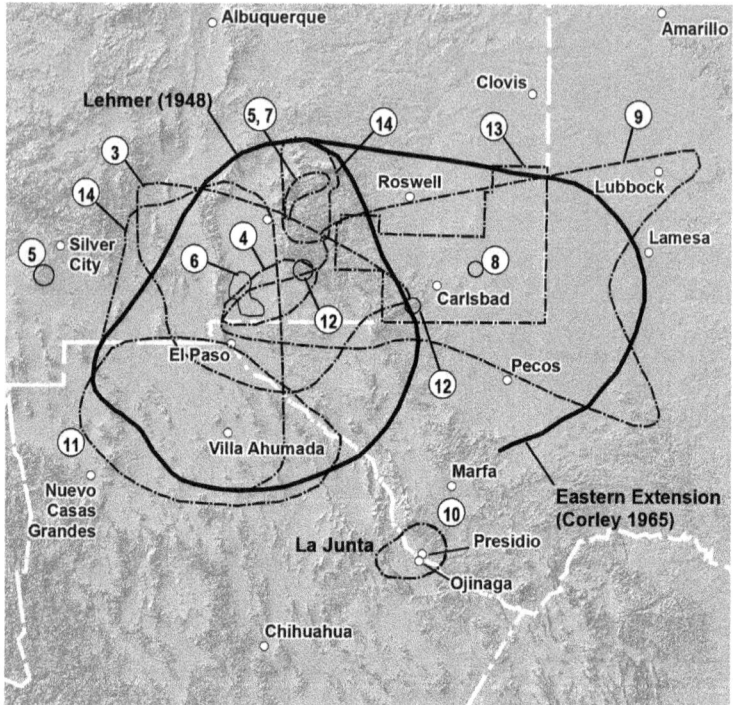

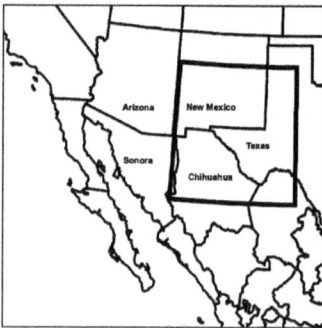

FIGURE I.I. *Regions of the Jornada Mogollon discussed in each chapter of the text. Short outlines are shown as continuous (rather than interrupted) lines to make them easier to see. Chapters 1 and 2 (dark continuous lines) address issues for the whole Jornada. Chapters 5 and 14 each focus on two separate regions, indicated by two separate outlines. The northeastern of the two regions discussed in chapter 5 is also the area discussed in chapter 7, as indicated by both a 5 and a 7 labeling the outlined area. Figure by Sandra L. Hannum.*

of Cultural Resource Management (CRM) reports and regional conference proceedings. However, recent large-scale CRM work in parts of the Jornada have amassed one of the largest data sets in the Southwest with up-to-date chronological, architectural, faunal, ceramic, obsidian sourcing, and other specialized studies. Other portions of the Jornada, while remaining much less researched, nevertheless are now well-enough understood to demonstrate tremendous variation and complexity in economic and social adaptations. The volume draws together results from these materials with chapters by some of the researchers currently most active in the area.

The concept of the "Jornada branch of the Mogollon culture" was an outgrowth of the gradual recognition of regional variation in the archaeology of the Southwest. The earliest syntheses of Southwestern prehistory were centered in the Colorado Plateau country of northeastern Arizona, northwestern New Mexico, southwestern Colorado, and southeastern Utah, and summarized in the "Pecos Classification" developed under the leadership of A. V. Kidder (1927). Although Kidder and others were well aware of regional variation in Southwestern prehistory (e.g., Kidder 1924), subsequent decades of research formally recognized this variation through taxonomic definitions that distinguished the northern "Anasazi" (or more recently "Ancestral Pueblo") cultural area from the southern Arizona Hohokam, the Mogollon of eastern Arizona and western New Mexico, and eventually the Colorado River–region Patayan. Over the decades, further subdivisions and transitional areas were identified among these large regional archaeological taxonomic divisions (e.g., Cordell 1984, 1997; Cordell and McBrinn 2012; McGregor 1941, 1965; Roberts 1935).

As these regions were delineated, an association between the major archaeological cultures and geographical ecological zones was often explicitly or implicitly noted: the Anasazi with the Colorado Plateau highlands, the Hohokam with the Sonoran Desert of southern Arizona, the Patayan with the Colorado River valley and adjoining highlands, and the Mogollon with the mountainous environment fringing the southeastern end of the Colorado Plateau. But each of these cultural areas was also recognized to subsume substantial environmental and cultural diversity as well.

In the case of the Mogollon, internal divisions were formalized with the definition of a series of geographical "branches" delineated over more than a decade of research (Wheat 1955:8). One of the last major subdivisions added was the Jornada branch of the Mogollon (hereafter Jornada),[1] defined by Lehmer (1948) as a broad swath that extended the Mogollon over much of the basin-and-range as well as the mountainous highlands of south-central New Mexico, a small part of Trans-Pecos Texas, and a section of north-central

Chihuahua. A more recent proposal by Corley (1965) roughly doubled the Jornada and extended it further into western Texas (figures 1.1, 1.2), that is, well into the fringes of the area commonly considered the "Southwest" of the United States. Identifying the Jornada's cultural links in additional areas to the south and east remain topics of research (see Kenmotsu, chapter 10, and Cruz Antillón et al., chapter 11, both in this volume).

The net result is that in many ways, the Jornada Mogollon with its eastern extension is both the largest and arguably the most "peripheral" of the divisions of the major archaeological areas of the Southwest. The Jornada is often regarded as marginal with limited relevance to the Southwest in general and to the Mogollon in particular. It is frequently viewed as a monotonous extension that is of minimal research interest compared to the dynamic Mogollon core area in the mountains of western New Mexican and eastern Arizona (Lekson et al. 2004). This volume is intended to counter this imbalance both in the attention and understanding afforded the region. The large data sets that have been, and continue to be, collected from across the Jornada illustrate that cultural processes demonstrated in other regions of the Southwest—changes in subsistence, technology, mobility, and land tenure, among others—align with the developmental trends in the Jornada. Specifically, contributors to the volume use their data to highlight three major topics: the Jornada's environmental and cultural diversity; the region's developmental trends that parallel those elsewhere in the Southwest; and, issues of broad anthropological interest.

THE ENVIRONMENT OF THE JORNADA

The Jornada is anything *but* monotonous, encompassing almost the full range of environments encountered in the Southwest (figure 1.2). Dry desert lowlands prevail in Chihuahua and the Basin Lowlands of southern New Mexico and in the vicinity of El Paso, Texas (hereafter referred to as the Western Jornada).[2] The transition to a xeric environment in these lowlands was well underway by 9,000 years ago as desert scrub and succulents began to dominate the vegetation (Abbott et al. 2009:2–52). Broad-valley riverine habitats are found along the Rio Grande as it cuts through the region from the lowlands around Las Cruces, New Mexico, flowing southeast to demarcate the border between Chihuahua, Mexico, and Texas. The Pecos River, east of the area included in Lehmer's original map, is another significant riverine habitat of the Jornada flowing past Roswell, New Mexico, in the north, then southeast through New Mexico and delimiting Trans-Pecos Texas. In contrast to the relatively narrow Rio Grande valley, the Pecos valley is broad and

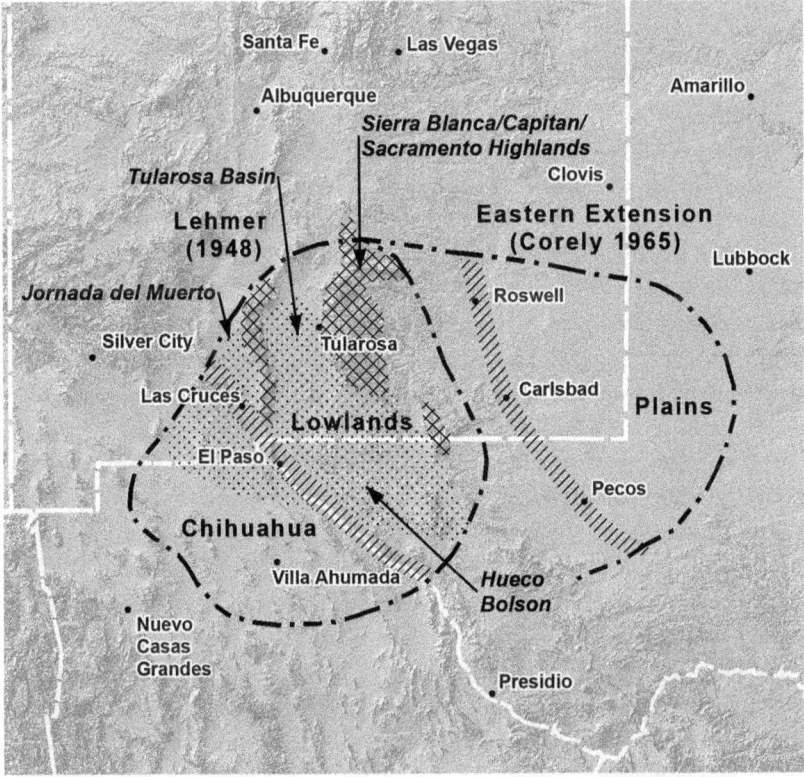

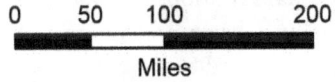

FIGURE 1.2. *Schematic outlines of the major subdivisions of the Jornada Mogollon region discussed in the text. Figure by Sandra L. Hannum.*

gently slopes west to highland foothills; to the east it also slopes gradually through areas of sand hills, including the area known as the Mescalero Plain (see Railey, chapter 13, this volume) to the escarpment marking the edge of the Southern Plains. The Pecos is also characterized by several major western tributaries, notably the Rio Peñasco near Artesia, New Mexico, and particularly the Rio Hondo, which creates what Wiseman (2013) characterizes as the "Roswell Oasis" near Roswell, New Mexico.

In the original definition (Lehmer 1948), the Jornada extended only as far east as the eastern foothills of the Sierra Blanca and Capitan Mountains, but the subsequent eastward extension of the Jornada culture area (Corley 1965) encompasses portions of the Southern Plains and prominent sandhills in west Texas and extreme southeastern New Mexico. Many archaeologists do not consider this part of the Jornada, and the nature of this region's cultural pattern in relation to other parts of the Jornada remains an important topic of research. In this volume we refer to this area simply as the Eastern Extension. In addition to these ecosystems, the Jornada includes piñon-juniper as well as ponderosa forest and subalpine highland ecosystems. These include (from west to east) the Organ Mountains separating Las Cruces and the Tularosa Basin, Otero Mesa, the Sacramento Mountains, Sierra Blanca, the eastward-extending finger of the Capitan Mountains, and the Guadalupe Mountains that straddle the New Mexico–Texas border. For the purposes of this volume we refer to these mountain systems collectively as the *Sierra Blanca/Capitan/Sacramento Highlands*, though environmentally and culturally they encompass substantial variation that warrants finer subdivision.

Finally, a basin-and-range desert environment of internally drained valleys interspersed by northwest–southeast trending low mountains (similar to parts of the Western Jornada Lowlands and the low-lying parts of the Eastern Extension) characterizes northern Chihuahua. This region encompasses a substantial part of the Jornada culture area, which we refer to simply as the Southern Jornada Mogollon.

GENERAL OUTLINE OF CULTURAL HISTORY IN THE JORNADA

Cultural patterns among the distinct microenvironments of the Jornada and across time range from highly mobile hunting-and-gathering groups with limited archaeological visibility to aggregated and relatively sedentary agricultural communities. Multiple prehistoric ethnic groups are also probably represented (see Wiseman, chapter 14, this volume). Various regions of the Jornada exhibit much of the same range of cultural developments seen elsewhere in the Southwest, as well as unique ones. In the review of the Jornada's culture history that follows, we begin with the Late Archaic period and then broadly describe the Formative period (AD 200–1450) across the area—including trends in architecture, settlement systems, land use, and subsistence—to present the context for the subsequent chapters.

The material cultural variability characteristic of the Formative-period Jornada was not yet notably developed during the Late Archaic period (1800 BC– AD 200) and many regions share similar trends. Across the Jornada there was an increase in the number of sites and features in those sites, suggesting a rising population. In contrast to earlier periods, Late Archaic sites are also found in all environmental zones whether in the Tularosa Basin Lowlands, Otero Mesa, the Sierra Blanca/Capitan/Sacramento Highlands, the Southern Jornada Mogollon, southeastern New Mexico, or the Texas Trans-Pecos (Cruz Antillón et al., chapter 11, and Railey, chapter 13, both this volume; Kelley 1984; Mauldin and Miller 2009; Miller and Kenmotsu 2004:229; Phelps 1998). Structures commonly consisted of small, shallow, basin-shaped depressions (Dering et al. 2001; Miller and Kenmotsu 2004), often surrounded by hearths and pits (Graves et al. 2014:197). In some areas, such as the Sierra Blanca/Capitan/Sacramento Highlands, no structures are known, either due to contrasting settlement patterns or, more likely, limited research. Where found, sites usually contain no more than one or two structures and researchers believe they represent the remains of extended family encampments. However, as a departure from this model, recent excavations at site LA 91759 in the Western Jornada revealed a "dense cluster of pithouses and pits with a common extramural activity area to the east" radiocarbon dated between 50 BC and AD 150 (Graves et al. 2014:197), indicating that in this portion of the Jornada Late Archaic settlement patterns were undergoing changes that have not been detected in other regions.

Subsistence continued to focus on hunting and gathering throughout most of the Jornada. Rockshelters with Late Archaic components have yielded large quantities of deer and other large-mammal bone; fauna at lower-elevation sites are dominated by rabbit and hare (jackrabbit) species. Dart points changed to smaller corner- and side-notched forms in the latter portion of the period. Data from the Sierra Blanca/Capitan/Sacramento Highlands and their edges provide conclusive evidence that cultigens (maize and beans) also were a part of Late Archaic subsistence in and around the highlands near the Western Jornada (Campbell and Railey 2008; Railey and Turnbow, chapter 5, this volume; Wiseman 1996b)—see data from two rockshelters overlooking the Tularosa Basin Lowlands, Fresnal Shelter (LA 10101; Tagg 1996) and Tornillo

Shelter (LA 71687;[3] Upham et al. 1987), as well as the Sunset Archaic site (LA 58971) and several other Late Archaic sites located in the Hondo Valley further north and east. Several of these sites had multiple large, bell-shaped storage pits suitable for crop storage (Raily and Turnbow, chapter 5, this volume; Campbell and Railey 2008; Wiseman 1996b). To date, other regions of the Jornada do not exhibit this same early adoption of cultigens.

The Formative in the Jornada

As elsewhere in the Southwest, hallmarks of the Jornada's Formative period are typically the manufacture of ceramics, the increased presence of substantial houses, and the use of the bow and arrow. The exact timing of the appearance of these new technologies remains imprecisely known and probably varied across the region, with the earliest-dated pottery in the Western Jornada around AD 200, followed in the eastern portion of the region around AD 500 (Campbell and Railey 2008:17; Miller 2005a; Railey 2011:13–14; 2015:30; Wiseman 1996b:188) (figure 1.3). The number of ceramic types found across the region led to Lehmer's division of the ensuing Formative archaeological sequence in the Jornada (within his 1948 boundaries) along a north–south split into two phase sequences (figure 1.3). In the Sierra Blanca/Capitan/Sacramento Highlands, he proposed a northern sequence of the Capitan, Three Rivers, and San Andres phases;[4] the ceramic types manufactured in that region are (from earliest to most recent) Jornada Brown, Broadline Red-on-terracota, Three Rivers Red-on-terracotta, Chupadero Black-on-white (thought by Lehmer to be intrusive, but now known to be locally manufactured), Corona Corrugated, and Lincoln Black-on-red, as well as types associated with Lehmer's southern (our "Western Jornada Lowlands") sequence described below, and intrusive from distant regions such as Mimbres and northern Chihuahuan types. Jane Kelley (1984 [original 1966]) divided this highlands region (with an extension northward into the Jicarilla Mountains) into two additional parallel Formative-phase sequences (Early and Late Glencoe phases in the south, and Corona and Lincoln phases in the north), with her southern sequence associated particularly with the persistence of pithouse architecture and high percentages of brownwares in contrast to the development of pueblo architecture and prevalence of more-decorated wares in the north. Although Kelley (1984) originally dated the start of both highland sequences ca. AD 1100, subsequent research has extended the Formative in this region to about AD 500.

In the Western Jornada Lowlands, Lehmer proposed his southern sequence of the Mesilla, Doña Ana, and El Paso phases; Miller (2005a) modified the

Date	Western Jornada (generic periods)	Western Jornada	Sierra Blanca/Capitan/Sierra Blanca Highlands South	North	Eastern Extension	Eastern Extension (generic periods)	Date
	Late Prehistoric	Late Prehistoric	Late Prehistoric	Late Prehistoric	Late Prehistoric	Late Prehistoric	
A.D. 1450		El Paso	Late Glencoe	Lincoln	Ochoa		A.D. 1450
A.D. 1275/1300		Late Doña Ana	Middle Glencoe	Corona	Maljamar	Late Formative	
	Formative		Early Glencoe				
A.D. 1150		Early Doña Ana					A.D. 1150/1100
A.D. 1000		Late Mesilla	unnamed Early Formative		Querecho	Early Formative	
A.D. 650		Early Mesilla			Hueco		
A.D. 200/400			Late Archaic			Late Archaic	A.D. 500/550
	Late Archaic	Hueco (Archaic)					

FIGURE 1.3. *Major Jornada regional chronologies; dates approximate. Not all local phase sequences are listed. After Kelley (1984 [originally 1966]), Miller (2005a), Miller et al. (2016); Railey (2015, 2016); Whalen (1981a, 1994b); Wiseman (1985b, 2014, 2016b).*

sequence by defining an Early Doña Ana phase (AD 1000–1150) and a Late Doña Ana phase (AD 1150–1300). The local ceramics for this sequence are El Paso Brownware, El Paso Bichrome, and El Paso Polychrome; instrumental neutron activation analysis (INAA) has shown all were manufactured in the Tularosa Basin (Miller and Ferguson 2010) and the polychrome vessels were widely traded to other regions of the Jornada and other regions of the Southwest (see Hill, chapter 9, this volume; Kenmotsu, chapter 10, this volume; and Cruz Antillón et al., chapter 11, this volume). The phase sequence for the Western Jornada Lowlands is also used in the Southern Jornada Mogollon region in north-central Chihuahua. In the eastern portions of the Jornada, including the Texas Trans-Pecos east of the Tularosa Basin, a number of phase names have been proposed over the decades (Collins 1968; Corley 1965; Jelinek 1967; Leslie 1979). Recently, Railey (2015) proposed a simplified temporal scheme for far southeastern New Mexico: Early Formative (AD 500–1150) and Late Formative (AD 1150–1450). That temporal scheme for southeastern New Mexico and the Trans-Pecos in Texas is used in this volume.

As noted, the hallmarks of the Formative—the appearance of ceramics, substantial houses, and the bow and arrow—indicate changing adaptations across the Jornada. In turn, they initiated a trend toward sedentary or semisedentary settlements, varying degrees of agricultural dependency, and social integration. These changes are associated with changes in settlement size, land tenure, and technology (coarse- versus fine-grained lithics, vessel size and shape, etc.)

(Boggess et al., chapter 8, this volume; Hogan 2006; Miller and Kenmotsu 2004; Railey 2015). This trajectory, which played out in the Jornada between AD 200 and 1450, was a pattern that has been identified, with differing forms, timing, and emphases, throughout the American Southwest. Below we provide more detail on specific aspects of the changes in the Jornada related to architecture, settlement patterns, land use, and subsistence during the Formative.

Architectural and Settlement Changes

Throughout the Jornada, architectural forms began with small, shallow, basin-shaped huts of the Late Archaic (Hogan 2006; Miller and Kenmotsu 2004; Railey 2015). These types of structures are quickly built and imply they were used for a limited time by mobile residents (Gilman 1987). In the Western Jornada they began around AD 200, but by AD 500/600 these types of structures or slightly more substantial ones, associated with ceramics and arrow points, have been identified throughout the Jornada (see Rocek, chapter 2, this volume. for a discussion of variation in these patterns). The one to three structures present at the sites suggest they housed a small number of seasonally mobile households. By the eighth century, round and rectangular pithouses replaced the huts in most regions. The pithouses were more formally constructed and often larger, requiring greater labor effort to build them. Such structures suggest an increased length of stays and a lower level of mobility. Some sites in the Western Jornada have notably large pit structures that are inferred to have a communal function (e.g., Lehmer 1948; Whalen 1994b). Around AD 1000, formal pit rooms—square in shape, shallower than the pithouses, often containing prepared caliche or adobe-plastered floors, and hearths with raised plastered collars—began to replace the pithouses. In the Western Jornada Lowlands and in the Late Glencoe phase of the Sierra Blanca/Capitan/Sacramento Mountain Highlands, these pit rooms are often found in one or more parallel rows (Kelley 1984; Miller et al. 2010). The energy expenditure to construct these rooms and their more formal features indicate they were occupied for yet greater periods of time. Moreover, the presence of several pit rooms at any one site argues that settlement size was increasing.

Settlement changes in the Early Formative in southeastern New Mexico and Trans-Pecos Texas differed in some regards from the other regions. In southeastern New Mexico, Railey (chapter 13, this volume) presents evidence of population abandonment of some areas due to drought conditions but a few sites contained nucleated settlements around oases. In the Texas Trans-Pecos, the evidence is meager outside of the Tularosa Basin. The few substantial investigations of Formative sites there indicate a continuation of small family groups living in small huts as they had during the Archaic (Hines et al. 1994). Nonetheless, they too used bows and arrows and their sites contained potsherds from the Western Jornada and goods from regions to the south or southwest, indicating they were aware of the developments in these areas.

Construction of pit rooms continued throughout the Formative, but around AD 1300 construction of contiguous-room pueblos began in most regions of the Jornada and continued until AD 1450. The El Paso–phase pueblos of the Western Jornada have received greater attention due to the quantity of CRM work at federal installations in the Tularosa Basin. These pueblos are largely found along the alluvial fans at the base of the Organ Mountains or near large playas that periodically fill with water (Carmichael 1986; Whalen 1977, 1978). The majority are small- or intermediate-size linear roomblocks of fewer than 20 rooms, but three have 100 rooms or more, and two others have over 50 (Miller et al. 2010:5–10, 36). Seventeen have plazas, and those with seven or more rooms contain large communal rooms; both the communal rooms and plazas are thought to have functioned as integrative facilities (Miller and Graves 2009:357). A particularly well-studied example is Madera Quemada Pueblo (LA 91220), a 13-room pueblo near Coe Lake Playa, occupied for only four or five years between AD 1300 and AD 1350. Like many other El Paso–phase pueblos, it was ritually burned upon abandonment (Miller and Graves 2009).

In the southern (Glencoe phase) sequence of the Sierra Blanca/Capitan/ Sacramento Highlands, true pueblo architecture is not apparent but dense clusters of subrectangular to rectangular abutting pithouses (exemplified by the Bonnell Site, LA 612 [Kelley 1984]) appear to fulfill a similar settlement function. Larger, apparently communal rooms are present. In the northern (Lincoln phase) Highland sequence, pueblos did develop, often plaza-oriented or linear in form, typically consisting of around a dozen to over a hundred rooms (Kelley 1984; Natker 2016; Wiseman 2016b). Few of these have been excavated, but examples offering some data include the Hiner Site 1 Pueblo near the northern end of the highlands; this site consisted of three pueblos, two of which were square buildings with a central plaza; the third was a linear room block (Kelley 1984:43, 185–194). Five contiguous rooms were excavated in the largest structure, which was estimated to have had 120 rooms. Earlier components underlay the excavated rooms. The Robinson site (LA 46326) is similarly constructed around a large central plaza and contains perhaps 150 contiguous rooms as well as some outlying roomblocks (Kelley 1991). Limited excavation at Robinson failed to identify a communal room, but some other Lincoln-phase pueblos such as the Block Lookout site (LA

2112) have them. Unlike their placement in El Paso–phase pueblos, these structures tend to be offset from the roomblocks or be inside the plaza areas (Wiseman 1996a, 2016b).

Pueblos or other aggregated sites were also constructed in the Jornada's Eastern Extension (Miller et al. 2016; Railey 2016). Prior to the Late Formative, the archaeological data suggest this region "was peripheral to—but not unaffected by—demographic and subsistence changes" elsewhere in the Jornada (Miller et al. 2016:21; see Railey, chapter 13, this volume, for a detailed analysis). Here the settlement, subsistence, and social developments between AD 1300 and 1450 in part parallel those taking place to the west, with aggregation into larger settlements of multiple rooms. These, however, show rapid change and a diversity of architectural forms ranging from substantial pueblos near Roswell, New Mexico (generally included in the Lincoln-phase taxon of the highlands to the west), to less-compact linear arrangements of surface rooms, to collections of pit structures found over a broader portion of the Eastern Extension. The best-known examples of the former pattern fall toward the end of the Late Formative and include the fourteenth- to early fifteenth-century Henderson (LA 1549) and Bloom Mound (LA 2528) pueblos; examples of the latter include the mid-thirteenth- to early fourteenth-century Rocky Arroyo (LA 25277) and Fox Place (LA 25277) sites in the "Roswell Oasis" (Wiseman 2013) on the west edge of modern Roswell (Speth 2004b, 2008; Speth and LeDuc 2007; Wiseman 2002, 2013). In the Eastern Extension of far southeastern New Mexico, the Merchant site (LA 43414) combines linear room alignments with slab "*cimiento*" foundations and a few isolated rooms, for a total of at least 21 surface rooms (Miller et al. 2016). This site is classified as part of the fourteenth- to early fifteenth-century Ochoa phase of the Eastern Extension region chronological sequence (figure 1.3), and is part of a broader scatter of relatively little-studied Late Formative village sites in this area (Railey 2016).

Some Eastern Extension sites had communal or ceremonial architecture or other features. Bloom Mound had a deep pit structure with a presumed ceremonial function (Speth 2008). A deep kiva at Fox Place had a horned serpent plastered on its walls (Wiseman 2002). Henderson Pueblo, with an estimated 130 rooms, had a large earth-oven complex that "served as the principal communal and ritual focus" for the village of some 80 individuals (Speth 2004a:421), though excavation identified no communal architecture. In addition to its surface rooms, the Merchant site had two pit rooms, dug through hard-pan caliche, that probably served communal and ceremonial functions (Miller et al. 2016:21, 405).

Subsistence Patterns in the Jornada

Reliance on cultivated crops versus the collection and hunting of wild plants and animals is clearly tied to changes in settlement intensity, architectural forms, and social organization. The extant archaeological record for the various regions of the Jornada illustrate a general increase in the importance of cultivated plants (specifically maize and beans) over the Late Archaic and Formative sequence, but non-domesticated foods remained important in many cases.

In the Western Jornada, maize, and to a lesser extent beans, were part of the subsistence foods as early as AD 200 but ubiquity ratios show that these domesticates were far from the primary dietary staples (Miller and Kenmotsu 2004; see Miller and Kenmotsu, chapter 3, this volume, and Condon and Vasquez, chapter 4, this volume, for detailed explorations of the Western Jornada subsistence sequence). As in the Late Archaic, rabbit species were the primary protein staple in the small sites in the basin while larger mammals served that purpose in the rockshelters and uplands. Several dozen wild plant taxa have been identified in pits, hearths, and structure remains from the small sites dating to the Mesilla phase. A continuing concern with understanding the subsistence patterns of the Mesilla phase in the lowlands is the often uneven recovery of plant remains, especially from sites in the basin proper, where preservation rates are quite low (Miller and Kenmotsu 2004). By the Early Doña Ana phase (AD 1000–1150), however, settlement moved from the basin to the alluvial fans that ring the edge of it. Recovery of plant remains at those sites is higher and shows that while the ubiquity of cacti/succulents continues to increase, so do maize and beans. In the subsequent Late Doña Ana and El Paso phases, the ubiquity of maize continues to increase. Beans and cacti/succulents, however, decrease (see Miller and Kenmotsu, chapter 3, this volume, for a discussion of the reasons for this decrease and how they are linked to architectural forms and settlement intensity; see Miller and Montgomery, chapter 12, this volume, for an exploration of burnt-rock middens and the role of pit-baked cacti/succulents from the Archaic through the Formative and into the historic period).

Unlike the Western Jornada Lowlands, early Formative evidence from the Sierra Blanca/Capitan/Sacramento Highlands begins around AD 500 and indicates that maize ubiquity was much higher than it was in the lowlands, despite substantial residential mobility (Campbell and Railey 2008; Railey and Turnbow, chapter 5, this volume; Rocek 1995, 2007a). Large bell-shaped pits at Late Archaic (see discussion above) and Early Formative sites also reflect the early importance of agriculture in this region. This carries over into later periods with significant evidence of farming in the Late Formative. At a number of later sites in the Roswell Oases, however, this evidence is combined with large numbers of bison bones, suggesting that bison hunting and/or trade onto the Southern Plains was part of a broader regional pattern (see below) (Speth 2004b; Wiseman 2013).

Southeast of the highlands, beyond the Roswell area, evidence of farming is evident in the recovery of maize as well as possible agricultural features at the Late Formative Merchant site. Finds of maize occur at a few other sites in this region but wild-plant resources are clearly important (Miller et al. 2016). Evidence of bison hunting increased across the area and in the broader Southern Plains after about AD 1250 (Miller et al. 2016; Railey 2016:111). The degree of reliance on agriculture in the Late Formative villages of the Eastern Extension remains a topic of research.

In the Eastern Extension of western Trans-Pecos Texas, ceramics have been recovered, but evidence of subsistence other than hunting and gathering is lacking, although it should be noted that few subsurface investigations have been undertaken. Demographic fluctuations described by Railey (chapter 13, this volume) suggest potential shifts back and forth between settled and mobile communities over time, and the movement of ceramics and other resources show substantial connections between mobile populations in the Eastern Extension and village groups in the highlands and basins to the west and northwest, as well as movement within individual regions as well (in this volume, see Miller et al., chapter 6; Lynch and Rocek, chapter 7; Boggess et al., chapter 8; and Hill, chapter 9).

The Southern Jornada Mogollon of northern Chihuahua is by far the least-explored region. As outlined by Cruz Antillón et al. in chapter 11, the region's architecture, ceramics, and presumably subsistence show strong ties to patterns seen in the Western Jornada Lowlands, though they also show a broad pattern of interaction with and influence by the Casas Grandes culture to the west. Currently most information for this area is based on surface data and excavations of a few pueblos resembling those of the El Paso region.

Abandonment and the End of the Formative

The end of the Formative period across the Jornada is marked by the disappearance of settled aggregated communities. The timing of this remains imprecisely known, but across much of the region it seems to fall in the early to mid-fifteenth century AD, suggesting a broad pan-regional environmental factor, a cascade of interacting social and/or economic changes, or, most likely, a combination of these. The same period is marked by the disappearance of occupation at Paquimé and at substantial sites in other portions of the southern Southwest within and beyond the Mogollon (Phillips and Gamboa 2015; see also chronometric analysis in Railey, chapter 13, this volume). A few Late Formative sites on the edge of the northern Sierra Blanca/Capitan/Sacramento Highlands have evidence of violence (Speth 2008; Wiseman 1997), though this cannot account for the full scale of the abandonment. By the time of Spanish contact, the Jornada area was occupied by relatively dispersed and mobile groups, but the villages of the Late Formative were no longer occupied.

In sum, a sequence from Archaic hunting and gathering through early agriculture, early pithouse settlements, and later pueblos is found across the Jornada, but some regions retained hunting and gathering adaptations, with persistent ephemeral or pithouse architecture (see figures 1.1 and 1.3). The data now show numerous, and sometimes quite abrupt, transformations occurred *within* any one of these broader patterns; the hunting-gathering manifestations as well as the agricultural populations display a dynamic range of shifting adaptations. The Jornada has a large and still-growing data set offering important insights into the range of "big issues" of central anthropological interest. As noted above, the adoption of agriculture (as well as variation in the rate of its adoption or rejection), shifts in mobility, and patterns of aggregation as well as social and political organization all play out in the regional archaeological sequence. Furthermore, the Jornada's geographic position makes it ideal for studying additional issues, such as those of interaction at both the local and interregional scale (for instance, Plains–Southwest, Southwest–Mesoamerican), ecological complementarity (for instance, farmer–hunter-gatherer, lowland–highland), ethnic diversity, and shifts in economic adaptation beyond the adoption of agriculture (such as the apparent shift away from agriculture in a variety of environments in the Jornada over the last half millennium).

ORGANIZATION OF THE VOLUME

The chapters in this volume are organized to explore some of these broader issues. Figure 1.1 helps readers orient themselves to the geographic focus of each chapter, figure 1.2 shows some of the major geographical features referred to throughout the text, and figure 1.3 provides chronological cross-references.

The volume is divided into four sections. In the first, introductory section (Part I), the present chapter as well as chapter 2 by Rocek introduce the environmental and cultural diversity of the Jornada and describe major geographical and environmental divisions. Rocek uses variation in architecture to demonstrate some of the cultural variation within and among these regions, exploring the multivariate underlying causes of the differences (environmental, social, economic, etc.) and showing how the history of research in the Jornada has resulted in a biased perception that oversimplifies and underestimates this diversity.

The second section (Part II) focuses on subsistence and the development of the farming economies that were fundamental to the Formative adaptation. In chapter 3, Miller and Kenmotsu synthesize subsistence data from the best-known region of the Jornada, the Western Lowlands and the adjoining mountain foothills to the east. They demonstrate a highly dynamic mixture of strategies that included intensified acquisition of *both* gathered foods and domestic crops in the early second millennium of the current era, followed by (in some areas) a shift to more-focused agricultural intensification by the fourteenth century. Within that broader set of patterns, settlement systems remained dynamic and both economic and social patterns varied locally; the diversity also reflects interaction with groups from beyond the Jornada, such as in the Mimbres region to the west and in modern Chihuahua to the south.

In chapter 4, Condon and Vasquez focus more narrowly on subsistence and geographically on a smaller area within the Tularosa Basin, while extending the analysis back into the Archaic. Their results complement those of chapter 3, confirming the relatively late increase in agricultural reliance, but also finding increased wild-plant diversity early in the Formative and suggesting the continued importance of wild resources even in the later periods, when Miller and Kenmotsu's data suggest a narrower focus on agriculture. The combination of the two chapters confirms the diverse and dynamic nature of adaptations, even within the Western Jornada.

Then, in chapter 5, Railey and Turnbow summarize evidence demonstrating one particular dimension of subsistence variation within the Jornada: the contrast between the process of slow and gradual commitment to agriculture in much of the Western Jornada, documented in the previous two chapters, versus the relatively abrupt shift to agriculture several centuries earlier in the highlands. They draw on comparative data from the Mimbres highlands west of the Jornada region to show that this contrast may be part of a broader pattern of early agricultural reliance in the highlands of southern New Mexico. These results confirm other data that suggest both subsistence and social contrasts between the highlands and lowlands, and contradict a perception that groups in southern New Mexico lagged in the adoption of agriculture behind adjacent regions.

The third section (Part III) explores mobility, sedentism, and integration. In chapter 6, Miller and his coauthors describe a major payoff of CRM investment in a non-site survey strategy ("transect recording units," or TRUs) that allows artifact distributions to be studied across landscapes without the prohibitive cost of mapping each individual item. Analysis of large-scale distributions of sherds across a section of the Tularosa Basin has identified a series of previously unrecognized prehistoric trails. While some may reflect local trips for water and other resources, Miller et al. demonstrate that a disproportionate number of the ceramics found along these trails were not locally produced, suggesting movements across the basins linking to settlements in more distant parts of the Jornada. They also document the diversity of these trails and their likely functions ranging from local resource procurement to visits between settlements within and perhaps beyond the Jornada, and perhaps travel associated with ritual activities.

In chapter 7, Lynch and Rocek examine the degree of mobility by the "settled" farmers of the Capitan Highlands in the Early Formative period compared to both the Archaic and the Late Formative. Shifts in the procurement of lithic materials suggest that mobility was already limited by the Late Archaic and it appears to have decreased further in the Formative, with the greatest emphasis on local resources in the second millennium AD after pueblo architecture became common in many parts of the area. Despite the evidence of agricultural dependence among highland Early Formative pithouse sites described above, the lithic data imply that they exhibited a transitional degree of movement, with a gradual trend toward reduction that culminated with the greatest curtailment in mobility after the transition to pueblo occupations.

In chapter 8, Boggess et al. show a direct example of mobility through analysis of a late twelfth or early to mid-thirteenth century AD ceramic vessel at an ephemeral site in the Eastern Extension, east of the Pecos River. They demonstrate that the vessel was made in the Sierra Blanca/Capitan Highlands some 200 km to the northwest and that its use history included exposure to a broad array of foods, including locally available plants such as grass seeds and *Commelina* (dayflower, a weed often found infesting agricultural fields that might have existed in the area), but also hints of starchy foods such as acorns or agave as well as a range of others. Chemical indications of aquatic resources, likely fish, suggest a stop at the Pecos River as well. Thus, the chapter indicates either that individuals in the highlands traveled far into the lowlands to the east, or perhaps more likely, interacted with groups in that region who used highland-produced pottery as they followed a complex, highly mobile lifestyle.

In chapter 9, Hill synthesizes ceramic data over a wide region of southeastern New Mexico and west Texas, covering a good portion of the Eastern Extension and the eastern fringes of the Western Jornada. Consistent with the vessel described by Boggess et al. in the preceding chapter, he finds that the vast majority of the ceramics were imported either from the Sierra Blanca/ Capitan/Sacramento Highlands or from the Western Jornada Lowlands. This reinforces the evidence of long-distance eastward mobility by the agricultural and relatively settled groups in the highlands and Western Jornada and/or interaction between them and more mobile groups to the east. One ceramic type (Ochoa Indented, associated with the Ochoa phase villages described above) does not fit this pattern, but indicates limited ceramic production among the eastern groups.

Finally, the fourth section (Part IV) considers the borders of the Jornada, both in terms of geographical boundaries and lifestyle. In chapter 10, Kenmotsu examines who the occupants of the La Junta del Rios region on the Texas/Chihuahua border were, and what sort of lifeway their sites imply. Consistent with previous chapters, she finds significant indications of interaction with core Jornada regions and the suggestion of an actual migration event into this area. The La Junta population remained distinct and dominated by descendants of the local hunting-gathering populations, however, and a mixed economy and seasonal mobility persisted, along with interaction both to the west with Casas Grandes and to the north with the Jornada. The La Junta communities in fact outlasted both the Casas Grandes and Jornada settlements in whose company they had developed.

In chapter 11, Cruz Antillón et al. examine the question of Lehmer's (1948) inclusion of northern Chihuahuan groups in the Jornada. Their core finding is that Lehmer got it right; while the boundary between the Casas Grandes and Southern Jornada was fuzzy, they represent meaningful, distinct entities, and sites in northern Chihuahua do have distinctly Jornada characteristics. On the other hand, they also describe contact and flux along that border.

Chapter 12 by Miller and Montgomery examines terminal Archaic to Late Formative–period burned-rock middens (BRM), among the least glamorous of archaeological features, and a hallmark of what is often assumed to be ephemeral hunting-gathering occupation patterns restricted to the fringes of the Jornada. They show that the construction of these features varied greatly over time and shifted spatially as well, with use fluctuating in several pulses and showing a trend from intensive processing of foods in Western Jornada Lowland settings to less-intensive logistical use of higher-elevation features in the west and by mobile groups farther east. Most important, they suggest production of these features was not restricted to mobile populations but instead represented an important activity of the farming villages of the Western Jornada and adjoining eastern mountain foothills that likely used them for production of alcoholic drinks for religious and socially integrative functions.

In chapter 13, Railey synthesizes a large body of radiocarbon dates from the Eastern Extension in southeastern New Mexico recently available due to an innovative Bureau of Land Management program that pools CRM resources to fund theory-driven research projects. Railey documents trends from the Early Archaic through the Late Prehistoric, showing how populations fluctuated in response to major environmental changes. Mobile hunting-gathering groups dominated the far southeastern borders of the Jornada, but pockets of reduced mobility, agricultural production, and small-scale aggregation developed in the Ochoa phase in the western and central portions of this region in the second millennium AD. Beyond climate, he notes the impact of regional developments. These included the rise of the Plains bison trade in the mid-thirteenth century followed by the disappearance of the Casas Grandes system and of aggregated villages to the west and northwest across the rest of the Jornada and the broader Southwest.

Finally, Wiseman's discussion in chapter 14 explicitly lays out an argument for ethnic diversity *within* the area currently subsumed under the Jornada. Archaeologists have a history of casually equating material culture variation with distinct "cultures." The diversity in the Jornada as well as ethnographic and historically documented ethnic divisions demands exploration of this issue both in order to understand patterns in the Jornada itself and questions of ethnicity in prehistory generally. Using the distribution of house forms, non-domestic architecture, utility wares, freshwater-shell ornaments, and bone gaming pieces, he suggests that, at least in the Late Formative, the Western Jornada Lowlands, the southern Sierra Blanca/Sacramento Highlands, and the northern Sierra Blanca/Capitan Highlands respectively represent three distinct ethnic groups, and he has argued elsewhere (Wiseman 2000, 2002, 2003b) for additional ethnic divisions within the Jornada. These sorts of ideas are implicit in many taxonomic divisions suggested over the years in the Jornada, the Mogollon more generally, and in many other cases (e.g., Lehmer 1948), but Wiseman offers a clear, explicit argument and data, allowing for future testing and refinement of such hypotheses.

THE FUTURE OF JORNADA RESEARCH

The last several decades have brought great progress of many sorts to Jornada research: improvements such as a dramatically expanded body of data, innovative survey strategies and CRM research priorities, the clarification of chronological sequences, and the documentation of ceramic-exchange patterns. An array of critical data gaps remains, but so do exciting topics for future research. The expansion of data and improved methods reveal more about our ignorance of the area, but also makes a range of new research topics accessible.

To cite a few examples regarding the gaps: survey and even more excavation coverage across the highly diverse Jornada country remains tremendously uneven; coverage of the Texas portion of the Eastern Extension and of the Chihuahuan portion of the Jornada is particularly sparse (see discussions in Rocek, chapter 2, and Cruz Antillón et al., chapter 11, both in this volume). This volume describes many parts of the Jornada, but even here we do little justice to many regions, such as only touching on the complexity of the Roswell Oasis cluster of Plains-edge aggregated communities that flourished for a brief few centuries between the Capitan Mountains and the Pecos near modern Roswell, nor covering the Pecos valley to the north.

Beyond filling in the large data gaps, basic questions regarding the Jornada remain unanswered. The sociocultural composition of the Jornada as a whole and the subdivisions within it addressed by Wiseman in chapter 14 are major avenues for further research. A related question concerns the integrity of the Jornada over time; its deep ceramic and artistic traditions (Miller et al. 2012; Miller 2018b) suggest a coherence and an influence on adjacent regions rather than a weak reflection of the "core" Southwest.

More broadly, the question of Jornada identity is linked with two other issues. One is the role of the Jornada in the broader world, not only of the Southwest but the Plains and northern Mesoamerica as well. Several chapters here (see also Rocek and Rautman 2007) show that the Jornada was both at the receiving end of impacts from surrounding regions and an active participant in many of those events. A second related issue concerns the fate of Jornada populations after the mid-fifteenth century. The abandonment of villages raises questions about where descendant populations went and why, and about the origins of mobile groups living in the region in the historical period. Given the Jornada's diversity there is likely to be more than one answer.

Basic questions of subsistence and settlement (variation in the mode, timing, and pattern of adoption of agriculture, for instance) remain major issues despite the advances described in this volume, as are questions regarding the relations between different economic systems and social groups within the region. The structure of sociopolitical groups such as discussed by Miller et al. in chapter 6 and Miller and Montgomery in chapter 12 have barely been addressed. The environmental impacts considered by Railey in chapter 13 invite more environmental studies across the region.

The Jornada has long been viewed as peripheral, monotonous, and static, in short, not terribly interesting in comparison with surrounding areas. As the chapters in this volume demonstrate, the region is in fact none of these—it is dynamic and complex, and its inhabitants played a significant economic, political, and social role at multiple scales. The oft-cited irony of A. V. Kidder's account of hearing that the Southwest was a "sucked orange" with no more information to contribute (Givens 1992:150) applies well to the Jornada. Perhaps more than in many other regions of the Southwest, we have barely scratched the surface of a very rich soil.

NOTES

1. Throughout the volume, the designation *Jornada* applies to the area as a whole. References to portions of the Jornada will use the name(s) of the region(s).

2. We lump the lowlands of the Hueco Bolson with the Tularosa Basin in this volume under the term *Western Jornada Lowlands*, or *Western Jornada*, for simplicity. These are contiguous, graben valleys flanked by block-faulted mountain ranges and highlands (Abbott et al. 2009:2-1 to 2-3). The Tularosa Basin is in New Mexico while the smaller Hueco Bolson is largely in adjacent Texas (Figure 1.2). Together, they form a continuous valley that is oriented primarily north–south. The divide between them consists of a slight topographic rise.

3. The site has also been referred to both in print and in unpublished notes with the first two digits of its Laboratory of Anthropology identification number reversed (that is, as 17687). However, the New Mexico Cultural Resource Information System's Archaeological Resource Management System Record matches 71687 instead, and identifies LA 17687 as a site in northwestern New Mexico.

4. This phase sequence is not included on figure 1.3 since Wiseman (1985b) proposed its abandonment and few to no researchers in the region continue to use it; Kelley's (1984) highland-phase sequences described below have largely superseded it.

2

Jornada Huts and Houses

Implications of Formative
Architectural Diversity
in the Jornada

Thomas R. Rocek

DOI: 10.5876/9781607327950.c002

Beginning with Lehmer's (1948) original definition of the Jornada branch of the Mogollon, researchers have recognized that this branch encompasses a great deal of diversity. Lehmer's synthesis divided the Formative archaeological sequence along a north–south split into two phase sequences, with the Capitan, Three Rivers, and San Andres on the north paralleling the Mesilla, Doña Ana, and El Paso sequence to the south. Subsequent syntheses of the Jornada have devoted considerable discussion to the Jornada's regional differences (e.g., Wheat 1955:29–33). Jane Kelley (1984 [originally 1966]) further subdivided the northern highland portion of the region, splitting the Capitan/Sierra Blanca/Sacramento Highlands off from Lehmer's broader taxonomy and dividing the highlands into parallel northern and southern Formative-phase sequences. Meanwhile, Corley (1965) and Leslie (1979) argued for an extension of the Jornada eastward to encompass an even broader range of environmental and cultural patterns (see discussion in Rocek and Kenmotsu, chapter 1, this volume: figures 1.1, 1.2, and 1.3.).

Despite this early recognition of differing patterns across the Jornada, however, subsequent research has tended to emphasize a single broad characterization of the archaeological culture. This conventional narrative portrays Jornada populations as mostly dispersed mobile Archaic hunter-gatherers of the semi-arid lowland basins who, late in prehistory, briefly experimented with a Puebloan agricultural lifeway, before reverting to mobile foraging or abandoning the region altogether (e.g., Cordell and McBrinn 2012). As pointed to in chapter 1, the fallacy of this perspective can be seen from various angles. Here I focus on architectural patterns to illustrate the multiple patterns characteristic of the Jornada.

Many aspects of culture both shape and in turn are shaped by architecture; these span a spectrum from the physical function of structures in providing shelter from the elements to their role in housing social units to their symbolic function as representations of identity and ideology (e.g., Baldwin 1987; Hodder 2012; McGuire and Schiffer 1983; Rapoport 1969). Although archaeological evidence of structure construction, form, and size has played a significant part in interpretations of how the prehistoric occupants of the Jornada lived and who they were, this architectural variety is lost in many discussions of the region. In the discussion below, I suggest the historical reasons for the "homogenized" and simplified view of the Jornada and, and how the architectural differences actually serve to illustrate the multiple trajectories of development across the region.

HISTORY OF RESEARCH

After the pioneering work of the 1940s through 1960s established the basic parameters of the Jornada, research emphases shifted as the demands of Cultural Resource Management (CRM) combined with a theoretical orientation increasingly shaped by processual archaeology. This expansion beyond the initial focus on description and comparison of regional phase sequences developed in two major directions.

First, a tremendous expansion in the quantity of data and finer attention to temporal patterning from numerous new radiocarbon dates (e.g., Mauldin 1995; Miller 1996, 2005a; Miller and Kenmotsu 2004; Stewart et al. 1991; Whalen 1985; see also in this volume Miller and Kenmotsu, chapter 3; Miller and Montgomery, chapter 12; and Railey, chapter 13) decreased reliance on dates derived purely from ceramic and lithic cross-dating, and refined the boundaries of the phase sequences. Critically, this not only improved chronological control in general, but increased the evidence of contemporaneity among very different but geographically adjacent structures and settlements, even when lumped into the same phase.

This improved chronological control set the stage for the second trend. Following particularly from Whalen's (1981a) theoretical orientation regarding the pithouse-to-pueblo transition and subsequent reevaluations (e.g.,

Carmichael 1981, 1985; Hard 1983b; O'Laughlin 1981; Whalen 1994b), research on pithouse-period occupations came to focus heavily on functional variation among sites. This has resulted in the accumulation of a wealth of data documenting multiple contemporary structure and site types and the identification of patterning among pithouse architectural forms and their associated settlement patterns.

Paradoxically, however, the explosion in data and analyses of the recent decades also had two negative impacts, to a certain degree detracting from peculiar advantages enjoyed by the first few syntheses of the Jornada Mogollon in the 1940s through 1960s. First, Jornada research has come to have an element of what Kuhn (1962) called "normal science." While the explosion in data has certainly produced surprises and exceptions to broadly perceived patterns, there is a sense that sites can and should be organized into consistent settlement systems and that chronological patterns can be linked to a fairly straightforward trend from relatively mobile and minimally agricultural Late Archaic populations to more settled and agriculturally dependent Late Formative groups. This view reflects the great advances in our understanding of regional settlement data combined with a wealth of ceramic, lithic, and architectural information, as well as a growing body of subsistence data. Thus, we have come far beyond the largely site-based limited comparisons possible in the early years of Jornada research. But at the same time, there is a danger of overgeneralization and oversimplification. It is not easy to distinguish between the occasional peculiar site as a data outlier, explicable on some very particularistic basis, versus recognizing a distinct broader subpattern that contrasts with recognized regional trends.

Second, and again reflecting the tremendous advance in Jornada research, is a tendency toward regional specialization. This latter point has a certain irony; early researchers were forced to draw their examples from a broad area, and they themselves often roamed over many regions of the Southwest simply because of the paucity of available research projects and excavated sites. With the rise of CRM archaeology and the expansion of regional databases, current researchers logically focus their comparisons on the most appropriate data—typically sites and settlement patterns in the regions surrounding their research areas. This latter trend is particularly exacerbated by a tremendous imbalance in the scale of CRM within the Jornada, in which most large projects through the twentieth and first years of the twenty-first century were heavily concentrated around three large military bases located in the interior Western Jornada lowland portion of this region. For example, by 2008 over 878,000 acres (3,554 km², or more than 79%) of Fort Bliss had been surveyed and yielded almost 18,500 sites (US Army 2010:3–129); as of 2016, almost 21,000 sites had been identified (US Army Corps of Engineers, Tulsa District, and Directorate of Public Works Environmental Division, Fort Bliss 2016:ES-2) (figure 2.1).[1] Furthermore, the very nature of the basin environments, which are subject to considerable deflation, tends to make the Formative archaeological record more readily visible in that area than in some of the other zones of the Jornada.

Thus, much of what has come to be viewed as typical of the Jornada Mogollon could more accurately be described as typical of the western lowland Jornada Mogollon, or more accurately still, the Jornada Mogollon of the Tularosa Basin, Hueco Bolson, and adjacent regions surrounding and north of El Paso, Texas, and lying primarily in the basin portions of the basin-and-range topography. This is not to imply that researchers are ignorant of the moderate amounts of research in the riverine corridors or of the even more-limited work in the highland ranges or the regions to the east or south, but simply that the biased distribution of research and known sites disproportionately reflects trends in the western lowlands.

THE DIMENSIONS OF VARIATION IN FORMATIVE JORNADA ARCHITECTURE

Turning to architecture itself, as noted earlier, it is important to consider some of the major variables frequently recognized as influencing architecture (cf. Baldwin 1987; McGuire and Schiffer 1983; Rapoport 1969). These offer critical insights into the groups that produced the structures. While they can be organized and classified in many ways, I focus specifically on five factors here: ethnic or cultural tradition, type and degree of mobility, site function and seasonality, environmental setting, and social organization.

The question of differences between cultural traditions was central to the theoretical orientation of the earliest Jornada researchers. Just as work in the Mogollon area in general started with the issue of identifying the cultural distinctiveness of what was viewed implicitly as a discrete Mogollon *ethnic* group (e.g., Haury 1936), initial work in and around the Jornada region tended to emphasize the question of "regional affiliation" both for the identification of a distinctive Jornada pattern and the delineation of its geographic boundaries (e.g., Kelley 1984:151–163; Lehmer 1948:73–90; Peckham 1976; Wheat 1955:189–233). These arguments most often emphasized ceramic and, to a degree, lithic data, but also included architectural traits such as house depth and shape, presence or absence of ventilators, and so forth, and noted geographic patterning in the

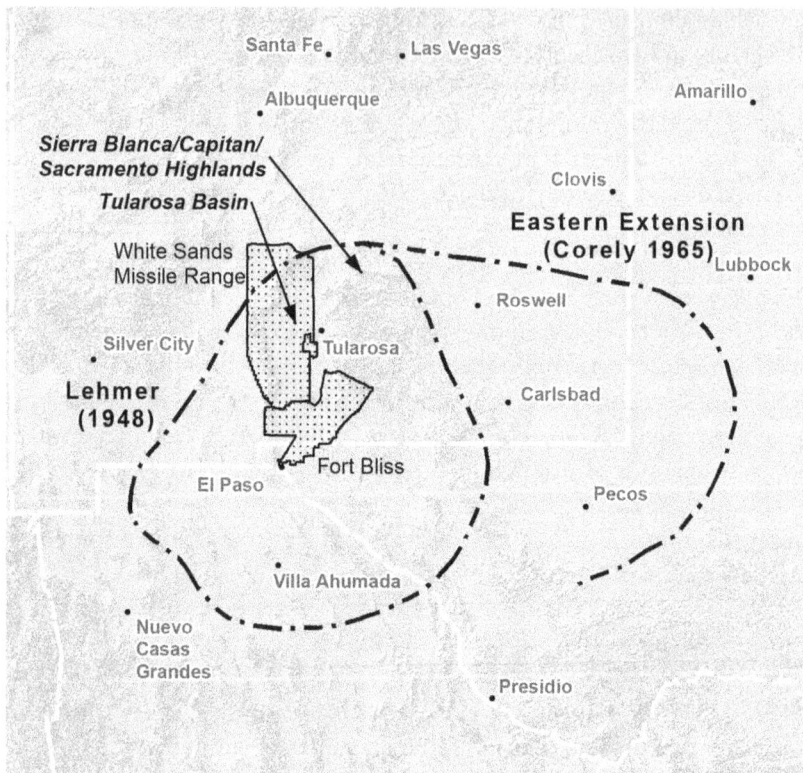

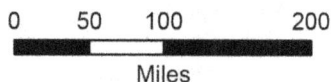

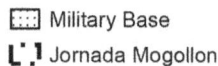

FIGURE 2.1. *Major military bases in the Western Jornada Lowlands (Tularosa Basin and Hueco Bolson) regions where the largest amount of Jornada research has been concentrated. Figure by Sandra L. Hannum.*

available architectural data. Along with the distribution of brownware ceramics, the late persistence of pithouses in the Jornada region was itself part of the basis for considering the Jornada a subdivision of the Mogollon pattern, and architectural variation within the Jornada contributed to the creation of the internal parallel geographic phase divisions mentioned above.

This emphasis on cultural identity decreased with the ascendancy of processual archaeology and criticism (e.g., Binford 1965; Speth 1988) of the paradigm of "breeding potsherds" that automatically attributed an equivalence between archaeological "cultures" defined on the basis of shared material culture traits and living "cultures" or "ethnic groups," concepts that themselves have often proved problematic even in ethnographic contexts.

Despite the cogency of this critique, the concepts of ethnicity and culture have remained topics of some of the research in the Jornada area (e.g., Kyte 1988; Wilson 2004; Wiseman 2000; 2002:170–174; 2003b; chapter 14, this volume). Furthermore, the renewed recognition of migration in the prehistoric Southwest and thus the importance of specific cultural links over time (e.g., Cameron and Duff 2008; Herhahn and Ramenofsky 2016; Hill et al. 2004; Mills et al. 2015; Stone 2003) serve as reminders that there truly *is* ethnic patterning in material culture that must form part of the explanatory framework of prehistoric material diversity. It is entirely likely that at various times the Jornada area encompassed multiple cultural groups that varied over time in their degree of integration, differentiation, or hostility. Likely patterns to consider for evidence of ethnic differences include the major north–south axis relating to the Ancestral Pueblo (or "Anasazi") versus Mogollon patterns and the east–west axis from the Rio Grande Valley, over the mountains and onto the Plains, as well as some of the more localized contrasts such as the Corona/Lincoln versus Glencoe phases in the Capitan Mountains, or perhaps broader divisions between lowland and highland groups (see chapter 1). Examples of suggestive patterning include a tendency for non-communal pithouses with ventilator shafts to be restricted primarily to the northern and western fringes of the Jornada, and of pithouse entries to be overwhelmingly south-facing in the Western Jornada Lowlands but more variable in other regions of the Jornada (Rocek 2011). Examination of this variation should not translate into the automatic assumption that architectural or any other material culture element necessarily is indicative of stylistically delimited ethnic groups, but it is appropriate to consider ethnic tradition and boundary maintenance among the dimensions structuring the architectural forms we observe.

On the other hand, attribution of ethnicity as a dimension of architectural variation must include at least four critical components: (1) clear identification of what attributes are being interpreted as marking cultural affiliation, (2) an explicit theoretical context for interpreting what represents ethnic tradition (e.g., Baldwin 1987; Stone 2003) rather than an ad hoc attribution of traits to cultural groups, (3) recognition of the dynamic nature of cultural patterns both as populations migrate and as ethnic boundaries are constructed or deemphasized over time, and (4) recognition of the potential for ethnicity to covary in complex and changing ways with other dimensions, such as site function or environmental settings. For instance, houses may pattern in certain ways due to the requirements of a given environment, but, at the same time, that environment may be occupied primarily by particular ethnic groups. In such a case, identifying the house styles in that area as specific to ethnicity or specific to the environment would be ambiguous. This latter caution regarding the potential for cross-correlations among multiple variables applies not only to this ethnic variable but to all of the other dimensions of variability I consider in the remainder of this chapter.

Moving from the ethnic dimension to others that are most heavily emphasized in the current literature of the Jornada region, three variables are closely associated with elaborateness of house construction. Much of the architectural literature of the Formative period is divided between surface pueblos and semisubterranean pit structures, and the later are subdivided into categories referred to as *huts* (Hard 1983a; Miller and Kenmotsu 2004:239) or simply *small houses* (Whalen 1994a:626) versus larger, more substantial *pithouses*. An additional category, typically identified as communal or ceremonial, consists of even larger and more substantial structures, or occasionally structures characterized by particular features such as benches or painting (e.g., Kelley 1984:85–88; Railey 2002:776 [with citations]; Shelley 1992:9; Whalen 1994b:51–53,135; Wilcox 2002; Wiseman 1996a; 2002). Leaving aside for now this communal or ceremonial category and the relatively substantial pueblos, the division between the small ephemeral *house* or *hut* versus more substantial *pithouse* potentially represents the intersection of at least three distinct underlying factors.

First, is a temporal pattern that is widely noted and generally assumed to relate to a trend toward decreasing *mobility*. The few known Late Archaic structures in the Jornada are typically small, shallow, and lightly built, with little evidence of prolonged repair. Subsequent periods in the Formative (expanding on a few earlier isolated cases observed toward the end of the Late Archaic [Graves et al. 2014]) show an increasing abundance of larger, deeper, more substantially constructed and more frequently repaired houses. This trend is widely interpreted as a consequence of greater permanence of settlement over time, culminating in the pithouse-to-pueblo transition in most areas.

Second is a *seasonal* and *functional* dimension linked to an annual settlement round. Beginning with the work of Whalen (1981a; see also Carmichael 1981, 1985; O'Laughlin 1981; Whalen 1994b), a well-established framework of interpretation partitions sites between villages or residential bases and more ephemeral collecting or other limited-activity sites. Some of the latter have no preserved features or architecture, but others have small structures that imply minimal investment in construction and maintenance.

A third variable is *environmental setting*. This variable encompasses factors such as temperature, precipitation, and wind, as well as availability of resources such as wood, clay, and water. It is clearly also correlated with both seasonality of settlement and the economic activities that influence mobility decisions. However, additional impacts on architecture relating directly to the environment derive from factors such as local climate and the availability of construction materials as well as resources such as firewood. Many current analyses of Jornada architecture consider environmental setting at a relatively fine scale of resolution, distinguishing basin or playa bottoms from basin edges, alluvial fans, adjacent slopes, and so forth (e.g., Graves et al. 1996; Peterson 2001, Appendix 3 [compiled by Graves]). This topographic variable is confounded with both the temporal trend in mobility and with variation within settlement rounds, since different portions of the settlement round concentrate in different environmental settings, and since among the most clearly demonstrated trends in the Western Jornada Lowlands region are shifts over time in the concentration of archaeological settlement locations (e.g., Whalen 1994a; Miller and Kenmotsu 2004). Thus, while early ephemeral structures are scattered over a wide range of environments in and around the basins, including in the basin bottoms themselves, later-period substantial architecture tends to be more tightly restricted to playa- and basin-edge settings and alluvial fans. Within this broader pattern is a possible trend for a greater concentration of later Formative pueblo sites down along playa edges and for basin-edge pueblos to be relatively rare and shifted downward toward the lower alluvial fans (Miller and Kenmotsu 2004:244–245). Discovery of at least one large pueblo above the eastern-basin alluvial fans in the highland foothills (Miller and Graves 2012) may indicate the existence of an additional component of the Late Formative settlement distribution (Nancy Kenmotsu, personal communication 2015; see also Miller and Kenmotsu, chapter 3, this volume).

Beyond the four factors of ethnic differences, temporal changes in mobility, seasonal settlement rounds, and local environments, at least one other set of variables—shifts in *social organization*—is of relevance to interpreting architectural patterns. House size and construction reflects not only the function of a site in a settlement round but also the nature of the social group(s) occupying the structures, and the composition and durability of the community occupying the site as a whole. Beyond house construction, social factors influence the presence and form of communal structures, communal features such as plazas, and shared walls among houses. Similarly, the type and placement of storage features and specialized features can reflect social organization (e.g., Rocek 1998; Wills 2001).

BIASED DATA

The pattering among these five core variables—cultural tradition, degree and pattern of mobility, site function within a seasonal settlement round, environmental setting, and intra- and interhousehold social organization—gives rise to the major concern of this chapter: the danger of a biased understanding of the Jornada region due to restriction of interpretations to a subset of the Jornada. As noted previously, the vast majority of research in recent decades has focused on the Western Jornada Lowlands and their immediate surroundings. Although in recent years more of this work has included areas of the adjacent Sacramento Mountain foothills and Otero Mesa, this still constitutes a limited portion of Lehmer's original Jornada region (figure 1.2). And while this area encompasses a considerable range of topography and ecological settings, that diversity is dwarfed by the differences across the surrounding regions. Three geographic regions (as shown in figure 1.2) are notably underrepresented in Jornada research: the Capitan/Sierra Blanca /Sacramento Highlands, the Eastern Extension, and the Southern Jornada region in northern Chihuahua. Furthermore, even within the relatively well-studied Western Jornada region, the riverine zone is poorly documented for reasons discussed below (figure 1.2).

The highland areas of the Capitan, Sierra Blanca, Sacramento, and Guadalupe Mountains on the east and the San Andres and Organ Mountains on the west, as well some of the slightly lower surrounding ranges, constitute a highly distinct environment. Recent research suggests that at least some of these areas have an evolutionary trajectory that is different from that of the adjacent lowlands. Although hunting is clearly important in the highlands and projectile points are notably abundant compared to the lowlands (Miller and Kenmotsu 2004:255), agriculture appeared earlier and much more abruptly in the highlands while evidence of a progressive increase in agricultural dependence over the course of the Formative is much less clear (Hard, Durst and Raymond 1996; Hard, Mauldin, and Raymond 1996; Howey and Rocek 2008; Railey 2008; Rocek 1995, 1997; see also Railey and Turnbow, chapter 5, this volume).

Architectural trends also differ significantly from those in the western low-lands. The few known Early Formative structures in the Sierra Blanca/Capitan/Sacramento Highlands region are markedly larger and more substantial than contemporary structures in the lowlands, but they display an unexpected trend toward *decreasing* rather than increasing size over time (Rocek 1998; see also Wills 2001; Campbell and Railey 2008:737–740). Thus, for instance, the Dunlap-Salazar site (LA 51344) in the Capitan Mountains has a series of structures 6 m or more in diameter dating from the sixth through early ninth centuries AD; by the early first millennium AD pit structures in the area such as those at the Bonnell site (LA 612) have roughly half the floor space (Rocek 1998, 2013; Rocek and Rautman 2012:115–116). This contrast with lowland patterns goes along with a widely noted trend for late persistence of pithouses in highland settings, and for construction of particularly deep pithouses at high altitudes (Stuart and Farwell 1983). Further complicating the pattern, settlements in the Capitan Mountains seem to have a distinctive pattern of large but *shallow* Early Formative dwellings (Rocek 1998, 2013; Rocek and Rautman 2012:116). The Late Glencoe phase in the southern Sierra Blanca Mountains (Kelley 1984) conforms to the pattern of persistence of pithouses in the highlands several centuries after freestanding surface and contiguous pueblo-style architecture comes to dominate in the lowlands as well as the northern portions of the Sierra Blanca/Capitan/Sacramento Highlands.

This highland area however suffers from the limited visibility and limited research described previously and thus generally receives only passing reference in summaries of the Jornada. The heavy emphasis on the lowland sequence that follows from the paucity of highland data is particularly ironic, given the traditional view of the Mogollon as predominantly a mountain adaptation (e.g., Wheat 1955:2), which reinforces the additional question of ethnicity. Do the highland sites reflect simply a subset of the same cultural pattern as in the lower-lying areas, or are distinct groups represented as well? Recognition of the contrast between the patterns is clearly a first step in addressing such a question (see also Wiseman, chapter 14, this volume).

Turning to a second region, the Eastern Extension of the Jornada region, the area east of Sierra Blanca/Capitan/Sacramento Highlands receives scant attention relative to its large size. Restricting discussion to just the western fringe of this eastern region along the base of the mountains, a striking diversity of forms occurs, most notably in the vicinity of Roswell (the "Roswell Oasis" [Wiseman 2013]). Here, a series of very small and shallow structures from the Townsend site (LA 34150; Akins 2003) resembles the ephemeral "huts" or "small houses" of the Western Jornada Lowlands. There appears to be a possible chronological trend toward slightly larger, deeper structures over time (Akins 2003:306), though the differences are small and all of the first-millennium houses fit the "hut" or "small house" pattern, well after much more-substantial architecture is known in the lowland basins west of the mountains. In the Late Formative period, after about 1200 or 1250, a complicated picture emerges. Henderson (LA 1549) and Bloom Mound (LA 2528) pueblos, dating after the mid 1200s and generally assigned to the Lincoln phase, incorporate surface adobe architecture along with partially subsurface subrectangular rooms reminiscent of the Late Glencoe phase in the highlands to the west. Perhaps overlapping in time or slightly earlier, nearby sites include Fox Place (LA 68188), a cluster of small, round structures comparable in size and depth to the huts of the preceding period but gathered around one larger rectangular ceremonial pit structure, and Rocky Arroyo (LA 25277), a cluster of larger, relatively deep subrectangular pithouses (Emslie et al. 1992; Speth 2008; Speth 2004; Speth and LeDuc 2007; Wiseman 1985a, 2002, 2013). Yet another small site, King Ranch (LA 26764), contains two additional isolated hut-type structures dating to this late period (Wiseman 1981a; 1988; 2002:183). Recent research on of patterns over a wider area of the Eastern Extension southeast and east of Roswell in New Mexico and west Texas adds even more examples of multiple settlement forms (e.g., Bandy 2011; Brown 2010; Brown 2011; Miller et al. 2016; Railey 2016; see also Railey, chapter 13, this volume).

Some of this bewildering variation is chronological, perhaps reflecting a shift from pithouse to pueblo over time, but it happens very rapidly, probably with overlap among patterns (Speth and LeDuc 2007). It occurs perhaps a bit later than the corresponding shift in both the Western Jornada and in the Lincoln phase in the Sierra Blanca/Capitan/Sacramento Highlands to the west, and even the terminal village occupation of the Roswell Oasis in the 1400s incorporates sunken rooms along with pueblo architecture. Partial parallels may be found in the Western Jornada Lowlands on the other side of the Sacramentos to the southwest. At the Jaca site (LA 6829) in the Tularosa Basin, Railey (Railey 2002) reports a number of small huts overlapping in age with early pueblo construction. Similarly, the early stage of construction of the El Paso–phase Firecracker Pueblo near El Paso includes subrectangular pithouses (O'Laughlin 2001a), but the details of timing, sequence, and architecture all differ (see figure 1.3). Furthermore, as with the highland sites, the economic context of the Roswell area pattern differs markedly from the Western Jornada Lowlands region. While the typical El Paso–phase sites of the latter region are dominated by maize agriculture, the eastern sites indicate unique combinations of large-scale maize farming along with intensive hunting as well, likely associated with trade in meat. This pattern includes large quantities of bison, for instance at both the Henderson-site pueblo and the Rocky Arroyo pithouse site (Speth 2008; Speth 2004; Wiseman 1985a), as well as birds and aquatic resources such as fish and mussels at several of the sites in the Roswell area (Akins 2003; Emslie et al. 1992; Rocek and Speth 1986; Speth 2004; Wiseman 1985a, 2002, 2013). These contrasts in economy and the Plains-edge location of the eastern sites also strongly imply differences in mobility from those of the Western Jornada occupants (Speth 2008; Speth 2004). And finally, the ethnic identity, or identities of these eastern groups is a subject of considerable speculation (e.g., Rocek and Speth 1986; Speth 2008; Speth 2004; Wiseman 2002; Wiseman, chapter 14, this volume), and may certainly differ from that of Western Jornada groups to the southwest, as well as from those in the mountains to the west.

While these examples from the highlands and the eastern margin clearly illustrate the regional diversity of the Jornada, they could be expanded to similar issues in the other regions of the Jornada culture area. Within the broader Western Jornada Lowlands, the riverine zone lying along the Rio Grande includes the Los Tules site (LA 16315), which figured prominently in Lehmer's (1948) original definition of the Early Formative Mesilla phase. Data from this area are poorly represented, in part due to the limited number of large CRM projects located there, but equally importantly due to historic agricultural and construction activities that have destroyed or obscured many of the Formative sites in this zone (Miller and Kenmotsu 2004:245–246). Unlike the highland region and the Eastern Extension of the Jornada, a few sites from the riverine zone *are* frequently incorporated in Jornada settlement studies, but the data from this area are nearly as scanty as those from the neglected areas to the east. Thus, the casual incorporation of a few riverine sites into the trends recognized in basins east of the river is questionable, both because of the limited and biased nature of the riverine data, and also because this region may well differ in economic history, settlement trajectory, and again plausibly in ethnic composition. The combination of a long growing season and readily available water along the river, for instance, suggests that the model of slow agricultural growth seen in the basin areas might not fit the riverine setting. Economic data from the river valley are very limited, however. The substantial architecture of Los Tules, with its deep construction, fairly large floor areas, and internal support posts also contrasts with the vast majority of Mesilla-phase architecture around the basin lowlands. Thus, even though Lehmer used the Rio Grande riverine setting to define this early period of his Southern Jornada Formative-phase sequence, it very likely forms a distinct development from the pattern that has subsequently been elaborated with data from elsewhere across the Western Jornada Lowands.

Finally, a drastically understudied region (called the *Southern Jornada Mogollon* in this volume) lies across the international border in Chihuahua (Cruz Antillón et al., chapter 11, this volume). Roughly a third of Lehmer's Jornada region lies in northern Chihuahua, and yet virtually no Mexican data are incorporated into most syntheses of the Jornada. This reflects both the limited data available for extreme northern Mexican archaeology and limited familiarity of many US archaeologists with this area. Once again, while both environmental and cultural continuities clearly link this region with the better-studied Jornada area to the north (Cruz Antillón et al., chapter 11, this volume) and the international boundary has no bearing on prehistoric patterning, it remains dangerous to simply extrapolate the patterns identified in the Western Jornada another 150 km to the south.

DISCUSSION

The point in describing these regional contrasts is not to argue for or against the utility of the concept of the Jornada Mogollon, an issue raised by others (e.g., Lekson 1988). Nor is it to suggest that these areas are unconnected to each other; in fact it is likely that some of the region's settlement systems straddled not just environmental subzones such as basin centers and edge slopes, but extended between major ecological divisions discussed here, such as riverine, basin, and highland (e.g., Lekson 1988; Hard 1983b). Rather, I argue that, given the complexity of the Jornada, the skewed distribution of research, and the biases in visibility of Formative sites, the normative view of trends in Jornada Mogollon archaeology in general, and architecture in particular, represents an incomplete picture of the broader regional pattern, and that not all of the site variation in the region can be subsumed into interpretations of sites within seasonal rounds of gradually decreasing mobility.

Such a characterization of the synthesis of Jornada architectural trends is oversimplified, but it reflects a real bias due to the domination of a western lowland, basin-centered view of the Jornada. The wealth of data that has come out of research in the central basins must serve to encourage exploration of the *diversity* in cultural identity, pattern and degree of mobility, site functions and seasonality within settlement rounds, environmental settings, and intra- and interhousehold social organization, as well as interactions among all of these across the Jornada region, rather than creating a homogenizing characterization of the whole region in terms of the patterns inferred from the lowland basins and their margins alone.

ACKNOWLEDGMENTS

Many thanks to helpful comments on a draft of this chapter by Nancy Kenmotsu as well as those of two anonymous reviewers.

NOTE

1. A recent welcome change has been the expansion of CRM research in far southeastern New Mexico through the implementation of the Bureau of Land Management's Memorandum of Understanding in 2008, subsequently converted to a Programmatic Agreement, and most recently extended through 2026 (Bureau of Land Management 2013, 2016). This program authorizes consolidation of funds from many small-scale energy-industry-related activities such as oil-well pad or access-road development and their allocation to coordinated and comprehensive research-driven projects (e.g., Railey, chapter 13, this volume). While very welcome, this expansion in research remains primarily focused on areas tied to oil and natural gas development.

Part II

Farming the Jornada Lowlands

3

Population aggregation, migration, and an increase in agricultural intensity in the Western Jornada Mogollon (Jornada) region during the Formative period parallel similar transitions elsewhere in the American Southwest and northern Chihuahua (Cordell et al. 1994; Gumerman 1994; Shafer 2003; Whalen and Minnis 2001a). In this chapter, we draw together macrobotanical data, burned-rock technology, architecture, and analyses of ceramics and obsidian from the lowland basins around El Paso and the western and southern Sacramento Mountains foothills (figure 1.2) to discuss changes in land use and settlement intensity both before and after AD 1000, a time that we believe was critical in the subsequent trajectory of regional prehistory. A robust local data set indicates that intensification of agricultural production in this part of the Jornada began around AD 1000[1] and sharply increased after AD 1150; then, from AD 1150 to 1300, the intensification was matched by intensive wild-plant processing. After AD 1300, domesticated-plant production continued but the contribution of wild plants to local diets dwindled dramatically. Several corresponding technological, settlement, and architectural patterns demonstrate correlations between these trends and the observed changes in subsistence and plant use. We explore the underlying factors for these changes—an interplay between climatic, demographic, and social factors—to suggest their wider implications within the greater Southwest and beyond.

Measuring Diversity

Land Use and Settlement Intensity in the Western Jornada before and after AD 1000

MYLES R. MILLER AND
NANCY A. KENMOTSU

DOI: 10.5876/9781607327950.c003

The chronological framework for the Formative period (AD 200/400–1450) used in this chapter is shown in figure 1.3. The Western Jornada sequence is taken from a recent realignment of the region's ceramic data with the broader Southwest (Miller 2005a). The phases generally follow those set forth by Lehmer (1948), but time intervals are adjusted to estimated ages from regional radiocarbon analyses. In addition, the Doña Ana phase, noted here as a key period in the intensification of agriculture, has been subdivided into two distinct phases.

Using macrobotanical data, burned-rock technology, architecture, and chemical analyses from recent excavations in the region, we have identified several important trends and transitions in Western Jornada prehistory between AD 600 and 1450. Developments during these centuries show increasing agricultural dependence—and ultimately agricultural specialization—culminating in population aggregation into pueblos between ca. AD 1300 and 1450.

THE PALEOBOTANICAL, TECHNOLOGICAL, SETTLEMENT PATTERN, AND ARCHITECTURAL EVIDENCE

To better understand the role of wild and domesticated plants in the overall subsistence of the people in the Western Jornada and how that subsistence changed during the Formative period, a study of paleobotanical samples from well-excavated contexts was undertaken (Miller 2005b). Initially, 38 prehistoric sites with 1,120 flotation samples were selected for review; the results are shown in table 3.1. Sites with fewer than four productive flotation samples (productive defined as a sample yielding subsistence remains) were eliminated. It should be noted that flotation samples from sites in the Western Jornada have been plagued by poor preservation. Dering et al. (2001) and Miller (2005b) argue that productive samples are most commonly recovered from sites that were intensively used. Not surprisingly, Mesilla-phase sites less frequently produce charred economic remains. However, we do not believe that the lower ubiquity vales in the pre-AD 1000 period reflect differences in preservation and float-sampling patterns because we only include productive samples in the analysis rather than the total of both productive and unproductive samples. Moreover, as shown in table 3.1, the total number of productive samples from Mesilla-phase sites outnumbers those from all other periods.

The final synthesis incorporates data from 1,003 flotation samples from 28 sites. (figure 3.1). Counts of charred subsistence or economic plant remains ranged from four to 345 per site with an average of 35 samples per site. In all, 402 samples (of the 1,003 flotation samples) were productive, representing 40%

TABLE 3.1. Frequency and ubiquity data

Time Period	Sites (N)	Samples (N)	Productive samples (N)	Productive samples (%)	Sample volume (liters)
Mesilla phase	18	697	205	29.4	2,611
Early Doña Ana phase	4	84	68	81.0	466
Late Doña Ana phase	3	55	54	98.2	428
El Paso phase	12	284	193	68.0	393
All time periods	37	1,120	520	46.4	3,898

of the samples. While a total of 18,960 charred subsistence or economic plant remains were cataloged from these samples[2] and 40 plant species were documented, we are here only concerned with four major genera or species: *Zea, Phaseolus, Prosopis*, and a combined cacti/succulent group (*Agave, Dasylirion, Yucca, Echinocereus, Mammilaria, Opuntia*). These four represent important domesticated (*Zea* and *Phaseolus*) and wild (*Prosopis, Agave, Dasylirion, Yucca, Echinocereus, Mammillaria, Opuntia*) foods that have been documented as important throughout the Southwest, including throughout the Jornada Mogollon (see, in this volume, Rocek, chapter 2; Condon and Vasquez, chapter 4; and Railey, chapter 13). It was anticipated that these species would serve as proxy measures for the dependence of local residents on agricultural production.

The study began in 1998 but was updated in 2005 (figure 3.2). The major difference between the original and updated studies is in mesquite: the original study indicated that mesquite dropped in the Late Doña Ana phase but with the 2005 data added, it remains stable during the AD 1150–1300 interval, with a more pronounced decline after AD 1300. Otherwise, the update shows little variation from the 1998 effort, indicating the results are reliable. The study establishes abundance measures for the four major subsistence items across time.

The study documents a trend of increasing agricultural dependence between AD 1000 and 1300. Corn shows a pronounced increase in ubiquity after 1150, as do beans (see figure 3.2). Of *greater importance*, however, ubiquity values for cacti and succulents increase to more than 50% between AD 1150 and 1300, but fall to less than 10% for components dating after 1300. The flotation samples from this time interval represent a variety of contexts, including refuse deposits

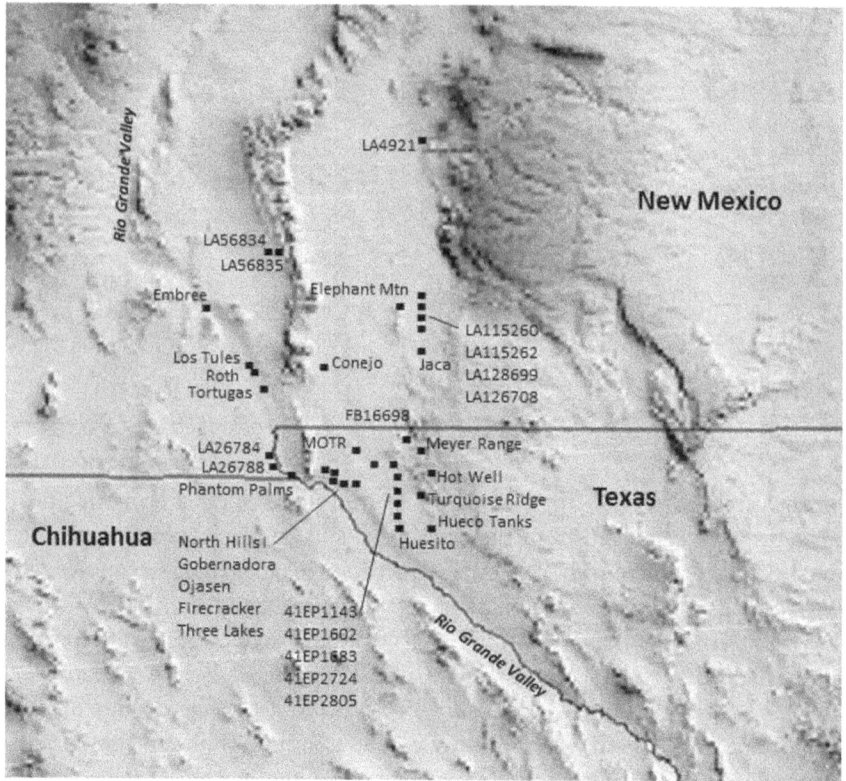

FIGURE 3.1. *Location of Jornada sites included in the paleobotanical study.*

in pithouses, middens, pits, domestic hearths, and plant-baking pits. This pattern indicates that exploitation of *both* domesticated and non-domesticated food resources intensified during the Late Doña Ana phase in the Western Jornada, but domesticated food dominated after AD 1300. To address underlying factors creating dual intensification of domesticated and non-domesticated plants during this period, we review several corresponding technological, settlement, and architectural patterns to demonstrate the correlations between these trends and the observed changes in subsistence and plant use.

TECHNOLOGICAL PATTERNS

Burned-rock thermal features are a common aspect of regional technology. They provide corroborative data for the macrobotanical study, particularly one

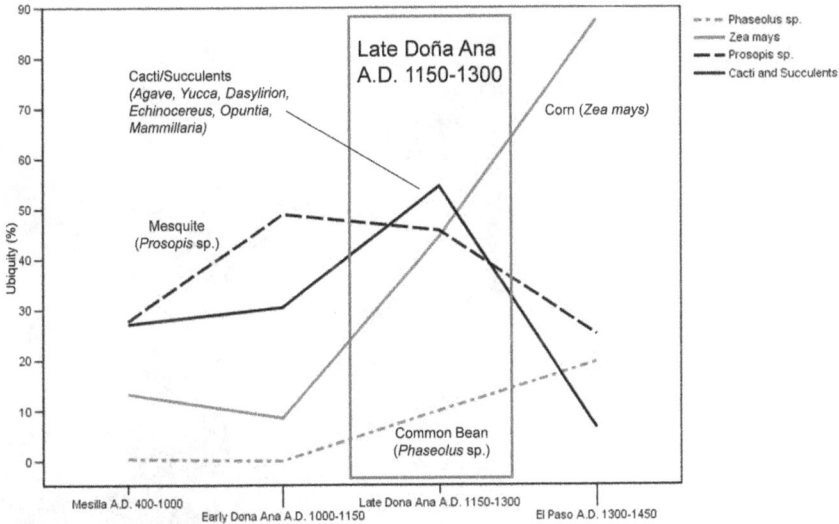

FIGURE 3.2. *Summary of plant ubiquity (1,120 samples, 520 productive).*

form of thermal features termed *rock-lined pits* (Condon, Hall, et al. 2006; Miller et al. 2012; Miller and Kenmotsu 2004; Quigg et al. 2002). Rock-lined pits are formally constructed burned-rock baking facilities used to parch seeds and process cacti and succulents. Some of the largest botanical inventories in the region have been recovered from these features. Examples in figure 3.3 show their formal construction and associated burned-rock discards that capped the features during cooking. The 73 burned-rock middens (BRMs, rock-lined pits used for plant baking with associated burned-rock discard middens) at LA163794, ranging from 3 m to 16 m in diameter, illustrate the size variation of these rock-discard areas. Moreover, some BRMs at the site have a single rock-lined pit while other BRMs have several, suggesting multiple-use episodes (Miller et al. 2012).

A review of over 3,000 economic and subsistence plant remains recovered from rock-lined pits from sites throughout the same study area as the ubiquity study shows a clear dominance of various cacti, including *Opuntia* (prickly pear), *Echinocactus/Echinocereus* (hedgehog or candle cactus), and *Yucca baccata* (datil, or banana yucca) (Miller 2005b; Miller and Lowry 2006; figure 3.4). Less-commonly identified but still important species are mesquite, chenoams, *Portulaca* sp., corn cupules and kernels, and various medicinal plants as well as several unidentified seeds. Recent pollen and macrobotanical research on BRMs with rock-lined pits in the southern Sacramento Mountains both

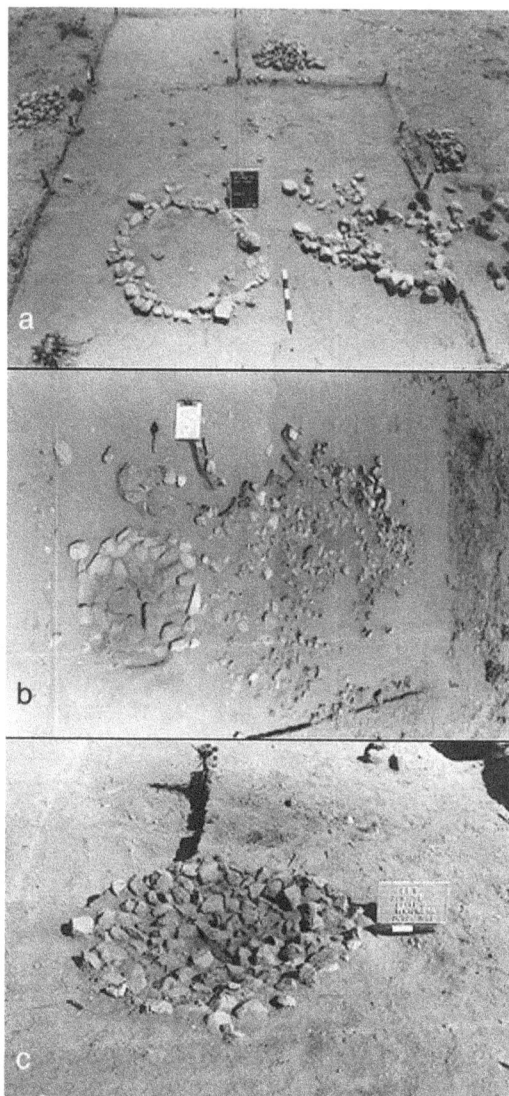

FIGURE 3.3. *Examples of rock-lined pits and associated burned-rock discard middens: (a) North Hills (41EP355), Feature 54; (b) Ojasen (41EP289), Feature 1; (c) LA37156, Feature 7. The North Hills and Ojasen sites are situated on the distal alluvial fans of the Franklin Mountains on the western edge of the Tularosa Basin; LA37156 is in Wildcat Canyon in the Sacramento Mountain foothills.*

corroborates and expands these findings (Miller and Montgomery, chapter 12, this volume; Miller et al. 2011; Miller et al. 2012). The widespread presence of agave and yucca (datil), including agave vascular fibers and a partial agave heart at LA 163813 (Miller et al. 2012) and charred agave fibers and cholla buds recovered from 10 rock-lined baking pits at other sites (Miller et al. 2011), demonstrates these features were used to bake/roast/dry succulents,

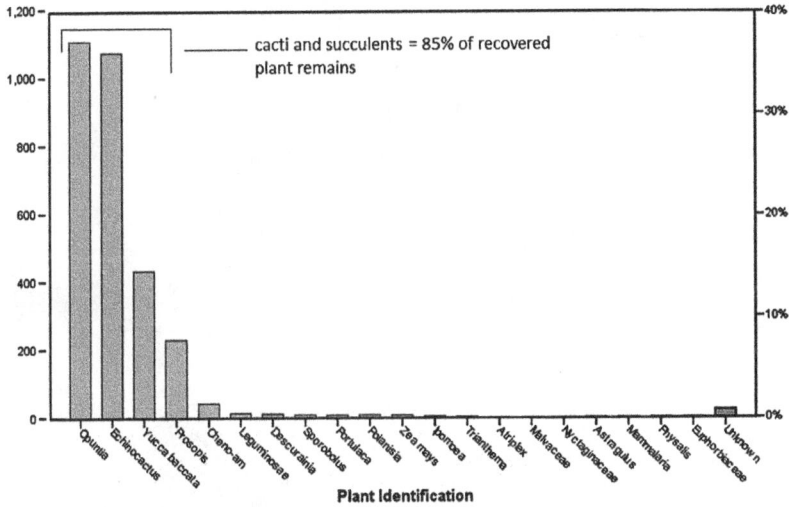

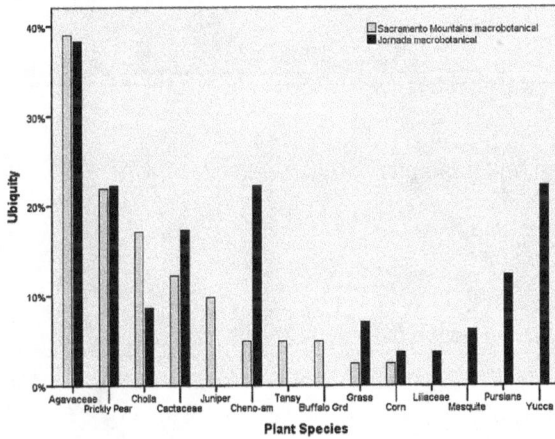

FIGURE 3.4. *Summary of plant remains from rock-lined pits: (a) summary of plant remains recovered from rock-lined pits (n = 3,149); (b) summary of plant species ubiquity values from plant-baking pits in the southern Sacramento Mountains and Western Jornada (from Miller et al. 2013: figure 7.6).*

as has been described for several historic Native American groups across the Southwest (Bell and Castetter 1941).

The sample of such plant remains is dwarfed, however, by the thousands of seeds from cacti, cholla buds, and datil pods recovered in these features. The substantial counts of these seeds and plant parts are indisputable evidence that

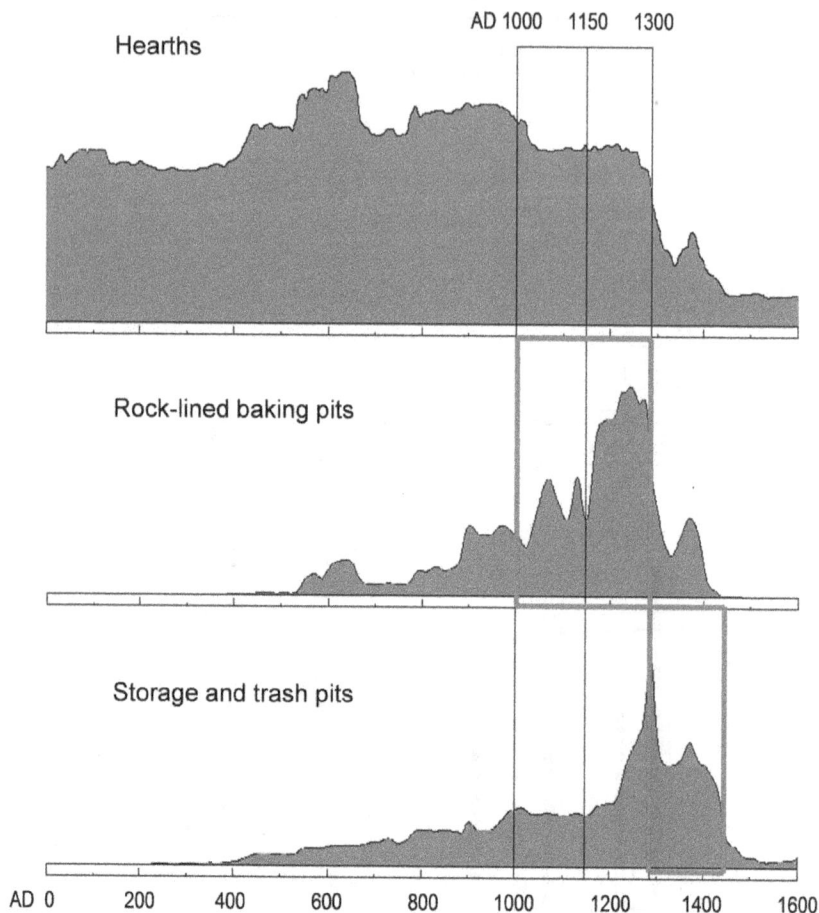

FIGURE 3.5. *Summed relative probability of radiocarbon dates for thermal features, rock-lined pits, and storage and trash pits. Bold rectangle outlines denote time periods discussed in the text.*

other plant species in addition to leaf succulents were also baked, roasted, or parched in them. This larger and more expansive multifunctional role of BRMs has been underestimated throughout the Jornada Mogollon region, including in the Western Jornada, but similar multifunctional roles, ranging from baking ovens for processing cacti to parching features for seeds and acorns, have been proposed for the large BRMs throughout central Texas (Black and Creel 1997; Ellis 1997). A large, well-preserved rock-lined pit at the Ojasen site (41EP289) in the Tularosa Basin (see figure 3.1) had over 10,000 amaranth seeds clustered within a small area of its western edge (Miller 1989) that clearly represents a spill event that occurred while the seeds were being parched in or on the feature and not from some incidental cause or background seed rain. The presence of taxa such as Ipomoea (Morning glory), *Polanisia, Astragalus,* and *Physalis* may indicate that, in addition to economic and subsistence uses, the features may also have been used for medicinal or ritual use.

Figure 3.5 shows summed probability histograms of radiocarbon dates across time for various features. Rock-lined pits became increasingly common after AD 1000, especially between AD 1150 and 1300. This correlates with the marked increase in cacti and succulents in flotation samples (see figure 3.2). After AD 1300, rock-lined pits decreased, which matches a decrease in cacti recovered at pueblos that O'Laughlin (2005) has identified in the Tularosa Basin lowlands. As rock-lined pits decreased, there was an increase in storage pits, reflecting increased agricultural production (see similar results in Condon and Vasquez, chapter 4, this volume). Formal refuse pits also increased during this same time, indicating patterned disposal that correlates with increased sedentism that indirectly points to agricultural production. These data support the notion that, after AD 1300, in addition to becoming more agriculturally dependent, Western Jornada populations were more agriculturally *specialized*. In contrast, a quite different pattern prevailed earlier. The lack of formal pit construction and near absence of storage and refuse pits between AD 200 and 1000 fit with evidence from Mesilla-phase sites that show greater mobility and movement in small family groups (Miller and Burt 2007; O'Laughlin 2002; Whalen 1994b).

SETTLEMENT PATTERNS

These trends are also reflected in the chronology of various feature types found across differing landforms within the Tularosa Basin and Sacramento Mountain foothills. Intensification of cacti and succulent processing and agricultural intensification were generally contemporaneous phenomena (see figure 3.2). This apparent intensification of both traditional plant processing and agricultural production occurring in tandem across different environmental zones marks an important transition in subsistence and settlement for this portion of the Jornada region.

Specifically, the transition is reflected in the chronology of the use of various feature types across differing landforms. Miller and Kenmotsu (2004) and Church et al. (2009:8–15) have shown marked differences in preferred landforms prior to and after AD 1000. Prior to AD 1000, use of the Sacramento Mountains is limited, whereas use of the interior lowland basins and Otero Mesa is relatively heavy. After AD 1000 settlements on the alluvial fans increase—locations in the basins with access to both playa and runoff water for agriculture and cacti/succulent communities are favored. The interval between AD 1150 and 1300 is intriguing—it appears to represent a dual settlement system for residential occupations when utilization of both alluvial fans and playa margins was roughly equivalent (see Miller and Graves 2009). However, pronounced differences existed in occupations of these two zones. Residential occupations were situated primarily in proximity to playas (Dering et al. 2001; Miller and Graves 2009); occupations along the alluvial fans consisted primarily of thermal features, occasionally associated with isolated pithouses, suggesting utilization of those landforms for seasonal harvesting of cacti (Kludt 2007:263; O'Laughlin 2002). These patterns are also apparent in the trends of plant-baking pits between the lowland basins and higher elevations in the Sacramento Mountains. Figure 3.6 contains the summed probability of radiocarbon dates for rock-lined baking pits from the Sacramento foothills versus the Tularosa Basin Lowlands region. Plant-baking pits are common throughout the lowlands beginning at around AD 600, but show a slight decline after AD 1000. In contrast, the numbers of plant-baking pits in upland settings increases dramatically after AD 1000, a pattern that may reflect exhaustion of fuelwood resources (see Miller and Montgomery, chapter 12, this volume). Finally, dense settlement in the Western Jornada during the agricultural period of AD 1300–1450 was concentrated near playas and river valleys. This settlement correlates with the decline in utilization of wild foods, as shown in figure 3.2.

In the Sacramento foothills, many thermal features are BRMs used for the bulk processing of succulents (Bell and Castetter 1941; Ferdon 1946; Komulainen et al. 2009; Miller et al. 2011; Stowe et al. 2009). Use of these features began during the period AD 200/400–1000, continuing through the Early Doña Ana phase until more-intense processing of both domesticated and non-domesticated resources began in the basin. This early focus on preparation of these larger features warrants more study. First, they may indicate an earlier advent of dual agricultural/cacti/succulent processing in the Sacramento foothills, although the reasons remain unclear. Second, the size of these features can be impressive, reaching from 15 m to 30 m in diameter at LA 37155 (Miller et al. 2011:133). Third, construction of these features would have required collection of substantial quantities of rock and wood for heating in addition to the digging of large numbers of *Agave* or other bulbs that

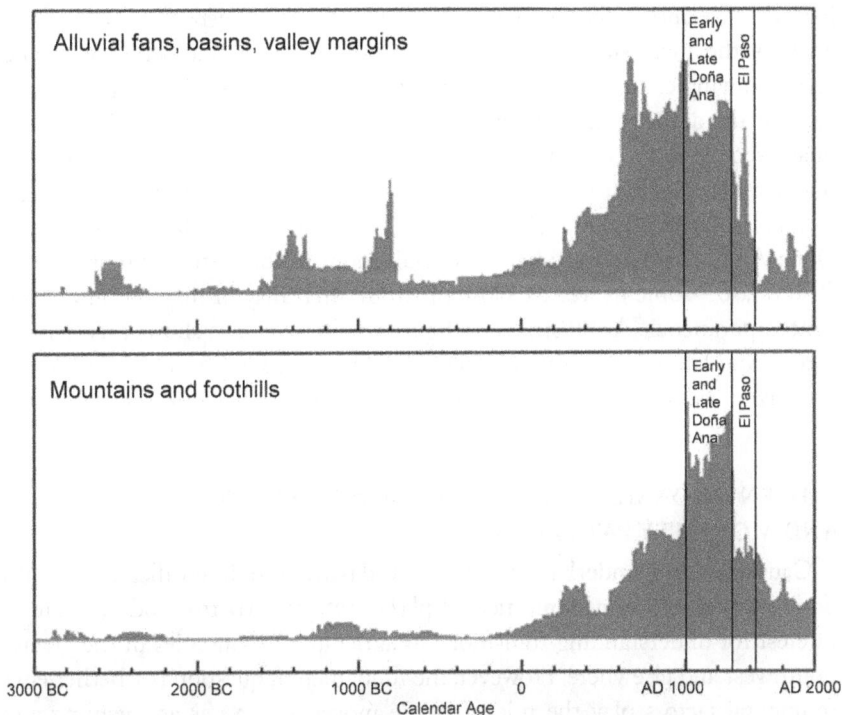

FIGURE 3.6. *Chronological trends (summed relative probability) in the construction and use of plant-baking pits in (a) the uplands (Sacramento foothills and Otero Mesa) versus (b) the Tularosa Basin Lowlands. Vertical lines denote Formative-period phase divisions at AD 500, 1000, 1300, and 1450.*

would be collectively roasted in them. Finally, the roasting process itself was a several-day event. Such a labor output suggests the features were part of a larger social event, perhaps an annual communal gathering where families cooperated for mutual benefit and shared information, renewed friendships, and possibly traded goods or marriage partners (for more on these features, see Miller and Montgomery, chapter 12, this volume).

ARCHITECTURAL PATTERNS

The subsistence, technology, and settlement trends are paralleled by changing architectural forms across the chronological sequence with an increasingly coherent and formal organization of residential settlements in the Western

Jornada. The most conspicuous and widely referenced aspect of this period involves the increasingly formal organization of residential settlements and accompanying changes in architectural form. Figure 3.7 provides a generalized view of the architectural sequence. That sequence roughly approximates the phase sequence for the Western Jornada. It illustrates the shift from informal, circular hut and pithouse constructions (Mesilla phase) to increasingly formal, isolated pitrooms (Early Doña Ana phase) to surface rooms (Late Doña Ana phase) and ultimately to multiroom pueblo settlements in the El Paso phase—some in relative close proximity that may or may not have been contemporaneous. As illustrated in figure 3.7, the sequence shows increasingly formal and labor-intensive architectural changes and is associated with more organized use of space, such as more-patterned refuse disposal through time.

THE ENVIRONMENT, REGIONAL DEMOGRAPHY, AND MOBILITY PATTERNS

Causal factor(s) underlying these observed patterns of intensification of both domesticated and non-domesticated plants between AD 1150 and 1300 are of interest for understanding transitions to agricultural economies in the greater Southwest and elsewhere. However, the fundamental question is whether environmental factors play the role of prime mover, serving as an enabling and catalytic process, or rather act as limiting influences. In the Western Jornada, environmentally deterministic models are common (Kludt 2007; Miller and Church 2008). In this regard, it is important to note that dendrochronological reconstruction of precipitation based on remnant tree stands in the Organ, Sacramento, and Magdalena Mountains of the southern Rio Grande basin present evidence of episodes of severe and persistent drought at ca. AD 1000, 1150, and 1275–1300 (Grissino-Mayer et al. 1997), indicating intervals of major climatic change correlating with the patterns discussed above. Despite this evidence, we argue that demographic and social changes—most notably those associated with increasingly restricted territories—played a heavy role in the intensification of wild and domesticated foods during the Late Doña Ana phase. In support of this interpretation we examine changing territorial mobility ranges using recent geochemical analyses of obsidian and ceramic samples.

Over 1,600 obsidian artifacts from the Western Jornada have been sourced in the past 20 years (Miller and Shackley 1997). It was once thought that most obsidian recovered from sites in the region was procured from secondary gravel deposits in the Rio Grande valley, but we have now determined that around 8%—a substantial proportion—of obsidian materials at Western

Huts / Shallow Circular Pithouses		
Subrectangular / Rectangular Pithouses		
Individual Surface Rooms		
Contiguous Room Pueblos		

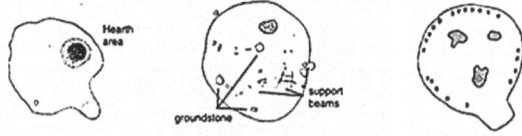

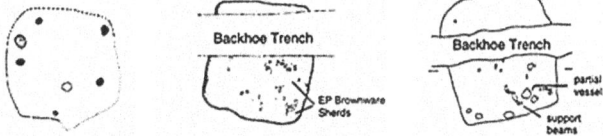

FIGURE 3.7. *Generalized schema of the architectural sequence (top to bottom) in the Western Jornada (after Miller and Kenmotsu 2004).*

Jornada sites derive from source outcrops in northern Chihuahua. It is important to note that Chihuahuan obsidian artifacts in regional sites are disproportionately represented by bifaces, projectile points, and other formal tools, thus suggesting their transport to the region in tool kits of mobile groups whose territorial ranges included much of the basin-and-range region of the Jornada and northern Chihuahua (Miller and Kenmotsu 2004).

The graph in figure 3.8a illustrates the distribution of Chihuahuan obsidian across time both as a proportion of obsidian within each period and as a proportion of Chihuahuan obsidian across time periods. Both show pronounced decrease in Chihuahuan obsidian during the Formative period, particularly during the Early and Late Doña Ana phases and the El Paso phase, followed by a notable increase during the Protohistoric/early historic period. It is important to acknowledge that prior to the Early Doña Ana phase and following the El Paso phase, populations in the Jornada had a greater mobility than during the period from AD 1000 to 1450 (Carmichael 1986; Miller and Burt 2007; Whalen 1994b).

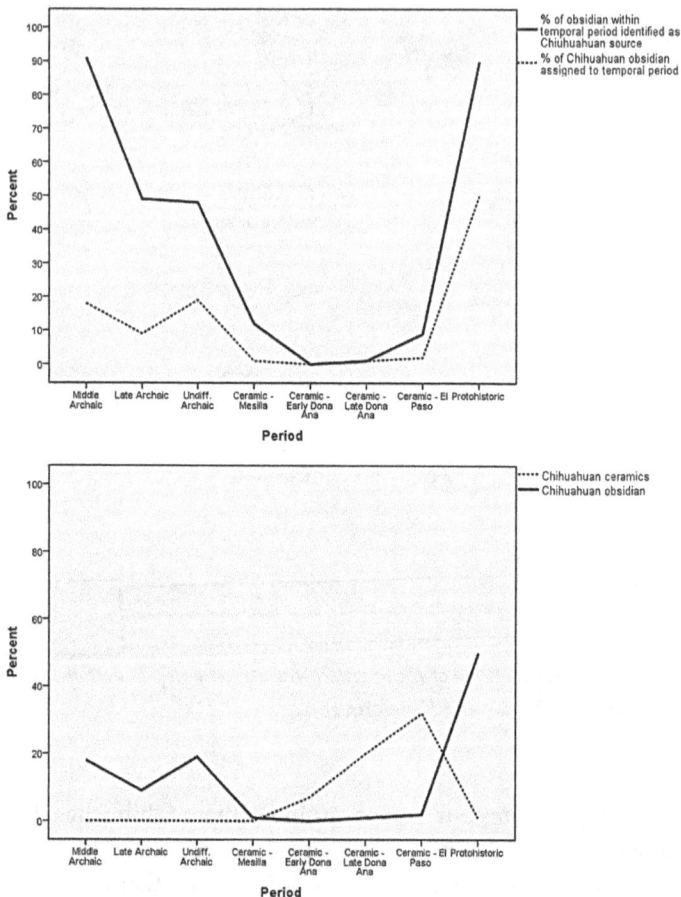

FIGURE 3.8. *Proportions of Chihuahuan obsidian in Western Jornada sites: (a) across time (solid line is proportion of obsidian per period deriving from Chihuahuan sources; dashed line is percentage of all Chihuahuan obsidian in Western Jornada sample assigned to each period); (b) Chihuahuan obsidian (solid line) compared to Chihuahuan ceramics (dashed line).*

As illustrated in figure 3.8b, the proportion of ceramics from the Casas Grandes region of northern Chihuahua negatively covaries with proportions of Chihuahuan obsidian during the Formative period. The graph is intended to provide a general or heuristic impression of obsidian and ceramic distributions to support the inference that territorial ranges of the Archaic period had become circumscribed during the Formative period. If we accept the premise that most Chihuahuan obsidian arrived in the Jornada as part of mobile tool kits (rather than through exchange), then this provides striking evidence that territories of hunter-gatherer groups—once taking in much of the basin-and-range province of south-central New Mexico, far West Texas, and north-central Chihuahua—was increasingly restricted during the Formative period. The graph in figure 3.8b suggests that those restrictions lifted at the close of the El Paso phase. As obsidian arriving in mobile tool-kits subsided beginning in the earliest part of the Formative, ceramics from Chihuahua begin to be found in western Jornada sites, peaking in the El Paso phase and quickly decreasing after AD 1450. It is generally believed that these ceramics came to the Western Jornada through exchange (Brewington and Shafer 1999; Dering et al. 2001; Miller and Graves 2009). Although the mechanisms of that exchange merit further study (see Ford 1983), the spike in Chihuahuan ceramics during the period when mobile territories were restricted indicates continued interaction with neighbors to the south in the form of trade.

Local demographic and mobility trends can also be studied through instrumental neutron activation analysis (INAA) of ceramics from the Jornada and the Mimbres region to the west (see Hill, chapter 9, and Kenmotsu, chapter 10, both in this volume; also, Brewington and Shafer 1999; Creel et al. 2002; Ferguson and Glascock 2007; Miller and Burt 2007). Distributions of El Paso Brownware compositional groups further highlight demographic pressures and territorial circumscription within the Western Jornada region. As of 2002, over 650 El Paso Brownware INAA samples had been analyzed from 30 sites located across all sectors of the Tularosa Basin, the Sacramento Mountains, and the Rio Grande west of the Tularosa Bolson. Miller (2002; see also Miller and Ferguson 2010) analyzed these samples to examine the variety and diversity of the chemical groups represented at sites of different time periods, identifying six geochemical compositional groups among them. Kintigh's (1994) Monte Carlo analysis of richness (the number of chemical groups identified per sample) versus sample size (the total INAA sample) was employed. The results demonstrate that sites prior to AD 1150 (Mesilla and Early Doña Ana phases) generally fall within a 90 percent CI indicating these sites have the expected number of chemical groups (figure 3.9a). In contrast, most later sites fall well below the 90% plot, indicating they have significantly fewer chemical groups present among their respective INAA samples.

The second and more concise means of examining mobility used the observed diversity among El Paso Brownware INAA chemical groups within

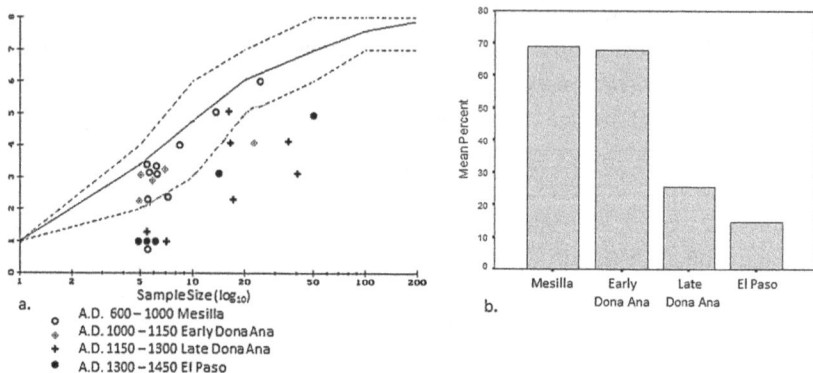

FIGURE 3.9. *Chemical group variety and diversity among El Paso Brownware ceramics across time: (a) Monte Carlo analysis of richness versus sample size for numbers of ceramic INAA groups per site; (b) percentage of non-local ceramics (i.e., from an INAA group other than from a site's locale) averaged by phase.*

Western Jornada region (figure 3.9b). Here, the proportion of the INAA samples from each site representing chemical groups originating from areas outside the local INAA production area where a site is located can be seen. The differing proportions represent a proxy measure of El Paso Brownware ceramics produced in different areas of the Western Jornada that were deposited at a given site. The graph shows that non-local production areas are significantly lower at sites dating after AD 1150.

Although exchange cannot be ruled out, we believe that much of the evidence of non-local production prior to AD 1150 represents actual movement of vessels by populations that were more mobile than their later counterparts (see Miller and Burt 2007). It has become apparent during the many intensive surveys conducted at Fort Bliss and elsewhere in the central basins of the Western Jornada that it is difficult to find a quarter-square-kilometer area that does not contain prehistoric ceramic debris. The decrease in richness values and proportions of non-local chemical groups present at sites occupied after AD 1150 suggest much more circumscribed territorial ranges after that time than existed for earlier periods.

Mimbres Black-on-white (Mimbres B/W) sherds are commonly found in Western Jornada sites dating from AD 1000 to 1150. Recent INAA studies of Mimbres B/W ceramics from the region west of the Jornada offer intriguing evidence regarding demographic pressures and social processes that at first seem to contradict some of the foregoing statements. When closely examined, however, they support the increasing social pressures.

As recently reported by Creel (2013), the statistical analysis of the INAA from a large number of whole Mimbres vessels, many of which are from the AD 1000–1150 time frame, "has resulted in the identification of some 35 chemical compositional groups most of which have been linked with varying levels of confidence to production locales." Of interest is the increasing number of compositional groups through time and the fact that they represent a greater range of production areas both inside and outside of the Mimbres heartland during the Classic or post–AD 1000 period (particularly post–AD 1100) (Creel 2013; Ferguson and Glascock 2007). This was a period of expansion of Mimbres populations into new areas, including the eastern Mimbres and Rio Grande valleys (Hegmon et al. 1999). That expansion is manifested by the greater variety of compositional groups represented among vessels exchanged with Western Jornada populations. During the Mimbres Classic period and the Early Doña Ana phase, and particularly the latter decades of these time intervals, evidence exists of increasingly diverse and widespread exchange systems. During this period the first hints of regional resource and demographic stress and territorial competition become evident.

Other studies indicate little use of Mimbres ceramics as status or prestige items (Creel 2006a; Gilman and Powell-Martí 2006:7; Shafer 2006), suggesting that common prestige-based or peer-polity exchange systems may not be appropriate models. Also, the distributions of the Mimbres chemical groups among Western Jornada sites are very random, indicating that alliances and highly formalized social relationships were not common among the populations of the two regions. This finding is intriguing, suggesting social groups in the Western Jornada were highly informal and fluid, and that maintaining formal relationships with such ephemeral "polities" required different forms of social arrangements than those common among more stable, formal, and established social and political entities.

Review of several temporal and distributional aspects of the INAA compositional data suggests that the most parsimonious explanation for the distribution of Mimbres vessels in the Western Jornada between AD 1000 and 1150 involves processes of boundary maintenance during times of increasing resource stress, demographic pressures, and circumscribed territorial ranges. We suggest that the highly mobile Jornada groups in the Western Jornada Lowlands during these 150 years interacted with the encroaching agriculturalists from the Mimbres region in ways that may have been demonstrative and symbolic.

A recent study of Mimbres ceramic distribution in the Western Jornada (Miller 2005c) shows that settlements where Mimbres B/W represent more than 5% of the total collection are clustered in the segments of the Rio Grande valley known locally as the Hatch/Rincon valley and the Mesilla valley near Las Cruces, New Mexico (see figure 1.2). Several sites in this area contain more than 20% Mimbres B/W. These locations are in closest proximity to the Mimbres region, and one site included in the INAA study, the Rio Vista site, is actually a Classic Mimbres pueblo in the Rio Grande valley. Another cluster of sites with significant proportions of Mimbres B/W is located in the El Paso segment of the Rio Grande valley.

The proportions of Mimbres B/W show a pronounced decline at settlements located to the east of the Rio Grande valley in the Tularosa Basin region. In fact, several of the eastern settlements actually have only trace amounts of Mimbres B/W and most have less than 0.5% of Mimbres B/W. This represents a significant decrease from the proportions observed at sites in and near the Rio Grande valley. Notably, this decrease occurs across distances of less than 40 km (25 miles) and in some cases only 20 km (12 miles). To those accustomed to distance decay or falloff models (see Renfrew 1975, 1977), operating at scales of hundreds of kilometers or even one hundred kilometers, the precipitous decline of Mimbres B/W distributions over such short distances is an observation that deserves closer consideration.

Review of the distributional and compositional data suggests a fluid process of exchange and social interaction operated between these groups. This differed from groups with more formal, regularized intergroup interaction, such as is suggested by the evidence for structured exchange networks operating in the central Rio Grande valley in the 1400s that Eckert and Cordell (2004:40) argue "potentially signal[ed] more stable social alliances than had existed earlier." The interaction in the Western Jornada included a continual cycling of various Western Jornada groups in contact with Mimbres populations. Thus, as an alternative explanation, it is proposed that the distributional and compositional data on Mimbres ceramics from the Western Jornada region indicate that unique strategies were required to create and perpetuate social relationships between sedentary Mimbres settlements encroaching further toward the east and the ephemeral polities of constantly shifting Western Jornada populations who were finding access to resource patches increasingly restricted (Miller 2005c).

Group identification and boundary maintenance intensify in situations where people compete for space and resources (Hitchcock and Bartram 1998; Lightfoot and Martinez 1995) and more conspicuous forms of boundary maintenance will emerge during periods when subsistence, social, and economic change is strongest and boundaries are under increasing pressure. For example, Hitchcock and Bartram (1998) conducted an ethnoarchaeological study of some 28,000 km² of the Kalahari Desert where 22 distinct ethnic groups compete for land and resources. Land tenure is hotly debated among foragers (San groups) and agropastoralists (Tswana groups) alike. Land is "often perceived as a social and ideological dimension" of both sociopolitical systems (Hitchcock and Bartram 1998:22) and San bands and Tswana descent groups each have rights over particular blocks of land and the resources on those blocks. Forager and agropastoralist territories are marked by naming them, giving them well-known boundaries in oral history, and through the known presence of burial areas and other sacred sites. Despite the continual debate over the territory among all groups, or perhaps because of the debate, all groups generally respect each other's territorial and social boundaries.

These are precisely the conditions occurring between the Western Jornada and Mimbres regions between AD 1000 and 1150. Interaction between farmers and foragers in such situations often includes conflict and competition over land. Such conflict between different land-use strategies requires some type of resolution. In some cases, it can lead to conflict. In the ethnographic case studied by Hitchcock and Bartram (1998:23), it is resolved through abundant available information of access rights to specific blocks of land, along with affinal ties through marriage, trade partnerships, and exchange networks. In other cases, the conflict and competition over land may lead to conspicuous forms of boundary maintenance and territorial marking, and we believe that this is the type of resolution seen in the archaeological record in the Western Jornada between AD 1000 and 1150.

The concept of territorial marking via exchange is compelling because, under conditions of emergent boundary tensions and increasing social relationships, the exchange of distinctive items—such as Mimbres B/W and El Paso Brownware vessels—may have allowed individuals and social groups to profess and display membership and to symbolically convey their presence within a region. For the Western Jornada groups there appears to have been an almost conspicuous attempt to establish and demonstrate boundaries. It is noteworthy that the El Paso Brownware ceramic tradition undergoes a significant change during this period. After some 600–800 years of plain brownware production, it is during this time interval of increasing exchange of Mimbres Style III vessels that painted designs are first added to El Paso Brownware vessels, and these design trends undergo two additional episodes of increased complexity and elaboration between circa AD 1000 and 1150. This is further evidence of attempts by Western Jornada populations to demonstratively and symbolically signal their identity as "Jornada" and convey information about their territorial rights and access to resources to encroaching agriculturalists from the Mimbres region.

PLANT UBIQUITY AND SETTLEMENT INTENSITY

To conclude, the paleobotanical data used in this study are robust and offer important insights into prehistoric trends of plant use, including intensification of both non-domesticated and domesticated species. The corresponding technological, architectural, and landscape trends from the Western Jornada are also based on firm empirical evidence.

Causal factors underlying the trends are less clear, but suggest that increasingly reduced territorial ranges, demographic pressures, and social factors need to be considered in addition to the commonly invoked environmental factors. There must be an important underlying cause that led to the relatively sudden intensification of cactus and succulent processing after AD 1000 with a concomitant rise in agricultural production (see figure 3.2). Although agricultural production continues to rise after AD 1300, use of cacti and succulents drops significantly after that date. (The chapter 4 data set of Condon and Vasquez in this volume confirms the dominance of maize from AD 1300 to 1450, but in their sample it was accompanied by the use of wild seeds to enhance local diets). Because both cacti and succulents generally have slow growth/replacement rates, their overexploitation may have led to increasing scarcity, thus motivating the increasing reliance on agricultural production as a supplement and, later, a replacement for them.

A more parsimonious explanation for these patterns—and one that is provisionally supported by geochemical sourcing data—involves population growth and movement. However, it is possible that these patterns do not reflect population growth within the Western Jornada region, but rather reflect extraregional factors resulting in reduced territorial ranges available for exploitation. That is, population growth per se may not have occurred within the Western Jornada. Instead increasing intensification of land use within the region and in adjacent parts of the Jornada Mogollon region and the Mimbres to the west, resulting from more restricted territories, could have taken place while population levels remained relatively stable.

It is also clear that such developments may not be best detected at the site or regional scale of analysis, but instead will require a larger scale of reference and the work of researchers from several regions. We would like to bring these significant trends to the attention of the larger Mogollon and Chihuahuan research communities. Clearly, the correspondence between major transitional events at around AD 1000, 1150, and 1275/1300—not only in the Western Jornada, but in the Mimbres valley, Eastern Mimbres area, and northern Chihuahua—are cause for deliberation, and the demographic trends proposed in this chapter have wider implications for population aggregation, migration, and other settlement trends throughout the greater Southwest.

NOTES

1. In chapter 4 (this volume), Condon and Vasquez, with a different data set from the western lowlands, find similar but slightly different ubiquity trends.

2. It should be noted that some 10,000 of the charred-plant remains are from two spill or processing events involving cheno-ams (Miller 1989).

4

Evaluating Plant Utilization and Subsistence Economies in the Western Jornada

Current Trends and Perspectives

Peter C. Condon and Javier Vasquez

The present study continues the discussion on regional subsistence economies introduced by Miller and Kenmotsu in chapter 3 of this volume, with a focus on Late Archaic and Formative-period mixed-plant usage in the lower Tularosa Basin of the Western Jornada region. In a consistent thread that runs through these two chapters, the authors recognize shifts in regional subsistence economies that are symptomatic of broader changes in cultural dynamics. Ultimately, the value of data presented in this chapter complements those presented in chapter 3 and together they move forward the discussion of the process of subsistence change on a regional scale.

As presented by Miller and Kenmotsu, the archaeological community has recognized shifting economic patterns including broad-spectrum resource exploitation and changing plant utilization during the first millennium AD. In the Western Jornada, this change has been particularly well studied on the training lands of Fort Bliss in the Tularosa Basin, the focus of this chapter (Church et al. 2009; Condon et al. 2010; Hard 1983a; Kenmotsu and Pigott 1977; Mauldin 1995; Miller and Kenmotsu 2004; Miller et al. 2009; Whalen 1994a; figure 4.1; see also figures 1.1, 1.2). For the lower Tularosa Basin, gradual change in the regional subsistence economy marked by resource specialization and increased use of plant domesticates is recognized after AD 1000. Specialization of subsistence economies appears to coincide with increased population

DOI: 10.5876/9781607327950.c004

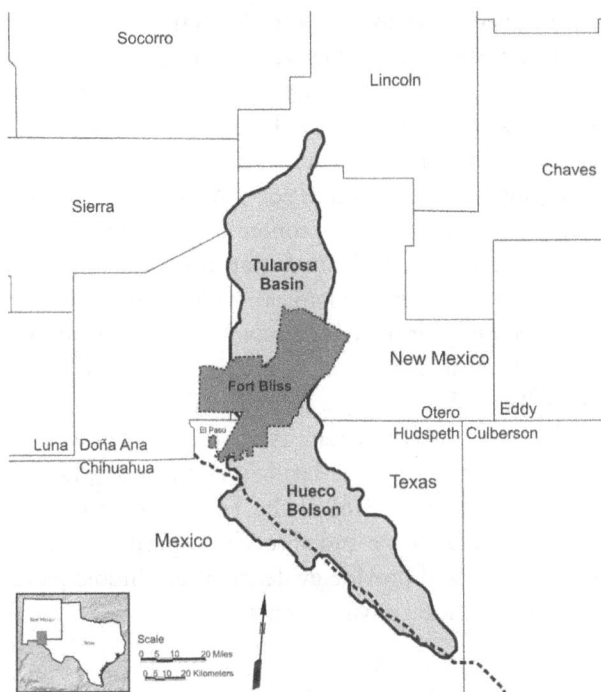

FIGURE 4.1. *Study area map showing the geographic relationship between the Tularosa Basin, the Hueco Bolson, and the Fort Bliss Military Reservation.*

aggregation, favorable environmental conditions, and the rise of social networks after AD 1000/1200 (Abbott, Hall, and Miller 2009; Carmichael 1986; Cordell, Doyel, and Kintigh 1994; Church et al. 2002; Grissino-Mayer et al. 1997; Lukowski et al. 2001; Mauldin 1995; Miller and Kenmotsu 2004; chapter 3, this volume).

Increasing resource stress, population aggregation, and the destabilization of regional exchange systems after AD 1300, however, point toward a changing socioeconomic dynamic that may have necessitated a continued emphasis on subsistence diversity and the use of non-domesticated plant species (Leonard 1989; Wills and Huckell 1994). This last finding differs from the pattern discussed by Miller and Kenmotsu, who identify a sharp regional decline in wild cacti and succulent exploitation after AD 1300. The discussion offered in this chapter differs from chapter 3 in that Miller and Kenmotsu focused specifically on cacti and succulents; the present authors included all identified wild species and identify continued heavy use of a broad spectrum of wild resources. Thus, the two studies augment one another as an examination of Late Formative subsistence economy, differentiated land use, and risk-management strategies in the lower Tularosa Basin and Hueco Bolson (Church et al. 2002; Condon and Swanson 2012; Condon, Hermann, et al. 2008, 2010; MacWilliams et al. 2009; Miller, Kenmotsu, and Landreth 2009; Miller et al. 2011).

In this chapter, we evaluate the economic contribution and relative significance of non-domesticated plants during the Late Archaic through the Formative period by comparing botanical evidence from a series of excavation projects carried out over the last decade. We examine 170 macrobotanical samples collected from feature fill at 83 prehistoric sites across Fort Bliss in New Mexico and Texas. Each sample yielded a calibrated radiocarbon age that was placed within the Middle-to-Late Archaic period (n = 52, including the Fresnal and Hueco phases) or the Mesilla phase (n = 77), Doña Ana phases (n = 25), or El Paso phase (n = 16) of the Formative period (see figure 1.3). These data indicate the presence and absence of specific plant species within the 83-site study group and provide evidence of diachronic patterns of plant utilization in relation to local environments.

PROJECT LOCATION

The training lands of Fort Bliss fall within the Mexican Highlands section of the basin-and-range province of the western United States (Fenneman 1931). This province encompasses much of the Chihuahuan Desert, in which two basin drainage systems critical to this study are located. The Hueco Bolson and Tularosa Basin are internally draining basins that form a north–south corridor, running from central New Mexico, south through far west Texas, and into northern Mexico (Abbott et al. 1996; Fenneman 1931; Keller and Baldridge 1999; cf. Lukowski et al. 2001). These intermontane lowlands are divided topographically along state lines; however, mesquite-stabilized dunes, interdunal deflation basins, seasonally active drainages, and basin playas are consistent elements of both landforms (Knowles and Kennedy 1958).

A gentle rise separates the Tularosa Basin from the Hueco Bolson; the two basins are bounded to the west by the Franklin and Organ Mountains and to the east by the Sacramento and Hueco Mountains (Fenneman 1931; Hawley and Kottlowski 1969; Hawley 1975; Orr and Myers 1986). The prehistoric sites analyzed for this study lie in the basin/valley proper, or along the adjoining alluvial-fan margins.

METHODS OF ANALYSIS

Analysis followed standard macrobotanical laboratory procedures as outlined by Cummings and Kováčik (2013), Diehl (2003), and Holloway (2012). Between 4 and 10 L of fill matrix were collected from each of the 170 features. Features included small hearths from the interior of pithouses and/or adobe-walled structures, extramural hearths, and to a lesser extent, both small and large burned-rock roasting pits (Condon et al. 2010; Miller and Kenmotsu 2004).

Between 2 and 6 L of fill matrix was processed through a Dausman flotation system, with the light fraction separated from the heavy fraction; up to 150 mL of the light fraction was analyzed per sample. After weighing, the light fractions were passed through a series of nested sieves (US Standard 4-mm, 2-mm, 1-mm, 0.5-mm, and 0.25-mm openings). Plant materials were sorted into two categories: carbonized wood and charred seed/fruit/maize fragments.

Subsequently, a subsample containing up to 24 wood-charcoal fragments greater than 1 mm in size were selected, a fresh break initiated, and the cross-section examined using a stereoscopic microscope at 70x magnification for greater clarification. Wood charcoal and charred seed/fruit/maize identifications were referenced using Leney and Casteel (1975); Dering (2014); Martin and Barkley (1961); Montgomery (1977); Musil (1963); and Schopmeyer (1974).

After identifications were complete, a correlating subsample of charred material was submitted to Beta Analytic, Inc., Miami, Florida, and/or the Paleo Research Institute, Golden, Colorado, for Accelerator Mass Spectrometry (AMS), and, to a lesser extent, standard radiocarbon analysis. The resulting calibrated radiocarbon dates range between 2470 BC and AD 1420. Figure 4.2 presents the summed-probability cumulative-age distribution of the 170 samples (OxCal 4.1). The macrobotanical analysis yielded an index of 21 charred-plant species (and an "indeterminate" category) upon which to evaluate the subsistence economies for the Middle-to-Late Archaic and the Formative periods (Condon and Swanson 2012; Condon et al. 2005, 2007, 2010; Condon, Hermann et al. 2006; Condon, Hall, et al. 2006; Condon, Kuehn, et al. 2008; Kenmotsu and Pigott 1977).

Frequency percentage was then calculated for each cultural phase to provide a measure of occurrence within the sampled time period (table 4.1). Frequency percentage was calculated by dividing the number of times a specific species was identified within the sampled features (e.g., in the Fresnal phase, *Prosopis* n = 12 out of 18 samples) by the *cumulative* number of positive species identifications (e.g., 22 positive species identifications within 18 samples, resulting in a ubiquity of 66.67%).

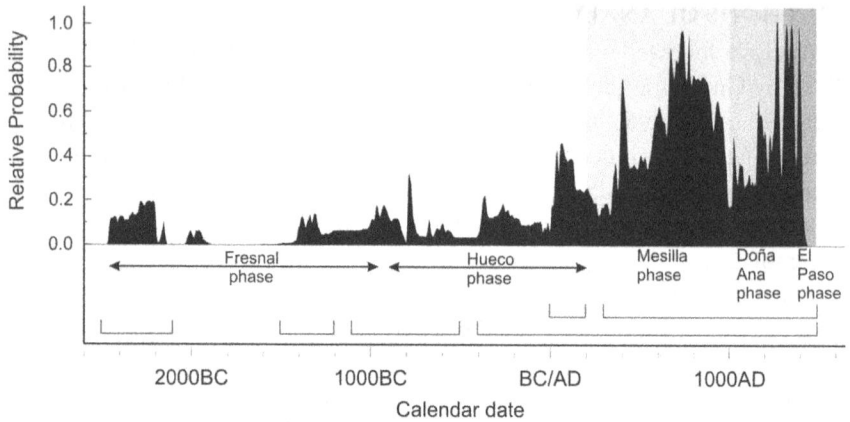

FIGURE 4.2. *Summed probability histogram for the 170 samples selected for the study. Shading demarcates Formative period phase divisions.*

In addition, taxon ubiquity percentages were calculated to provide a comparative measure of plant-use frequency through time. This approach assesses presence and absence of a species among multiple samples (Popper 1988). Ubiquity percentage was calculated by dividing the number of species by the total number of flotation samples assigned to a cultural phase (Adams 2004) (see table 4.1).

RESULTS OF ANALYSIS

The light-fraction analysis from 170 features yielded 21 identifiable domestic and non-domestic taxa; unidentifiable wood charcoal and indeterminate charred seed/fruit species were grouped into separate categories. Recording both type and frequency, the following results were identified (figure 4.3).

Eighteen samples recovered from 11 sites dated to the Fresnal phase (2470–900 BC) of the Middle Archaic period. These samples returned five taxa, with *Prosopis* (*n* = 12, 54.54%) the most prevalent fuel wood. Seed/fruit species were limited in occurrence; only *Chenopodium* (*n* = 1, 4.54%) and *Helianthus* (*n* = 1, 4.54%) were recovered.

Thirty-four features collected from 23 sites date to the Hueco phase of the Late Archaic period (1000 BC–AD 200). Five species were identified: again, fuel wood is dominated by *Prosopis* (*n* = 29, 58.0%). Seed/fruit species include *Juniperus monosperma* (*n* = 1, 2.0%) and *Celtis occidentalis* (*n* = 1, 2.0%). *Zea mays* is identified in 2.0% (*n* = 1) of the samples. The presence of charred maize during this period falls in line with current models of maize introduction of positive species identifications for each time period (e.g., in the first row 22 positive species identifications within 18 samples).

Cultural phase	Sample (N)	Sites (N)	Species ID Count	Chenopodium sp. Goosefoot	Helianthus sp. Sunflower	Poaceae sp. Grass Seed	Portulaca Purslane	Opuntia sp. Prickly Pear	Brassicaceae Mustard Seed	Yucca elata Yucca	Quercus undulata Acorn
Common Name											
Fresnal	18	11	22								
Frequency %				4.54	4.54						
n				1	1						
ubiquity				5.56%	5.56%						
Hueco	34	23	50								
Frequency %											
n											
ubiquity											
Mesilla	77	39	124								
Frequency %					4.03	0.8	0.8	1.61			
n					5	1	1	2			
ubiquity					6.49%	1.30%	1.30%	2.60%			
Doña Ana	25	3	38								
Frequency %								5.26		7.89	
n								2		3	
ubiquity								8.00%		12.00%	
El Paso	16	5	55								
Frequency %				7.27		5.95	7.27	1.81	1.81		3.63
n				4		3	4	1	1		2
ubiquity				25.00%		18.75%	25.00%	6.25%	6.25%		12.50%

continued on next page

TABLE 4.1—*continued*

Cultural phase	Sample (N)	Sites (N)	Species ID Count	Amsinckia *Fiddleneck*	Sphaeralcea (ambigua) *Globemallow*	Celtis occidentalis *Hackberry*	Juniperus monosperma *Juniper*	Fabaceae *Legume*	Indet. Seed/Fruit *n/a*	Zea *Maize*	Most Common Fuel
Common Name											
Fresnal	18	11	22								
Frequency %											54.4
n											12
ubiquity											66.67%
Hueco	34	23	50								
Frequency %						2	2			2	58
n						1	3			1	29
ubiquity						2.94%	8.82%			2.94%	85.29%
Mesilla	77	39	124								
Frequency %					0.8		3.22	0.8	1.6		45.96
n					1		4	1	1		57
ubiquity					1.30%		5.19%	1.30%	1.30%		74.03%
Doña Ana	25	3	38								
Frequency %										18.42	34.21
n										7	13
ubiquity										28.00%	52.00%
El Paso	16	5	55								
Frequency %				1.81	1.81			1.81	1.81	21.81	25.45
n				1	1			1	1	12	14
ubiquity				6.25%	6.25%			6.25%	6.25%	75.00%	87.50%

and expansion in the Jornada region (Miller and Graves 2015b; Miller and Kenmotsu 2004; Toll 2006; cf. Lentz 2006).

Sites with Early Formative/Mesilla-phase components offer the first observable increase in plant diversity. Twelve plant species from 77 samples, representing 39 sites, dated between AD 200/400 and 1000. As illustrated in figure 4.3, five species are possible fuel: *Prosopis* (n = 57, 45.96%) once again occurs with the highest frequency. The identification of both Pinaceae and *Cercocarpus*, however, points toward the exploitation of more upland fuel sources that thrive beyond the immediate environment of the study area.

Seven of the 12 taxa (58.33%) were identified as charred seed/fruits. Of the 12 species, *Helianthus* (n = 5, 4.03%), *Juniperus monosperma* berry (n = 4, 3.22%), and *Opuntia* (n = 2, 1.61%) are the most prevalent. Interestingly, while the number of seed/fruits increases during the Mesilla phase, cultigens are nearly absent in the sample.

Twenty-five (25) samples collected from three sites date to the Early and Late Doña Ana phases (AD 1000–1300) and show a noticeable shift in fuel-wood preference. Unlike the preceding Mesilla-phase samples, the Middle Formative–period sites reveal an increase in the use of *Atriplex/Sarcobatus* (n = 13, 34.21%) rather than *Prosopis* (n = 5, 13.15%) as a possible fuel source. The underlying factors behind this change are intriguing, yet unclear; they may relate to access rather than to an increase or decrease in resource use.

Seed processing is evidenced by charred *Yucca* sp. (n = 3, 7.89%) and *Opuntia* (n = 2, 5.26%) seeds. Similar to the increase in cultigens seen by Miller and Kenmotsu in the period AD 1000–1150, charred *Zea mays* cupules and kernel fragments make up 18.42% (n = 7) of our cumulative sample.

Sixteen samples from five sites date to the El Paso phase (AD 1300–1450). These samples were by far the most diverse, yielding multiple species from each light fraction. This abundance may relate to the sedentary nature of the occupations, which often facilitates the accumulation and storage of multiple resources at a single locale. This stands in contrast to highly mobile groups that may access a restricted range of plant species at any given time; processing and consumption rather than economizing and storage are potentially reflected in these divergent subsistence strategies.

For the El Paso phase, although *Prosopis* again supplants *Atriplex/Sarcobatus* in percentages, fuel-wood diversity remains generally consistent with *Prosopis* (n = 14, 25.45%) and *Atriplex/Sarcobatus* (n = 8, 14.54%) as the predominate fuel sources.

Nine seed/fruit-bearing species were identified in the El Paso phase, the majority present in relatively low quantities. Species with the highest

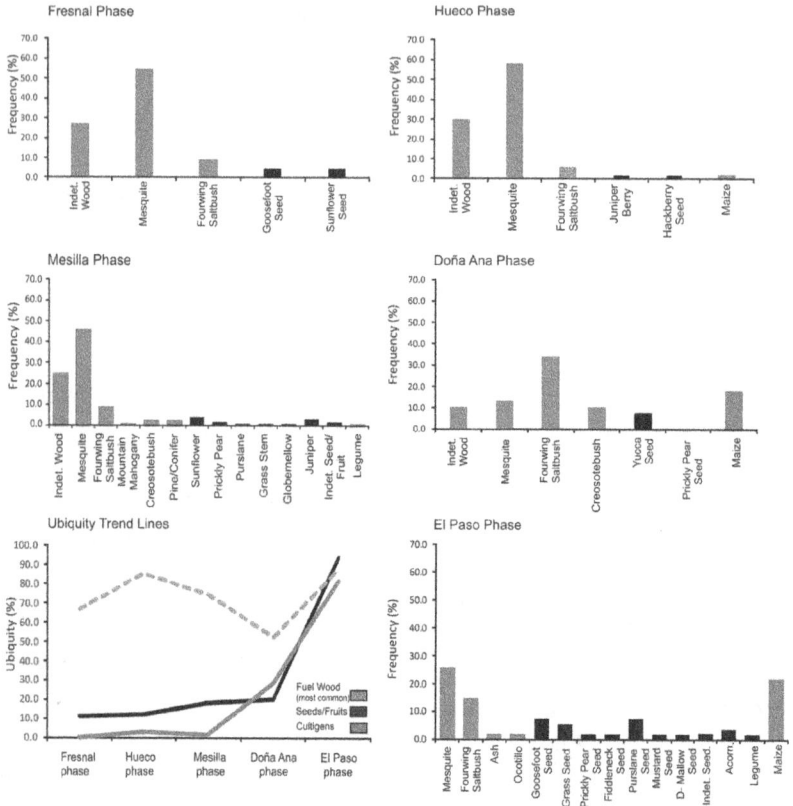

FIGURE 4.3. *Frequency-distribution graphs showing species distribution by phase, and trend-line graph (bottom left) illustrating ubiquity through time.*

occurrence included *Chenopodium* (*n* = 4, 7.27%), *Portulaca* (*n* = 4, 7.27%), and Poaceae (*n* = 3, 5.95%). In addition, charred *Quercus* shells (*n* = 2, 3.63%) were collected from two separate features.

Finally, *Zea mays* was identified in 75% (*n* = 12) of the 16-feature sample group, representing 21.81% of the total species count for the phase. The increased presence of *Zea mays* provides the strongest evidence for the use of cultigens during the Late Formative period, which compares with Miller and Kenmotsu's findings (chapter 3, this volume). However, the recovery of seven charred-seed/fruit species identified for the El Paso–phase sample group suggests that non-domesticated plants continue to play a critical role in the Late Formative subsistence economy.

CONCLUSIONS AND DISCUSSION

The plant remains identified in this study reveal two general but nonetheless critical subsistence patterns. The first highlights a subsistence economy that is reliant on a narrow range of non-domesticated plants—these findings support patterns discussed by Miller and Kenmotsu in chapter 3 of this volume. For example, samples assigned to the Fresnal and Hueco phases of the Archaic produced similar fuel-wood patterns and a nearly equal number of seed species. Both frequency and ubiquity trends show that *Prosopis* is the preferred fuel source for the pre-Formative period. In addition, three separate seed/fruit species were identified for the Middle and Late Archaic period. The presence of non-cultivated species follows currently known trends for the Late Archaic period, in which wild plants dominate the subsistence record and domesticated plant species, such as maize, played a less critical role for mobile hunter-gatherers in the region.

Plant species assigned to the Mesilla phase reflect increased diversity in both fuel-wood selection and seed-plant exploitation. These findings reinforce the subsistence, and by proxy, mobility patterns identified by Miller and Kenmotsu in chapter 3 for the later Mesilla phase (AD 600–1000). The range of fuel wood expands to include *Cercocarpus* and Pinaceae—both upland species that occur with lower frequency than the more widespread *Prosopis* or *Atriplex/Sarcobatus*. Non-domesticated seed-producing plants includes six species. The diversity of the samples suggests a more robust plant selection and tentatively the onset of regional intensification (Miller and Kenmotsu 2004:249).

The range of plant species for this time period may also be influenced by the type of archaeological site from which the samples were obtained. Many of the Mesilla-phase features were excavated at residential sites. Storage pits and durable ceramic vessels may provide better preservation and account for better plant recovery. The near absence of cultigens for the Mesilla sample group may be explained by sampling bias and/or may be indicative of the early stages of agricultural intensification. It should be noted that Miller and Kenmotsu, with their different data set, also found few cultigens from Mesilla components.

Nonetheless, maize and legumes dated at Fresnal Rockshelter and High Rolls Cave indicate that domesticates were regionally used, at least as a supplemental resource, by ca. 1350 BC (Bohrer 1981; Lentz 2006). By AD 1000, it is clear that cultigens play a more critical role in the region, with maize ubiquity increasing with time in the archaeological record (Miller and Kenmotsu 2004; Miller et al. 2009).

The second pattern highlights plant selection after AD 1000 and provides evidence for increased agricultural production in the region; these findings generally parallel interpretations described in chapter 3. Localized fuel-wood selection is indicated by the frequency/ubiquity trends, with the absence of *Cercocarpus* and Pinaceae and a higher frequency of *Prosopis* and *Atriplex/Sarcobatus*. This pattern may reflect more immediate access tempered by increased territorialism. As noted by Miller and Kenmotsu (chapter 3), increased sedentism and resource selection characterize the region post–AD 1000.

Fuel-wood diversity is moderate for the El Paso phase and may reflect increased regional intensification/territorialism, resulting in resource stress. Intensification is interpreted as the depletion in fuel-source selection, resulting in the increased use of *Prosopis* and *Atriplex/Sarcobatus* rather than more durable and sustainable hardwood sources.

The number of remains of seed-producing plants noticeably increases after AD 1000, as does the recovery of domesticated plant remains for the study group. An upward trend in charred maize is first observed in the Early and Late Doña Ana phases and continues into the subsequent El Paso phase. This is in keeping with the ubiquity values observed in Miller and Kenmotsu's (2004:249; chapter 3, this volume) analysis. Exploitation of wild seed-bearing plants seem to parallel this increase in domesticated plant usage; of particular note are *Yucca elata* and *Opuntia* sp. seeds for the Early and Late Doña Ana phases. The ubiquity trends for the El Paso phase show increased finds of seed-producing taxa, with a focus on *Chenopodium, Portulaca*, and Poaceae. However, it is important to note that while the ubiquity of non-domesticated plants is higher in the El Paso phase, the ubiquity values tend to be dramatically lower than the values of cultigens such as *Zea mays*.

Non-domesticated plant use during the El Paso phase presents the first clear divergence from the model provided by Miller and Kenmotsu in chapter 3. The differences in non-domesticated plant usage may reflect differing sampling strategies. Miller and Kenmotsu rely heavily on data recovered from specific feature types: rock-lined hearths or plant-baking facilities, and correctly focus on cacti/succulent data relating to these feature types; other non-cacti fruit/seed-bearing plants were omitted in their study.

In contrast, the emerging emphasis on cultigens tends to correlate with socioeconomic changes and climatic shifts experienced in the region after AD 1000, a period that postdates a 100-year interval of below-average rainfall (Grissino-Mayer et al. 1997). The return to average or above-average precipitation rates occurs after AD 1040, when cultigens appear to play a more pivotal role in the region. Subsistence specialization depends on the correct conditions to support the growth and harvest of domesticated plant species. Success allows high-yield economies that focus on fewer resources, but are susceptible to failure from a variety of fronts, including environmental, social, and political influences (Leonard 1989).

This interpretation tentatively applies to the subsequent El Paso phase, when localized intensification of agriculture flourishes after AD 1300 along with the emergence of greater sociopolitical complexity. The results of this study suggest that intensive agricultural economies may mediate risk through multiple combined strategies, including but not limited to the development of social networks, specialization, and, to some extent, subsistence diversification. While the ubiquity data generally show low values for seed-producing plants, the frequency data indicate a broad increase in the diversity of plant species during the El Paso phase. This pattern may also correlate with the moderate increase in fuel-wood taxa during the same period.

Diversification as a risk-management mechanism in the Formative period should not be viewed as a singular response but, perhaps more accurately, as one of several integrated strategies employed to offset socioeconomic failure. Improved storage capabilities after AD 200/400 introduced technological factors that managed risk during the Formative period. Moreover, the development of social networks, particularly after AD 1300, served as an effective risk-management strategy during the El Paso phase, one that may have temporarily eased regional ecological constraints. To this end, an earlier study carried out by Miller and Kenmotsu (2004) identified a regional focus on agriculture and a reduced role in wild-plant exploitation after AD 1300 (Miller and Kenmotsu 2004; chapter 3, this volume). The current study, smaller in scale, offers a similar pattern for cultigens, but tentatively suggests that non-domesticated plants, and specifically seed-bearing species, may retain extended value in the region despite the development of a more specialized resource economy after AD 1300. Moreover, possible overexploitation and slow recovery of cacti and succulents, as suggested by Miller and Kenmotsu (chapter 3), may have increased the economic value of resources not as susceptible to depletion.

Thus, non-domesticated plants, and specifically seed-bearing species, continue to play a role in regional subsistence strategies during the agriculturally focused Late Formative period. While the degree of reliance is uncertain, even a supplementary role provides an economic contribution, and thus a viable component to the subsistence economies of the region.

ACKNOWLEDGMENTS

This study is the result of research supported by the United States Army, Department of Public Works, Environmental Division, Conservation Branch,

Fort Bliss, Texas. To this end, gratitude is expressed to Brian Knight, Belinda Mollard, Sue Sitton, and Martha Yduarte. Myles Miller provided invaluable assistance with the radiocarbon analyses. Luis Sierra created the primary botanical database from which much of this study was based. Two anonymous reviewers provided valuable insight and editorial direction. Finally, the authors would like to extend their thanks to Tom Rocek and Nancy Kenmotsu for their insightful review, constructive comments, and boundless patience.

5

As with most other late prehistoric cultures in the American Southwest, one of the most important underpinnings of the Jornada Mogollon was the development of maize-based farming. Thus it behooves us to examine the origins and development of farming in this region. But the topic of early farming, here and in the greater Southwest, potentially encompasses two different issues: first the initial introduction of maize, and second the development of dependence on farming as an important focus of the subsistence economy. As numerous researchers have pointed out, the mere presence of maize does not necessarily signal a major subsistence shift or reliance on farming for nutritional needs, and in most places there appears to have been a significant time lag between the initial appearance of maize and high dependence on farming (e.g., Wills 1992; Wills and Huckell 1994).

To put the origins and development of farming in the Jornada into a clearer perspective, it helps to expand the geographic scope a bit. Accordingly, we examine late preceramic developments in the Jornada region in relation to neighboring areas, including the Mimbres and Casas Grandes areas to the west. This comparison suggests a broad pattern involving early farming dependence in wooded highland areas of southern New Mexico—encompassing both the Jornada and Mimbres areas—with highly mobile hunting-and-gathering economies persisting until ca. AD 1000 in the adjacent desert lowlands of the Jornada and eastern Mimbres areas.

Farming Dependence in Southern New Mexico

Earlier Than We Thought

JIM A. RAILEY AND
CHRISTOPHER A. TURNBOW

DOI: 10.5876/9781607327950.c005

Thanks to investigations at a handful of caves and rockshelters, southern New Mexico has provided some of the most frequently cited evidence for early maize in the Southwest (e.g., Dick 1965; MacNeish 1993:319; Martin et al. 1954; Martin et al. 1952; Tagg 1996; Upham and MacNeish 1993; Upham et al. 1987; Wills 1988a:108–109). With respect to more farming-based economies, however, until recently southern New Mexico (and adjacent portions of west Texas) had produced little evidence from the preceramic time frame, and thus appeared to contrast with southeast Arizona and northwestern Chihuahua. As a result, well into the last decade, researchers concluded that farming-dependent economies did not begin until AD 500–600 in the highlands of southern New Mexico, and not until ca. AD 1000–1100 in the lowlands (Brown 1998; e.g., Hard 1997; Huckell 1996:345; LeBlanc 1983; Rocek 1990, 1991, 1995; Whalen 1994a, b; Wills 1988a). This remained the received knowledge even after evidence of significant farming dependence and storage, dating back to approximately 2,000 years ago, had already been discovered in the Rio Hondo Valley of the Sierra Blanca Highlands portion of the Jornada (Wiseman 1996b).

Using this perceived knowledge as a starting point, Doleman (2005) sought to explain what appeared to be a significant time lag between the beginnings of farming dependence in southeastern Arizona (ca. 1200 BC) and southern New Mexico (ca. AD 500). In the same volume, Hard and Roney (2005) sought to explain the contrast between the early appearance of farming along the Rio Casas Grandes in Chihuahua, and its much later appearance in the nearby Southern Jornada Mogollon. But whereas Hard and Roney focused their contrasting case on the lowlands of the Southern Jornada region, Doleman looked at all of southern New Mexico in his discussion of early farming, and in this respect there are some problems with his model.

Doleman followed Wills and Huckell's (1994) argument that cultivation of maize was never casual, given that this plant demands extended seasonal attention for its planting, tending, and harvesting. As such, maize farming introduced potential scheduling conflicts for groups still dependent on hunting and gathering. According to Doleman's model, these conflicts could be resolved "by occupying residential loci that offered easy access to both agriculturally productive land and favored foraging areas" (Doleman 2005:118). Such loci were situated where short-distance vertical mobility, encompassing a range of environmental zones and their seasonally successive resource blooms, was possible. Doleman argued that such conditions prevailed within the tightly spaced basins and ranges of southeastern Arizona, but not so much in southern New Mexico, where basins and ranges are more widely spaced.

Doleman also pointed to dissimilarities in precipitation and biological diversity between the two areas. Hard and Roney (2005) include these same factors among those they used to explain the long time lag in the appearance of early farming between the Rio Casas Grandes valley in Chihuahua, and the lowland areas of the nearby Southern Jornada region. But for Doleman it was primarily physiographic spatial structure that explains the long delay before farming dependence took hold in southern New Mexico.

Doleman's explanation can be challenged on both theoretical and substantive grounds. On the theoretical front, he did not fully account for the possibility of short-distance vertical mobility along the edges of southern New Mexico's vast basins. Although the sizes of the basin floors differ considerably between southeastern Arizona and southern New Mexico, there is much less difference in the widths of mountain ranges between the two regions. This is important because most of the vertical resource zonation occurs within the mountains and along basin edges. In other words, it is easily conceivable that Archaic hunter-gatherers in southern New Mexico and west Texas could have practiced the sort of short-distance, logistical mobility that Doleman argued was more feasible in southeastern Arizona.

More directly undercutting Doleman's explanation is the archaeological evidence itself. Besides Wiseman's (1996b) discoveries, prior to the appearance of Doleman's essay, additional new evidence was already published showing that farming-dependent economies in southern New Mexico did not, in fact, make a "last-minute appearance" (Doleman 2005:122). That evidence came from a large-scale excavation along New Mexico Highway 90 (NM 90), in the Big Burro Mountains of the Mimbres region (Turnbow 2000). Discoveries from that project showed that farming dependence began no later than the early first millennium BC—only a few centuries later than nearby southeastern Arizona and northwestern Chihuahua. A few years later, excavations along US Highway 70 (US 70) in the Hondo Valley in the Sierra Blanca Highlands showed that farming dependence and storage began there no later than the late first millennium BC (Campbell and Railey 2008)—even earlier than what Wiseman (1996b) had found in this same valley. Like Wiseman's and the NM 90 discoveries, those from the US 70 project also seem to have been overlooked in at least some subsequent discussions of early farming developments in the Southwest (e.g., Gregory et al. 2011). Nonetheless, it is now abundantly clear that significant dependence on farming in southern New Mexico—in both the Mimbres and Jornada regions—was hardly a "last-minute" development, although the evidence is restricted to highland areas. The NM 90 and US 70 discoveries prompt us to reconsider the development of farming in

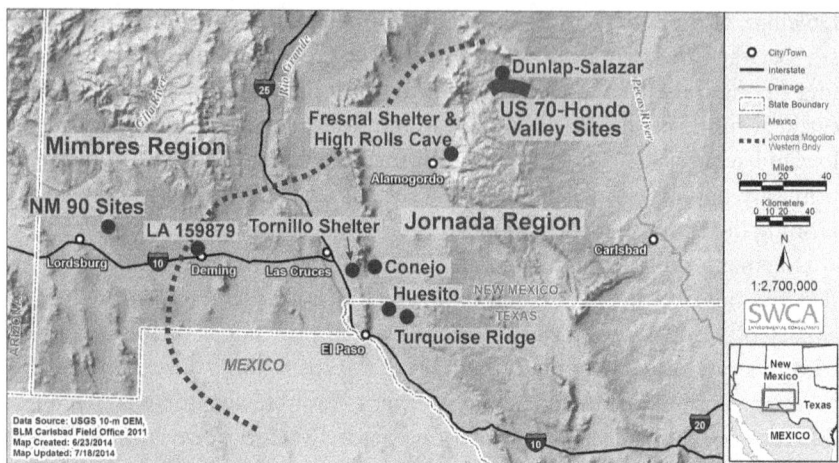

FIGURE 5.1. *Southern New Mexico and adjacent areas, showing sites mentioned in the text.*

southern New Mexico and neighboring areas (figures 1.1 and 5.1), and explore the regional and local diversity in the preceramic origins of Mogollon culture here (see also Rocek, chapter 2, this volume).

FARMING DEPENDENCE

Since this chapter is concerned with farming dependence, we should first clarify what we mean by this term. One measure of agricultural dependence is maize *ubiquity*, which is a simple percentage of the flotation samples from a site (or site component) containing maize (Rocek 1995). Multiroom pueblos tend to have more maize than do pithouse sites, but this does not necessarily mean that agriculture was more important for pueblos. Rather, pueblo sites may have more maize simply because they were occupied on a more sustained basis, and contain characteristics lacking in many pithouse sites, such as sub-stantial (and spatially discrete) trash middens, more visible maize remains (such as charred cobs), and storage and processing rooms where abundant maize remains are sometimes found. Dry rockshelters and caves may also contain more-abundant maize remains than do open sites, again not necessarily due to differences in farming dependence, but because of superior preservation condi-tions. Using ubiquity of charred maize from flotation samples helps to neutral-ize the effects of preservation, and different kinds of occupations and contexts, and as such has been offered as a more reliable indicator of farming dependence than simple maize abundance. An important caveat, however, is that maize ubiquity may not always be a straightforward indicator of relative agricultural dependence, since intersite variability in the fragmentation of charred remains may affect identification potential (and, hence, ubiquity values).

Another potential indicator of farming dependence is storage facilities, among the more distinctive of which are cylindrical and bell-shaped pits. The use and effectiveness of deep, underground pits for storing grains and other foods is well documented historically, ethnographically, and experimentally (e.g., Currid and Navon 1989; DeBoer 1988; Gronenborg 1997; Martinek 1998; Reynolds 1974, 1979a, 1979b; Robinson 1963; Wilson 1987:87–97), although evidence also indicates some loss of grain—sometimes substantial—to spoilage is to be expected with underground storage facilities (see Diehl and Davis 2016:338, and references therein). In the American Southwest, the vast majority of known storage pits occur at sites where there is evidence of substantial dependence on farming (e.g., Campbell and Railey 2008; Geib and Spurr 2000:191; 2002:236; Gilman 1987; Huckell 1995; 1996:343–347, 351; Huckell et al. 2002; Huckell et al. 1995; Mabry and Doolittle 2008:64; Mabry et al. 1997; Rocek 2007a; Sayles 1983:125–131; Turnbow 2000; Van Dyke et al. 1998:85–86). The close association of bell-shaped and cylindrical storage pits with farming is, in fact, a global phenomenon (e.g., Andersson 1973:171–174; Blitz 1993; Blomster 1998; Bogucki 1999:275; Borhegyi 1965; DeBoer 1988; Drass 1998; Flannery 2009; Flannery and Winter 1976; Jelks 1967; Martinek 1998; Peregrine and Ember 2001; Reina and Hill 1980; Reynolds 1974; Shook 1951; Syms 1974; Wilson 1987; Winham and Calabrese 1998:289; Winter 2009:28–29, 34; Yerkes et al. 2009:1082, 1084–1085). Thus the occurrence of deep storage pits (bell-shaped or otherwise) can usually (but not always) be taken as an indicator of farming, and the numbers and sizes of such pits may be used to help gauge not only storage capacity but also agricultural dependence. Their presence has also been linked to concealment under conditions of seasonal mobility (DeBoer 1988). But bell-shaped and other underground storage pits are hardly restricted to seasonally mobile human groups, as they are also found in sedentary settings cross-culturally (Currid and Navon 1989:67; DeBoer 1988:9–10; Gronenborg 1997; Mannessier 1950; Robinson 1963; Staller et al. 2006; Tristam 1898:488), an apparent testimony to their effectiveness in preserving food and, perhaps in some cases, concealing stores from nosy neighbors or sociopolitical overlords. At any rate, we can expect bell-shaped and cylindrical storage pits to occur in at least the early stages of a long-term trajectory involving a shift from mobility to sedentism. This is precisely what appears to have happened in southern New Mexico, where large storage pits are associated with pithouses, but largely disappear once people began living in multiroom pueblos (e.g., Gilman 1987; Rocek 1995). In the discussion below we use evidence of maize ubiquity and storage pits in the southern New Mexico Mogollon region to address the timing of agricultural dependence.

NM 90 IN THE MIMBRES REGION

Although this volume is focused on the Jornada and the NM 90 project area lies well to the west, in the Mimbres region, the environmental conditions and discoveries here underscore the precocious nature of farming dependence in highland areas of southern New Mexico relative to the surrounding lowlands, and parallels the situation in the Jornada area. The NM 90 sites were strategically placed at the boundary of two of the richest ecosystems in the Big Burro Mountain highlands and beside a broad floodplain probably suitable for early farming (see figure 5.1).

Excavations at the Forest Home (LA 78089) and Wood Canyon (LA 99631) sites revealed evidence of three discrete, preceramic farming settlements with maize and wild-seed dates between 895 BC and AD 200 (Turnbow 2000). Each had small pit structures surrounded by storage and roasting pits, burials, and ground-stone caches, all associated with thick (0.3–0.6 m) cultural deposits and dense concentrations of burnt rock and artifacts. The presence of maize and large storage pits suggests that by 800 BC farming may have taken on a more economically significant role in the Mimbres region than previously assumed (Brown 1998:233; LeBlanc 1989).

Food production is evident from the maize and squash identified from macrobotanical, pollen, and phytolith samples (Bozarth 2000; Huckell 2000). Maize ubiquity (measured here by the percentage of samples containing maize among all flotation samples that had preserved charred seeds) is viewed as a basic measure of its importance, but could be skewed by the poor preservation of the Wood Canyon macrobotanical remains. Still, maize ubiquity was 41% from the earlier Wood Canyon component with both structures and all sampled bell-shaped pits containing charred maize kernels or cobs. Around four hundred years later, the Forest Home component had 91% maize ubiquity and also produced tobacco and squash. Maize pollen and phytolith ubiquity at the components were comparable to that from flotation.

Like the US 70 sites, large bell-shaped or cylindrical storage features were present at each NM 90 component with the earliest (ca. 800 BC) having five bell-shaped pits with a mean estimated volume of 1,364 L. Using Huckell et al.'s (2002) storage-pit capacity formula, a pit of this size could hold 16,647

Archaic maize ears. Even if not all of the pits were used in any one year, and even with some loss of stored grain to spoilage, they indicate that the population was producing and/or gathering a significant food surplus not recognized during earlier periods.

The intensity of occupation (i.e., increased labor investment to construct storage pits, structures, and graves) of the NM 90 components suggests greatly reduced residential mobility similar to that of preceramic settlements excavated along US 70 in the Sierra Blanca Highlands. The relatively high maize ubiquity and storage capacity at the NM 90 sites indicate that food production had already assumed an important role in the local economy by 800 BC. Wild plants and cultivars imply multiseasonal occupation during at least the spring, summer, and fall, and Hunter-Anderson (1986), Whalen (1994b), and Huckell et al. (2002) propose that large-scale, on-site storage could indicate an overwintering strategy. Site occupants may, perhaps, have hidden their crops before leaving for winter hunts, revisiting their stores as needed before finally consuming their stockpiled food during the lean spring-planting period.

US 70 IN THE HONDO VALLEY

The Hondo Valley lies in the northern portion of the Jornada (see figures 1.1 and 5.1) and is, by far, the largest drainage in the Sierra Blanca/Capitan/ Sacramento Highlands. Heading in high-elevation, subalpine and alpine conifer forests and grasslands, the Hondo watershed descends eastward through ponderosa pine, Mogollon chaparral, and piñon-juniper zones, before entering the semidesert grassland and steppe that extends from the lower foothills across the vast lowlands of the Pecos River valley. Flanking the local streams are narrow floodplains, with soils that are well-suited to farming, and indeed are heavily farmed today. Before the past century these streams supported a healthy aquatic biome including rich stocks of fish and mollusks (Arntzen and Speth 2004; Speth and McKay 2004; Speth et al. 2004). In short, the Hondo Valley offered a bonanza of resources, and prehistoric peoples had access to a variety of closely spaced resource zones.

A widening of US 70 along the Rios Hondo and Ruidoso prompted an intense flurry of excavations in the early 2000s (Campbell and Railey 2008; Railey 2010). The most significant discoveries of the US 70 project came from nine prehistoric residential sites. Six of these are clustered along a stretch of the Rio Ruidoso, flanked by piñon-juniper and Mogollon chaparral biotic communities in the highlands; the other three are in the semidesert zone downstream and to the east. Over 90 radiocarbon dates from these sites (figure 5.2),

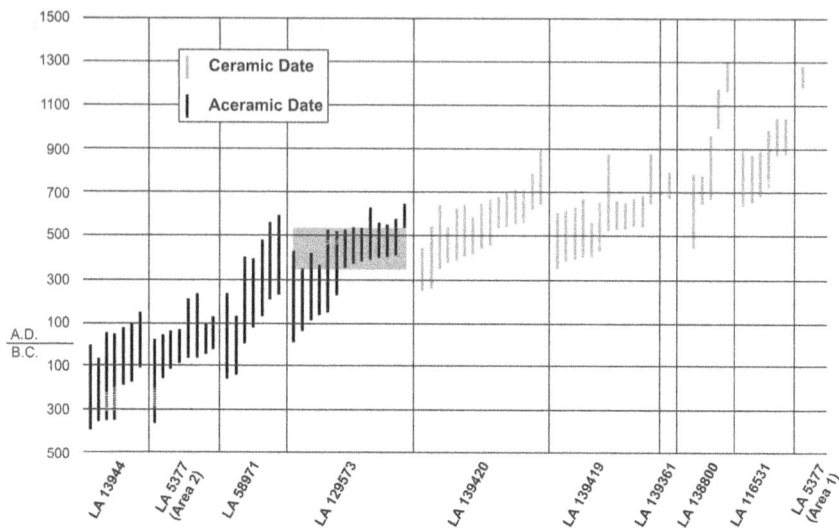

FIGURE 5.2. *Distribution of calibrated (two-sigma) radiocarbon dates from the US 70–Hondo project. The shaded areas denote the minimum ranges for the aceramic dates from LA 129573 (adapted from Campbell and Railey 2008:711, figure 32.2).*

including some from the Sunset Archaic site (LA 58971) obtained previously by Wiseman (1996b), show that they collectively span ca. 300 BC–AD 1100. Among other things, the dates indicate that ceramics first entered the valley around AD 530–540, and projectile points suggest the bow and arrow arrived just prior to this date.

Among the most notable findings of this project was that substantial investments in maize-based farming and storage began much earlier in the Sierra Blanca Highlands than was previously thought. A pattern of high maize ubiquity, bell-shaped storage pits, and thick, rich midden deposits was discovered at site after site in the US 70 investigations, covering a collective occupation span of ca. 300 BC–AD 1100. Four of the sites (LA 13944, LA 5377 Area 2, Sunset Archaic [LA 58971], and LA 129573) are preceramic and collectively date from ca. 300 BC to just after AD 500. Maize ubiquity (among flotation samples with charred seeds) ranges from 81% to 100% among the four preceramic sites in the sequence. Moreover, every bell-shaped storage pit from which flotation samples were processed contained maize, and this was the same for both preceramic and ceramic sites. Charred cobs and cupules indicate that maize was grown within or near these sites. Beans were found in one of the bell-shaped pits at the Sunset Archaic site. Wild-plant foods were also represented. Numerous dropseed grass seeds were recovered from one bell-shaped pit at LA 129573, and a mesquite seed was also found at this site (suggesting consumption of mesquite pods, as the seeds themselves are rock-hard and inedible). Walnut shell was found at LA 139944. The Sunset Archaic site also produced *Chenopodium*, tansy mustard, piñon, and dropseed.

A total of 68 bell-shaped storage pits was excavated at the Hondo Valley sites, with 36 of these at the preceramic sites (these include eight bell-shaped pits excavated at the Sunset Archaic site by Wiseman). The preceramic ones range 0.5 m to 2.9 m in maximum (basal) diameter (mean = 1.6 m; standard deviation = 0.6 m). There are no clear size trends through time, although the four pits from LA 139944—the earliest site in the sequence—have the largest mean diameter (2.2 m), and there is no increase in the size of bell-shaped pits between the preceramic- and ceramic-period sites. Volumes were not measured for the Hondo Valley bell-shaped pits, but they are larger on average than those from the NM 90 sites. They are similar in size to (but still slightly larger than) six bell-shaped pits excavated at the early ceramic-period site (ca. AD 550–850) of Dunlap-Salazar (range 1.0–1.8 m; mean = 1.46 m), located along the Rio Bonito to the north (Rocek 1991).

The US 70 sites hosted sustained occupations. All have thick middens rich in artifacts, and the bell-shaped pits and other features are full of redeposited trash, including charred maize. Recognizable remains of house structures are notably rare to absent in the US 70 sites, however. The preceramic area at LA 5377 included three oval-to-circular features that ranged from 2.3 m to 2.8 m in maximum diameter and were a meter in depth. These may have been pit structures, although no internal hearths were found, and they may have been storage facilities rather than domiciles. At LA 129573, a structure was inferred from six postholes and an adobe-lined hearth, but its overall dimensions and character could not be clearly discerned. Site LA 129573 was the largest and richest of the four preceramic sites, and was strategically located at the confluence of the Rios Bonito and Ruidoso, which join to form the Rio Hondo.

In summary, the Hondo Valley discoveries push back the beginnings of farming-dependent economies in the Sierra Blanca Highlands several centuries prior to the previously accepted date of ca. AD 500. High maize ubiquity, charred cob fragments and cupules, beans, numerous bell-shaped and other storage pits, and rich midden deposits all point to a pattern of intensive site occupations and heavy investment in both farming and storage. Some degree of seasonal mobility may be evidenced by the dearth of recognizable structure remains, but in the Hondo Valley a pattern of farming dependence continued, with no evident change, throughout the first millennium AD.

HIGHLANDS VERSUS LOWLANDS: THE GEOGRAPHY OF EARLY FARMING DEPENDENCE IN SOUTHERN NEW MEXICO

Discoveries in highland areas of both the Mimbres and Jornada regions not only push back the origins of farming dependence in southern New Mexico to the first millennium BC, but also prompt us to reconsider the historical geography of farming developments in the region. Perhaps more than any other environmental aspect, the beginnings of maize cultivation and early transition to heavy investments in farming were dependent on available water (including both precipitation and local runoff) coupled with rich biotic zones and favorable local floodplain conditions.

Half a century ago, Haury (1962) concluded that maize became important in more mesic uplands hundreds of years before it became economical for populations in the more arid lowlands. However, more recent investigations found some of the earliest evidence for farming dependence in lowland areas of the southern Southwest. These include evidence from the Santa Cruz Valley in Arizona, where maize dating to around 2100 BC is associated with some of the earliest, farming-based communities in the Southwest (Mabry 2005). Less than 40 km south of the New Mexico boot heel in Chihuahua, Cerro Juanaqueña and similar *trinchera* sites are large, intensively occupied farming communities dating to around 1250 BC. They are positioned on commanding hilltops along the Rio Casas Grandes (Hard and Roney 2005). They are only slightly higher in elevation than basin-floor sites in the Jornada region, but next to the Rio Casas Grandes, and the local floodplain offered one of the best places for farming in the North American Southwest.

In southern New Mexico and adjacent portions of the Jornada Mogollon region, both initial maize cultivation and intensive farming got a head start in highland areas, while in the nearby desert basins high mobility and hunter-gatherer economies appear to have persisted much longer. The corridor along the Rio Grande represents something of a wild card, as evidence from here remains rather slim. The earliest maize remains in southern New Mexico are found near the Rio Grande, at the Tornillo Rockshelter near Las Cruces (figure 5.1). A composite sample of cobs from Tornillo returned a calibrated (one-sigma) date of 2030–830 BC (Miller and Kenmotsu 2004:227; Upham et al. 1987; Wills and Huckell 1994:42). Hard and Roney (2005:171) argue that the Rio Grande floodplain was perhaps ill-suited to early farming, due to frequent destructive flooding and irregular flow. Still, it is possible (if not likely) that at least certain locales along the Rio Grande were, in fact, suitable to early agricultural developments. The Tornillo Rockshelter maize may have been grown in the nearby Rio Grande floodplain, but the shelter's occupants may also have farmed the adjacent bajada slope of the Organ Mountains, where precipitation runoff and/or active springs may have provided the necessary water. Thus, although the Tornillo Rockshelter is close to the Rio Grande, evidence for early floodplain farming along the river remains somewhat equivocal.

Elsewhere on the basin floors and other lowland areas of southern New Mexico and adjacent portions of the Mogollon region, there is little evidence of maize cultivation and use—and essentially no evidence of farming-based communities—through the end of the first millennium AD. Preceramic maize microfossils (and possible macrobotanical maize), starch, and residues are reported from lowland sites stretching from the boot heel to far southeastern New Mexico (Boggess 2011; Brown and Brown 2011; Davis et al. 2002; Fish et al. 2006:26;5 Lentz et al. 2013; O'Laughlin 1980; Yost and Scott-Cummings 2011). However, the precise dating and/or identification of some these remains have been questioned (Miller and Burt 2007; Miller and Kenmotsu 2004:226), and only one of these is accompanied by macrobotanical maize. That one exception, LA 159879 (Lentz et al. 2013), includes only a single charred maize kernel. Moreover, these sites (including LA 159879) lack substantial midden deposits and none contains storage pits. Well-dated, preceramic contexts in lowland areas of the Jornada region often lack macrobotanical food remains, a pattern common to sites of highly mobile hunter-gatherers (O'Laughlin 2002:684), and when such remains are present they consist of wild plants such as cheno-ams, sunflower, wild barley and buckwheat, and various species of Agavaceae (Miller and Kenmotsu 2004; Railey 2013:68–61; see also in this volume Miller and Kenmotsu, chapter 3, and Condon and Vasquez, chapter 4).

There is little change in this lowland pattern during the Early Formative period in the Jornada region, ca. AD 500–1000 (see Dering 2007; Miller and Kenmotsu 2004:248; Railey 2013:58–61). That is, macrobotanical remains continue to be very low in frequency (or absent) at open-air sites, and the remains that are found tend to be wild plants. The best evidence of early farming from the desert floor comes from the Mesilla-phase sites of Huesito (Whalen 1981a, 1981b), Conejo (Goldborer 1988; Hard 1988; Miller and Burt 2007), and Turquoise Ridge (Whalen 1994b) (see figure 1.3). Huesito lies on the interior basin floor, while Conejo and Turquoise Ridge are both basin-edge sites located on opposite sides of the Tularosa Basin–Hueco Bolson lowlands. Maize ubiquity is less than 10% at Huesito and Conejo (regardless if measured by percentage of total flotation samples or only those containing charred seeds). Huesito is a very late Mesilla-phase site, dating to around AD 1000, and was apparently used as a camp for summer collecting activities. The maize at this site does not necessarily indicate that it was grown in the interior basin floors. At Turquoise Ridge, maize ubiquity (as measured among flotation samples containing charred seeds) was similarly low, at 7.3% for the early component (AD 500–750), but increased to 27% in the late component (AD 750–1000). The latter value is still much lower than those at the preceramic Hondo Valley and NM 90 sites. Storage pits, including both bell-shaped forms and others that might be collapsed bell-shaped pits, were present in both early and late components at Turquoise Ridge (Whalen 1994b:54–55). But these appear to be small in comparison to those at the Hondo Valley sites and, interestingly, most are located inside structures. Taken together, the evidence suggests that there was comparatively little investment in farming in the basin floors of the Jornada region prior to the Late Formative period.

In the upland areas of southern New Mexico, a very different story unfolds with respect to early farming developments. Among the earliest evidence of farming in the highlands comes from Fresnal Shelter (Tagg 1996) and High Rolls Cave (Lentz 2006), where maize dating perhaps as early as 1400 BC has been recovered. These sites contain abundant uncharred perishable materials, and as such offer a much more complete picture of subsistence than any open-air site possibly could. These two sites are located across a canyon from each other on the western escarpment of the Sacramento Mountains above Alamogordo. They are situated at the juncture of four biotic zones, including the piñon-juniper woodland and a narrow riparian strip along the canyon bottom. Along with maize, a wide variety of wild plants and other cultigens (beans, tobacco, and presumably cultivated amaranth) are present in the botanical assemblage, including seeds of wild grasses that were collected in different seasons.

The superior preservation at Fresnal Shelter and High Rolls Cave makes comparing maize ubiquity with open-air sites somewhat problematic. At Fresnal, Bohrer (1981:45) reports maize ubiquity of 50% and 57% in flotation samples collected from strata and pit features, respectively (see also Miller and Kenmotsu 2004:227). It is unclear, however, if this includes both charred and uncarbonized specimens. At High Rolls Cave, carbonized maize ubiquity in flotation samples appears to be between 23% and 33% (Bohrer 2006:tables 18.4 and 18.5). This is higher than in either component at Turquoise Ridge but lower than both the NM 90 and Hondo Valley habitation sites. The principal occupation at High Rolls occurred between ca. 1310 and 940 BC, earlier than any of the NM 90 or Hondo Valley components. If maize dependence in the region was less at this time than it was in the later centuries of the Late Archaic, then this could explain the apparently lower maize ubiquity at High Rolls Cave.

It remains unclear, however, how the maize-ubiquity values at Fresnal and High Rolls may also be affected by the seasonal occupation of these sites (see Miller and Kenmotsu 2004:228). Their rich botanical assemblages contain species from both the nearby desert floor and the upland and riparian zones. The biotic zones are closely packed in the vicinity of these two sites, and occur in response to slope aspect as well as elevation. Fresnal Shelter and High Rolls Cave are, in fact, so close to the desert-basin floor that they could almost be considered basin-edge sites. Moreover, the terrain on the western escarpment of the Sacramento Mountains is exceptionally rugged and steep, biotic zones occur in rather narrow bands that are broken into patches by slope aspect, and drainages flow through narrow canyons that in many places are ill-suited to substantial habitation sites. The abandonment of Fresnal Shelter and High Rolls Cave by AD 250 may indicate the unsuitability of the locally rugged terrain for substantial investments in farming and/or site occupations. With increased farming dependence, people likely began to spend more time at substantial settlements closer to their agricultural fields, which were located in areas especially favorable to farming. That probably did not include the narrow canyon where Fresnal and High Rolls are located. Farming dependence and reduced mobility were already well established in the Hondo Valley, on the other side of the mountains, where the longer, wider valleys offered conditions much more conducive to the development of farming-based economies. Some of the valleys on the west side of the Sacramento Mountains, including Tularosa Canyon, also offered at least stretches suitable for early farming, although currently the earliest evidence of farming communities here dates from the later part of the Early Formative period (e.g., Del Bene et al. 1986; Wiseman 1991).

CONCLUSION

Evidence to date suggests that farming-based economies in southern New Mexico emerged no later than the first millennium BC and were largely restricted to favorable zones in highland areas. In the adjacent desert lowlands of the Jornada region, at least, a more mobile, largely hunting-and-gathering lifeway (with little or no farming) persisted until AD 700–1000, and domesticates remain rare at lowland sites dating prior to AD 1000 (in this volume see Miller and Kenmotsu, chapter 3, and Condon and Vasquez, chapter 4; also Miller and Kenmotsu 2004:248). The evidence from NM 90 and the Hondo Valley forces a reevaluation of existing ideas about the beginnings of farming dependence in southern New Mexico, including Doleman's

(2005) model. In particular, the NM 90 and Hondo Valley discoveries point to contrasting subsistence-settlement patterns in the highlands versus the basin floors during the late preceramic and into the Early Formative period, as opposed to a more monolithic, pre-AD 500 hunter-gatherer pattern. Moreover, the mobility model involving seasonal moves between lowlands and uplands is unevenly applicable in southern New Mexico. Many of the small, narrow mountain ranges here do not penetrate the piñon-juniper and encinal/chaparral woodlands, or contain only a limited extent of these critical zones. Access to the piñon-juniper woodlands along the precipitous western front of the Sacramento Mountains requires movement up and down very steep and rugged terrain. However, some places on the western side of the Sacramentos—such as stretches along Tularosa Canyon—hosted farming-dependent communities by Early Formative times (if not earlier). In contrast, vast expanses of woodland zones exist on the broader, gentler eastern slope of the Sierra Blanca/Capitan/Sacramento Highlands and in the Gila Mountains in southwestern New Mexico. In these areas, the woodland zones could have been easily accessed by groups moving up from lowland areas (social conditions permitting). The Rio Hondo drains the largest watershed on the east side of the Sacramento and Guadalupe Mountains, and it and other rivers on the eastern slope provided natural access routes between the highlands and lowlands.

It is possible that some (if not most) highly mobile Late Archaic and Early Formative groups living on the basin floors had no access to the woodland zones. If so, these groups relied instead on the Chihuahuan Desert biome. This zone offered food resources that were, overall, less seasonally sensitive than those in the woodland zones, but also more dispersed, and they required greater mobility and more frequent relocation of residential camps. Some early farming may have occurred along the Rio Grande, but due to a paucity of data this important riverine zone remains a wild card in our understanding of early agricultural developments in the Jornada region. Floodplain conditions along much of the Rio Grande in southern New Mexico may not have been favorable for early agriculture (Hard and Roney 2005:171), but it seems likely that at least stretches of this major river's floodplain could have been farmed. At any rate, evidence from the Jornada *lowlands* suggests little or no dependence on farming until perhaps as late as AD 1000.

In light of the current evidence, Doleman's (2005) model appears to be only partially correct at best, and then only with respect to at least some lowland groups. His model does not account for the pre–AD 500 farmers now known to have occupied the highlands of southern New Mexico. Moreover, the influence of region-wide landscape factors that Doleman points to in drawing a contrast between southeastern Arizona and southern New Mexico requires some reassessment. In some areas, such as the western front of the Sacramento Mountains, movement between the basin floors and highlands involved short (but steep) distances similar to those in southeastern Arizona. There is evidence for early farming dependence at some localities here, such as Tularosa Canyon, but not until relatively late in Early Formative times. With the NM 90 and Hondo Valley findings, it now appears that more localized environmental variability is responsible for the settlement-subsistence dichotomy between the highlands and lowlands of southern New Mexico. The prolonged pattern of high mobility, with little or no farming, in the basin lowlands of southern New Mexico is perhaps still attributable to the environmental factors highlighted by Doleman (i.e., the much greater extent of basin floors in southern New Mexico as opposed to southeastern Arizona). But other environmental factors noted by Hard and Roney (2005), including low precipitation levels, may also have played a role. Substantial reliance on farming was certainly possible along the basin edges of the Jornada region, as evidenced by Turquoise Ridge and the many Late Formative sites with maize and other cultigens found there. But basin-edge farming is not clearly evident until ca. AD 500, and even then it appears to have been more casual relative to the highlands until after ca. AD 1000. The development of farming-based, Jornada Mogollon communities along the lower edges of mountain slopes may have depended in part on investments in water-management infrastructure, including artificial reservoirs (Bentley 1993; Leach et al. 1993; Scarborough 1988).

At any rate, Late Archaic and Early Formative hunter-gatherers in the desert lowlands seem to have been more or less locked into a highly mobile forager pattern, in an environment that did not offer the diversity and concentration of food resources found in the higher-elevation woodlands (especially during the autumn months) and riparian zones of the highland rivers and streams. To the extent that desert-floor groups did not have access to these productive upland zones, and were unable to invest in water-management infrastructure along basin edges, their only option may have been to carry on with a residentially mobile, hunter-gatherer lifeway. Conditions across much of the Jornada lowlands simply were not conducive to the early adoption of farming as a strategy to increase foraging effectiveness because the dispersed nature of the resources—and consequent high degree of mobility required to exploit them—precluded the kind of settlement focus necessary to plant and tend cultigens.

The subsistence-settlement dichotomy between the basin and highlands also raises questions about the geography of early farming across the southern Southwest, the route(s) through which maize first arrived in southern New Mexico and westernmost Texas, and how heavy dependence on farming got its start in the region. As evidence from the Tucson area and Rio Casas Grandes demonstrate, early farming-based economies were indeed possible in the desert lowlands of the southern Southwest, along floodplains where conditions were just right and precipitation levels were higher than in the Jornada lowlands (Hard and Roney 2005; Mabry 2005). In southern New Mexico, early farming prevailed in highland areas that constitute biotically rich "islands" separated from each other by up to 100 km (62 miles).

How maize reached these areas remains an intriguing question. One possibility is that farming technology spread among mobile hunter-gatherers, and those occupying (or with access to) favorable highland zones made the earliest shifts to high farming dependence and reduced mobility in the region. In this scenario, mobile hunter-gatherers across the southern Southwest were carrying around enough maize seeds that, by the late second millennium BC, maize had reached the Mogollon highlands and the eastern side of the Tularosa Basin, and, sometime before 100 BC, had arrived on the eastern slopes of the Sierra Blanca/Capitan/Sacramento Highlands. In an alternative scenario, groups already possessing farming technology purposefully migrated—up to 100 km in some cases and across territories occupied by hunter-gatherers—to favorable highland areas in southern New Mexico, where they established and expanded farming-based communities. Such moves would necessarily mean that groups acquired and maintained knowledge of geographic conditions well beyond their original home ranges. A combination of these scenarios is of course possible as well. At any rate, early farming dependence found a toehold in favorable highland environments, with their vast woodland zones, precipitation levels higher than in the desert lowlands, and snowmelt runoff feeding perennial streams (such as the Rio Hondo and its tributaries) that provided water for crops during the otherwise dry spring-planting season.

High farming dependence in the preceramic time frame may have occurred in parts of the Jornada Mogollon region where the evidence has not yet been found. This could include other drainages along the eastern front of the Sierra Blanca/Capitan/Sacramento Highlands. The Rio Hondo is the largest watershed in the highlands, and was probably one of the most favorable environments for prehistoric farming anywhere in the Jornada Mogollon region. But farming was also practiced along the Rio Peñasco, although the evidence dates after AD 1000 (Jennings 1940). Still, a big question is whether or not preceramic farming dependence, documented in the Hondo Valley, extends to other highland valleys in the Sacramento and Guadalupe Mountains. The Rio Grande floodplain also remains a big question mark. If it was also a center of precocious agricultural developments, then it would present a lowland exception to the southern New Mexico pattern of the restriction of preceramic farming dependence to highland areas.

The arrival of maize and other crops were apparently also part of a broader complex of imported behavioral traits from Mexico. This includes the practice of notching incisors (as evidenced by a young adult burial in one of the Early Formative sites in the Hondo Valley) and potential indicators of interaction with Mexico at the Fresnal–High Rolls sites, including sandal- and coiled-basketry technologies shared by these sites and other caves in the Hueco Mountains to the south (Lentz 2006:259–260). Whether these traits point to immigrant populations of early farmers into southern New Mexico, or adoption by indigenous folks of non-subsistence material practices along with early maize and farming techniques (or some combination of both), remains one of the big questions surrounding the beginnings of farming in the region. At any rate, this important foundation of Jornada Mogollon culture was much more geographically variable than has been acknowledged, farming-dependent economies appeared here much earlier than previously thought, and received knowledge about the geography of early farming in southern New Mexico is no longer supported by the archaeological record.

PART III

Mobility within and beyond the Lowlands

6

Deciphering Prehistoric Trails and Unraveling Social Networks in the Tularosa and Hueco Basins

Myles R. Miller,
Tim Graves, Moira Ernst,
and Matt Swanson

The discovery and delineation of linear distributions of ceramics marking the pathways of prehistoric travel corridors is one of the more significant discoveries of the past decade of fieldwork in the Western Jornada region, specifically within the Tularosa and Hueco Basins. The linear distributions of ceramic artifacts, referred to as trails or pathways, have been a common revelation of high-resolution transect recording unit (TRU) surveys[1] on Fort Bliss Military Reservation (Camarena-Garcés et al. 2011; Ernst and Swanson 2012; Graves et al. 2002; Graves et al. 2013; Kludt et al. 2007; Kludt, Stowe et al. 2007; Leckman 2010; Leckman and Chavez 2013; MacWilliams et al. 2010; Miller and Graves 2015a; Phillips and Leckman 2012; Phillips et al. 2011; Swanson and Graves 2011).

To date, 17 trail segments varying in length from 360 m to nearly 5 km have been identified during TRU surveys of the Tularosa and Hueco Basins (figure 6.1), and together these segments comprise nearly 20 km of mapped pathways. The pathways are defined by a series of 15-m-by-15-m TRU survey cells containing ceramic artifacts and pot breaks that are arranged along relatively narrow, linear corridors. Another 21 trails were identified by examining the distribution of ceramic isolates recorded during earlier conventional transect surveys of the basins (Camarena-Garcés et al. 2011), revealing a network of over 280 km of trails crossing the southern Tularosa and northern Hueco Basins. Several of these trails

DOI: 10.5876/9781607327950.c006

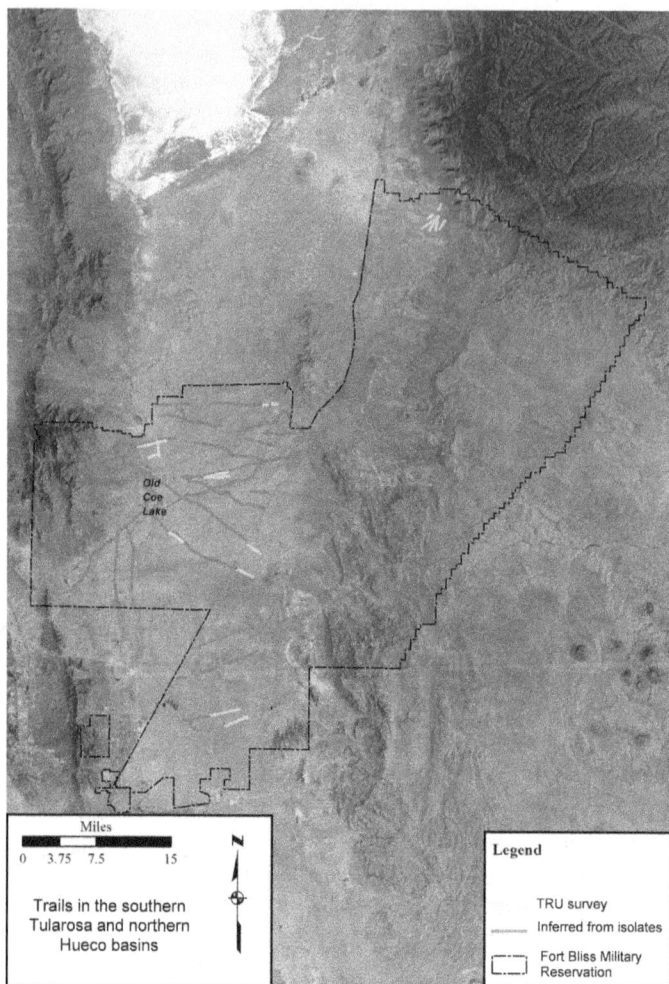

FIGURE 6.1. *Trails and trail segments identified through TRU survey and analysis of ceramic isolated finds in the Tularosa and Hueco Basins.*

were subsequently linked to segments identified during TRU surveys, thus confirming their existence.

The following chapter reviews the attributes of the pathways and the methods by which they are identified in the field, alternative explanations of their formation and function, and their significance for a broader understanding of movement, connectivity, and place in the prehispanic American Southwest.

Compositional analysis of ceramics from two trail segments is used to examine competing theories of the origin and function of the trails. The discovery and study of Jornada pathways have implications for social interaction and network analysis within and beyond the Western Jornada. Trails can be integrated into regional analyses of larger patterns of social, community, and economic organization across the landscape, going beyond the conventional focus on individual and isolated settlements. The use of the refined survey methods that revealed the existence of the pathways may be used in other regions to identify corridors of movement and connectivity across the American Southwest and Mexican Northwest.

TRAILS IN THE SOUTHWEST

The Western Jornada trails were not intentionally constructed roads as found in the Chaco and Mimbres regions (Creel 2006b; Vivian 1997a, 1997b), but rather appear to be preferred routes of travel and communication used over a considerable period of time. Based on the production spans of ceramic wares and types found along the trails, it appears that most were used during the latter phases of the Formative period, specifically the Late Doña Ana phase (AD 1150–1300) and the El Paso–phase pueblo interval (AD 1300–1450). However, the presence of earlier El Paso Brownware types and other ceramics indicate that the pathways could have been used as early as AD 500, suggesting that some pathways may have had a long history of use. Many of the trails lead to and from clusters of pithouse and pueblo settlements centered on prominent alluvial-fan-margin playas at the edges of the basins.

The existence of prehistoric and historic trails traversing the desert landscapes of the American West and Southwest has been known since the late 1800s. Hubert Bancroft (1890) described trails in the Mojave Desert and Adolph Bandelier (1892) gave an account of traveling along trails across the Pajarito Plateau in north-central New Mexico. There has been considerable fieldwork, research, and speculation about hundreds of trails preserved on desert pavement surfaces of the Sonoran and Mojave Deserts of southern Arizona and southeastern California, beginning with Francis and Patricia Johnson (Johnson and Johnson 1957), Julian Hayden (1965, 1967), Robert Heizer (1978), and most intensively by Malcolm Rogers (1939, 1941, 1966). Studies of these trails proceeded through the 1980s (Brown and Stone 1982; Stone 1986) and have been the subject of renewed interest during the past decade (Becker and Altschul 2003; Darling 2009; Darling and Eiselt 2003; Pailes 2014; White 2007).

In New Mexico, Harold Colton (1964) described the trail system of the Zuñi region, including pilgrimage trails leading to and from Zuñi Salt Lake. More recent studies in northern New Mexico have examined trails and ritual sites associated with trails on the Pajarito Plateau and Galisteo Basin (Snead 2002, 2008a, 2008b), while Ferguson et al. (2009) and several researchers have examined the symbolic and social contexts of Zuñi trails. To the south, Swanson's (2003) and Pitezel's (2011) analyses of Chihuahua *atalayas*—hilltop signaling sites or shrines—describe trails leading from these hilltop sites to Paquimé and other Medio-period settlements in the Casas Grandes region. A growing body of method and theory grounded in geographic information systems, remote sensing, ethnography, landscape considerations, and phenomenological approaches has been applied to prehistoric trail research, yet overall the study of trails and our understanding of their function and meaning are relatively recent developments (Snead 2008a; Snead et al. 2009; White and Surface-Evans 2012).

The discovery of trails in the Tularosa and Hueco Basins of southern New Mexico and far west Texas is an even more recent phenomenon and the economic and social function of the newly discovered trails remain speculative. Kludt, Church, and Kuehn (2007) and Kludt, Stowe, et al. (2007) proposed that trails were formed through a "habitual activity" process and they linked trail formation to an increasing stability of departure and destination points on the landscape. Stability (i.e., sedentism) can result in patterned and consistent use of corridors between the departure and destination points, thus creating pathways cleared of vegetation and worn by foot traffic. However, even under conditions of settlement stability, for a trail to form in the first place there had to be a reason for such traffic. Kludt, Stowe, et al. (2007) suggest that the trails identified at the northern margins of McGregor Range on the Fort Bliss Military Reservation were used to transport water from playas or springs.

The inference that trails lead to and from water sources has been a repeated theme among early studies of trails in the Jornada region. The first studies involved short segments less than 2 km in length and noted that they were generally oriented toward fan-margin playas located several kilometers away (Kludt, Church, and Kuehn 2007; Kludt, Stowe, et al. 2007) or were found to originate near the margins of a large playa (Graves et al. 2002). However, there was no evidence if such trails ended at a playa or passed around its margins and continued onwards from another side. The water source and transport inference was made on these partial data as well as the fact that higher numbers of ceramic olla *pot breaks* (small clusters of sherds representing a single broken vessel) were found along the pathways.

However, it is equally likely that the trails represent pathways of communication and exchange between major pueblo settlements or clusters of pueblo settlements near playas. It is also likely that trails led to resource areas of particular importance, such as the turquoise mines in the Jarilla Mountains or across major avenues of travel such as mountain passes (see Willis et al. 2002). Surely, some pathways led to pilgrimage sites, to mountaintop shrines, to Hueco Tanks, Picture Cave, and other sites with concentrations of rock art, and to other locations of ritual importance and spiritual power in or adjacent to the Tularosa and Hueco Basins.

To explore these and other ideas regarding the function of the trails, the ceramic assemblages marking segments of pathways crossing two prehistoric sites in south-central New Mexico, LA 95071 and LA 169230, were examined. The TRU survey of a 1,065-acre parcel (Swanson and Graves 2011) that recorded LA 95071 and LA 169230 also identified segments of two prehistoric trails that extended more than 4 km across the east–west distance of the survey parcel. Each site was a low-density multicomponent distribution of hearths and artifacts across the basin floor, and both trails passed through the sites and extended beyond the survey parcel. While the trails were not designated as separate sites from the surrounding distributions of hearths and artifacts, it was proposed that the trail segments within the sites contributed to their National Register of Historic Places eligibility and thus merited further consideration along with the non-trail portions of each site. Accordingly, excavation efforts at the two sites included the collection and analysis of representative samples of ceramic artifacts collected from the trails. Vessel forms were examined, although it was uncertain whether this variable would provide insights since it is likely that jars/ollas were used for transport of both water and foods, valuable goods, and perhaps fermented beverages such as mescal. In an attempt to identify the origin of ceramic vessels broken or discarded along the trails, samples of the sherds from each trail segment were submitted for instrumental neutron activation analysis (INAA).

The results of the INAA study are detailed later in this chapter. We first provide a description of the trails that have been identified to this point, their unique attributes and how they differ from other trail systems in the Southwest, and various interpretations of their function and meaning. The INAA data support an interpretation that the pathways served multifunctional and multidimensional social and economic roles for travel, transport, and communication among diverse communities rather than simply as avenues for local water or resource collection. Having established their multidimensional role, a preliminary typology derived from studies of trails in the Sonoran Desert

(Darling 2009) is proposed, along with some thoughts on future analysis directions in light of how such pathways represent material manifestations of landscapes, movement, and social networks in the prehispanic Southwest.

WESTERN JORNADA TRAILS: DELINEATION AND DESCRIPTION

The trails that formed across the Tularosa and Hueco Basins appear to have been informal pathways where repetitive foot traffic displaced a small amount of topsoil and reduced or killed off the natural grassland vegetation cover. It does not appear that rocks had been cleared from the path or that any other form of labor had been expended to create or maintain the trails in a fashion similar to trails in the Sonora and Mojave Desert regions. Figure 6.2 provides an impression of what a typical Jornada footpath may have looked like as it traversed the grasslands of the Tularosa Basin during the Pueblo period.

Paleoenvironmental and geomorphic studies have determined that the interior basins of this portion of the Jornada region were stable grasslands until recent times. Overgrazing and drought during the latter part of the nineteenth and early twentieth centuries resulted in severe soil degradation and radically altered vegetation patterns throughout southern New Mexico; the most visible change being the widespread expansion of mesquite and creosote shrub communities (Buffington and Herbel 1965; Gardner 1951; York and Dick-Peddie 1969). The present-day coppice dune topography of the interior basins is a result of the combined factors of drought, overgrazing, and soil erosion during the late 1800s and early 1900s.

The past century of eolian soil displacement and erosion has created a context where the physical manifestations of the ancient trails or footpaths are no longer visible. In other words, once-visible paths, trails, or series of meandering paths that crossed the stable grasslands of the Tularosa and Hueco Basins have since eroded away, leaving only a distribution of ceramics to mark their former locations. The segments of Jornada trails through sites LA 95071 and LA 169230 differ significantly from the well-preserved trails on stable and ancient desert pavement surfaces of the Sonoran and Mojave Deserts (figure 6.3) that can be easily identified and traced through conventional surveys, aerial photographs, and even satellite imagery. In contrast, the Jornada trails are linear scatters of ceramics on eroded landforms that can be detected only through the intensive archaeological survey methods and GIS mapping that are components of the TRU method.

These ceramic patterns are of interest in and of themselves. Breternitz (1957) notes that one of the more common artifact classes associated with trails in

FIGURE 6.2. *Modern footpath through a terrain of grass, yucca, and cholla in the mountain foothills of southern New Mexico. Prehistoric trails across the Hueco and Tularosa basins probably had a similar appearance.*

the western Papagueria of Arizona are linear scatters of ceramic sherds. These include isolated sherds, but more often they comprise pot breaks located within 3 m of a physical trail crossing the desert pavement. Indeed, pot breaks are also a consistent feature along Jornada trails that have been identified to date (Camarena-Garcés et al. 2011; Kludt, Church, and Kuehn 2007; Swanson and Graves 2011), but scatters of isolated ceramic sherds are much more common (figure 6.4). This observation leads to another important question: if the breakage of vessels along the trails resulted in relatively intact "potbreak" features, then what process of breakage, loss, or discard created the scattered sherd distributions seen everywhere else along the trails?

FIGURE 6.3. *Examples of trails in the southern Southwest: (top) example of a trail crossing a desert-pavement surface of western Arizona (from Darling 2006); (bottom) a segment of what constitutes a typical Jornada trail examined in this chapter—a linear scatter of ceramics across the eolian sands at LA 95071. Reprinted with permission of the Cultural Resource Management Program, Gila River Indian Community, Sacaton, Arizona.*

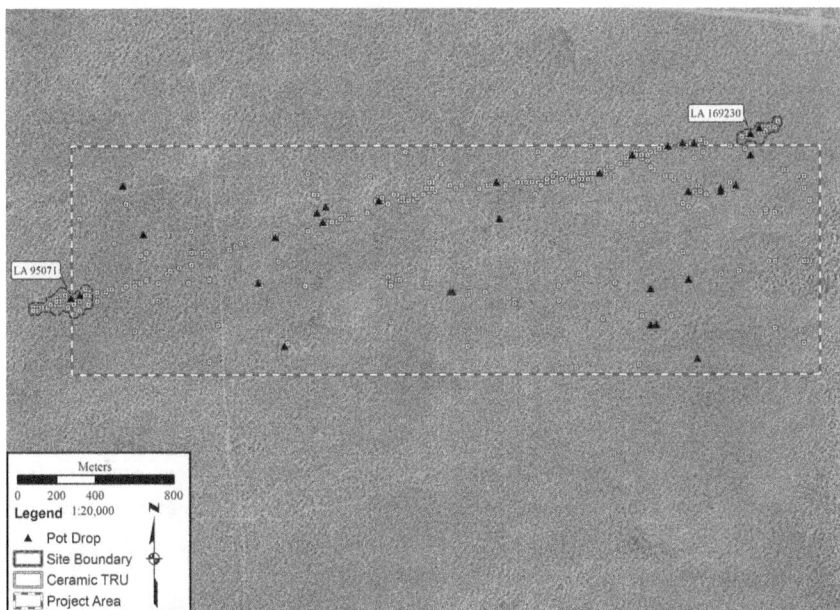

FIGURE 6.4. *Example of a Jornada trail corridor identified through TRU survey at Fort Bliss, illustrating the linear distribution of ceramic-positive TRU cells, pot breaks, and typical width of the corridor. Segments of the trail passing through LA 95071 and LA 169230 were investigated as part of this study.*

In turn, this brings up another important and curious aspect of the Jornada pathways: the linear ceramic distributions actually occur within and across bands measuring up to 50 m in width (see figure 6.4). The displacement and movement of sherds on dynamic eolian landscapes may have contributed to a small degree of artifact displacement and movement (Mauldin et al. 1998; Wandsnider 1988), but such geoarchaeological transformation can account for movements of only a few meters and surely does not explain the bands of sherds scattered across distances of 20–50 m. The width of some segments may be due to the inclusion of isolated sherds and collections of sherds within campsites or sherds that are part of the continuous, low-density background scatter of artifacts present across the desert basins of the Jornada, thus artificially contributing to the width of the trails. However, the majority of trail segments extend far beyond the defined boundaries of sites, and the inclusion of sherds from background artifact scatter cannot account for the high numbers of sherds that are consistently arranged along linear bands.

A more satisfying explanation is that the wide, linear ceramic distributions represent multiple, parallel, and shifting pathways within a designated travel corridor. Several factors may have contributed to the formation of multiple pathways. Doña Ana–phase pithouse villages and many El Paso–phase pueblos were comparatively short-term settlements, occupied for five years or less (Miller and Graves 2009). Some trails may have fallen into disuse or been temporarily abandoned when a settlement or cluster of settlements was abandoned in a particular area, only to be reused several years later when a settlement or settlement cluster was again occupied. Moreover, if the frequently interpreted function of water transport is valid, the trail segments may have been temporarily abandoned as certain playas dried up. During periods of disuse, the trails would have been overgrown with vegetation, and subsequent reuse of the travel corridor may have followed a parallel course that differed slightly from the abandoned pathway. If line-of-sight factors influenced the location and orientation of trails (Phillips and Leckman 2012), then abandoned corridors could have been reused, based on traditional knowledge.

Pathways may also have shifted due to periodic phenomena with shorter time spans. Trail segments may have become overgrown with vegetation or cut by arroyos during heavy summer rains, and low-lying segments through bajos may have flooded and become muddy, resulting in the creation of new paths parallel to the original corridor. A similar process can be seen among the modern dirt roads in the Tularosa Basin, where erosion, mud, and other obstacles lead to the creation of multiple parallel tracks (figure 6.5).

A final and intriguing explanation is that some aspects of the width of Jornada ceramic corridors represent what Snead (2008b) and Marshall (1997) describe as twinned or doubled pathways common among trails on the Parajito Plateau and even documented along certain Chaco roads. Such twinned pathways may have been created during pilgrimages or ritual processions requiring dual corridors to and from certain locations.

INTERPRETATIONS OF THE FUNCTION AND MEANING OF WESTERN JORNADA TRAILS

The identification of pathways in the Tularosa and Hueco Basins is a phenomenon of the past few years of TRU surveys, and accordingly the study and interpretation of the trails is at a preliminary stage. Sophisticated GIS analyses have been undertaken, including least-cost path (LCP) and line-of-sight analyses (Phillips and Leckman 2012; Ernst and Swanson 2012).

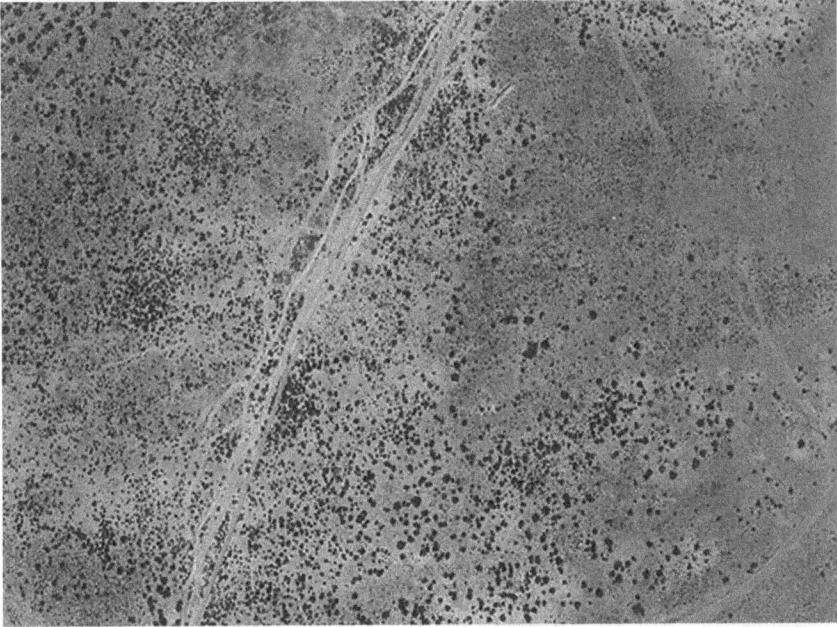

FIGURE 6.5. *Multiple parallel tracks within a modern road corridor in the eastern Tularosa Basin.*

Geomorphological studies have examined the geomorphic context, preservation, and age of the trails (Kludt et al. 2007; Rachal 2013).

To date, most interpretations regarding the origin and function of the trails have embraced a processual, utilitarian perspective, viewing the trails as resulting from the transport of water from sources in springs or playas to settlements (Kludt, Church, and Kuehn 2007; Kludt, Stowe, and others 2007; MacWilliams et al. 2010; Phillips and Leckman 2012). Water transport is an appealing interpretation since it explains both the apparent playa origin and destination points for many trails as well as the linear patterns of ceramics and ceramic pot breaks as resulting from what have been assumed are broken water transport vessels. Yet not all analyses have arrived at the conclusion that trails resulted from water transport. A least-cost path analysis of trails recorded in a survey parcel a few kilometers to the east of Old Coe Lake playa in the Tularosa Basin concluded that the pathways did not lead to the playa or to water sources in the Organ Mountains west of it (Ernst and Swanson 2012).

Salt transport has also been mentioned, perhaps in a manner similar to the ritual pilgrimages to obtain salt from evaporate pans along the Gulf of

California and the Zuñi region of west-central New Mexico (Ferguson et al. 2009; Lumholtz 1912; Rea 1997; Titiev 1937). However, studies of local playas determined that the only viable salt source in the Tularosa and Hueco Basins is the saline evaporate pans of Lake Lucero on White Sands Missile Range. Most of the trails reviewed in this and other studies lead to and from playas such as Old Coe Lake, which salinity measurements of water and soil samples have conclusively established are not saline playas (Miller and Graves 2009). This is not to deny that salt was transported prehistorically from Lake Lucero along routes similar to the historic nineteenth-century Euro-American San Andres Salt Trail (Bowden 1962; Freeman 1981; Hawthorne-Tagg et al. 1998). Indeed, one of three westernmost trails identified during the study of ceramic isolates (Camarena-Garcés et al. 2011) closely parallels the course of the historic San Andres Salt Trail. While salt trails originating at Lake Lucero may have existed, salt transport does not explain the origin of trails leading to and from non-saline playas at the eastern and western margins of the two basins.

As an alternative to such utilitarian interpretations, the social, ritual, economic, and landscape/spatial dimensions of trails and their interrelationships with geographic space and prehistoric social fields can be explored. In a comprehensive landscape and GIS analysis of prehistoric trails throughout the Papagueria region of southwestern Arizona, White (2007) found that trail functions and meanings were not uniform and that univariate explanations involving water or food resources did not adequately explain the distributions and orientations—and thus the functions—of the trail networks:

> The social landscape of the Sonoran Desert was not a geographic and functional monolith, used in only a set number of ways by all of its permanent, semipermanent, and transient inhabitants throughout prehistory, but instead exhibited a high degree of subregional variation motived by strong local intracommunity ties and sacred/ritual concerns in addition to energy-efficient long-distance travel motivated by exchange. (White 2007:9)

The passage quoted above best describes our intuitive concept of the origin and function of the trails and pathways of the Jornada region. In addition to travel and movement of basic goods, trails are also viewed as "complex, tangible metaphors of interaction and association" (Snead 2008a:203). The water-transport hypothesis does not seem to "hold water," so to speak, although admittedly there is little solid empirical data aside from the few existing GIS analyses to argue the matter one way or the other.

It is entirely possible that the perceived origin and destination points of trail segments at playas were not associated with playas per se, but rather were associated with the clusters of pueblo settlements that existed around these important water sources. From this perspective, it is thought that the pathways were formed through various social processes and reflect communication and movement among settlements, resource areas, and ritual or sacred areas. Communication and movement included people, goods, and ideas, and reflected social ties, power relationships, and status and leadership roles among communities. It is also possible that the ceramic sherds found along trails were from vessels that were used for liquid transport, but a different type of liquid than water: fermented mescal or corn beer.[2] Fermented mescal could have been an important commodity transported from pueblo settlements near agave communities in mountain foothills for communal feasts at settlements in the lowlands (see also Cruz Antillón et al., chapter 11, this volume). As noted earlier, it is likely that certain pathways led to places of power and spirituality on the landscape, including springs, mountaintop shrines, caves, and rock-art localities. It should be noted that trails linking pueblo settlements probably differed in social and economic function from trails connecting settlements and ritual sites; perhaps the latter type of trail did not involve transport of ceramics and therefore may be difficult or impossible to detect through TRU surveys and other methods.

The alternative interpretations of water transport as opposed to multidimensional social and economic interaction were examined through studies of trail segments at LA 95071 and LA 169230. Analyses included GIS mapping, geomorphological analysis, and INAA analysis of samples of sherds collected from the trail segments (Graves et al. 2013). The geomorphological investigations concluded that stable dune ridges existed in the area of the trail segments across both sites, although the upper Holocene sediments of LA 95071 had been stripped at some point in the past (Rachal 2013). The trail may have followed the more stable elevated dune ridges across the survey parcel, a pattern detected among other trail segments in the region (Phillips et al. 2011). Ceramic studies focused on El Paso Brownware sherds collected along the trail segments and compositional analysis of random samples drawn from the site collections.

INAA OF CERAMICS FROM TWO TRAIL SEGMENTS

The trails and pathways identified through the TRU survey method were defined by distributions of ceramic artifacts, and indeed the linear distributions of scattered sherds provide the only form of material culture with which to analyze and interpret the trails. Future surveys of trails found in more stable geomorphic and topographic settings may reveal the presence of cairns, trail markers, and ritual items or deposits, but presently ceramics represent the only material culture available for study.

Conventional attribute and functional analysis of ceramic sherds collected from trail segments has proven unproductive. Sherds are usually small and rim sherds are rare, and thus it has been difficult to identify a robust sample of functional vessel forms. In a study involving 2,100 sherds identified along trail segments south of Old Coe Lake playa, only four rim sherds were present that could be identified to a specific vessel shape and subsequently applied to Braun's (1980) functional categories (MacWilliams et al. 2010). Despite the small sample size, the range of vessel forms identified among the rim sherds was used to infer that the trail segments could have been involved in water and salt transport from Old Coe Lake playa.

The assumption that certain El Paso Brownware vessel forms were exclusively associated with water transport is unfounded. Large El Paso Brownware ollas were used for transporting and caching quantities of shell, turquoise, and other valued goods. The Bald Eagle cache (Wooldridge 1979) located east of the Tularosa Basin in the Sacramento Mountains consisted of two large El Paso Polychrome ollas containing 50,009 items of marine shell, calcite, slate, and turquoise.

The use of INAA offered an alternative approach for modeling ceramic function and transport along the trails. This method provides an indirect or proxy approach to interpreting the function of the trails by providing insight into the manufacturing locations of vessels found along the trails and therefore, by extension, a measure of vessel movement along these travel corridors. The INAA data can identify general geographic production areas of the El Paso Brownware ceramics collected from the trail segments. Production areas identified during the past two decades of work include the northeast, east, and west Tularosa Basin, east and west Hueco Bolson, the Mesilla Bolson that surrounds Las Cruces, and several areas in the Sacramento and Guadalupe Mountains, in addition to brownware production areas in more distant regions such as the Mimbres-Mogollon region, the Southern Plains of New Mexico, and the La Junta region of Trans-Pecos Texas (Miller and Ferguson 2010, 2014; see also Hill, chapter 9, this volume).

The interpretation of the INAA geochemical data and distributions of compositional groups and production areas is based on a model developed under the following assumptions. If the trails were used primarily for water transport, it would be expected that the ceramic assemblages would have minimal chemical compositional variability, since most vessels would have been transported between a single settlement or settlement cluster and a water source. In addition, the majority of vessels would have a local geochemical production signature, since water transport and storage vessels are usually part of site furniture and represent local production for local use (Arnold 1988; Skibo 1992).

Conversely, if the trails were created through long-term systems of communication, exchange, and social relationships between multiple settlements and settlement clusters, it would be expected that the ceramic assemblages would consist of vessels produced at multiple locations across the region and accordingly would exhibit multiple chemical compositional groups. In addition, locally produced vessels would be a minority, since most of the vessels would have been transported from distant settlements across the Western Jornada basins and perhaps even further from the Sacramento and Guadalupe Mountains.

In order to explore this model, 40 sherds were submitted to the Missouri University Research Reactor for INAA. The total sample was divided into two sets of 20, selected from the linear ceramic distributions across LA 95071 and LA 169230. The 20 sherds were randomly sampled from the total collection of El Paso Brownware ceramics collected along each trail segment. Only sherds within the trail segments were sampled; sherds from the surrounding site areas were not included.

Five production areas and a group of unassigned chemical profiles were identified among the INAA sample.[3] The counts and proportions of these groups are listed in table 6.1. Three of the sherds have low probabilities of group membership and cannot be assigned to a known geochemical group with confidence. It remains uncertain if these are statistical outliers of existing groups or represent chemical groups and production areas that as yet remain unsampled and unidentified.

The five production areas identified include the Tularosa Basin Southwest, Tularosa Basin Northeast, Hueco Bolson West, Mogollon/Mesilla Valley, and one chemical group for which the production area remains undetermined. The Tularosa Basin Southwest group represents the production area closest to the trail segments. It is a well-defined chemical group of secure provenance and includes ceramic paste samples from the floor of a room at Madera Quemada pueblo, located just 7 km to the west of the trails. Accordingly, the Tularosa Basin Southwest group would be considered the "local" production group associated with occupations and land use around Old Coe Lake playa, including water transport from the playa.

Figure 6.6 plots the geographic locations of these groups in relation to the trails. Prior studies of El Paso Brownware production and distribution using

TABLE 6.1. Chemical compositional provenance groups in ceramic trails

Chemical Group	LA 169230 segment		LA 95071 segment		Combined segments	
	n	%	n	%	n	%
Hueco Bolson West (Group 1033)	10	50.0	7	35.0	17	42.5
Tularosa Basin Northeast (Group 2164)	7	35.0	9	45.0	16	40.0
Mesilla/Mogollon? (Group 82)	—	—	2	10.0	2	5.0
Tularosa Basin Southwest (Group 32)	**1**	**5.0**	**—**	**—**	**1**	**2.5**
Provenance unknown (Group 61B)	1	5.0	—	—	1	2.5
Unassigned	1	5.0	2	10.0	3	7.5
Total sample	20		20		40	

Note: **Bold** indicates the local group.

INAA have determined that local production groups account for 40–60% of the total INAA sample from individual Western Jornada settlements (Miller and Ferguson 2010). In stark contrast, the closest production area—the Tularosa Basin Southwest chemical group—accounts for only 2.5% of the INAA sample from the trails. Rather than local production, the most common of several production areas represented in the sample (unassigned samples may represent other production areas or outliers) are centered in the northeast Tularosa Basin and western Hueco Bolson. The production areas represented in the samples extend across much of this portion of the Jornada region and clearly show that the vessels transported along the pathways were produced at multiple locations across the landscape and perhaps even beyond in the Mogollon region. Considering these data in relation to the model outlined above, the INAA chemical and provenance data best support the interpretation of trails as pathways resulting from social relationships between settlement clusters and places beyond. Those social relationships may have subsumed several things—feasting and transport of food and mescal, transport of socially valued goods, and other factors.

As proposed by the model, if the trails were created through long-term systems of movement, communication, exchange, and social relationships between multiple pithouse and pueblo settlements, then the ceramic assemblages would consist of vessels produced at multiple locations across the region and accordingly would exhibit multiple chemical compositional groups. It is likely that the trails did not lead to and from playas for water transport,

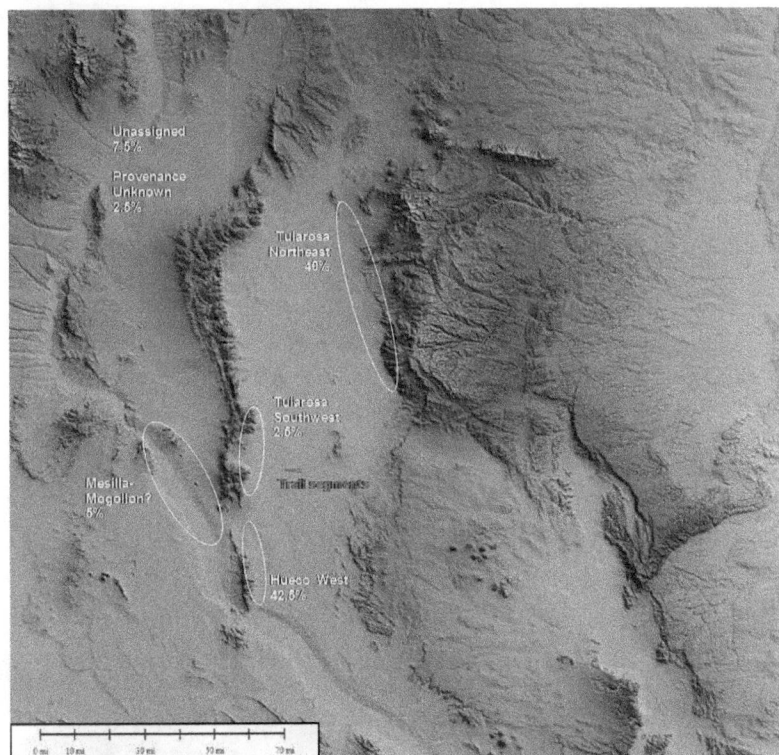

FIGURE 6.6. *Plot of the geographic locations of INAA compositional groups in relation to the trail segments at LA 95071 and LA 169230.*

but rather to the clusters of villages positioned around the playas and major alluvial-drainage networks leading from the mountains (figure 6.7). The INAA study offers further data and insights regarding the functional role of trails and pathways in the social and economic landscape of the prehistoric Jornada region. However, the issue is far from resolved and will require additional GIS, artifact, and compositional studies to determine if the patterns observed during this study hold true for other trail segments.

DISCUSSION OF WESTERN JORNADA TRAILS AND SOCIAL NETWORKS

The analysis of two segments of prehistoric pathways through LA 95071 and LA 169230 focused on alternative explanations of their function: as corridors

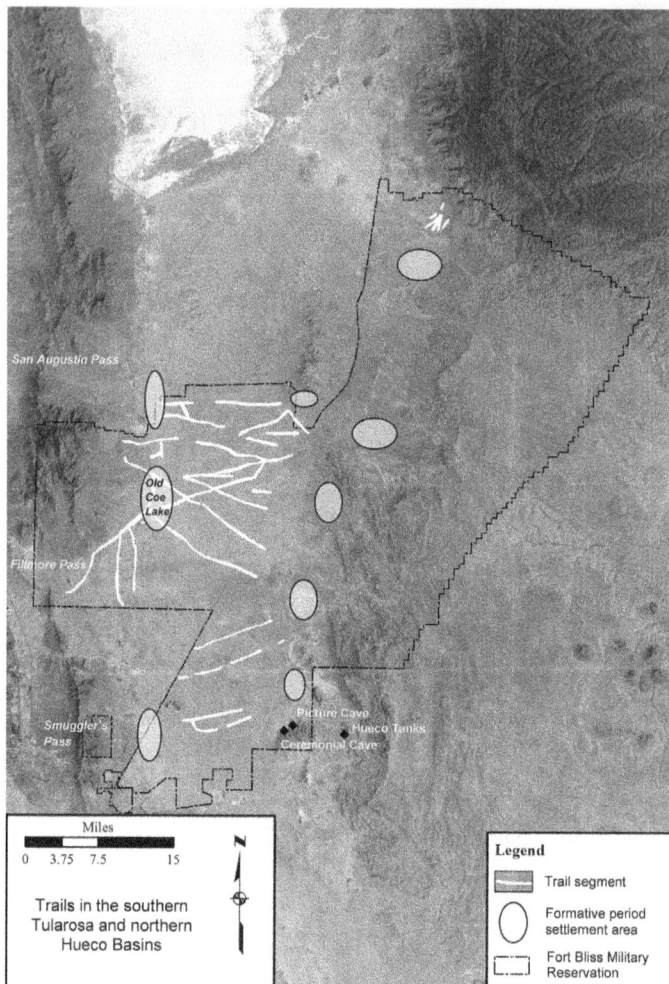

FIGURE 6.7. *Trails, settlement clusters, and ritual locations mentioned in the text.*

for water transport or for social movement and communication. The INAA chemical and provenance data support the interpretation that the trails were formed and sustained through various social processes, reflecting communication and movement among settlements, resource areas, and ritual or sacred areas. These may have included movement of food, mescal, and people for feasts, the transport of socially valued goods, journeys to spiritually charged locations, and other factors. It is likely that the trails did not lead to playas but rather to the clusters of pueblos positioned around the playas. Further evidence of the connection with settlement clusters is that, rather than terminating at playas, several trails appear to lead east to arable lands along major alluvial floodplains leading from the Hueco Mountains and Otero Mesa escarpment that were also the locations of late prehistoric settlement clusters.

These conclusions are not intended to disparage or discount the idea of water transport; under certain circumstances it is likely that water was transported along the pathways. The present study attempts to go beyond the water-transport hypothesis as a monothetic explanation, offering instead a broader perspective on social processes involved in the formation and maintenance of pathways.

Ethnographic and archaeological evidence indicate that a variety of trail types and trail formations existed across the western and southwestern deserts. Darling (2009:75, figure 4.5; see also Darling and Eiselt 2003) presents a useful model of trail types in the Sonoran Desert of southern Arizona based on modes of travel—including type I, II, and III trails. *Type I trails* are interregional pathways that connect primary zones of prehistoric settlement in different river valleys and alluvial fans, often by crossing hinterlands such as mountain ranges, waterless plains, and other types of uninhabited and oftentimes hazardous space. *Type II trails* lead to resource areas beyond the primary zones of settlement. *Type III* trails involve ritual travel such as salt journeys, pilgrimages, and ceremonial journeys to sacred places. An important aspect of type III trails is that they often bypass settlements and may continue far beyond the local settlement region. The model also mentions a fourth and unnumbered type of trail, termed a *local path*, which connects primary zones of settlement within the same valley or geographic zone.

Darling's model provides a useful departure point for modeling and identifying variation among Jornada trails. We would expect a similar range of trail types and attendant social or economic functions to be represented among the Jornada trails, although some differences in their manner of formation and their function should be anticipated, owing to the different social, ecological, and economic landscapes of the Jornada and Papagueria regions. It must be noted that the INAA study was designed to test the competing water-transport versus multifunctional interpretation of trail formation and function, but was not designed to examine which of the four trail types of Darling's model best applies. Nevertheless, some insights can still be gained from the INAA compositional and distributional data.

Type I trails and local paths are examined below. Type II trails leading to resource areas would be expected in the Jornada, and indeed two of the more recently identified trail segments may characterize this type. Leckman and Chavez (2013) identify several trails leading to canyons in the southern Sacramento Mountains that may have provided access to agave fields, baking pits, and other resources. An even more localized example of a type II trail may be a 300-m-long trail leading from a complex of pueblo settlements at LA 91406 to a nearby playa (Miller and Graves 2015a). Perhaps this is an example of a water-transport trail and a future INAA study of the ceramics marking this trail would reveal the presence of a local production group as opposed to the cross-basin distributional patterns described above.

Type III trails undoubtedly existed but may be the most difficult to identify, even with high-resolution TRU survey methods. At present, no trail segments have been identified that would lead to the westernmost foothills of the Hueco Mountains where some of the most significant rock art and ritual cave sites in the Jornada are located: Ceremonial Cave, Picture Cave, and Hueco Tanks (see figure 6.7). Whether this is an artifact of the lack of intensive survey coverage in the southern Hueco Bolson or the different nature of this trail type (e.g., no ceramics, used less intensively) remains a subject for future investigation. The objects carried along ritual journeys, such as the prayer sticks and other ritual paraphernalia deposited in Ceremonial Cave (Cosgrove 1947; Creel 1997) or the minerals, fossils, and crystals procured in the mountains and left in termination deposits at pueblo settlements (Miller and Graves 2009), were placed in ritual spaces rather than scattered across the desert. To further complicate matters, in the absence of ceramic markers, prehistoric trails leading to hilltop shrines and caves may be obscured by, or confused with, paths created by twentieth-century ranching, hunting, and military use, and even paths created by looters and avocational archaeologists visiting rock-art sites.

This is unfortunate because type III trails are critical to a fuller understanding of the relationships between prehistoric communities and surrounding landscapes. Darling (2006, 2009) links oral tribal histories and sacred journeys narrated in Akimel O'odham (Pima) songs to material and physical traces of movement along ancient desert pavement trails in southern Arizona. Such practices result in a cognitive geography situated in both mind and landscape as the lines of words in songs and lines of trails across the terrain are relationally and metaphorically constitutive of each other. Other acts, such as the placement of shrine offerings and recitation of prayers, all contribute to the manner in which movement and connectivity enact and reify social memories (Anschuetz and Wilshusen 2010; Snead 2008a; Van Dyke 2007, 2009). The Hopi perceive trails as metaphorical umbilical cords that spiritually link villages to outlying sacred places on the landscape (Ferguson et al. 2009). Certain ritualized trails connecting villages to other villages and to sacred places on the landscape may have been viewed in a similar fashion by Jornada groups, and research is currently focusing on identifying trail or clan markers in rock-art panels adjacent to pathways and travel corridors.

Although the prognosis for finding type III trails appears rather discouraging, there are some intriguing possibilities. Salt was probably transported from Lake Lucero, and it is not beyond the realm of possibility that such travels involved ritual pilgrimages similar to the Zuñi example. The crystals and sheets of gypsum precipitates recovered from pueblo settlements across the Jornada (Miller and Graves 2009) are testament to the fact that Lake Lucero was a common destination for this mineral. Intensive surveys around the lake bed may reveal the presence of multiple trails originating from the salt pans. Residue analysis of ceramic vessels and pot breaks along these trails may identify high concentrations of mineral salts. Non-local vessels may have been used during certain rituals or to transport ritual items. Future surveys may also locate trails leading toward Hueco Tanks or to prominent peaks. Small-scale, targeted surveys designed to find evidence of trails leading from the canyons where rock art and cave sites are located may be an option for future research.

Returning to type I trails and local paths, an important observation is that these two types are pathways of communication between settlement zones as opposed to routes to resource areas or special landscape features, as with types II and III. In light of the prevalence and importance of type I-Local pathways in the Western Jornada, this form of trail was given a formal type designation. Accordingly, for the study of Western Jornada trails it is useful to consider the local paths as type I-Local trails as opposed to type I-Regional trails.

In some cases it is even possible that type I-Regional and type I-Local paths might be the same entity, in the sense that a type I-Regional trail entering the Tularosa Basin and encountering a site may continue onwards to another site within the basin. In certain cases it should be possible to differentiate the type I-Local and type I-Regional segments of a continuous regional and local pathway on the basis of the ceramic wares and compositional groups comprising the ceramic scatters delineating the two segments.

Type I-Regional trails are rare in the Western Jornada sample, but this is likely due to survey bias. The most propitious areas for finding type I-Regional trails is near the margins of intermontane basins, but these regions have been undersurveyed due to the concentration of survey efforts within the basin interiors. One example may have been found: the westernmost of the trail segments identified by Camarena-Garcés and others (2011) leading toward Fillmore Pass between the Organ and Franklin Mountains may be a type

I-Regional trail that connected the Mesilla and Tularosa Basins (see figures 6.1 and 6.7). On the basis of a GIS least-cost path analysis of possible routes between site clusters on the east and west side of the Franklin Mountains, Willis and others (2002) propose that certain passes in the Franklin Mountains were pathways for travel and communication. Again showing deeper connections between past and present trail corridors, the primary pathway identified in their analysis is Smuggler's Pass along Fusselman Canyon, the main passage across the Franklin Mountains. As suggested by its historic name, the pass was a well-known corridor for smuggling cattle and other goods. Several rock-art sites are known along Fusselman Canyon and certain panels may be associated with the prehistoric use of this travel corridor.

Hypothetically, type I-Regional trails would have extended beyond the Jornada region and connected with the Mimbres Valley, Casas Grandes, Chupadera Mesa, and other adjacent locales. The application of TRU survey methods beyond the limits of Fort Bliss may someday identify type I-Regional trails connecting settlements and regions across southern New Mexico. Moreover, owing to the interregional nature of type I-Regional trails, it is likely that non-local ceramics will be more common among this class of trail. Indeed, perhaps the distributions of isolated Chupadero Black-on-white sherds found across southern New Mexico and Trans-Pecos Texas might mark the locations of type I-Regional pathways.

Last but not least we consider the category of type I-Local pathways. Despite its apparent subordinate status to the numbered trails in Darling's model, type I-Local paths are the most common type represented among the present sample of 30 or so pathways identified through TRU surveys and the analysis of ceramic isolated finds at Fort Bliss. This may be another artifice of survey bias; the vast majority of TRU and conventional surveys have focused on central basins and distal alluvial fans where it would be expected that local paths connecting settlements and settlement clusters would predominate. The compositional and distributional results of the preliminary INAA study would best match the expected distributional patterns arising from the use of this type of trail. The majority (82.5%) of El Paso Brownware sherds found along the trail segments were from vessels produced at settlements located some distance from the trails but located nevertheless within the Tularosa-Hueco Basin.

The type I-Local trails link settlements and settlement clusters across the 30–60-km-wide Tularosa and Hueco Basins (see figure 6.7). Presently, the majority are east–west corridors, but north–south trails have been identified near the Organ Mountains and other trails have northeast–southwest or northwest–southeast orientations. These trails currently comprise the primary body of data on location, orientation, artifact content, age, and other important variables for analysis. They comprise a local network of associations, movement, and social fields across space and time. We have just begun to explore their potential.

SUMMARY

This chapter reviewed current discoveries and research on the recently discovered trails and pathways in the Tularosa and Hueco Basins. A preliminary typology of trails derived from studies of trails in the Sonoran Desert is proposed, along with preliminary interpretations of their formation and function and some thoughts on future analysis directions. The research on Jornada trails is in its infancy, and the "unraveling" of social networks mentioned in the title of this chapter would more accurately be described as the untying of a few threads. However, regardless of whatever the current status of research may be, the web of trails and all they represent clearly demonstrate the profound research potential of these archaeological features.

Trails can be integrated into regional analyses of social and community organization across the landscape, going beyond the conventional focus on single pithouse or pueblo settlements. Adler (2002) and Varien and Potter (2008) question the concept of a prehispanic Southwest "community" when analysis is restricted to a single settlement. Expanding on this view, the conceptual space formed by the web of settlements, social groups, trails, sacred places, and resource areas creates a broader conceptual and cognitive landscape of movement and connectivity.

These concepts of community and landscape must be viewed within the context of geographic space. Darling (2009), Gorenflo and Bell (1991), Snead (2008b), White (2007) and others suggest that the analysis of trails is ultimately tied to conceptions of space and how space and social fields interact and influence each other. In addition to physical features of the landscape, the movement of people, goods, and ideas we see materialized in the formation of trails was constrained by the social fields of communities. Thus the choices of which path to take, which path to continue taking, and which path to abandon were structured by such phenomena.

At any rate, whether dealing with analytical abstractions of communities and social fields across spatial dimensions, or somewhat more grounded studies of economic relationships, regional exchange networks, and political economies, the identification of multiple pueblos linked by trail systems can serve to expand our conception of community formation and dynamics among Southwest pueblo groups from the Hohokam to the Jornada and allow for a more comprehensive analysis of settlement organization and social production across the landscape. The variability among type I-Local trails, their age profiles, and their associated material culture—including ceramic densities, proportions of non-local types, residues in jar fragments, chemical compositional groups, existence of shrines and trail markers, the presence of other artifact types—may provide insights into community organization and shifting social fields. Social network analysis can identify patterns of centrality among trail systems that reflect social inequality (Pailes 2014). Changing social ties or alliances between groups and settlements, the abandonment of settlements or settlement clusters and movement of the resident populations, the increasing ritualization seen during the Pueblo period, and the presence and influence of non-local prestige goods might all be reflected to some extent in the material culture of the trails.

These discussions clearly establish the archaeological significance of Western Jornada trails, particularly in light of the current focus on landscape, place, movement, and social networks in the American Southwest. Trails both reflected and structured movement across space and embodied the human role in structuring the landscape. As such, the Jornada trails are material manifestations of social arrangements and social production during the Formative period of southern New Mexico and far west Texas. Taking a broader view in light of current revelations from social network analysis in the Southwest (Borck et al. 2015; Mills et al. 2013), these trails are tangible, physical evidence of the development and change of networks and nodes at the microscale level of analysis (after Mills et al. 2015) that are otherwise identified through the distributions of decorated ceramics and other items within and among settlements. The networks of pathways, settlements, and spiritual locales in the Western Jornada region provide a lengthy and profound "chronicle of life and dwelling" (Ingold 2000:189) in a portion of the prehispanic Southwest.

ACKNOWLEDGMENTS

The authors wish to extend their appreciation to Tom Rocek and Jim Railey for the invitation to participate in the 2010 SAA symposium and subsequent invitation to add this study to the volume. The TRU surveys and studies of Western Jornada trails could not have been possible without the support and funding provided by the Conservation Branch, Environmental Division, of

Fort Bliss Military Reservation. Brian Knight, chief, and archaeologists Sue Sitton, Chris Lowry, Belinda Mollard, and Martha Yduarte have supported and encouraged the study of the trails during the past decade. Sue Sitton supported the inclusion of INAA in the data-recovery program for the trail segments through LA 95071 and LA 169230. GIS specialists Brock Boven and Kevin Vaughn contributed to the analysis and produced several figures used in the chapter. The contributions of Trevor Kludt, Phil Leckman, Sean Phillips, and David Camarena-Garcés to our knowledge and understanding of Jornada trails must be acknowledged; several discussions in this chapter are built upon their work. Matt Peeples and Lewis Borck provided comments on a draft version of the chapter and the senior author expresses his appreciation for their insights and suggestions, and the authors thank thank two anonymous reviewers for their thoughtful comments. Finally, we thank Tom Rocek and Nancy Kenmotsu for their extreme patience, editorial guidance, and support for this chapter.

NOTES

1. The existence of the pathways and trails discussed in this chapter has been recognized only within the past decade. They were discovered through the use of the high-resolution TRU (transect recording units) survey method. This method was developed for lowland desert environments with discontinuous artifact scatters typical of the central basins of the Western Jornada. A brief discussion of the survey method is in order because the discovery and definition of the pathways are intrinsically linked to the use of the TRU survey method and the manner in which it enables archaeologists to tease out details such as trails that cannot be detected by visual means or through traditional transect surveys.

The TRU method is an intensive and comprehensive 100% inventory of designated survey parcels. Transect lines in survey blocks are oriented along the north–south axis of the parcel and standard transect spacing is 15 m. The grid system is positioned so that the southwest corner of the transect grid is placed on the southwest corner of a Universal Transverse Mercator (UTM) square kilometer. A transect recording unit cell (TRU) measures 15 m by 15 m in size, and every TRU cell along a transect is examined by the crew person assigned to that transect, providing complete coverage of the parcel. Each crew person is equipped with a handheld personal data assistant (PDA) unit and global positioning system (GPS) unit to record cultural and natural observations within each TRU cell. The field supervisor and crew chiefs are equipped with high-resolution handheld GPS units and use this equipment to ensure that field crew maintain consistency and accuracy in transect coverage.

Upon discovery of artifacts or features, the UTM coordinates of the TRU cell are entered into the PDA. All artifacts within each 15-m-by-15-m TRU cell are tallied by class and entered in the PDA using dropdown menus and standardized codes. In a similar manner, features and architectural remains are classified, assigned a number, and the locality is plotted with the GPS unit for exact provenience. The immediate environment, geomorphic context, human or natural impacts, and any impediments to visibility such as dense vegetation or recent alluvium that could obscure artifacts are noted. Once this information is recorded and saved into the PDA, the crew person continues along the transect until another positive TRU is encountered and the recording process is repeated. Upon completion of the field day, the data collected on the PDA are downloaded in a database format to a laboratory computer and reviewed for consistency and errors. The data are then mapped in a GIS program and examined for spatial errors.

An important aspect of the method is that sites are not defined in the field, but instead are defined in the laboratory by processing the spatial data through GIS subroutines. Sites are defined through specific density and distance criteria. The raw TRU cell data are processed through a series of Boolean statements and site-positive TRU units (cells that met criteria for artifact counts) are established. Sites are defined on a uniform distance criterion based on a 30m buffer between site-positive cells. Once sites are defined, the boundaries and other TRU information are converted to GIS shapefiles for further analysis and evaluation.

The TRU method meets the description and criteria of a total survey as defined by Ebert (1992). However, it is unlike the 100% point-proveniencing method of "non-site" and earlier total survey methods used in the region (Camilli et al. 1988). In contrast, the TRU method of using 15-m-by-15-m data-collection units provides a means of achieving the needs of archaeological inventory and evaluation across tens of thousands of acres and for conducting landscape-scale archaeological research without the infeasible and unrealistic time and cost burdens of landscape survey methods based on 100% point-proveniencing of cultural materials. The TRU method serves as both a "site" and "non-site" method, providing the necessary information for the evaluation and management of sites while also providing high-resolution distributional data for studies of prehistoric landscape use, settlement pattern, geomorphic conditioning of surface distributions, and other research pursuits. The only minor drawback to the use of TRU data for spatial and distributional studies is that the 15-m-by-15-m recording units create particular scalar effects and constraints on the data (Miller 2007a). Spatial patterns at scales of less than 15 m cannot be discerned, nor can scales of 16 m, 17 m, 20 m, or 25 m and so on be isolated until a multiple of 15 is reached (e.g., 30 m, 45 m, 60 m). While this may present some problems for small-scale intrasite spatial analysis, the data resolution and quality are clearly sufficient for spatial studies of intersite and landscape distributions (Miller 2007a, 2007b).

The benefits of the TRU method can be applied to the domains of both cultural resources management and archaeological research. The combination of standardized field recording methods and GIS site definition serve to reduce considerably the subjective and ambiguous nature of site boundary definition—a problem that has long troubled site identification and management at Fort Bliss and elsewhere across the deserts of the Jornada region. It is not uncommon to find sites that have had four or five different boundary definitions that often vary by several thousands (or even tens of thousands) of square meters. These problems are considerably reduced through the use of standardized TRU survey methods. Site boundaries are defined on the basis of a standardized distance criterion between TRU cells with well-defined content attributes. The effects of idiosyncratic and biased (unconsciously or consciously) site definitions are considerably reduced and, in some cases, eliminated by the use of standardized GIS-based site-definition procedures.

To date, over 150,000 acres have been surveyed at Fort Bliss using the TRU method. The cumulative total represents one of the most detailed and extensive compendiums of surface material-culture distributions for archaeological research in North America. The use of the method during large-scale survey plays to its particular strengths as a total survey method and allows for multiscalar studies of material distributions and relationships across broad areas. Of relevance to the present study, the method allows for different classes of material culture, artifact types, or features to be plotted and their spatial relationships mapped across broad landscapes. It is this capability for high-resolution landscape mapping that revealed the presence of trails or pathways. Plots of ceramic-positive TRU cells revealed linear patterns of ceramics extending across the desert basins. Further analysis, such as plotting potbreaks, found that this specific form of ceramic feature was typically associated with the linear patterns of ceramics.

2. Mescal may have been transported from baking pits in the mountains to settlements and subsequently between settlements, but it is less likely that maize beer would have been moved in such a manner. Using local stores of maize, corn beer was probably brewed in large El Paso Polychrome ollas that remained on site.

3. The counts and proportions in Table 6.1 differ slightly from an earlier analysis presented in Graves et al. (2013) that used an outdated classification. The data in Table 6.1 incorporate the most recent comprehensive classification of El Paso Brownware chemical compositional groups (Miller and Ferguson 2014). The major differences from the prior classification is that the Tularosa Basin East group has been subsumed within the overall Tularosa Basin Northeast group and that several previously unassigned samples are now securely placed within compositional groups. The different classifications and production locations do not alter the interpretations, but in fact enhance them because the identified provenance areas are of even greater distance from the trails than previously identified.

7

The Dunlap-Salazar Site Lithic Sources and Highland Pithouse-Period Mobility in the Jornada

Shaun M. Lynch and Thomas R. Rocek

The Formative period, the approximate American equivalent of the Old World "Neolithic Revolution," is generally interpreted as a time of "settling down" by communities adopting agriculture, investing in substantial houses, and establishing permanent farming villages. In this chapter, we consider the nature of this transformation in the highlands of the Jornada by examining one of its fundamental aspects, changing mobility ("settling down"). To do this we analyze shifts in stone raw-material selection and acquisition in the Formative pithouse period in the Sierra Blanca/Capitan/Sacramento Highlands to examine how sedentary these early Formative sites are.

To study changes in mobility, we examined debitage from the Dunlap-Salazar pithouse site (LA 51344) and other nearby sites in Lincoln County, New Mexico. We assessed the approximate travel distances to the raw-material source areas, as well as the distribution of the raw materials themselves, and compared data from the early Formative pithouse-period sites with Late Archaic and Late Formative pueblo-period sites. Given the expectation that pithouse occupations were transitional between high mobility in the Archaic and greatly reduced mobility in the Pueblo period (e.g., Gilman 1987), we predicted that the raw materials would reflect substantial mobility in the pithouse period despite the "settled village" appearance of pithouse sites and in contrast to the succeeding Pueblo period. Our results are consistent with this

DOI: 10.5876/9781607327950.c007

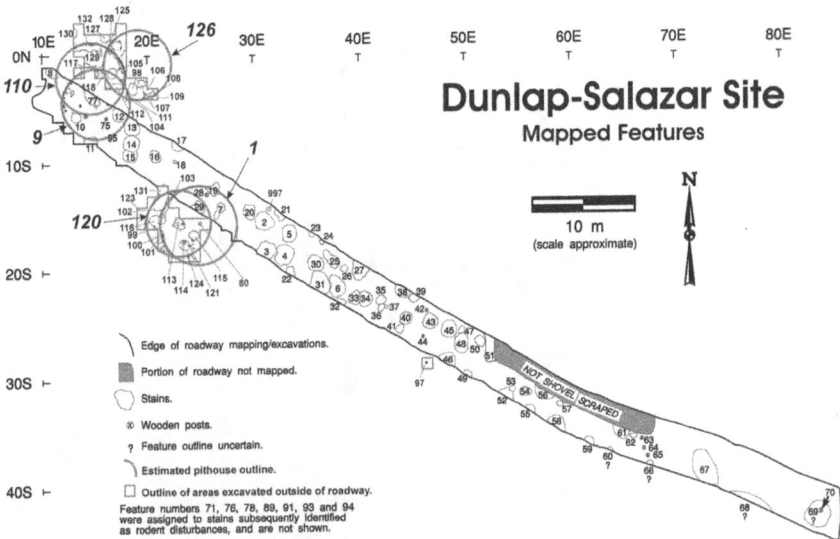

FIGURE 7.1. *Map of Dunlap-Salazar site (LA 51344) features.*

expectation, suggesting that the shift to committed sedentism characteristic of the Formative was gradual, despite the earlier and apparently rapid rise in agricultural dependence in the highlands (in this volume, see Rocek and Kenmotsu, chapter 1; Rocek, chapter 2; and Railey and Turnbow, chapter 5). We also find hints of a trend *within* the pithouse period toward decreasing mobility over time. While focused specifically on this one portion of the Jornada Mogollon, the study illustrates how research within this region has implications for broader, worldwide patterns of early village formation, demonstrating the complexity of the Formative/Neolithic transition.

The Dunlap-Salazar site (figure 7.1, 7.2; see also figure 1.2) has yielded the richest data on the early pithouse period in the Sierra Blanca/Capitan/ Sacramento Highlands region. Features on the excavated portion of the site include over 40 storage pits, many large and bell shaped, and at least five (and probably significantly more) pithouses, though not all are contemporary with each other (figure 7.1). A large series of high-precision AMS measurements on short-lived materials (seeds, twigs, etc.) dates these features from about cal. AD 550 to 800/850 (for a fuller description of the site, see Rocek 2007b, 2013).

Dunlap-Salazar is characterized by very high maize ubiquity and rank abundance (i.e., rank order among taxa of counts of macrobotanical specimens), and both squash and bean cultivation are also indicated (Rocek

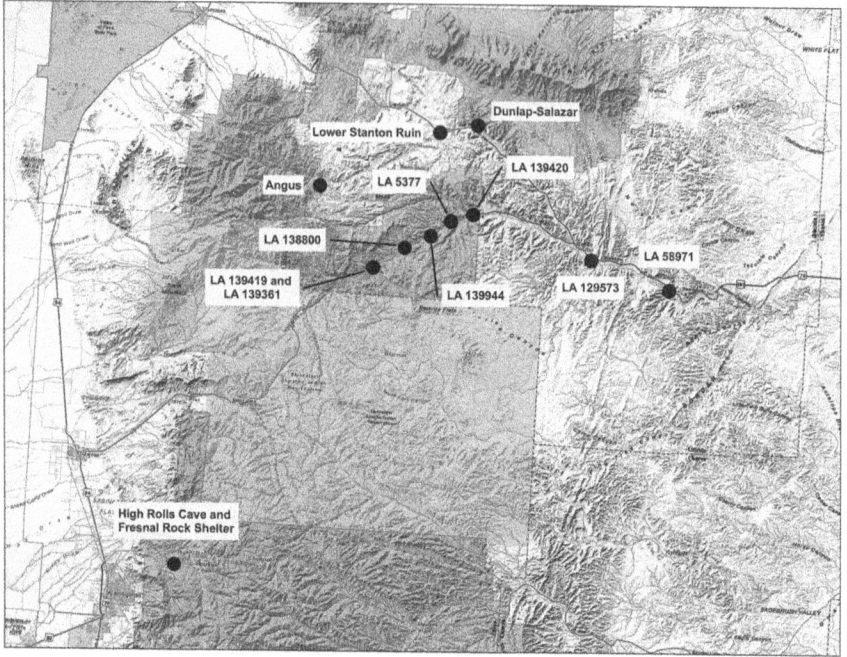

FIGURE 7.2. *Map of sites mentioned in the text.*

1995, 2013), all of which indicates heavy agricultural reliance as might be expected in the Formative (in this volume, see Rocak and Kenmotsu [chapter 1], Rocek [chapter 2], and Railey and Turnbow [chapter 5] for a discussion of this highland Formative pattern of early agricultural dependence in broader regional context). Combined with the number and size of the substantial structures and storage features, it is evident that the inhabitants invested much effort at this site location. However, ethnographic and archaeological evidence suggests that pithouse architecture and extramural, subterranean-pit storage are consistent with significant mobility (DeBoer 1988; Gilman 1987; Kelly 1992; Rocek 1995; Wills 1988b), and thus our lithic debitage research is designed to examine mobility independently of either subsistence or architectural data.

In order to assess the nature of the Dunlap-Salazar occupation, we estimated how far and how often the site's occupants traveled by evaluating sources of stone represented in the site's debitage assemblage. Debitage represents every stage in tool production and is abundant at many sites in the available comparative archaeological sample from the highlands (McNally

2002:143). Focusing on debitage rather than finished tools reduces the problem of small sample sizes and biases caused by differences in transport among tool classes as well as those introduced by artifact surface collection (cf., Smith and Harvey 2018). Previous research on ceramics recovered from Dunlap-Salazar (Howey and Rocek 2008; Rocek 2007b:2) demonstrated the dominance of locally manufactured brownware ceramics in the highlands and offered no indication that the inhabitants engaged in large-scale trade. Therefore, we assume that while small quantities of exotic lithic materials at the Dunlap-Salazar site may be the result of trade, large quantities of materials are likely to reflect direct procurement via travel to source areas.

For our study, we used Browman's (1976) exploitable territory threshold model, which is designed to estimate how far hunter-gatherers and agriculturists will travel to obtain certain resources. Browman proposed theoretical distances, along an ordinal scale, that people are willing to travel from their residences to collect resources and then used ethnographic data from a range of societies to quantify these distances. Since he gathered supporting data from multiple time periods and geographic areas, the approximate distances should be fairly robust estimates of typical mobility patterns in such groups. Based on Browman's results, we identify the *local* area as the 8-km range that Browman (1976) found to be the typical distance traveled by ethnographic agricultural populations. Browman found a typical hunter-gathererer procurement range up to 35 km, which we use to define our *regional* range. We define *long-distance* procurement as anything beyond 35 km.

Applying this model, we collected information from the geological literature and maps of south-central New Mexico to estimate the minimal distances the inhabitants would have had to travel to procure the raw materials found in the Dunlap-Salazar debitage collection, and classified them into local, regional, or long-distance categories. This approach does not allow us to demonstrate that a particular piece of debitage originated at a particular location, but permits us to estimate roughly what percentage of raw material might have come from within 8 km or 35 km, or from over 35 km away from the site, respectively. We did not choose Browman's model in order to describe each population represented by the archaeological sites in our study as more "agricultural" or "hunter-gatherer." Agriculturalists and hunter-gatherers, as documented both ethnographically and archaeologically, use varying degrees of mobility both seasonally and on longer time scales (Kelly 1992; Randolph 2001). As mentioned above, other more direct lines of evidence indicate the subsistence strategies of these populations. Rather, we used Browman's model as an independent basis for quantifying and comparing mobility.

Next, we used the same geologic information to classify each lithic type as coming from a primary or secondary source in order to address the variable of abundance (Andrefsky 1994; Dibble 1991). Primary sources are in situ outcrops of stone that are concentrated, occur in large pieces, and can be readily located during procurement trips. Secondary sources, such as river gravels, are more diffuse across the landscape and typically have been transported from primary localities by geological processes that also decrease their size and quantity. Due to these characteristics, secondary resources require more time and mobility within a procurement area to obtain an amount comparable to that of a primary resource. All of the lithic sources for the regional and long-distance materials are primary in nature, however, and the distinction between primary and secondary is only relevant for local sources in this study.

For the comparative portion of the study, we compiled published data on lithic materials from other pithouse-period sites, and from Late Archaic and pueblo sites from the region surrounding the Dunlap-Salazar site (figure 7.2). This includes a large series of sites from Campbell and Railey's (2008) report on the Hondo Valley south of Dunlap-Salazar, in addition to several other excavation reports with large samples. All of the sites are in the Sierra Blanca/ Capitan/Sacramento Highlands with the exception of one (LA 57971), which is located in the foothills on the east edge of the highlands. A total of 12 comparative sites, all with lithic sample sizes over 150 pieces, are included.[1] For each site, we applied the same procedure that we used for Dunlap-Salazar for classifying each raw-material type in the respective site's lithic sample according to source type (primary vs. secondary) and potential procurement distance. Combining all of these data, we calculated the relative proportions of local (primary and secondary), regional, and long-distance materials (table 7.1).

RESULTS

In the discussion that follows, we examine the data for trends over time (figure 7.3A). As discussed below, several of the patterns show trends, but an examination of residuals from regression analysis shows that none of the patterns is linear; therefore we use two non-parametric measures, Spearman's rank correlation coefficient (ρ) and Kendall's rank correlation coefficient (τ), to assess change over time and to evaluate statistical significance. All tests are one-sided, based on the hypothesis that mobility decreased over time.

None of the 13 sites used for the intersite analysis has a substantial quantity of long-distance resources, nor is there a significant trend over time in long-distance materials ($\rho = -0.27$, $p > 0.18$; $\tau = -0.17$, $p > 0.21$). While

TABLE 7.1. Raw-material counts and percentages from all 13 sites

| Site | Period | Raw Materials | | | | | | | | | | Totals | |
| | | Primary Local Resources | | Secondary Local Resources | | Regional Resources | | Long-Distance Resources | | Other Materials | | | |
		N	%	N	%	N	%	N	%	N	%	N	%
Fresnal Shelter	Late Archaic	637	39.3	782	47.9	196	12	17	1	0	0	1,632	100
High Rolls Cave	Late Archaic	734	13.5	4,523	83.1	180	3.4	0	0	0	0	5,437	100
LA 139944	Late Archaic	140	18.8	596	79.9	7	0.9	2	0.3	1	0.1	746	100
LA 5377	Late Archaic	36	14.8	184	75.7	4	1.6	1	0.4	18	7.5	243	100
LA 58971	Late Archaic	57	17.3	240	72.9	12	3.6	0	0	20	6.2	329	100
LA 129573	Late Archaic	653	21	2,190	70.4	25	0.8	78	2.5	165	5.3	3,111	100
LA 139420	Pithouse	384	39.1	437	44.5	131	13	9	0.9	21	2.2	982	100
LA 139419	Pithouse	165	35.2	198	42.2	8	1.7	0	0	98	21	469	100
Dunlap-Salazar	Pithouse	693	43.5	240	15.1	580	36	80	5	0	0	1,593	100
LA 139361	Pithouse	82	50.6	28	17.3	21	13	0	0	31	19	162	100
LA 138800	Pithouse	208	47.5	221	50.3	0	0	0	0	10	2.2	439	100
Angus	Pueblo	2,077	90.2	122	5.3	84	3.7	7	0.3	11	0.3	2,301	100
Lower Stanton Ruin	Pueblo	1,001	62.2	361	22.4	248	15	0	0	0	0	1,610	100
Totals		6,867	36	10,122	53.1	1,496	7.9	194	1	375	2	19,054	100

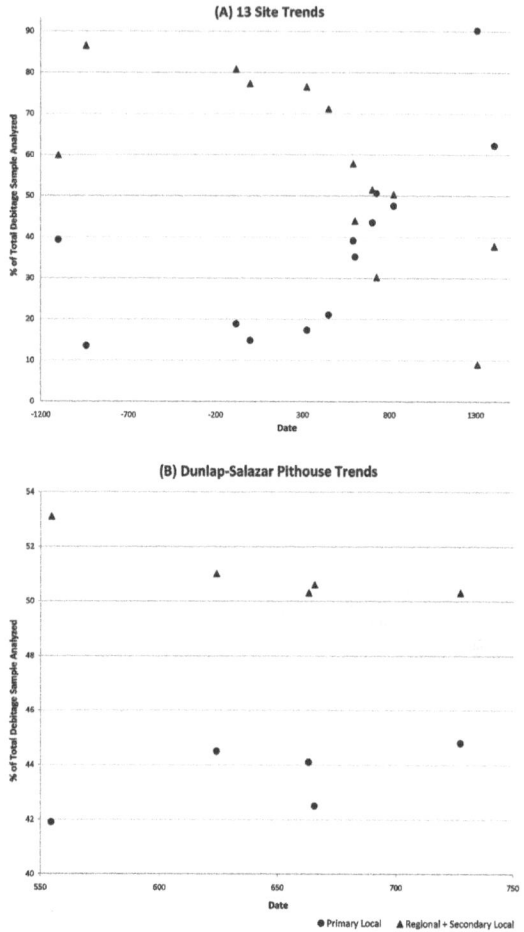

(A) 13 Site Trends

(B) Dunlap-Salazar Pithouse Trends

● Primary Local   ▲ Regional + Secondary Local

FIGURE 7.3. *Raw material percentages: percentage of local primary and percentage of local secondary plus regional materials at (A) all 13 sites and (B) the five pit structures excavated at Dunlap–Salazar (LA 51344).*

populations during the Paleoindian and Early Archaic periods in many parts of North America likely obtained high percentages of long-distance resources via extremely high mobility (though cf. Speth 2018), it is evident that such procurement strategies were no longer relied upon in this region by the Late Archaic period. Interestingly, there is also not a significant trend for regional ($\rho = 0.29, p > 0.83$; $\tau = 0.18, p > 0.78$) or a combination of regional and long-distance resources ($\rho = 0.23, p > 0.78$; $\tau = 0.15, p > 0.74$). Rather, mobility is already more closely restricted to the local level by the Late Archaic period in this portion of the Jornada highlands (see also discussion in endnote 2 below).

However, among local resources we find significant trends for an increase in *primary* materials ($\rho = 0.81$, $p < 0.001$; $\tau = 0.69$, $p < 0.001$) and a decrease in secondary ones ($\rho = -0.76$, $p < 0.002$; $\tau = -0.64$, $p < 0.001$). Further, the combination of secondary local and regional materials yields the strongest trend for a decrease in these resources over time ($\rho = -0.86$, $p < 0.001$; $\tau = -0.74$, $p < 0.001$), consistent with our expectation of a decrease in mobility. This latter test is not completely independent from the two preceding tests, but it combines *all* of the materials that we hypothesize reflect relatively high mobility (secondary local and regional) while leaving out materials that *cannot* be attributed to direct procurement (the "other materials" that cannot be sourced and the limited amounts of long-distance resources most likely acquired via trade). In essence, then, this is the inverse of the trend toward an increase in primary local materials, but with the "noise" of unsourced and traded materials removed, it shows the strongest temporal trend. Thus, over time inhabitants of the region were gradually decreasing their reliance on diffuse secondary local and more distant regional resources and proportionately increasing their use of concentrated primary local materials.

The strength of the temporal trend of the *combined* local secondary with regional materials indicates that site inhabitants of successive periods decreased reliance on secondary local and regional resources in varying combinations, with the balance of variation reflecting intersite variable mobility strategies. Occupants of some sites may have swapped secondary local resources and others swapped regional resources in favor of highly accessible local resources; ultimately both of the less-easily collected resources declined over time in favor of the easily procured (primary) local materials.

The shift away from secondary local materials is specifically the result of declining importance over time of chert, which is the only secondary local resource found among the 13 sites. This pattern is consistent with the analysis of Greenwald (2008), who showed that, among the Rio Hondo Valley sites, chert is abundant at Archaic sites and low at Formative sites. This trend is consistent with the expected consequence of decreasing mobility over time as the regional inhabitants gradually procured more local resources from primary sources at the expense of secondary sources.

To examine more precisely the pattern of change during the Early Formative, we narrow our analysis to the pithouse-period sites in our sample. This decreases our sample to merely five sites, and so statistically significant results are unlikely. However, there remains a strong suggestion of an increase in primary local resources among the five pithouse sites over time *within* the Early Formative, although not attaining a .05 level of significance ($\rho = 0.8$,

$p < 0.06$; $\tau = 0.6$, $p < 0.08$). The data do not provide support for a decrease in secondary local resources over time ($\rho = -0.1$, $p > 0.44$; $\tau = 0.0$, $p = .5$). Data for regional resources or, as in the comparison among all 13 sites, the *combination* of both secondary local combined with regional resources are consistent with a decreasing trend, though in this case not as strong as the increase in primary local resources and, given the small number of cases, not approaching the .05 level of significance ($\rho = -.5$, $p > 0.19$; $\tau = -0.4$, $p > 0.16$; these results are the same for either regional resources alone or the combination of regional and secondary local materials together). Thus, the trends are marginal but are consistent with decreased mobility for the inhabitants of the five pithouse sites over time, although a larger sample of sites would be needed to make a more compelling case.

To examine this pattern further, we also performed an intrasite comparison among the five known pithouses at Dunlap-Salazar that span the relatively brief period from the mid-sixth century through the early ninth century AD (figure 7.3B, table 7.2). While, as expected, primary local materials increase over time ($\rho = 0.6$, $p > 0.17$; $\tau = 0.4$, $p > 0.24$) and secondary local resources decrease ($\rho = -0.6$, $p > 0.17$; $\tau = -0.4$, $p > 0.24$), again these results all fail to attain statistical significance due to the small sample size. Intriguingly, however, the combination of secondary local and regional resources shows a strong decrease over time at Dunlap-Salazar that exceeds the one-sided .05 significance level ($\rho = -0.82$, $p < 0.05$; $\tau = -0.73$, $p < 0.04$). This trend and the increase in primary local resources were the strongest findings in the 13-site analysis as well, and, while clearly the data do not permit a strong argument in this case, they are consistent with our thesis that the inhabitants were gradually moving around the landscape less and less.[2]

DISCUSSION

At an intuitive level, our study is based on the expectation that raw-material collection occurs in the context of mobility: the more people move across the landscape, the more likely they are to collect non-local raw materials. A more formal version of this argument derives from the model of Parry and Kelly (1987), who argue that mobile populations produce lightweight, high quality, curated formal tools with multiple functions in order to limit carrying weight. In contrast, sedentary populations do not require easily transportable tools and make them from locally available materials, typically of low quality, discarding and replacing the tools as they become inefficient. Thus, groups use more low-quality and local chipped stone as they become more sedentary.

TABLE 7.2. Debitage raw-material counts and percentages from the five pit structures excavated at Dunlap-Salazar (LA 51344)

		Raw Materials								
Pithouse	Median Date of Use	Primary Local Resources		Secondary Local Resources		Regional Resources		Long-Distance Resources		Totals	
		N	%	N	%	N	%	N	%	N	%
9	554.5	75	41.9	41	22.9	54	30	9	5	179	100
1	624	138	44.5	57	18.4	101	33	14	4.5	310	100
110	663	198	44.1	50	11.1	176	39	25	5.6	449	100
126	665.5	131	42.5	38	12.3	118	38	21	6.8	308	100
120	727.5	155	44.8	54	15.6	120	35	17	4.9	346	100
Totals		697	43.8	240	15.1	569	36	86	5.4	1,592	100

Notably, Parry and Kelly's model ties shifts in raw-material use specifically to residential mobility—people who move their residences need more portable and curatable tools, made of better materials.[3]

Railey (2010) has recently proposed an alternative theory explaining changes in lithic raw-material selection over time, suggesting that the introduction of the bow and arrow corresponds better with the shift toward the decreased prominence of secondary materials in debitage assemblages than does a reduction in mobility (Railey 2010:20). Using some of the same data that we have borrowed from his work, he points out that the shift toward the bow and arrow occurred at around AD 500–700 in the Jornada Mogollon, coinciding with the changeover toward decreased production of large bifaces and the drop in chert abundance. Making a larger atlatl dart involves a complex biface reduction process that requires large pieces of high-quality raw materials and produces many retouch flakes. In contrast, producing small arrow points directly from flakes requires smaller high-quality raw materials and produces smaller, less-readily recovered retouch flakes. In addition, arrow production conserves high-quality materials much better than dart production because it creates fewer errors and uses less material. Railey (2010:21–22) suggests that these biases, rather than shifts in mobility, explain why site assemblages post-dating the bow and arrow are disproportionately skewed against the small flakes produced during arrow manufacture and seem more expedient than site assemblages that predate it.

Our results are consistent with either interpretation, since the argument applying to lithic-procurement strategies, in contrast to the lithic-reduction strategies above, yield the same expectations in our study. Specifically, tool production that entails large-biface reduction requires larger pieces of high-quality lithic materials as compared to small-flake-shaping for arrow points. This is consistent with the trend in our results of decreasing use of secondary local resources (which are composed solely of the high-quality chert in our sample). In the earlier periods, populations most likely traveled relatively more (either residentially or logistically) to collect large pieces of the less-abundant chert to acquire the larger sizes and quantities needed for dart production than did the later arrow-producing populations. Thus, under either the Parry and Kelly or Railey interpretations, the shift toward local resources from the Archaic through the Pueblo periods implies a progressive decrease in mobility as people collected a smaller amount of the rarer and harder to collect secondary high-quality material (i.e., chert) and relied more on abundant (primary) materials of lower qualities.

Our lithic analysis cannot differentiate between residential and logistical mobility. Parry and Kelly's (1987) theory would imply that the trend of decreased mobility in the Late Archaic through Pueblo periods is one of a decrease in *residential* mobility—people moving their residences less frequently and thus getting less picky about what materials they use; this is also what the architectural arguments (e.g., Gilman 1987) imply. Andrefsky's (1994; see footnote 3) modification of Parry and Kelly's model and Railey's (2010) alternative hypothesis suggest that the trend toward increased use of lower-quality materials may reflect a reduction in *logistical* mobility as people travel less to procure the less-abundant chert and use fewer large chert cores to make dart points. However, these latter interpretations don't contradict a change in residential mobility as well.

Even if residential mobility is sharply restricted at Formative pithouse sites such as Dunlap-Salazar, significant numbers of people were periodically going out beyond the typical day range to procure stone or other resources (i.e., they engaged in more logistical mobility), and did this more regularly and/or farther than was typical in the Pueblo period, although less than earlier in the Formative or in the Archaic. Dunlap-Salazar inhabitants may also have been continuing a limited, regional-scale residential mobility pattern that is comparable to, but more restricted than, that which characterized the Late Archaic. Despite the ambiguity about the form of mobility, our findings suggest that Formative-period sites, as exemplified by Dunlap-Salazar, expressed different mobility patterns from both the immediately preceding and immediately succeeding periods and that change was occurring over the course of the period covered by Dunlap-Salazar as well.

These findings are intriguing in light of the evidence of the movement of ceramics from the highlands into adjacent lowland areas (see Boggess et al., chapter 8, and Hill, chapter 9, both in this volume), since they are consistent with contact or even group movements among the various regions of the Jornada. More directly, they have implications regarding the nature of early Formative (or early Neolithic) "hamlets" or "villages" such as Dunlap-Salazar, where agriculture is clearly well established but settlement and social changes remain poorly understood. The evidence of continuing but changing mobility suggests a process of transition over the course of the Formative rather than an abrupt settling into a fully formed sedentary village pattern (see Rocek 2013 for a discussion of further evidence of settlement flux at Dunlap-Salazar). Whether or not Dunlap-Salazar qualifies as a "village" with significant logistical mobility, or remained relatively residentially mobile, the occupants of early Formative pithouse-period sites in the Sierra Blanca/Capitan/Sacramento Highlands traveled more than villagers of the Late Formative pueblo era in the region, but the data show a trend over time in the direction of the those later villages. The high resolution of this recent Jornada research allows us to document this process and provide a comparative basis for examination of the Formative/Neolithic process elsewhere in the Southwest and beyond.

ACKNOWLEDGMENTS

We wish to thank Coleen and Joe Salazar and the late Rosalie and Ralph Dunlap for their friendship, help, and tremendously generous support of the work at LA 51344. The work was supported by grants from the American Philosophical Society, the National Geographic Society, and the National Science Foundation (grant no. 9600581).

NOTES

1. Although the emphasis is on debitage, and only debitage data were used from the Dunlap-Salazar site, the published comparative data are variable in how data were compiled and thus partial debitage counts or counts of artifacts were sometimes included. For instance, the Angus site sample total of 2,301 is based specifically on flake data (Zamora and Oakes 2000:142) while the data from the Hondo Valley project (Campbell and Railey 2008:484) include *all* lithic specimens. However, given the restriction of our study to large samples and the relatively low number of non-debitage included in any of the totals, these minor variations in how the data were tabulated do not appear to have a significant impact on the results.

2. It should be noted that the trend in regional resources by themselves is weakly *positive* in two of the three analyses described above: $\rho = 0.29, p > 0.83; \tau = 0.18, p > 0.78$ for all 13 sites, $\rho = -0.50, p > 0.19; \tau = -0.40, p > 0.16$ for the five pithouse sites, and $\rho = 0.60, p > 0.82; \tau = 0.40, p > 0.69$ for the five pithouses on the Dunlap-Salazar site (all one-sided tests for H_0 that mobility was increasing). The two positive correlations contradict our expectations, but do not approach statistical significance. Furthermore, consistent with our thesis, in all of these cases the combination of regional and local secondary resources together shows as strong or stronger *decreasing* trends over time than do local secondary resources by themselves (and in two of the cases, the 13 sites and the five pithouses, this negative trend is stronger than the positive trend in local primary resources alone). Thus, while the pattern in regional resources by themselves is unclear, the overall results appear consistent with our expectations.

3. Andrefsky (1994) argues that Parry and Kelly's model is incomplete; the availability of lithic resources, classified by abundance and quality, also affects tool production across all types of settlement patterns. He suggests that while informal tools are typically made from poor quality and formal tools from high-quality materials that occur in low abundance, informal tools can also be made from the latter when such quality materials are abundant. Mobile groups who live in an area of abundant low-quality materials can easily acquire enough low-quality materials as part of their residential mobility round to make satisfactory informal tools and thus need not make formal tools out of the high-quality materials. In contrast, sedentary inhabitants living in an area of sparse low-quality material have two options: make longer, yet infrequent, logistical trips to higher-quality materials for formal tool production or make frequent short trips in order to acquire enough of the sparse low-quality material to make a requisite number of informal tools. This model addresses raw material use vis-à-vis logistical mobility, and complicates the simple correlation of formal tools made on high-quality material with mobile adaptations versus informal tools on low-quality materials with limited mobility. However, it should be noted that in the present study, raw material availability remained roughly constant (barring significant depletion of source areas by overuse); thus, given that the comparisons here are *relative* ones among time periods, Andrefsky's points regarding the importance of raw-material availability is of secondary concern.

8

The Eastern Extension of the Jornada Mogollon has often been given short shrift in treatments both of Southwestern archaeology and of Southern Plains archaeology, the disciplines that might lay claim to that part of southeastern New Mexico east of the Sacramento Mountains and extending into Texas. As Speth and Newlander point out, this region lies on the eastern edge of the Jornada Mogollon culture area, and is sometimes viewed as a "'backwater' occupied by 'less-developed' cultures that somehow missed the boat while important things were happening elsewhere" (Speth and Newlander 2012:153). When other prehistoric Southwestern groups came to live in more sedentary-looking settlements such as pueblos and grew corn, beans, and squash in carefully managed fields, people in the Eastern Extension seemed to follow a hunter-gatherer lifestyle for a much longer period, compelled by the agricultural unsuitability (read "poverty") of the landscape (see Akins 2003; Dering 2005; Doleman 2005).

For archaeologists working in the Southern Plains, the Eastern Extension lacks the analytic charms of the Southern Plains, nor are its sites blessed with abundant, easily visible, Florence, Alibates, or Edwards chert. These lithic resources can show mobility and trade across much of the Southern Plains, as opposed to the locally available gravels that are shaped into expedient tools and left on the landscape, along with only an occasional sherd, to form thousands of "picked over,

What's for Supper?

The Contents of a Complete Vessel Found in Southeast New Mexico

Douglas H. M. Boggess,
Chad L. Yost,
David V. Hill,
Linda Scott Cummings,
and Mary Malainey

DOI: 10.5876/9781607327950.c008

deflated, surface manifestations" (Speth and Newlander 2012:153) in southeastern New Mexico.

During the course of data recovery at what appeared, at least in places, to be one such "picked over, deflated, surface manifestation," LA 149260 (the Rascal Rabbit site) we recovered a complete late-twelfth- to mid-thirteenth-century Jornada Brown bowl in situ within a thermal feature. We submitted sherds from the vessel and the fill from within and beneath the vessel for a variety of analyses. These analyses document a pattern of mobility and interaction that brought pottery and perhaps maize from farming villages 200 km to the northwest and fish from riverine environments 30 km to the west within sight of the Maroon Cliffs on the Mescalero Plain in the Eastern Extension of the Jornada area (Corley 1965; Leslie 1979; see also Railey, chapter 13, this volume). Likely local resource use including consumption of *Commelina erecta* (whitemouth dayflower) and small seeded grasses is also indicated. Far from the technologically impoverished marginal groups that conventional accounts attribute to this region of the Jornada, the research demonstrates use of a sophisticated mixture of resources and tools drawing on a broad area of central and southeastern New Mexico.

The Rascal Rabbit site (figures 8.1 and 8.2) is located on Tower Hill, approximately 30 km east of Carlsbad (and the Pecos River), overlooking Highway 62/180. Site LA 149260 was initially recorded and described in a survey report prepared by Railey and Mullen (2006) with subsequent data recovery carried out as part of a Bureau of Land Management land exchange (Boggess 2011). Data recovery yielded 531 artifacts from surface and buried contexts and identified three datable ash-and-charcoal-stain features (Features 1, 4, and 9), which produced calibrated AMS dates ranging from AD 780 to 1280. A reworked dart point suggested a possible Late Archaic component, and the presence of Chupadero Black-on-white and Corona Corrugated suggests that the use of Rascal Rabbit may have extended at least into the early fourteenth century AD.

Much of Rascal Rabbit was buried within a 75-cm-thick sand sheet, except for the western margin of the site where a bladed road cut down to the caliche with an eroded hardpan surface on its margins. This hardpan was covered with a diffuse scatter of burned caliche and heat-altered sandstone measuring 24 m from north to south by 3 m from east to west designated "Feature 4" (figure 8.3) Trowel scraping resulted in discovery of a 70-cm-by-60-cm ash-and-charcoal stain near the top of the slope on the northeast portion of the feature.

Once the less than 2 cm of blowsand and the upper fill of the ash-and-charcoal-stain feature had been removed from the west half of the feature, the rim of a bowl became visible at the southern end of the stain (figure 8.4). After

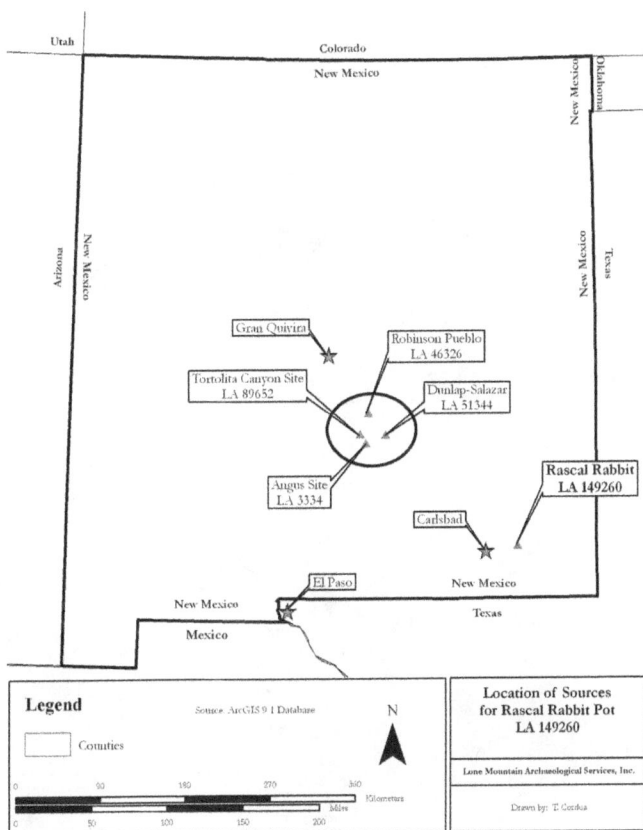

FIGURE 8.1. *Location of Rascal Rabbit site (LA 149260) and possible points of pottery manufacture.*

removing the west half of the feature outside of the rim, we confirmed the presence of a complete bowl of what appeared to be Jornada Brown, given a polished exterior lacking visible "popcorn" temper. The fill within the vessel was left in place and the fill surrounding and below the vessel was removed from the west half of the feature which proved to be a basin-shaped ash-and-charcoal feature 14 cm deep. The bowl, its contents, and the remainder of the feature were then removed as one item. Although complete and held in place by surrounding sediments, the bowl had cracked into 49 sherds. The bowl measures 19.5 cm in diameter and has a depth of 9 cm (figure 8.5) and it appears to have been left in situ, sitting within a small fire pit. Its discovery presented an opportunity to obtain data concerning the origins and resources

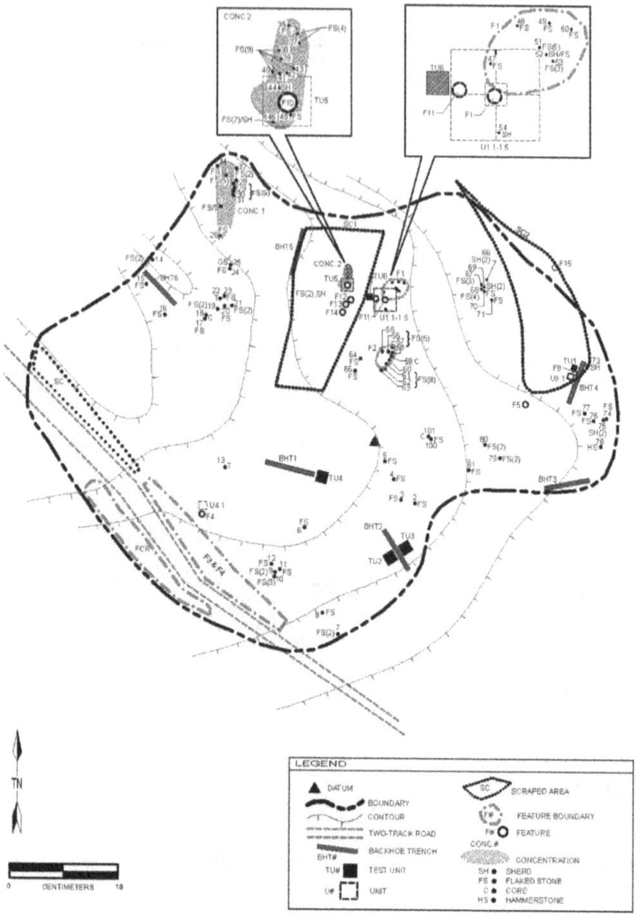

FIGURE 8.2. *Plan view of LA 149260, the Rascal Rabbit site.*

consumed within the bowl and the feature that preserved it, data that argue for a rich and varied subsistence base and the far-ranging mobility of the site's occupants.

Sherds from the vessel itself, fill of the feature beneath the vessel, and fill within the vessel were submitted for a variety of analyses, including petrography, lipid residue analysis, and Fourier Transform Infrared Spectroscopy (FTIR). Feature fill from beneath the vessel was submitted for flotation, AMS dating, and pollen, starch, and phytolith analyses. The fill of the vessel itself was also submitted for pollen, starch, and phytolith analyses.

FIGURE 8.3. *View of Feature 4, the Rascal Rabbit site.*

Because we employed two different techniques for examining residues on the bowl—lipid residue analysis and FTIR—a brief description of these two techniques is provided in more detail in an appendix. These analyses, when taken together, confirm each other and reveal the geographic extent of the available resource base and also identify a previously unrecognized potential economic plant resource.

PETROGRAPHIC ANALYSIS

Petrographic analysis of a sherd from the bowl suggests that the bowl may have been manufactured in the Sierra Blanca/Capitan/Sacramento Highlands (see figure 1.2; see also Hill, chapter 9, this volume), ca. 200 km west of the Rascal Rabbit site. The paste from the bowl is a medium brown color and contains 15% sediments that were derived from a source of syenitic composition (Hill 2011). The predominate mineral that occurs in the paste, both as isolated mineral grains and in the sparse rock fragments, is untwinned alkali feldspar. Trace amounts of microcline and quartz are also present in the

FIGURE 8.4. *View of Rascal Rabbit bowl, as it first appeared.*

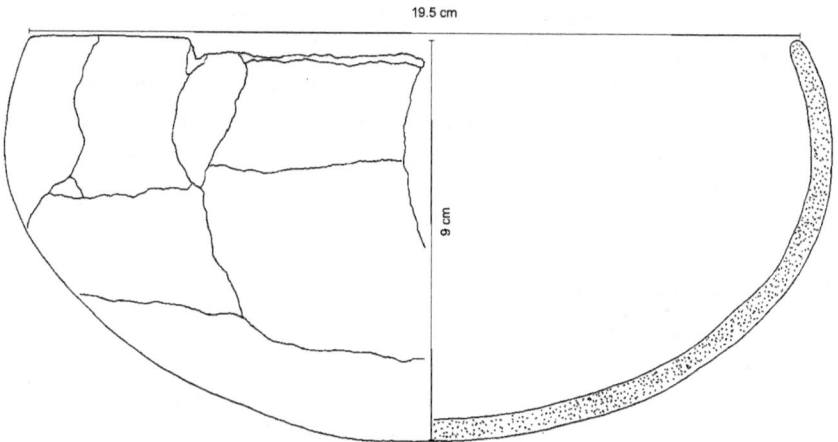

FIGURE 8.5. *The Rascal Rabbit bowl.*

paste as isolated minerals and in the rock fragments. Black opaque inclusions, likely weathered biotite, are present in the rock fragments as well. Mineral grains and rock fragments range from fine to coarse in size, based on the Wentworth Scale for describing the size of sediments. The rock fragments suggest that the syenite was equigranular. However, the presence of isolated coarse-sized grains of untwinned alkali feldspar in the ceramic paste indicates that the texture of the syenite was more variable than indicated by the rock fragments alone.

Petrographic analysis of brownware pottery from Robinson Pueblo (LA 46326) showed that the majority of its sherds contained syenite (Stewart et al. 1990), which is present in the Sierra Blanca area (Allen and Foord 1991). Robinson, a Lincoln-phase pueblo dating to the late thirteenth century, is located at the north end of the Sierra Blanca/Capitan/Sacramento Highlands region of the Jornada, on the eastern side of the Patos Mountains, about 5 km north of the town of Capitan, New Mexico. These areas are therefore potential points of manufacture for the bowl found at Rascal Rabbit (figure 8.1).

LIPID RESIDUE ANALYSIS

A single sherd from the bowl was submitted for lipid residue analysis (Malainey 2011). The fatty acid composition of the residue extracted from the sherd from the Rascal Rabbit bowl resembled that of decomposed medium-fat-content foods, which can result from the preparation of plant products, such as mesquite, corn and cholla, and/or from animal products, such as freshwater fish, terrapin, *Rabdotus* snail, and late winter, fat-depleted elk. The source of the residue was likely plant, given the presence of a plant-derived sterol β-sitosterol (Dudd and Evershed 1998; Evershed 1993; Evershed et al. 1997; Malainey 2007). The level of C16:1 (palmitoleic acid) in the residue of the sherd was very high; this fatty acid is known to be elevated in the decomposed cooking residues of certain fish and birds, suggesting that fish or birds has also been cooked in the vessel.

FOURIER TRANSFORM INFRARED
SPECTROSCOPY ANALYSIS (FTIR)

PaleoResearch conducted a FTIR analysis of another sherd from the Rascal Rabbit bowl (Cummings et al. 2011; see appendix for methodological details). The FTIR analysis yielded peaks representing the presence of absorbed water, fats/oils/lipids and/or plant waxes, protein, aromatic rings, humates, cellulose and carbohydrates, and arabinogalactorhamnoglycan, a polysaccharide. Water may have been absorbed from the surrounding ground or may have collected in the vessel during episodes of precipitation. The Rascal Rabbit site is located on a hilltop that overlooks a draw that may have received runoff at certain times of the year, but more reliable natural springs would have been present at the base of the nearby Maroon Cliffs, a short walk of 3 to 5 km to the east.

Matches with raw and baked pulp suggest that *Agave* was contained in this vessel in both its raw and cooked forms. The Mescalero Apache, who ranged throughout southeastern New Mexico, at least in the historic period, if not earlier, are named for their consumption of mescal, a food made from agave (see also Miller and Montgomery, chapter 12, this volume). The Mescalero roasted plant hearts and young leaves, baked "roots," and roasted or boiled agave stalks (Castetter 1935; Whitehead and Flynn 2016). Raw agave leaves are toxic, containing saponins that could be used as soap and to kill fish (Whitehead and Flynn 2016:96)

Other matches included possible (but not conclusively matching) contributions from *Zea mays* cupules and raw *Zea mays* kernels, starchy roots and tubers, and oak nutshells, as well as cooked fish meat. Based on this analysis, we can say it appears the inhabitants of the site had been cooking fish they harvested from the Pecos River or Black River, located ca. 30 km from the site; we are unable, however, to identify the particular species or types of fish that were being used within the bowl collected from Feature 4. It should be noted that a uniface collected near a feature elsewhere at Rascal Rabbit and tested for protein residue yielded a positive to gizzard shad antisera. Gizzard shad are identified as a native fish of the Pecos drainage system (Propst 1999:table 2).

SAMPLES FROM BENEATH THE VESSEL

As stated above, charcoal was submitted from the fill beneath the vessel for AMS dating. This charcoal produced a 2σ date of cal. AD 1185–1200 and AD 1205–1280 (Cummings et al. 2011; PRI-09-08-534). Charcoal from beneath the vessel was analyzed by both McBride (2011) and Cummings et al. (2011) and both analysts identified this material as *Condalia* (javelina bush). The flotation sample from beneath the vessel produced uncharred remains of local *Mollugo* (carpetweed), *Portulaca* (purslane), and *Talinum* (flameflower), and the pollen analysis of this sediment found high-spine Asteraceae (sunflower family), along with *Prosopis* (mesquite), *Pinus* (pine), *Quercus* (oak),

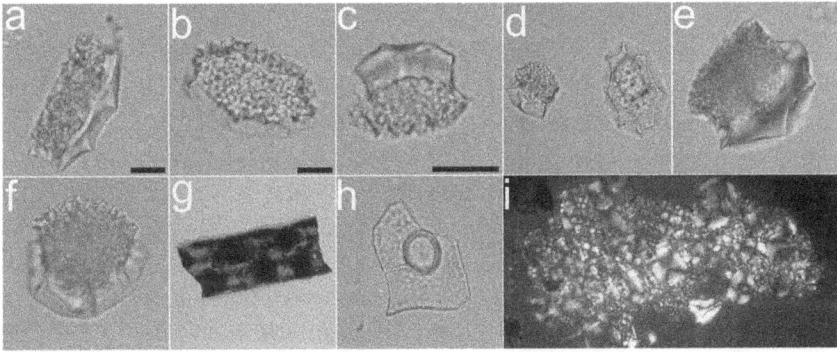

FIGURE 8.6. *Micrographs of phytoliths and starch grains recovered from samples associated with the vessel. All micrographs taken at approximately 400x magnification. Scale bar in a, b, and c equals 10 µm. (a–f) Commelina erecta seed epidermis phytoliths in various orientations. Large Commelina phytolith morphotype in (a) side view (long axis 36 µm) and (b) top view. (c) Small Commelina phytolith morphotype in side view (18 µm; note change in scale). (d) Large (top view) and small (side view) morphotypes in the same field of view. Another of the large morphotype in (e) side view and (f) bottom view. (g) Asteraceae seed hull epidermis phytolith. (h) Cyperaceae achene (seed) phytolith likely derived from Cyperus or Scirpus. (i) Large cluster of mostly grass-seed starch, with some root/tuber types as well. This starch cluster was recovered from residue removed from the interior surface of one of the vessel sherds.*

Artemisia (sagebrush), low-spine Asteraceae (ragweed family), Brassicaceae (mustard family), cheno-am, *Ephedra* (Mormon tea), Geraniaceae (geranium family), and Poaceae (grasses)—all consistent with environment on and around Tower Hill.

The pollen sample also contained starches: (both unaltered and cooked) grass seed and *Hordeum/Elymus*-type (little barley grass, wild rye, and/or wheatgrass) seed starch. The identifiable phytoliths recovered from beneath the vessel indicate the presence of hundreds, if not thousands of seed coat (endotesta) phytoliths from whitemouth dayflower *Commelina erecta* (figure 8.6a–f), numerous Asteraceae seed hull epidermis phytoliths (figure 8.6g), as well as sedge (Cyperaceae) achene (seed) phytoliths (figure 8.6h), another possible food source. The phytolith sample also contained water organism microfossils in the form of concentricysts and freshwater sponge spicules and spherasters, possibly derived from water once contained in the vessel. Most of the materials from beneath the vessel appear to be the remains of locally available (or potentially so) plants

SAMPLES FROM WITHIN THE VESSEL

Sediments from the interior of the vessel were also analyzed for pollen, phytoliths, and starches. Pollen from within the vessel included more cheno-am and slightly more Poaceae than found in the soils beneath the vessel, suggesting grass seeds had been present in the vessel. The vessel fill also contained a root- or tuber-type starch. Phytolith analysis of the fill yielded primarily an environmental record. No *Commelina* phytoliths were observed during the 300-phytolith count, and only two were observed during the subsequent scan for rare and underrepresented types. This is important because if *Commelina* seeds were being blown into the vessel after abandonment, their phytoliths would have been present at much higher levels, suggesting that the two represent seeds that the vessel's owners put into the bowl. Residue from the interior surface of the vessel was also examined for phytolith and starches. *Commelina* phytoliths were present in this residue, suggesting their likely transfer from vessel residue to vessel fill. One large cluster comprising hundreds of grass-seed starch grains was also recovered (figure 8.6i). It should be noted that in the sediment beneath the vessel, 71 out of 301 phytoliths were derived from *Commelina*. This is an extraordinary concentration that remains unprecedented. As of this writing, *Commelina* phytoliths have been recovered by coauthor Yost from over 30 prehistoric and historic sites in North and South America, with 17 of these sites located in New Mexico (table 8.1). *Commelina* phytolith concentrations at these sites rarely exceed 1 or 2 per 300 total phytoliths counted. Thus, the phytolith evidence suggests that whitemouth dayflower seeds (whole or processed) were contained in this vessel and that their remains may have washed or leaked out into the underlying soil.

Discussion of *Commelina*

Commelina erecta or dayflower is a perennial herb that grows in clumps, and flowers from spring to fall. It can be found growing in rocky woods and hillsides, scrub oak woods, pine woods and barrens, sand dunes, hummocks, shale barrens, roadsides, railroad rights-of-way, fields, and occasionally as a weed in cultivated ground (Faden 2000). Dayflower seeds are an important winter food for quail, and the current distribution of this plant on the New Mexico landscape reflects the habitat and range of various quail species in southeastern New Mexico at present (Cummings and Kováčik 2013:35–38). As noted above, *Commelina* phytoliths (mostly *Commelina erecta*) have been identified in 48 samples from 30 prehistoric and four historic-era archaeological sites in North and South America. For Jornada sites in southern New Mexico, 24 samples

TABLE 8.1. Summary of New Mexico sites with *Commelina erecta* phytoliths

PRI Project #	Site	County	Commelina phytolith recovery	Cultigen & wild plant food evidence (1 = same sample, 2 = same site)	Site/Feature Age or Affiliation
08-48	FB 17153	Doña Ana	Midden	(1) Maize pollen and phytoliths	Late Formative
08-60	LA 51225	Doña Ana	Sherd	(1) Maize cupules, wild potato starch (2) Maize pollen and phytoliths, *Gossypium* seed	AD 1100–1250
08-95	LA 149268	Eddy	Backhoe trench	(1) None (2) Grass-seed starch	AD 640–770
09-08	LA 149260	Eddy	Vessel	(1) Maize lipid & FTIR signatures (2) Grass-seed starch, tuber starch	AD 1185–1200
09-22	LA 99434	Eddy	A) Buried stain B) Buried stain	A(1) Maize starch B(1) None	A) AD 540–650 B) AD 1280–1400
09-29	LA 36985	Otero	Groundstone	(1) Maize FTIR signature (2) Maize kernels and small charred seeds	AD 610–665
09-140	FB 9153	Doña Ana	Mano	(1) Torn cheno-am pollen, legume pollen & CaOx phytolith, *Hordeum/Elymus*-type starch	Early Formative
09-140	FB 223	Doña Ana	Metate	(1) Deteriorated starch (seed or root)	Early Formative
10-63	LA 103961	Doña Ana	Buried stain	(1) cf. Maize starch, grass-seed starch	Jornada Mogollon
10-63	LA 129534	Doña Ana	Buried stain	(1) cf. Maize starch, grass-seed starch	Early Archaic to Mesilla phase
10-63	LA 129535	Doña Ana	Buried stain	(1) Cyperaceae achene (seed) phytoliths	Late Mesilla to Doña Ana phase
10-63	LA 129543	Doña Ana	A) Buried stain B) Buried stain	A(1) *Hordeum/Elymus*-type starch B(1) cf. Maize starch, *Hordeum/Elymus*-type starch	Mesilla to El Paso phase

continued on next page

TABLE 8.1—*continued*

PRI Project #	Site	County	Commelina phytolith recovery	Cultigen & wild plant food evidence (*1 = same sample, 2 = same site*)	Site/Feature Age or Affiliation
11-76	LA 171726	Eddy	A) Buried stain B) Buried stain	A(1) Grass-seed starch, baked cactus fruit FTIR signature B(1) Grass-seed phytoliths (dendriforms) and Cyperaceae achene phytoliths, baked cactus fruit FTIR signature	550–400 BC
12-13	LA 118226	Eddy	Buried stain	(1) Grass-seed phytoliths (dendriforms) and Asteraceae-seed phytoliths, cf. maize phytolith, *Prosopis* endocarp	Jornada Mogollon
12-67	LA 172823	Eddy	Buried stain	(1) Maize and squash phytoliths, grass-seed starch, charred acorn, and *Eragrostis* seed	AD 970–1030
12-114	LA 111429	Sierra	Buried stain	(1) Grass-seed phytoliths (dendriforms), grass-seed starch, prickly-pear fruits and pads, yucca caudex, seeds from cheno-ams, spruge, dropseed, and other grasses	AD 1490–1600 to AD 1950
12-137	LA 174561	Eddy	Buried stain	(1) Maize phytoliths, Cyperaceae-achene phytoliths, Asteraceae-seed phytoliths, grass-seed and/ or maize starch, root/tuber starch	AD 650–710 and AD 740–770

from 17 sites (out of an estimated 100 sites examined between 2008 and 2014) yielded *Commelina* phytoliths, with nine of these samples (37.5%) also yielding diagnostic evidence of maize (table 8.1). Of the 15 sites lacking evidence of cultigens, all but two yielded phytolith, starch, or macrofloral evidence of seed processing. The intriguing question regarding the recovery of *Commelina* seed phytoliths is whether their presence at archaeological sites is a reflection of their intentional use, or whether the dayflower plant is simply adventitious of anthropogenic disturbance (and a relationship with quail who might favor these subsequently bushy disturbed areas). So far, the evidence, although favoring anthropogenic disturbance, appears to be mixed in a few cases. On one hand, *Commelina* roots and greens are edible (Sturtevant 1919), and the seeds are enclosed in a modified leaf-like structure called a spathe, which could easily be cooked with the rest of the plant. Also, the seeds are relatively large, edible, and pop (and taste) like popcorn when parched, so they may be targeted as well for consumption. However, the weedy nature of this plant also makes the unintentional consumption scenario just as plausible. Incidentally, the fact that the seeds pop after just a few minutes exposure to direct heat may in part explain their paucity in macrofloral records. Also, charred *Commelina* endosperm fragments actually resemble charred maize-kernel endosperm and may simply be unidentified or misidentified in macrofloral samples.

Commelina is a well-documented weed of today's agricultural fields worldwide; in Texas, 20 dayflower seeds per 1 kg of processed white rice seed is typical (Wilson 1981). Eichhorn et al. (2010), in their study of *Commelina* plants and phytoliths in West Africa, have linked the occurrence of different species of *Commelina* with specific types of anthropogenic disturbance, such as cultivated fields, heavily fertilized fields, periodically inundated fields, village vegetation, ruderal plant communities, and fallow fields. *Commelina*-seed phytoliths have been recovered from archaeological investigations of historic-era agricultural fields in Connecticut (Yost 2010a) and Canada (Yost 2010b), as well as from stone-lined prehistoric agricultural fields at Coctaca in Argentina (Yost and Scott-Cummings 2010a) and canal-irrigated field samples at Las Capas, near Tucson, Arizona (Yost 2015). At Las Capas, maize pollen and phytoliths, and *Commelina erecta* and *Commelina dianthifolia* phytoliths in Stratum 504 (800–730 BC) samples, were ubiquitous. Since maize and *Commelina* phytoliths have also been recovered in tandem from sherd residue, groundstone tools, hearths, and in two cases, storage pits from sites in Minnesota (Yost 2012) and Georgia (Yost and Scott-Cummings 2010b), there must be an explanation for its presence in both unprocessed and processed foodstuffs. *Commelina erecta* (the species at most of these sites) can grow one to two feet in height. Maize that was planted deep may only grow two or three feet high, and the lowest ears would be well within the reach of *Commelina erecta* stems and this may account for its widespread presence, as small viney stems and inflorescence parts become intertwined with husks. Another possibility is that *Commelina* may have been used as a buffering layer and steam generator for earth oven or related cookery, as *Commelina* plants are mucilaginous and have about 12% water content by weight. And finally, *Commelina* plants have antimicrobial properties (Ibrahim et al. 2010) and may have been added to harvested or processed foodstuffs to prevent spoilage.

The association of dayflower with disturbed contexts, such as agricultural fields and roadsides, suggests that its presence can often be tied to human activity. While the widespread removal of grass by grazing may have led to the creation of a loose sandy dunal landscape (Hall 2002), it may also be that the activities that create archaeological sites caused small patches of vegetal disturbance where *Commelina* might gain a foothold. Whether *Commelina* comes to be present or not, these weakened patches of desert floor may be the most susceptible to eolian erosion, leading to the oft-noted association between dunal blowouts and archaeology in southeastern New Mexico. *Commelina* had been found on perhaps 17% of the sites from which Cummings and Kováčik (2013) examined samples across southern New Mexico between 2008 and 2013. In 2013, 69% of 500 radiocarbon samples collected by the Carlsbad BLM across southwestern New Mexico as part of a research project funded by their Permian Basin Programmatic Agreement program (see Rocek, chapter 2, endnote 1, this volume) yielded *Commelina* phytoliths (Cummings and Kováčik 2013). This frequency and distribution suggest that the plant does not represent ubiquitous disturbance vegetation that is always associated with human activity. Rather there is a "synergistic relationship between the distribution of this plant, the habitat and range of the quail, and probably also the distribution of thermal features (disturbance) on the landscape" (Cummings and Kováčik 2013:35). In the case of the Rascal Rabbit bowl, whether *Commelina* came to be in the Tower Hill vicinity as a result of past human activity or not, it was present in sufficient concentration to argue for its very deliberate placement in this bowl.

DISCUSSION

The analyses described above indicate that this Jornada Brown bowl was made in the mountains some 200 km to the west (see figure 8.1), used to transport, cook, and/or process cooked and uncooked agave, acorn, possibly maize, and fish, either prior to its deposition in Feature 4, or as part of a stew containing all the ingredients for which we found evidence. At Feature 4, the vessel appears to have been placed above a javelina bush–fueled fire sometime between cal. AD 1185 and 1200 or AD 1205 and 1280, where it was used to cook or warm grass seeds and whitemouth dayflower greens and/or seeds.

Pottery has been thought to have developed as part of the "Neolithic toolkit"—that is, a suite of technologies tied in with increasing sedentism and agriculture (e.g., Arnold 1988; Forenbaher and Miracle 2005) and therefore out of place among fully mobile seed-gatherers. Eerkens (2003) has argued that mobile groups in the western Great Basin could use ceramics in quantity, despite frequent moves, as ceramics could be cached across the landscape at favored locations. Cached ceramic vessels are often found in other parts of New Mexico, secreted away in rocky alcoves, but are not encountered in the sands in southeastern New Mexico. A lack of cached vessels in the local archaeological record may be a reflection of poor site-preservation rather than human behavior, as a vessel buried in loose and rapidly deflating sands lacks the protective rocky "shell" that other parts of New Mexico provide in abundance.

Eerkens (2003:729) is concerned with how mobile groups may have scheduled ceramic production in conjunction with the best season to be moving around the landscape, foraging. Arnold (1988) and Eerkens (2003) both argue that sedentary groups tend to make pottery, semisedentary groups make pottery less often, and fully nomadic groups do not seem to make pottery at all. Eerkens makes the case that "occupational redundancy in areas with resources suited to mass collecting and boiling, especially small seeds, should be better correlated with pottery use" (Eerkens 2003:736). Eerkens's thoughts concerning pottery use were prompted by his work in the Great Basin but are borne out by discoveries elsewhere in the world.

The earliest Asian and sub-Saharan African ceramics are not associated with sedentism or agriculture. Early ceramics dating from 20,000 years ago from south China and sherds from Ounjougou in Mali dating prior to 9400 BC are related to intensification in the use of small-seeded grasses (Huysecom et al. 2009; Kuzmin 2006; Richerson et al. 2001; Wu et al. 2012). It is therefore no surprise that a presumably nomadic or seminomadic group would use a ceramic bowl to cook small seeds in the grasslands of southeastern New Mexico. Nor should it be unexpected that such a vessel would contain the residues of other locally available plant resources such as agave, and acorns, likely obtained from *Quercus havardii*, the shinnery oak.

As Hill (2009; see also chapter 9) has recently pointed out, the majority of the brownware ceramics recovered in southeastern New Mexico appear to have originated in the Lincoln County porphyry belt, which encompasses the mountainous regions of southeastern New Mexico (in the Sierra Blanca/Capitan/Sacramento Highlands portion of the Jornada) or from the El Paso area. Some sherds of Chupadero Black-on-white analyzed for the Intrepid Potash project appear to have originated even further west in the Chupadera Mesa area on the northern fringe of the Jornada region. According to Akins (2003), Wiseman (2002), and most recently Hill (2009; chapter 9, this volume), the presence of these brownware vessels in the desert of southeastern New Mexico may represent a seasonally mobile phase for the residents of the Sierra Blanca/Capitan Highlands and Tularosa Basin regions of the Jornada or an active trade in ceramics between more sedentary pottery-producing horticulturalists and hunter-gatherer groups.

Maize has remained an unknown but suspected economic plant east of the Pecos until recently, despite recovery of a charred maize cupule from Site LA 104607, a Formative-period site near Bear Grass Draw (Clifton 1995; see Railey, chapter 13, this volume). Clifton's excavation was conducted prior to the construction of a well pad, and like most compliance-related "gray literature" in southeastern New Mexico, remained barely known outside of the regulatory offices that collect such documents. Then Condon, Kuehn, et al. (2008) discovered maize starch on a piece of groundstone at another Formative-period site also near Bear Grass Draw. Boggess (2009) subsequently found evidence indicating the processing of maize in the Jornada's Eastern Extension during the Formative period, as well as some evidence suggesting Late Archaic maize processing (Boggess 2010; 2011). Maize remains were found at LA 149279, located to the northwest of Tower Hill at the HB Potash mine, in a thermal feature that produced a 2σ date of cal. 790–510 BC (Beta-254033) (Boggess 2011). Maize was also recovered at LA 159599, on the western slopes of Tower Hill, in a thermal feature that has produced a 2σ date of cal. 760–400 BC (Beta-261691) (Boggess 2010). More recently, staff at the Carlsbad BLM collected 500 radiocarbon samples from stain features at a variety of sites throughout southeastern New Mexico, including a stain feature at Site LA 43414, (the Merchant site), a Late Formative habitation site an estimated 45 km east of Rascal Rabbit. This sample contained maize kernels and a cupule that had a 2σ date of cal. AD 1384–1428 (PRI-13–050–405Z) (Cummings and Kováčik 2013). The most recent work at the Merchant site has recovered maize cupule and cob fragments, as well as maize pollen, though most dates collected during the 2016 excavations at the Merchant site fall between AD 1300 and 1400 and post-date the Rascal Rabbit bowl (Miller et al. 2016). Phytoliths from two other samples in this BLM study suggested the Late Archaic and Late Formative samples were of the popcorn-type of maize (Cummings and Kováčik 2013:38).

However, despite the expanding body of maize discoveries in the Pecos River Corridor within the Eastern Extension, there has yet to be evidence that the maize was grown in any of the locations investigated, only that maize had been cooked in firepits in those locations. As Railey (chapter 13, this volume) notes, while Late Formative "villages" developed in the highlands and parts of the Eastern Extension, none has yet been identified in the Pecos River

Corridor. Nonetheless, the occupants of Rascal Rabbit cooked maize within the vessel found in Feature 4, either at the Rascal Rabbit site or at whatever location they had previously occupied. The source of the maize found at the site is unknown, but it is tantalizing and not entirely unreasonable to hypothesize that the local occupants of Rascal Rabbit and the other sites in the vicinity either maintained garden plots in more favorable locations or obtained the maize from agriculturalist neighbors, such as the inhabitants of the Sierra Blanca/Capitan/Sacramento Highlands, the Tularosa Basin, or an as yet unidentified nearby site similar to the later Merchant site.

If a group left the Sierra Blanca/Capitan/Sacramento Highlands or even the Tularosa Basin and made their way to Tower Hill, they may have brought maize with them and it is very likely that they came into contact with the Pecos or Black Rivers, both of which provide a habitat for fish, including the gizzard shad (which lives in flowing water). At the closest points, the Pecos River is, in its present course, approximately 30 km west of Tower Hill and the Black River is 32 km southwest of Tower Hill. Although the fish residue in the Rascal Rabbit bowl may not have been created during preparation of a meal at Rascal Rabbit, the positive reaction to gizzard shad antisera on the uniface collected elsewhere on this site suggests that fish were obtained from one of the rivers and the tool and the bowl used to process these fish were brought to the Tower Hill area. It is possible that this vessel was deliberately cached in this location, and other examples of cached vessels in southeastern New Mexico have not survived the coming of cattle and the attendant deflation of the landscape. Rascal Rabbit and neighboring sites in the Tower Hill area may be examples of "occupational redundancy" that Eerkens has argued for in the Great Basin with mobile groups returning to favored locations over time (Eerkens 2003).

Unambiguous evidence of *Commelina erecta* seeds and/or greens from the Jornada Brown vessel is intriguing, and adds to the mix of evidence from across North America indicating both purposeful and perhaps inadvertent incorporation of dayflower plant remains to processed and stored foodstuffs. It also supports the possibility mentioned above of the existence of small-scale horticulture in the Late Formative along the Pecos River Corridor. Although rarely documented in North and South America, *Commelina* has reported medicinal and subsistence uses. Infusions of dayflower were used by the Navajo as an aphrodisiac (Wyman and Harris 1941), and were used to treat tuberculosis (Moerman 1999). The Maya added *Commelina* to their maize dough to aid fermentation in the preparation of *pozol* (Austin 2004). Although its exact purpose at the Rascal Rabbit site is unknown, increasing awareness of the presence of this plant at archaeological sites via phytolith analysis will undoubtedly shed light on a plant that may have been, until now, an invisible component of the archaeobotanical record. At a minimum, micro-botanical *Commelina* remains may serve as useful indicators of anthopogenic landscape disturbance or even in certain cases, ancient agricultural activities, possibly even in the Eastern Extension.

The discovery of a complete vessel within the very feature in which it was used provided us with an opportunity to examine the contents of the feature and the vessel. Although the observation is not new, the find also supports the relationship between the ceramic-producing sites in the Sierra Blanca/Capitan/Sacramento Highlands and the Western Jornada Lowlands with sites in southeastern New Mexico.

At a methodological level, the analysis of this vessel allowed us to compare fatty lipid analysis with FTIR. While lipid-residue analysis and FTIR are differing analytical techniques that examine similar data sets and provide different resulting sets concerning the residues on the vessel, the combination of lipid-residue analysis and FTIR served to complement each other and appeared to offer some confirmation of each other's results.

At a broader level, the relationship between the adoption of ceramic technology and small-seed processing found in other parts of the world is supported by this find in southeastern New Mexico. Moreover, the discovery of this vessel on an eroded surface typical of the Eastern Extension shows that eroded sites still have data to offer, especially if several analytical techniques are applied. Finally, any model of Formative-period mobile gatherers in southeastern New Mexico should not rely overly on descriptions provided by later Spanish explorers of poverty-stricken wretches, having nothing, and collecting prickly pear pads across the desert. The brownware sherds that are scattered throughout the Eastern Extension of the Jornada represent more than occasional scraps of trade. Rather, they reflect a broad and complex social and economic system that relied both on exploitation of local resources and on a network of trade and mobility that involved the movement of people and a range of food resources as well as the archaeologically more visible pottery. The people who left their bowl at Rascal Rabbit appear to have entered what are now the dunes of southeastern New Mexico with a network of social ties to the west, a detailed knowledge of local resources, and larder of foods obtained elsewhere, reflecting a level of sophistication to the Eastern Extension of the Jornada that is not widely recognized.

Lipid and FTIR Analyses

Lipid Analysis

Mary Malainey

Lipids are a broad category of compounds that are insoluble in water; those of archaeological interest include fatty acids, triacylglycerols, sterols, waxes, and terpenes. Fatty acids are the major constituents of fats and oils (lipids) and occur in nature as triglycerides: that is, three fatty acids attached to a glycerol molecule by ester-linkages.

The identification criteria used herein were developed by analyzing the fatty acid compositions of more than 130 uncooked Native food plants and animals from western Canada using gas chromatography (Malainey 1997; Malainey et al. 1999a) and examining the effects of cooking and degradation over time. Malainey (1997; Malainey et al. 1999b) determined that levels of medium-chain fatty acids can be used to distinguish degraded experimental cooking residues (Malainey 1997; Malainey et al. 1999b). In her studies, higher levels of medium-chain fatty acids, combined with low levels of both $C18:0$ and $C18:1$ isomers, were detected in the decomposed experimental residues of plants, such as roots, greens, and most berries. In contrast, high levels of $C18:0$ indicated the presence of large herbivores, while moderate levels of $C18:1$ isomers, with low levels of $C18:0$, indicated the presence of either fish or foods similar in composition to corn. High levels of $C18:1$, isomers with low levels of $C18:0$, were found in residues of beaver or foods of similar fatty acid composition. The criteria for identifying six types of residues were therefore established experimentally; and a seventh type, plant with large herbivore, was inferred.

Malainey and colleagues (2000a, 2000b, 2000c, 200d, 2001; Quigg et al. 2001) have continued research to understand the decomposition patterns of various foods and food combinations (Malainey et al. 2000a, 2000b, 2000c, 2001; Quigg et al. 2001) and the collection of modern foods has expanded to include plants from the Southern Plains so that the fatty acid compositions of a variety of food plants from that region have been determined. Experimental residues of many of these plants, alone or in combination with deer meat, have been prepared by boiling foods in clay cylinders or using sandstone for either stone boiling (Quigg et al. 2000) or as a griddle. In order to accelerate the processes of oxidative degradation that naturally occur at a slow rate with the passage of time, the rock or clay tile containing the experimental residue was placed in an oven at 75°C. After either 30 or 68 days, residues were extracted and analyzed using gas chromatography. The results of these decomposition studies enabled refinement of the identification criteria (Malainey 2007).

High-temperature gas chromatography is used in lipid-residue analysis to separate and assess a wide range of lipid components, including specifically the fatty acids, long-chain alcohols and hydrocarbons, sterols, waxes, terpenoids, and triacylglycerols (Evershed et al. 2001). The molecular structure of separated components is elucidated by high-temperature gas chromatography with mass spectrometry (HT-GC/MS) (Evershed 2000).

Sterols are particularly useful for distinguishing animal-derived residues, which contain cholesterol and significant levels of both triacylglycerols, from plant-derived residues, indicated by plant sterols, such as β-sitosterol, stigmasterol, and campesterol, and only traces of triacylglycerols (Evershed 1993; Evershed et al. 1997; Dudd and Evershed 1998). Terpenoid compounds, or terpenes, are long-chain alkenes that occur in the tars and pitches of higher plants. The use of GC and GC/MS to detect the diterpenoid, dehydroabietic acid, from conifer products in archaeological residues extends over a span of 25 years (Shackley 1982; Heron and Pollard 1988).

Fourier Transform Infrared Spectroscopy (FTIR) Analysis

Linda Scott Cummings, Chad Yost, Kathryn Puseman, and Melissa K. Logan

Infrared spectroscopy (IR) is the study of how molecules absorb infrared radiation and ultimately convert it to heat, revealing how the infrared energy is absorbed and showing the structure of specific organic molecules. One of the primary advantages of FTIR is that it measures all wavelengths simultaneously. It has a relatively high signal-to-noise ratio and a short measurement time. Each peak in the spectrum represents either a chemical bond or a functional group. Since molecular structures absorb the vibrational frequencies or wavelengths of infrared radiation, the bands of absorbance can be used to identify the composition of the materials under study. Carbohydrates, lipids, proteins, and other organic molecules are associated with specific wave number bands (Isaksson 1999:36–39). The infrared spectrum can be divided into two regions—the functional group region and the fingerprint region. These two groups are recognized by the effect that infrared radiation has on the respective molecules of these groups. The functional group region is located between 4 and 1.5 kHz. The molecular bonds display specific characteristic vibrations that identify fats, lipids, waxes, lignins, proteins, carbohydrates, and so on. The fingerprint region, located below 1.5 kHz, is influenced by bending motions, which further identify the molecules present.

Using FTIR, it is possible to identify various types of organic compounds and eventually recognize different types of materials such as plant or animal fats or lipids, plant waxes, esters, proteins, carbohydrates, and more. Specific regions of the spectrum are important in identifying these compounds. The results of the identification of specific wavelengths can be compared with commercial or laboratory-created analytical standards to identify the specific types of bonds present in different materials. By combining the results of the analysis of individual samples with all of the reference materials in the PaleoResearch library, the percentage match with individual reference items can be displayed. For instance, plant lipids or fats are identifiable between 3 and 2.8 kHz. A match might be obtained on this portion of the spectrum with nuts such as hickory, walnut, or acorn, or with animal fats or corn oil. Recovery of high-level matches with several types of nuts (in this example) indicates that nuts were processed. If the match with the library is for meat fats, then the signature is more consistent with that produced by meat rather than plant parts such as nuts.

For this study, a mixture of chloroform and methanol was used as a solvent to remove lipids and other organic substances that had soaked into the surface of the ceramic. This solvent and sample were placed in a glass container and allowed to sit, covered, for several hours. After this period of time, the solvent was pipetted into an aluminum evaporation dish, where the solvent was allowed to evaporate. This process leaves the residue of any absorbed chemicals in the aluminum dishes. The residue remaining in the aluminum dishes was then placed on the FTIR crystal and the spectra were collected. The aluminum dishes were tilted during the process of evaporation to separate the lighter from the heavier fraction of the residue. The lighter and heavier fractions are designated Upper (lighter fraction) and Lower (heavier fraction), respectively, in the subsequent analysis. FTIR is performed using a Nicolet 6700 optical bench with an ATR and a silicon crystal. The sample is placed in the path of a specially encoded infrared beam. The infrared beam passes through the sample and produces a signal called an "interferogram." The interferogram contains information about the frequencies of infrared that are absorbed and the strength of the absorptions, which is determined by the sample's chemical make-up. A computer reads the interferogram and uses Fourier transformation to decode the intensity information for each frequency and presents a spectrum.

9

The Circulation of Prehistoric Ceramics in the Eastern Extension of the Jornada Mogollon

David V. Hill

This chapter describes the results of recent studies regarding the sources of clays used to manufacture prehistoric ceramics recovered in the lowland deserts of the Eastern Extension of the Jornada Mogollon (Eastern Jornada) area located in southeastern New Mexico and west Texas (see figure 1.2). The area discussed here is bordered in New Mexico by the Sierra Blanca/Capitan/Sacramento Highlands to the north and west. The Texas portion of the area covers roughly the "sand hill" country of west Texas to the margins of the Southern Plains grasslands. This eastern boundary extends from Lubbock and Crosbyton in the Texas Panhandle south to Iraan, including the saline lakes east of the Guadalupe Mountains (Boyd 1997; Corley 1965; Lehmer 1948; Leslie 1979) (figure 9.1). These ceramic studies not only tell us something about the clay sources of pottery, but also contribute to local chronology-building and to archaeological theory, leading to a greater understanding of the interaction of horticulturalists and mobile peoples (Akins 2003; Hill 2009; Wiseman 2002).

In the following sections I summarize the major compositional studies that have been conducted to identify sources of prehistoric pottery in the study region. I then present a brief overview of the ceramic types produced in southern New Mexico and west Texas and highlight specific analytical studies that have been used to characterize their distinctive raw materials. Finally, I present physical and chemical

DOI: 10.5876/9781607327950.c009

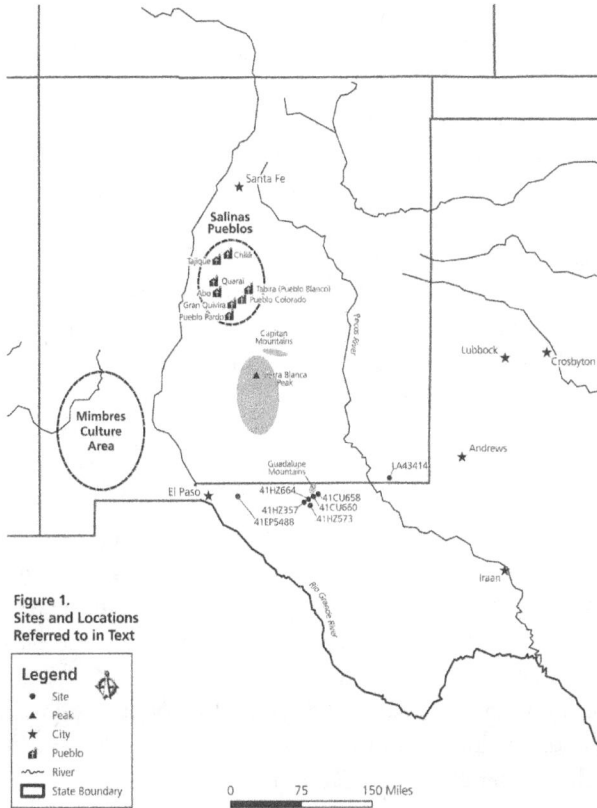

Figure 1.
Sites and Locations
Referred to in Text

Legend
• Site
▲ Peak
★ City
🏠 Pueblo
~~~ River
☐ State Boundary

0   75   150 Miles

FIGURE 9.1. *General study area and sites mentioned in the text.*

data from several studies to identify the manufacturing locales of the ceramics recovered at sites in this area as a means to understand how vessels circulated during the Formative period.

The Eastern Jornada area incorporates two major physiographic features: the Pecos River valley and the southern Llano Estacado. The Pecos valley in southeastern New Mexico is characterized by karst topography formed from the dissolution of evaporite minerals including gypsum, anhydrite, salt, and potash of the underlying Permian Artesia Group (Kelley 1971). Rising eastward at a slope of 1–5%, the Mescalero Plain lies between the Pecos River and the Llano Estacado escarpment and extends from Fort Sumner into the Texas Panhandle (see Railey, chapter 13, this volume, for environmental background of the Eastern Extension).

Prehistoric occupation in the Eastern Extension area was highly variable, with archaeological evidence of the contemporary presence of both settled and mobile peoples (see Railey, chapter 13). However, a few large sites, dating post–AD 1250, are located in the "Roswell Oasis" near Roswell, New Mexico, at the confluence of the Hondo and Pecos Rivers and have substantial architecture and extensive material inventories that often exceed hundreds of thousands of artifacts (in this volume, see Rocek and Kenmotsu, chapter 1, and Rocek, chapter 2; also Kelley 1984; Speth 2004b; Wiseman 2002).

Away from the Pecos River and its tributaries, scatters of ceramic sherds and chipped- and groundstone artifacts are by far the predominant archaeological manifestations (Hogan 2006). Sites both with and without architecture across the area exhibit repeated episodes of occupation (Hogan 2006). Where architecture is present away from major water sources, such as the Pecos, the ceramic evidence is much less substantial (Wheaton 2013; Zamora 2000). Sites with architecture dating after AD 1250 have been found associated with some of the larger playa lakes located east of the Pecos River valley (Bandy 2011; Brown 2010; Corley 1965; Leslie 1979). The limited investment in architecture and the presence of shallow midden deposits elsewhere in the region indicate episodic, repeated, or possibly year-round occupation of the playa lake sites. Evidence of maize is limited in the archaeological record of the sites located in the Eastern Jornada lowland deserts (Boggess 2009; Condon, Kuehn, et al. 2008; see also discussions in this volume by Rocek and Kenmotsu, chapter 1; Boggess et al., chapter 8; Railey, chapter 13).

SOURCES OF CERAMICS IN THE EASTERN JORNADA

The appearance and sources of plain-surfaced and decorated ceramics in the Eastern Jornada are areas of active research (Hogan 2006:4–16). One study places the introduction of ceramics area around AD 200 (Hill and Staley 1999). The temporal assessment is based on radiocarbon-dated features associated with undecorated ceramics at LA 22107 and LA 22122, two sites located on the western edge of Lea County, New Mexico, east-northeast of Carlsbad (figure 1.2) (Staley et al. 1996). Undecorated ceramics dating to the third century AD have also been documented in the El Paso area and eastern Mogollon sites located to the west of the Eastern Extension (Miller 2005a; Wilson 1999a). As described below, plain-surfaced and decorated ceramics from the El Paso region and other eastern Mogollon areas to the west and north are also commonly reported from more recent contexts in the Eastern Jornada.

Ceramics appear in artifact assemblages between AD 460 and 870 at the Townsend site near Roswell (Akins 2003; Maxwell 1986). However, in the adjacent Sierra Blanca Highland region, recent excavations along the Rio Hondo in Lincoln County reported that ceramics were not present until around AD 500 (Railey and Ruscavage-Barz 2008). Nonetheless, the uncertainty regarding the timing of the appearance of prehistoric ceramics in southeastern New Mexico is likely a function of the limited number of sites dating between AD 1 and 500. It is likely that ceramics appeared at different times across the area. As is discussed later, decorated and undecorated ceramics recovered from sites in the Eastern Jornada area were produced in different areas of southeastern New Mexico and west Texas.

Brown-colored utility wares are the most common types of pottery found in the Eastern Extension (Corley 1965). Classification of brownware ceramics in this portion of southern New Mexico and west Texas has relied primarily on surface attributes such as color and degree of polish and to a lesser extent visual identification of the mineral inclusions in the ceramic paste. However, prehistoric utility ware ceramics were commonly fired in an uncontrolled atmosphere that results in variation in the surface color by unevenly oxidizing their surfaces. Sherds of these plainware ceramics differ little from one another to the casual observer. Variation in paste color and the degree of surface polish used to classify the major brownware ceramic types in the region can overlap between different recognized ceramic types (Hill 2014; Wilson 1999b; Wiseman 2002). Also, the appearance of the surface of vessels, including the application of stone-polishing or other forms of surface smoothing, can be the result of cultural practices or reflect the properties of the ceramic clay (Bright and Ugan 1999; Hill 2012; Simms et al. 1997).

A confounding issue for establishing the appearance of ceramics is that most ceramics recovered from archaeological contexts in southeastern New Mexico and west Texas were made at a considerable distance from the sites of their ultimate deposition. To identify their source areas, two analytical techniques—petrographic analysis and instrumental neutron activation analysis (INAA)—have been used to measure their composition (Bishop et al. 1982; Neff and Glowacki 2002)

Petrographic analysis uses a polarized-light microscope to identify optically transparent minerals in ceramic clay bodies. Traditionally, inclusions observed in ceramics in the American Southwest have been viewed as an additive technology, though the presence of inclusions in the paste of ceramics should be viewed as a research question oriented toward the identification of the origin of the minerals present in ceramics, including whether the minerals were added to the clay body or are natural inclusions. To identify potential production sources, local clays and mineral samples collected near sites in areas of potential ceramic production should be analyzed for comparison with the ceramic samples. Petrographic analysis conducted in conjunction with the analysis of potential temper and clay resources leads to insights for identifying potential areas of production (Stewart et al. 1990). Where such data are not available, reference to relevant geological literature should be consulted in conjunction with ceramic petrographic studies.

INAA uses irradiation of samples to determine elemental composition for a wide range of materials including archaeological ceramics. INAA is a bulk analytical technique that combines data from both clay and non-clay inclusions. Together, petrographic analysis and INAA help to locate areas of ceramic production.

SOURCES OF PREHISTORIC CERAMICS RECOVERED FROM SOUTHERN NEW MEXICO AND WEST TEXAS

There has been some confusion regarding the origin and dating of the array of ceramics recovered from sites across the Jornada Mogollon region. This review is presented to clarify some of these details and to highlight several studies relating to local sources of ceramics. Through an understanding of the various sources it is possible to document nuanced patterns of ceramic circulation in the region.

CERAMICS PRODUCED IN THE TULAROSA BASIN

In the Tularosa Basin (figure 1.2), the majority of undecorated ceramics are classified as El Paso Brown (Lehmer 1948). Plain-surfaced ceramics in the Western Jornada began to be decorated in red or black designs by around AD 800/1000 with virtually all ceramics being decorated by AD 1300 (Miller 1995). Dates associated with El Paso Bichrome-Red and El Paso Bichrome-Black range between AD 800 and 1100/1250 (Miller 1991, 1995). By AD 1300 only El Paso Polychrome ceramics were produced in the Western Jornada and continued to be made until around AD 1450 (Miller 1995, 2005a). El Paso Polychrome vessels were widely traded across the Southwest, western Texas, northern Mexico, and as far northeast as south-central Kansas (Kenmotsu, chapter 10, this volume; Burgett 2006; Wedel 1982). As the lower two-thirds of El Paso Polychrome vessels are undecorated, it is likely that many of the El Paso Brownware sherds reported from the Eastern Extension represent the lower portions of El Paso Polychrome vessels. Thus, it is possible that some of the El Paso Brownwares are misclassified, a continual problem with the admittedly understudied plainware ceramics of any type (Hill 2014; Wilson 1999b).

El Paso Brown, Bichrome, and Polychrome sherds are characterized by a reddish-brown grading to black-colored paste and tempered with abundant coarse-sized angular fragments of quartz, white and pink alkali feldspar, and trace amounts of hornblende and brown biotite consistent with the use of granite as a tempering agent (Burgett 2006; Hill 1988). Brownwares of the El Paso tradition were produced primarily in the vicinity of El Paso, Texas, where granite is present in the nearby Franklin Mountains (Deen 1974; Harbour 1972).

CERAMICS PRODUCED IN THE LINCOLN COUNTY PORPHYRY BELT

To the northeast of the Tularosa Basin in the northern Sierra Blanca/ Capitan/Sacramento Highlands (see figure 1.2), plainware vessels, often highly polished and referred to as Jornada Brown (Howey and Rocek 2008; Jennings 1940; Stewart et al. 1990), continued to be produced until at least AD 1250 (Farwell et al. 1992). These ceramics were produced by prehistoric peoples living in and near what is known as the Lincoln County porphyry belt, which includes the intrusive rocks of the Sierra Blanca, Carrizo, Capitan, Jicarilla, and Patos Mountains (Allen and Foord 1991; Kelley 1984). The Capitan Pluton, which makes up the Capitan Mountains, is characterized as a Tertiary, compositionally zoned aplite to porphyritic alkali feldspar granite (Allen and McLemore 1991). The western end of the Capitan Pluton contains more quartz and has an equigranular texture. The eastern end is quartz poor and porphyritic, containing untwinned alkali feldspar, biotite, and hornblende (Allen and McLemore 1991). Other smaller mountainous areas within the Lincoln County porphyry belt are texturally and compositionally similar and may share a common origin with the contemporary Capitan Pluton (Allen and Foord 1991).

The western part of the Sierra Blanca region including Sierra Blanca Peak is part of the Sierra Blanca volcanic complex of Oligocene age. The Sierra Blanca volcanic complex has been divided into four formations: the Walker intrusive breccia, Church Mountain latite, Nogal Mountain syenite, and Godfrey Hills trachyte. Intrusive rocks include Rialto monzonite, Chavez Mountain monzonite, Three Rivers syenite, and the Bonito Lake stock, which includes biotite, syenite, andesite porphyry, quartz monzonite, and aplite dikes (Griswold 1959; Moore et al. 1991). Soils on the valley floors within the Sierra Blanca region are composed of loams and clay loams and frequently contain weathered fragments and mineral grains from the nearby intrusive rocks (Maker et al. 1971; Sidwell 1946). The presence of weathered fragments of local intrusive rocks and mineral grains in ceramic thin sections and samples of clay indicate that these sediments were used for the production of several types of ceramics in the region. Production of Jornada Brown pottery in in the Lincoln County porphyry belt has been documented through INAA and thin-section petrography of ceramics and local rock samples (Farwell et al. 1992; Garrett 1991; Hill 2009, 2014; Howey and Rocek 2008; Shah 1998; Stewart et al. 1990).

Another ceramic type from the Lincoln County porphyry belt is Chupadero Black-on-white, produced from AD 1050/1100 until about 1544 (Hayes et al. 1981; Wiseman 1982, 1986). Recent INAA and thin-section petrographic studies have identified five major sources for the production of this pottery type (Capone 2002; Clark 2006; Creel et al. 2002). These areas are at the Salinas Pueblos to the north-northwest of the Jornada and the Capitan and Jicarilla Mountains (at the north end of the Sierra Blanca/Capitan/Sacramento Highlands) (Creel et al. 2002) (see figure 9.1). One of the possible production locales has been identified by the presence of prehistoric pottery-making tools at LA 2315, in the Sierra Blanca Highlands just southwest of the Capitan Mountains (Farwell 1981). It has been suggested that some Chupadero Black-on-white pottery was also produced in the upper reaches of the Pecos River and its western tributaries (Clark 2006).

Other decorated types of pottery were possibly produced in the Lincoln County porphyry belt. Three Rivers Red-on-terracotta is made using a distinct light orange-brown firing clay and decorated with red geometric designs (Mera and Stallings 1931). Site LA 4921, located on the eastern side of the Tularosa Basin below the western edge of the Sierra Blanca Highlands is the type site for Three Rivers Red-on-terracotta (Bussey et al. 1976; Laumbach et al. 2002; Mera and Stallings 1931). The span of production for this type is poorly known but was probably between circa AD 1100/1150 and 1300/1350 (Wiseman 2002). Petrographic analysis of six sherds of Three Rivers Red-on-terracotta from LA 4921 in the low foothills just west of Sierra Blanca indicates that the sherds contained fragments of weathered granite (Southward 1979:98). Without additional comparative study and analysis of potential tempering material the source or sources of this type will remain unidentified.

Limited petrographic study has been conducted on the fourteenth-century ceramic type, Lincoln Black-on-red (Mera and Stallings 1931; Stewart 1979). The limited data show that Lincoln Black-on-red was made at several locations in the Capitan Mountains, possibly in some of the same communities as undecorated brownware (Kelley 1984; Warren 1992; Wilson 1999b; Wiseman 2016a, 2017).

Brownware vessels with red slips have also been reported from sites across southeastern New Mexico (Bussey et al. 1976; Laumbach et al. 2002; Peckham 1976). Red-slipped brownware ceramics have been classified variously as Jornada Red (Bussey et al. 1976) or red-slipped brownware (Jennings 1940; Peckham 1976; Wiseman 1981b). Red-slipped brownware was produced sometime between AD 500 and 1300 (Wiseman 2014:381) but the time of production is poorly understood. Early tenth-century dates have been reported from structures that yielded red-slipped brownwares at Taylor Draw (LA 6565) and site LA 71276, both of which are located in the northeastern edge of the Tularosa Basin (Levine 1997; Peckham 1976). At LA 86736, located near Three Rivers, also in the northeastern portion of the Tularosa Basin (just west of the Sierra Blanca Highlands), brownware ceramics with thin red slips were recovered from features dated to the eleventh century AD, based on their association with Style III Mimbres Black-on-white (Laumbach et al. 2002).

Playas Red and Playas Red Incised have the widest spatial distribution of the redware types, extending from the Arizona/New Mexico border to Eddy County, New Mexico. INAA studies of these two types have progressed enough to provide sufficient detail to identify particular sources of production (Speakman 2007).

Playas Red and Playas Red Incised were first identified during the analysis of Medio-period ceramics from Casas Grandes and were likely to have been produced in the vicinity of Casas Grandes (Sayles 1936b; Di Peso et al. 1974:volume 8). More recent research has demonstrated that Playas Red Incised was also produced in the Sierra Blanca/Capitan Mountain portion of the highlands, and in southwestern New Mexico as well as in Chihuahua (Bradley and Hoffer 1985; Warren 1992; Wiseman 1981b). Based on the original dating of the Casas Grandes Medio period, Playas Red and Playas Red Incised were dated to between AD 1060 and 1519, (Di Peso et al. 1974:volume 8). Subsequent redating of the Casas Grandes sequence indicates that Playas Red and Playas Red Incised were more likely to have been produced between AD 1200 and 1450 (Whalen and Minnis 2001b).

Survey and excavation in the Eastern Extension also yields corrugated pottery (Leslie 1979; Miller et al. 2016). In the sand hills of Texas and Lea County, New Mexico, the corrugated ware began production around AD 1300 and is known as Ochoa Indented Corrugated. Other corrugated wares were produced in the Gila and Mimbres drainages west of the Jornada Mogollon region (Anyon and LeBlanc 1984) as well as within the Jornada in the northern Sierra

Blanca/Capitan/Sacramento Highlands area (Kelley 1984; Wilson 1999b). In the highlands, corrugated ceramics were produced at the same time as plainwares and possibly in the same communities (Warren 1992).

OTHER PRODUCTION CENTERS OF CERAMICS
RECOVERED FROM THE EASTERN EXTENSION

Brownware ceramics have been documented to a lesser extent from survey along the Pecos just north of the study area (Jelinek 1967). South Pecos Brown, McKenzie Brown, and Roswell Brown were first identified between Fort Sumner and Roswell (Jelinek 1967). Some of these types are in need of revision (Chapman and Gerow 2006). South Pecos Brown is widely distributed in southeastern New Mexico (Jelinek 1967; Leslie 1979; Wiseman 2002). The distinctive angular, lavender-gray feldspar present in the temper of this type is indicative of an origin in the Sierra Blanca/Capitan Mountain region (Wiseman 2002; Wiseman et al. 1999).

Mimbres Black-on-white is also commonly reported from southeastern New Mexico (Chapman and Gerow 2006). Stylistic variation within Mimbres-series ceramic designations carry temporal significance (Anyon and LeBlanc 1984; Shafer and Brewington 1995). Style I, the former Mimbres Bold Face, was produced roughly AD 750 to 900. Style II began production sometime around AD 850, continuing until around 1010. Style III, or Mimbres Classic Black-on-white, was made between around AD 1010 and 1130 (Shafer 2003; Shafer and Brewington 1995). Mimbres Black-on-white pottery has been examined primarily through INAA. At least 10 areas of production have been identified (Dahlin 2003; Speakman 2007), all but one of which are located in southwestern New Mexico; the exception is an area on the Rio Grande in south-central New Mexico (Creel 2013).

COMPOSITIONAL ANALYSIS OF CERAMICS
FROM THE EASTERN EXTENSION

In a previous summary of petrographic analysis of a total of 203 brownware sherds recovered from 19 sites in southeastern New Mexico and 17 sites in west Texas (Hill 2009), the clear majority of the brownware was manufactured in either the El Paso region of the southern Tularosa Basin or in the Lincoln County porphyry belt in the northern Sierra Blanca/Capitan/Sacramento Highlands (table 9.1). The sites summarized in this study were scattered unevenly over a large area of southeastern New Mexico from the

TABLE 9.1. Sources of brownware ceramics from sites in the northern Sierra Blanca/Capitan/ Sacramento Highlands and the Eastern Extension identified through INAA and thin-section petrography (Hill 2014)

Locations for 2014 INAA/ Petrographic Analysis	N	El Paso area sources	Capitan/ Jicarilla source	Other source	Unassigned
Mountain sites	40	10	11	6*	13
Lowland sites	40	13	15	8†	4

* Includes four sherds that, based on petrographic analysis, are from a unique possible local source.
† Includes eight sherds that, based on petrographic analysis, are from a unique possible local source.

northwestern end of the Tularosa Basin of the Western Jornada to the Sierra Blanca/Capitan/Sacramento Highlands, extending along the Pecos River (particularly in southeast New Mexico east of the Pecos River to the east of Carlsbad and southwest of the Llano Estacado). In West Texas, the samples included sites up to about 100 km east of the New Mexico border and from about as far north as the latitude of Portales, New Mexico, south to a site east of Monahans, Texas (east of Pecos, Texas). Only a few sherds could not be attributed to production in the Tularosa Basin or the northern Sierra Blanca/ Capitan/Sacramento Highlands; these sherds were of unknown origin. The presence of brownware ceramics in southeastern New Mexico that originated in the Tularosa Basin and the highlands was also documented in an earlier petrographic study (Haskell 1977) but at that time comparative materials were not available to assign shreds to specific sources.

An additional recent study compared the sources of brownware ceramics from the Eastern Jornada desert lowlands of southeastern New Mexico with brownware ceramics in the Sierra Blanca/Capitan/Sacramento Highlands and the Western Jornada (Hill 2014) (table 9.1). A sample of 80 brownware sherds was selected for petrographic analysis and INAA. Forty of the brown-ware sherds were selected from four sites located in the highlands and an additional 40 brownware sherds were from five sites located in the Eastern Extension's desert lowlands east of the Guadalupe Mountains within about 25 miles of Carlsbad, New Mexico.

This study documented that there existed considerable circulation of undecorated brownware ceramics. The brownwares from the five lowland sites contain fragments of plutonic rock and isolated mineral grains from plutonic sources. Plutonic rocks are exotic to the area but are common in the Western Jornada area where ceramics tempered with granite have been documented previously in the El Paso area and in the Lincoln County porphyry belt in the Capitan Highlands to the northwest where aplite granite, monzonite, and quartz monzonite have been reported previously. The majority of the brownware ceramics have chemical signatures, characterized through INAA, that are shared with brownwares from the El Paso area and the Lincoln County porphyry belt. A few were assigned by INAA to a Mogollon composition reference group believed to originate in the western Tularosa Basin or west of the Rio Grande and a few more could not be assigned to any previously identified INAA composition group. These unclassified brownware sherds contained fragments of granite, quartz monzonite, or hornblende diorite and likely represent additional ceramics that were produced either in the El Paso area and/or the Lincoln County porphyry belt.

A great deal of archaeological research on sourcing of ceramics has been undertaken in the Western Jornada but much less has been done to the east, particularly in west Texas. Analysis of ceramics recovered from a recent CRM project that stretched through Trans-Pecos Texas from the east side of El Paso (and thus within the Western Jornada) to the Guadalupe Mountains located well east of the Tularosa Basin has produced substantial information regarding the production and distribution of ceramics from the Western Jornada into the Eastern Extension (figure 9.1, table 9.2).

Of the 286 sherds analyzed during the study, 216 (over 75%) were sourced to the Western Jornada; this includes the majority of both the plain brownwares as well as the El Paso decorated wares and Jornada Red sherds. Approximately 10% of the El Paso Brown, a quarter of the Three Rivers Redware, and over a quarter of the Jornada Brown derive from other, as yet unidentified sources. A few of the brownwares and El Paso decorated wares and the majority of the Three Rivers Redwares could not be assigned to a source group (table 9.2).

All of the Chupadero Black-on-white sherds in the study derive from the northern Sierra Blanca/Capitan/Sacramento Highlands area, and all five of the Mimbres Black-on-white sherds derive from sources to the west of the Jornada area, as did a single sherd of Mimbres Corrugated. Finally, the three Playas Red sherds could not be sourced (table 9.2)

Thus, these results indicate that the vast majority of sherds in this area were produced in the Tularosa Basin to the west or (in the case of Chupadero Black-on-white) the highlands to the northwest, and they also included rarer, more distant imports from the Mimbres area west of the Jornada.

OCHOA INDENTED: AN INDIGENOUS CERAMIC TYPE

Ochoa Indented Corrugated pottery is a readily distinguishable ceramic type that is found in southeastern New Mexico and the adjacent counties of

TABLE 9.2. INAA from the AT&T NEXGEN Fiber Optic Line (Hill and Wheaton 2009, 2010; Speakman 2007)

Ceramic Types	N	El Paso area sources	Capitan/ Jicarilla sources	Other sources	Unassigned
El Paso Brown	111	92	—	10	8
El Paso Bichrome	30	30	—	—	—
El Paso Polychrome	55	54	—	—	1
Chupadero Black-on-white	19	—	19	—	—
Jornada Brown	54	36	—	11	7
Playas Red	3	—	—	—	3
Jornada Red	2	2	—	—	—
Mimbres Black-on-white	5	—	—	5*	—
Mimbres Corrugated	1	—	—	1	—
Three Rivers Redware[†]	6	2	—	—	4

* The five sherds were classified as belonging to five previously identified sources in the Mimbres valley.

† Given that Three Rivers is rare in this region, these sherds may simply be well-finished local brownwares.

Texas. This type is characterized by tooled or fingernail-impressed exterior surfaces on a sand-tempered or sandy-textured clay body (Leslie 1965a; Miller et al. 2016:317–320). Although mentioned in earlier reports (Leslie 1965a; Runyan and Hedrick 1973:33–34), until recently the most detailed examination of this type remained Michael Collins's study of excavated materials from the Andrews Lake site near Andrews (figure 9.1) in the Texas portion of the Eastern Extension (Collins 1966). Ochoa Indented Corrugated is poorly dated in southeastern New Mexico. Recent reanalysis of old collections and new data indicated that Ochoa Indented Corrugated was produced at the Merchant site between AD 1300 and 1450 (Miller et al. 2016). Ochoa Indented Corrugated's association with El Paso Polychrome also supports a production span from the fourteenth to the fifteenth centuries (Leslie 1965a, 1965b; Miller 2005a; Miller et al. 2016; Pangburn 2012; Speth 2004a).

Recent INAA research suggests that at least some of the Ochoa Indented Corrugated pottery was produced in the southeastern New Mexico portion of the Eastern Extension (Alvarado 2008). Alvarado examined a sample of 28 sherds of Ochoa Indented Corrugated and a clay sample collected from the Merchant site (LA 43414) (Leslie 1965b). Twenty-five of the sherds in the sample share a common and possibly local origin (Alvarado 2008). Interestingly, the Merchant site is located on a playa lake where architectural features, including a surface pueblo and two possible kivas, have been documented (Leslie 1965a, 1965b; Miller et al. 2016). The clay sample collected near the site also has an elemental composition that falls within the 90% CI for compositional similarity with those 25 sherds of possible local origin, providing support for the hypothesis that these ceramics were produced at the site. Recent reexcavation of the Merchant site provided an opportunity for this larger analysis that confirmed Alvarado's (2008) earlier findings (Miller et al. 2016:391–395).

These results indicate that at least some pottery was produced in the far southeastern extent of the Eastern Extension in southeastern New Mexico and west Texas after AD 1300. If Ochoa Indented Corrugated represents a locally produced ceramic type in the lowlands of southeastern New Mexico and west Texas, the production of this unique ceramic type would represent the work of local peoples rather than being brought into the area from elsewhere. However, due to the small sample of Ochoa Indented Corrugated sherds that were examined in the study by Alvarado, they only hint at the potential sources of production of this type.

SUMMARY

Based on both petrographic analysis and INAA, two geographic areas appear to have served as the major sources of ceramics that have been analyzed from southeastern New Mexico and west Texas: the Tularosa Basin and the pueblo communities in the northern end of the Sierra Blanca/Capitan/Sacramento Highlands (Kelley 1984). The Tularosa Basin served as the primary source of production for the El Paso Brown, El Paso Polychrome, and El Paso Bichrome (red and black varieties) wares found at sites in the Eastern Extension. Additional production sources of El Paso Polychrome and El Paso Brownware have been tentatively recognized to the east of El Paso in Hudspeth County, west Texas, based on INAA alone.

Other brownware ceramics and Chupadero Black-on-white share a common origin in the Lincoln County porphyry belt of the northern Sierra Blanca/Capitan/Sacramento Highlands (figure 1.2). Ochoa Indented Corrugated appears to have an origin in the southeasternmost extent of the Eastern Extension in southeastern New Mexico and west Texas, and as such represents the only type of ceramic that was made in the Eastern Extension.

Future archaeological projects in southeastern New Mexico and west Texas should concentrate on further defining the variability in the paste and chemical composition of Ochoa Indented Corrugated ceramics. As Ochoa Indented Corrugated appears to represent the only locally produced pottery in the Eastern Extension, the type needs much more extensive study to determine its area of origins and production.

Except for Ochoa Indented Corrugated, it appears that virtually all of the ceramics recovered from archaeological contexts in the Eastern Extension of the Jornada Mogollon in southeastern New Mexico and western Texas were produced in adjacent portions of the Jornada Mogollon or Mimbres regions. Composition studies of ceramics indicate that some vessels were carried hundreds of miles from their origins (see also Boggess et al., chapter 8, this volume). In conjunction with ongoing examination of the sources of ceramics found in the Eastern Extension, archaeologists should also seek to understand the social mechanisms that created the distribution of imported ceramics across the landscape.

ADAPTIVE DIVERSITY AND THE EASTERN JORNADA MOGOLLON

The archaeological record of the Eastern Extension presents us with the probability of contemporaneous interacting groups who practiced a diversity of lifeways. Decorated and undecorated ceramics found in the Eastern Jornada originated primarily in pueblo communities in the Tularosa Basin and the Lincoln County porphyry belt of the northern Sierra Blanca/Capitan/Sacramento Highlands. In addition, some of the undecorated wares from the El Paso area found their way to communities in the Sierra Blanca and Capitan Mountains. Undecorated prehistoric ceramics originating from these two regions were often transported several hundred miles to sites within the Eastern Extension area (see also Boggess et al., chapter 8, this volume). Chupadero Black-on-white and Mimbres Black-on-white and its related types were brought to the Eastern Extension, the latter from even more distant locations.

The results of ceramic sourcing studies not only inform us about the sources of pottery in the Eastern Jornada area but also contribute to our understanding of the interaction of horticulturalists with full-time or seasonally mobile peoples and the origins of their populations (Akins 2003; Hill 2009; Sebastian and Larralde 1989; Wiseman 2002). Several investigators have proposed that the pueblo settlements of the Tularosa Basin do not appear to have been completely dependent on agriculture. Rather, they practiced a wide range of subsistence activities, including reliance on wild-plant foods more than horticulture (Carmichael 1986; Whalen 1977, 1978, 1994b; see also in this volume Miller and

Kenmotsu, chapter 3, and Condon and Vasquez, chapter 4, for a discussion of contrary chronological trends in the Western Jornada Lowlands). Given the abundance of ceramics that originate in the settlements of the Lincoln County porphyry belt highlands but are recovered in the Eastern Jornada, it is likely that these people were at least in part seasonally mobile as well.

Many peoples in the Eastern Jornada area may have lived in this rich environment as hunters and gathers. The ceramics recovered from the abundance of small sites in the Eastern Extension could represent trade between the seasonally settled and mobile groups (Sebastian and Larralde 1989:83). During wet years people from either seasonally or more fully mobile populations could have lived at the playa-lake settlements, pulling up stakes when the lakebeds shrank and the water turned brackish and returning to settled communities in the adjacent upland regions or living as mobile peoples (Speth 2004a; cf., Upham 1984).

At least one group of semisedentary people were present in the Eastern Extension east of the Pecos River, the peoples of the Ochoa phase. Ochoa Indented Corrugated ware is the only type of ceramic pottery made within the Eastern Jornada area. The exclusively fingernail-impressed decoration and vessel forms differing from ceramics of groups to the northwest and west indicate that the Ochoa Indented Corrugated was likely produced by an ethnic group that was distinct from the pueblos of the Tularosa Basin and the Sierra Blanca/Capitan/Sacramento Highlands. The limited amount of maize remains recovered from some Ochoa-phase sites indicates a more mobile adaption focused on the resources that were available within the Eastern Extension, such as acorns and mesquite beans. The preponderance of Ochoa Indented Corrugated at playa-lake sites located primarily in Texas and at the Merchant site demonstrate the manufacture of ceramics by these seemingly semi-horticultural people (cf. Eerkens 2003; Hill 2017, Jordan and Zvelebil 2009; Simms et al. 1997).

The Eastern Extension of the Jornada Mogollon was originally defined as the prehistoric occupation of a specific geographical landscape rather than based on a single cultural pattern's occupation of a region (Corley 1965; Leslie 1979). The area is a rich natural environment for examining the interaction between contemporary sedentary, semisedentary, and mobile peoples drawn from across southeastern New Mexico and west Texas. The area has access to water, not just in the Pecos River but from springs along the edge of the caprock and the abundance of playa lakes. Highly productive plant resources such as acorns and mesquite beans, along with the abundant mammals and waterfowl drawn to the area, would have provided an abundant and diverse food supply during non-drought years.

The region is an amazing environmental laboratory to explore the interaction of peoples from different ethnic backgrounds and practicing different lifestyles. Continued innovations in ceramic studies such as the studies described in this chapter serve to better define the sources of ceramics found in the Eastern Extension. This effort can best be accomplished by analysis of ceramics not only from within the area but also from surrounding regions that served as the sources of ceramics. Other studies are developing innovative methods for reconstructing portions of the prehistoric diet by extracting organic materials from the pore structures of ceramics (see Boggess et al., chapter 8, this volume). These same organic materials in sherds can now be radiocarbon dated. Clearly the Eastern Extension has much to contribute to the understanding of social processes such as cross-cultural interaction between sedentary and mobile peoples, seasonal migration and flexibility in subsistence, and settlement strategies in the archaeological record.

PART IV

Finding the Borders of Jornada Lifeways

10

La Junta de los Rios (La Junta), located some 250 miles southeast of El Paso, has long been at the center of a debate about its relationship with the Western Jornada. Beginning around AD 1200, pit structures and a small single-roomblock pueblo with the trappings of an El Paso–phase pueblo, are documented at sites in La Junta on both sides of the Rio Grande. The debate is important. It centers on whether these pit-structure communities resulted from indigenous development or from immigration, issues that are important topics of concern across the Southwest. Lehmer (1948), who defined the Jornada, was familiar with these archaeological manifestations but excluded them from his defined culture area. In contrast, his colleague, J. Charles Kelley (1986:132), concluded that the settlements were the result of significant immigration from the El Paso area. The debate remains unresolved, as does understanding La Junta's relationship with the Jornada or its place within the larger Pueblo or mobile hunter-gatherer worlds of which it was a part. If we place La Junta within the broader context of pit-structure communities as well as what is known as Pueblo IV, a period of demographic, economic, and sociopolitical reorganization across the Pueblo world ca. AD 1250–1600 (Adams and Duff 2004), herein extended to 1683, La Junta's place in these worlds, its community structure, and settlement pattern come into sharper focus.

In this chapter, I argue that the La Junta developments were influenced by social interactions with

Jornada Connections

Viewing the Jornada from La Junta de los Rios

NANCY A. KENMOTSU

DOI: 10.5876/9781607327950.co10

people living in the Western Jornada and Casas Grandes regions, but La Junta's responses to the Pueblo IV developments in the Jornada and elsewhere were muted, adopting some patterns but not others. I examine the evidence for migration from the Jornada, the La Juntans commitment to agriculture, and their settlement pattern. To the extent allowed by the data, I also suggest the types of land tenure operating in La Junta after AD 1200.

The discussion draws from Gilman's (1987, 1997) studies of ethnographically documented pit-structure communities and her application of these data to the pit-structure villages and agricultural dependency in southeastern Arizona,[1] a recent summary of the Pueblo IV period (Adams and Duff 2004), Spielmann's (1998, 2004) discussions of settlement clusters in the American Southwest, and Schriever's (2012) conclusions about land tenure at pithouse villages. The chapter also uses Schriever's (2012:419) concept of *persistent sites*, or places with evidence for "repeated, perhaps continual, residential occupation."

Below, I provide an overview of the Pueblo IV period in the Western Jornada (see figure 1.2). This is followed by evidence from La Junta for immigration, aggregation/settlement clusters, agricultural commitment, and land tenure. However, La Junta data sets are less than robust than in other regions of the Southwest. Extensive excavations were undertaken in the 1930s and 1940s by J. Charles Kelley or people working under his direction (Kelley 1939, 1949, 1951, 1986; Kelley et al. 1940). Unfortunately, except for one field school (Shackelford 1951, 1955), analyses and reporting of these remain incomplete, although publication of Kelley's dissertation (Kelley 1986) and his later work provide additional insights (Kelley and Kelley 1990). Recent investigations by Cloud and others (Cloud et al. 1994; Cloud and Piehl 2008; Mallouf 1990, 1995, 1999; Piehl 2009) offer data about possible social alliances, timing of local changes, and alternative interpretations of La Junta. Nonetheless, much remains unknown. We have an outline of the prehistoric beginnings of the district but detailed chronologies remain problematic and descriptions of most structures and their contents are uneven. Given data limitations, future work may result in alternative models of community structure and social networks for La Junta.

PUEBLO IV IN THE JORNADA

Around AD 1250/1300 the Pueblo IV period began across a region from "Taos . . . to south of the border with Mexico and from Flagstaff and the Verde Valley on the west to . . . the Plains on the East," where the archaeological record reveals important changes in sociopolitical organization (Adams and Duff 2004:4–5). The most visible change was growth of villages as many smaller pueblos and some whole regions were abandoned. Multiple families occupying larger villages (often in settlement clusters) required new or modified means to organize and integrate larger populations living together. Religion played an important role in this integrative process and village plazas, called "ritually sanctioned space" (Adams and Duff 2004:4), served as communal places where families interacted. Kivas, another focus of ritual activity, were often located in these plazas. Increased evidence of the katsina religion in rock art, kiva murals, and ceramic vessels is another sign of increased ritual activity (Adams 1991; Miller 2009; Schaafsma 1980, 2009). Another Pueblo IV trait was the manufacture in most regions of distinctive painted pottery that was widely traded as "significant quantities of goods [moved] in long-distance exchange" (Spielmann 2004:142).

Lekson and colleagues (2004:53) characterize the Pueblo IV period in the area from Albuquerque to Chihuahua City, Mexico, and from El Paso to New Mexico's boot heel as containing "Southern Pueblo districts" with several large villages—some clustered—and distinctive ceramic styles distinguishing one district from another. One district is the Jornada (figure 1.1). By AD 1450, many were abandoned, including the Jornada.

As noted in Rocek and Kenmotsu, chapter 1, and Rocek, chapter 2 (both in this volume), a wealth of data exists for the Tularosa Basin. There, El Paso–phase pueblo settlements date AD 1250/1300–1450. Many are small but often incorporate plazas, and most pueblos except the very smallest include communal rooms. The communal rooms and plazas are both thought to function as integrative structures (Miller and Graves 2009:357).

El Paso Polychrome, an outgrowth of a brownware tradition that began ca. AD 200–400, replaced earlier styles by AD 1250 in the Western Jornada, becoming the only pottery manufactured there between AD 1250 and 1450 (Miller 1995:212). Widely traded outside the Tularosa Basin, it represents 53% of the ceramic inventory at Henderson, a large pueblo in southeastern New Mexico (Wiseman 2004:68), approximately 16% of the ceramics from Villa Ahumada in Chihuahua (Cruz Antillón et al. 2004), and 38% of the non-local ceramics at Casas Grandes (DiPeso et al. 1974:8:141, 156), and it is the dominant pottery type at components in La Junta dating from AD 1250–1450. Petrographic analyses of El Paso sherds from Casas Grandes, Villa Ahumada, and La Junta reveal that their production was in the Tularosa Basin (Burgett 2007; Robinson 2004), as do instrumental neutron activation analyses (INAA) of El Paso Polychrome sherds from La Junta (Cloud 2004; Kenmotsu 2013; Speakman and Glascock 2005). Thus, while DiPeso et al. (1974:8:156) suggested that El Paso Polychrome represented "tin cans," its extensive distribution outside of the Tularosa Basin indicates the vessels had value, and denotes the Western Jornada's participation in the long-distance trade seen elsewhere during Pueblo IV. Around AD 1450, the El Paso–phase sites were abandoned and production of El Paso Polychrome ceased.

LA JUNTA DE LOS RIOS

The La Junta district was named in 1582 by Luxán (Hammond and Rey 1929), diarist for Espejo's expedition to New Mexico. La Junta de los Rios means "the joining of the rivers" because the Rio Conchos of Mexico confluences with and replenishes the Rio Grande at Presidio, Texas, and Ojinaga, Mexico (see figure 1.1). The confluence is within the Presidio Bolson, a small, narrow basin in the Chihuahuan Desert ringed by mountain ranges. Within the basin, the rivers meander and overbank flooding creates broad-level terraces that erode when meander belts shift. Sloughs and marshes form after periodic floods and storms (Kelley 1986).

Kelley and colleagues (1940) assigned the period after AD 1200 to three phases: La Junta (AD 1200–1450), Concepcion (AD 1450–1683), and Conchos (AD 1684–1750), a division still in use (table 10.1). Prior to AD 1200, sites consist of lithic scatters, hearths, and burned-rock features, with no evidence of pithouses, pueblos, sedentism, or farming (Cloud 2004:20; Kelley 1986; Seebach 2007:8).

Between AD 1200–1450 a semisedentary agricultural adaptation developed. Sites of this time period on the alluvial terraces or adjacent mesas investigated to date (figure 10.1) contain pithouse villages (Kelley 1986:72–77). One five-room surface pueblo (figure 10.2a) at the Millington site (41PS14) was interpreted as "an actual colony of El Paso phase people [in La Junta]" (Lehmer 1948:84). Cloud, using photographs from the excavations, has expressed concern about whether it actually was a "surface" pueblo because its floors appear to have been below the ground (personal communication, March 2012). It is here considered to be an El Paso pueblo because small El Paso pueblos often were partially constructed below ground; their average depth was 31.8 cm (Graves et al. n.d.:89). In addition, both Lehmer (1948:48) and Kelley (1986:82) saw the excavated structure and stated it represented an El Paso–phase pueblo. Moreover, Lehmer conducted field work in both regions and subsequently defined the Jornada. Finally, its approximate construction details match those of El Paso–phase pueblos (altars, common adobe walls, adobe-plastered floor, and three- or four-post roof supports [Miller and Kenmotsu 2004:240]).

TABLE 10.1. Current cultural historical sequence for AD 1200–1760 in La Junta*

Phase, Age Interval (AD)	Type Site	Architecture	Material Culture	References
La Junta, 1200–1450	Millington (41PS14)	Circular pithouses, rect-angular side-by-side pithouses; adobe floors, most are jacal in construction, one is of adobe bricks; one five-room pueblo in a shallow pit.	El Paso Polychrome with minor quantities of Villa Ahumada Polychrome, Ramos Polychrome, Playas Red, Playas Incised, Chupadero Black-on-white, and Three Rivers Black-on-white; Perdiz, Toyah, Fresno, Garza/Soto arrow points; side scrapers, flake drills, occasional beveled knives, oval pestles, sinker stones, bone rasps, and bone, stone, and turquoise beads; ground stone; shell ornaments	Cloud et al. 1994; Kelley 1986:72–75; Kelley et al. 1940:33; Mallouf 1999
Concepcion, 1450–1684	Millington (41PS1) Loma Alta (41PS15)	Continuation of circular and rectangular pithouses; some built side-by-side; floors of tramped gravel or refuse.	Chinati Plain, Chinati Scored, Chinati Neck-Banded, Capote Plain, Capote Red-on-brown, Paloma Plain, and Paloma Red-on-gray; Toyah, Perdiz, Fresno arrow points; ground stone; shell.	Cloud and Piehl 2008:20–22; Kelley 1940, 1986:77–84; Kelley et al. 1940: 35
Conchos, 1684–1760	Millington (41PS14)	Rectangular pithouses, many built side-by-side	Conchos Plain, Conchos Red-on-brown with some Spanish majolica; Toyah, Perdiz, Fresno arrow points; ground stone; shell, Spanish coins.	Cloud and Piehl 2008:23–24; Kelley 1986:84–88; Kelley et al. 1940:163

* Chronological placement of local phases was initially made by Kelley (1939, 1949, 1986), Kelley et al. (1940), and Lehmer (1948) through cross-dating of intrusive, tree-ring-dated ceramics and cultural traits from other regions, including the Jornada. In recent years, the chronological sequence these researchers established has been largely confirmed through radiometric dating of charred beams, roof fall, post molds, pits, and burials from La Junta–phase pueblos (Cloud et al. 1994:13, 35; Cloud and Piehl 2008; Mallouf 1990) and pits from a stratified campsite on the terrace of the Rio Grande within the Presidio Bolson (Cloud 2004:51, table 1).

Other structures at these sites dating to the same approximate time period differed (figure 10.2b–c). Also rectangular (ca. 3.4 m by 4.2 m), most rooms were constructed side by side in pits; where depth is reported, it ranges from 50 to 170 cm, although one room at Polvo (41PS21) was only 20 cm deep

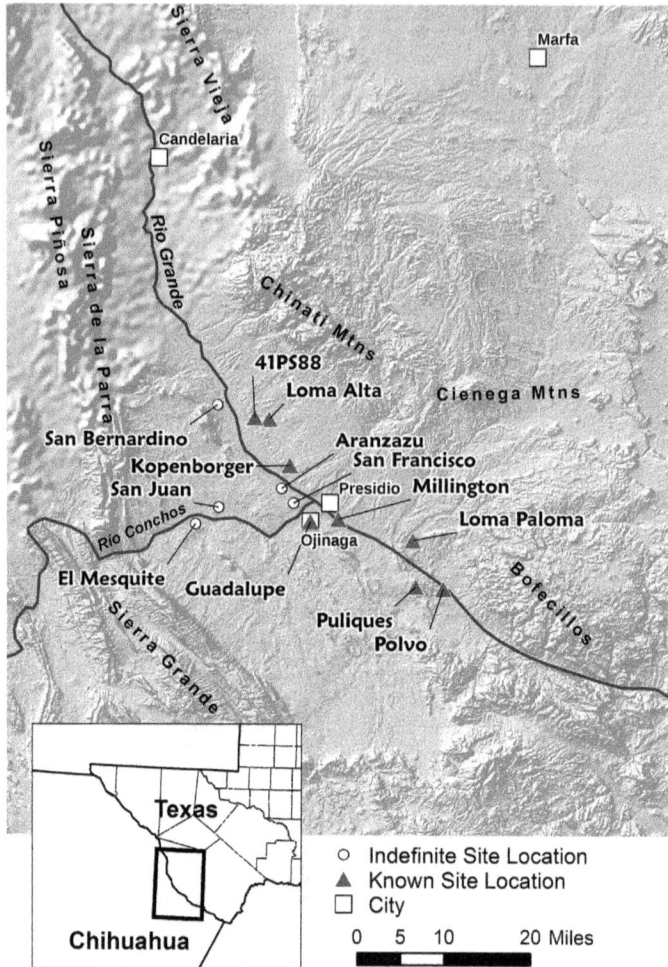

FIGURE 10.1. *Village sites in La Junta visited by the Spanish.*

(Shackelford 1951:28). At Loma Seca (Chihuahua E7–5), located ca. 8 km southeast of Ojinaga, two rows of these pithouses faced one another across a plaza with rooms in each row ca. 2–4 m apart (Kelley 1951). Some rooms, including at the surface pueblo, had adobe altars such as those found in some El Paso pueblos. Walls were constructed of wattle and daub, although one room at Polvo was of adobe bricks. Isolated rectangular pit structures were also present at these sites, as were smaller, sometimes deeper circular pit structures.

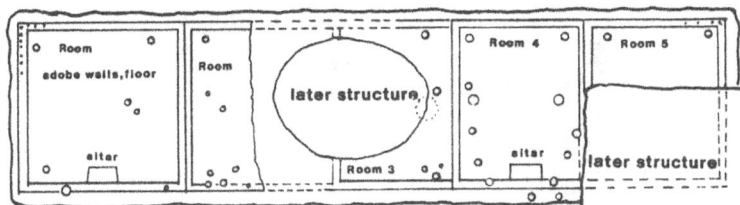

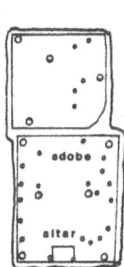
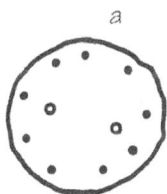
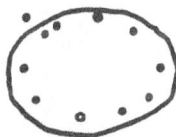

a

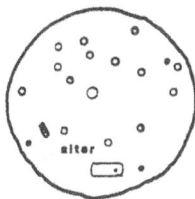
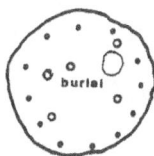

b

c

d

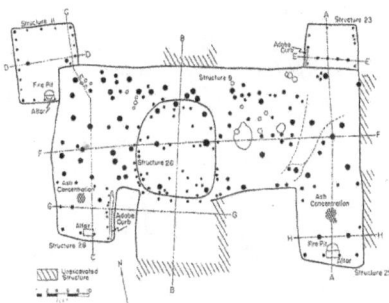
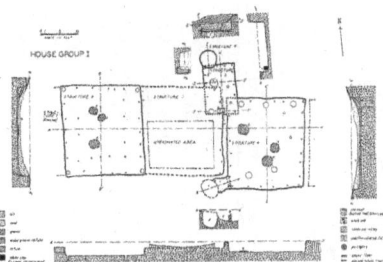

e

FIGURE 10.2. *Structure patterns in La Junta (after Kelley 1985): (a) the El Paso–style pueblo at Millington; (b) rectangular pit houses AD 1200–1450; (c) circular pit structures AD 1200–1450; (d) circular pit structures AD 1450–1684; (e) rectangular pithouses AD 1450–1684.*

Assemblages include chipped stone, shell, and groundstone (see table 10.1). El Paso Polychrome dominates the ceramic inventory until AD 1450. Other ceramic types (Villa Ahumada Polychrome, Ramos Polychrome, Playas Red, Chupadero Black-on-white, and Three Rivers Black-on-white) are recovered

TABLE 10.2. Assemblages from three villages in La Junta and Madera Quemada Pueblo*

Site and phases (reference)	El Paso wares	La Junta wares	Other wares	Ground stone	Debitage	Cores	Lithic Tools (arrow points)	Coarse Raw Material	Fine-Grained Raw Materials
Millington (41PS14), La Junta, Concepcion, Conchos phases (Cloud and Piehl 2008)	31	97	2	2	2,020		206 (41)	Uncommon in the collections (Cloud and Piehl 2008:126)	Described as "overwhelmingly chert" (Cloud and Piehl 2008:126)
Polvo (41PS21), La Junta, Concepcion, Conchos phases (Cloud et al. 1994)	14	222	33	16	8,657	39	222 (44)	Present in low numbers (Cloud et al. 1994:64–65)	Described as mostly consisting of "fine-grained cherts" (Cloud et al. 1994:64)
Loma Seca (Chihuahua E7–5), La Junta phase (Kelley 1951*)	644		31	7	Unknown	1	12 (1)	Unknown	Unknown
Madera Quemada, LA 91220, El Paso phase (Miller and Graves 2009)	17,310		441	205	1,489	59	362 (5)	1,747	163

* It is assumed that the deposits were not screened, and distinctions between course- and fine-grained lithics or types of groundstone were not made.

in small quantities. Table 10.2 illustrates the material culture recovered from three relatively well-reported villages, with an assemblage from Madera Quemada (an El Paso–phase pueblo in the Tularosa Basin) assemblage for comparison.

After AD 1450, side-by-side pithouses, isolated pithouses, and circular structures were built over most La Junta–phase structures, albeit larger in size (7.3 m by 8 m) than earlier (see figure 10.2d–e). Kelley (1986:82) hypothesized the larger rectangular pithouses housed several families. Little change exists in the artifactual inventory other than ceramics. In the place of El Paso Polychrome, several plainwares and, rarely, red-on-gray and red-on-brown styles were produced (Kelley et al. 1940:35–36). INAA studies indicate these wares were produced in La Junta (Kenmotsu 2013; Speakman and Glascock 2005), though the timing of their production is unclear. Kelley (1985:158) noted that excavations of components at Loma Alta (41PS15) postdating AD 1450 recovered only 20 sherds and two restorable pots. However, Loma Alta appears to have been largely abandoned before missions were established in 1683, and Kelley (1953:27–29) hypothesized the occupants moved to the nearby Kopenbarger site (41PS16), where Concepcion-phase ceramics are abundant. The lack of ceramics recovered at Loma Alta echoes Cabeza de Vaca's (Nuñez Alvar 1992) statements in 1535 that ceramics were not used; people cooked by dropping hot stones into gourds filled with water. He may have disremembered, but he and his companions were starving when they reached La Junta. Food preparation must have been a closely watched event. It is possible that production of local wares increased under the direction of the missions.[2]

Beginning in 1535, Spaniards traveled through the district describing "pueblos" on both sides of the Rio Grande and Conchos. Cabeza de Vaca (Nuñez Alvar 1992:284–287) described five. Later visitors described from five to eight, depending on how extensively they inspected the basin. Table 10.3 lists each expedition from 1581 to 1751, giving village names, names of native inhabitants, and population estimates provided in the documents. By the mid-eighteenth century hunter-gatherers with close ties to La Junta (Cacalotes and Cibolos) relocated into the basin by the Spanish are listed among the residents. Adult or elderly males were said to be leaders or "chiefs" of each settlement, and usually the leader at Guadalupe (modern Ojinaga) was described as the most exalted (Hammond and Rey 1929:63).

Data on architecture and subsistence recorded by the Spanish are consistent with the pithouses excavated at post–La Junta–phase sites. Luxán (Hammond and Rey 1929:60) said San Bernardino "resembled a pueblo as it was composed of flat-roofed houses, half under and half above the ground." Other

TABLE 10.3. Villages in La Junta visited by Spanish expeditions between 1581 and 1751

Modern name/site name, number (location) (from Kelley 1949, 1952, 1953)	Native Group (and Population) Visited, by Expedition							
	Rodríguez[a] June 1581	Luxán[b] December, 1582	Mendoza/ López[c] December 1683–June 1684	Traviña Retis[d] May–July 1715	Ydoiaga[e] November 1747	Rábago y Terán[f] November 1747	Vidaurre[g] November 1748	Celiz[b] August 1751
El Mesquite/ Mesquite Pueblo (base of Cuchillo Parado trail)	Amotomanco (Amotomanco, no number given)	No name given (Otomoaco/ Patarabuey, "many")	Santa Catalina (no names given, "Place of many people")	El Mesquite, Ntra. Senora de Loreto (Mesquites, 80)	El Mesquite (Mesquites, 77; Conejos, 40; others, 38)	Mesquital Pueblo (Mesquites, Cacalotes, no number given)		Mesquite (Mesquite, 9)
San Juan/ various (foot of Sierra Grande)	Amotomanco (Amotomanco, no number given)	La Paz (no name given, no number given)	Santa Catalina	San Juan Bautista (Cacalotes, 165)	San Juan Bautista (Cacalotes, 143; Conejos, 40; Cholomes, 38)	San Juan Bautista (Conejos; Cacalotes; Mesquite, no numbers given)	San Juan (no name given, no number given)	San Juan (no name given, 40 families)
San Francisco de la Junta (Junction of Conchos & Rio Grande)	No name given; planted a cross (no name given, no number given)	Santo Tomás, (Abriaches, 600)	Rancherias of Julimes	San Francisco de la Junta (Oposmes, 180 "three settlements separated by 300 m")	San Francisco de la Junta (Oposmes & Julimes, 167; Tecolotes, 50)	San Francisco de la Junta (no name given, no number given)	San Francisco de la Junta (no name given, no number given)	San Francisco de la Junta (no name given, no number given)

continued on next page

TABLE 10.3—continued

Modern name/site name, number (location) (from Kelley 1949, 1952, 1953)	Native Group (and Population) Visited, by Expedition							
	Rodríguez[a] June 1581	Luxán[b] December, 1582	Mendoza/López[c] December 1683; June 1684	Traviña Retis[d] May–July 1715	Ydoiaga[e] November 1747	Rábago y Terán[f] November 1747	Vidaurre[g] November 1748	Celiz[b] August 1751
Ojinaga/Guadalupe (beneath modern Ojinaga)		Santiago (no name, given, "the largest of all pueblos")		Nuestra Señora de Guadalupe (Polacmes, 550; also Cíbulos)	Nuestra Señora de Guadalupe (no name given, 172)	Nuestra Señora de Guadalupe (no name given, 53 families)	Nuestra Señora de Guadalupe (no name given, no number given)	Nuestra Señora de Guadalupe (no name given, no number given)
Possibly Ejido Parado hamlet/ Aranzazu (1.5 leagues up Rio Grande from San Francisco)				Nuestra. Señora de Aranzazu (Conejos, 71)				
Mimbres/Chihuahua E7-2 (12 miles up Rio Grande from San Francisco)	Not named; planted a cross (no name given, no number given)	San Bernardino (Otomoaco, no number given)	No name assigned (no name given, no number given)	San Bernardino (Tecolotes, no number given)	Abandoned pueblo of Tecolotes (Tecolotes, no number given)			

continued on next page

TABLE 10.3—continued

Modern name/site name, number (location) (from Kelley 1949, 1952, 1953)	Native Group (and Population) Visited, by Expedition							
	Rodríguez[a] June 1581	Luxán[b] December, 1582	Mendoza/López[c] December, 1683, June 1684	Traviña Retis[d] May–July 1715	Ydoiaga[e] November 1747	Rábago y Terán[f] November 1747	Vidaurre[g] November 1748	Celiz[b] August 1751
Loma Alta/41PS15, Shafter 7:3, (High ridge above Rio Grande)	Not named; planted a cross (no name given, 8-room "pueblo" with 300 people)	San Juan Evangelista (Otomoacos, 600)						
No modern town; 41PS88, Shafter 7:5 (Base of Loma Alta)		Rancheria below Loma Alta (no name given, no number given)						
Presidio/Kopenbarger, 41PS16, Shafter 7:4 (on north edge of Presidio)			Possible site of "grass" mission (no name given, no number given)	No name given (no name given, no number given)	Jacales described (Conejos, Mesquites, Cacalotes, no number given)			

continued on next page

TABLE 10.3—continued

Modern name/site name, number (location) (from Kelley 1949, 1952, 1953)	Native Group (and Population) Visited, by Expedition							
	Rodríguez[a] June 1581	Luxán[b] December, 1582	Mendoza/López[c] December 1683, June 1684	Traviña Retis[d] May–July 1715	Ydoiaga[e] November 1747	Rábago y Terán[f] November 1747	Vidaurre[g] November 1748	Celiz[b] August 1751
Pulicos/San Antonio de Puliques (Below Ojinaga on Rio Grande)				San Antonio de los Puliques (Puliques, 92)	San Antonio de los Puliques (Puliques, 115; Cibolos, 96; Pescados, 60)	Pueblo de Puliques (no name given, no number given)	San Antonio de los Puliques (no name given, no number given)	
No modern town/Loma Paloma, 41PS58, Shafter 8:1, 57B8-1 (on high bluff ca 8 km. SE of Presidio)				San Antonio de Padua (Puliques, 87)				

continued on next page

TABLE 10.3—continued

Modern name/site name, number (location) (from Kelley 1949, 1952, 1953)	Native Group (and Population) Visited, by Expedition							
	Rodríguez[a] June 1581	Luxán[b] December, 1582	Mendoza/López[c] December, 1683; June 1684	Traviña Retis[d] May–July 1715	Ydoiaga[e] November 1747	Rábago y Terán[f] November 1747	Vidaurre[g] November 1748	Celiz[h] August 1751
Polvo/Polvo, 41PS21, 57D2–3 (20 km SE of Guadalupe)			Tapalcomes (Tapalcomes, 87)	No name given (Chisos, 300)	Ruined pueblo of San Antonio de los Puliques (Tapalcolmes, no number given)	Abandoned Mission of Tapalcolmes (Puliques, Cibolos, Pescados, Tapacolines, 137 families)		
Presidio/Millington, 41PS14, Shafter 7:1, 57B7–1 (on SE edge of Presidio)		San Cristobal (Poxalmes, no number given, "many flat-roofed houses")	San Cristobal (no name given, no number given)	San Cristobal (Posalmes, 180)	San Cristobal (no, name given, no number given)	San Cristobal (no name given, total of 154, "well populated")	San Cristobal (no name given, no number given)	San Cristobal (no name given, no number given)

a Gallegos 1871; Hammond and Rey 1966.
b Espejo 1871; Hammond and Rey 1929.
c AGN 1689–1778.
d Ayer 1714.
e AGI 1751.
f AGN 1747b; AGI 1747c.
g AGN 1747a.
h AGI 1750.

descriptions consistently described dwellings as large, flat-roofed structures housing many people (AGN 1747a, 1747b, 1747c, 1748; AGI 1750; Ayer 1714; Gallegos 1871; Hammond and Rey 1929). Subsistence items included cultivated and non-domesticated foods. Cabeza de Vaca noted beans, calabashes, and corn; he was told that most villagers were away hunting "cows" (bison) (Nuñez Alvar 1992:287). In 1582, Luxán (Hammond and Rey 1929) observed beans, corn, and calabashes in each settlement and mentioned cultivated fields. Non-cultivated foods included mesquite, prickly pear, mescal, fish, and bison. By the mid-eighteenth century, crops in La Junta also included wheat, squash, melons, and tobacco (AGN 1689–1788), although Ydoiaga (Madrid 1993) noted floods periodically prevented cultivation.

The above data from La Junta mesh well with Gilman's (1987) argument that three conditions promote construction of pit structures: (1) cold winters, (2) biseasonal settlement pattern, and (3) reliance on stored foods while inhabiting pit structures. Gilman (1997:158, after Wills 1988b) notes that one type of stored food can be cultivated food and argues that "agriculture is initially used to maintain a hunting-gathering subsistence system [where] it composes a small proportion of the diet." Pit structures are used for a few weeks or months annually; in other seasons people move to gather native plants or other resources, a pattern that can endure for many generations. If agricultural dependency increases, pit-structure communities may transition to aboveground residences (but see Rocek [2007a; chapter 2, this volume] for examples of pithouse use and high agricultural dependency).

The first condition is a cold season, and similar to southeastern Arizona, La Junta has cool winters. Data in support of the biseasonal settlement pattern are thin, but Cabeza de Vaca was told most people were away hunting bison. If this was an annual event, a biseasonal settlement pattern operated. As well, people in La Junta had quite intimate knowledge of surrounding groups and gave accurate distances to them, suggesting they traveled widely. Information on storage in the villages, the third condition promoting pit-structure construction, is also meager, but Kelley (1986:81) excavated a circular pit at Loma Alta he suspected was for storage; two others were found at Polvo (Cloud et al. 1994; Shackelford 1951). Tentatively, then, the three conditions for pit-structure use existed in La Junta.

LA JUNTA, THE JORNADA, AND PUEBLO IV

Despite data limitations, it is clear that people in La Junta were aware of events in the Pueblo IV world. The ceramic evidence indicates they interacted with people from the Western Jornada and the Casas Grandes regions after AD 1200. During this time, they also began floodplain farming, which became part of their organizational strategy, affecting dwellings, mobility, and economic pursuits. The fact that they told Cabeza de Vaca about the pueblos is further evidence that they were aware of the Pueblo IV world. Yet, they were equally influenced by mobile hunter-gatherers to the south, east, and north of them, and by their own past. I agree with Mallouf (1999:84) that they were the direct descendants of the indigenous hunter-gatherers occupying La Junta prior to AD 1200. Below, I lay out my interpretations, but recognize data concerns. What is presented represents a working hypothesis.[3] The discussion focuses on La Junta's evidence for migration, aggregation, commitment to agriculture, and land tenure.

Migration and Aggregation

A hallmark of the Pueblo IV period was the movement and aggregation of people into large villages, often in settlement clusters (Adams and Duff 2004:4; Spielmann 2004:141). La Junta followed this pattern of migration, aggregation, and settlement clusters in a manner influenced by Pueblo IV developments but without fully embracing them. The best evidence for migration comes from Structure 2 at Millington, the five-room pueblo dating sometime between AD 1250 and 1450 (Kelley 1985:156; see also figure 10.2a) that appears to have been designed and constructed by people from the Tularosa Basin. Its construction details followed the Western Jornada template, two broken El Paso Polychrome ollas lay on the floor, and corn and corn husks were recovered from the floors and from the roof-fall debris. Kelley (1985:150; 1986:82; Kelley and Kelley 1990:10) suspected the pueblo was the oldest occupation at Millington and thought the ensuing development of pithouse communities and farming in the Presidio Bolson was the result of significant migration from the Tularosa Basin.

I agree there was migration based on the construction of the pueblo. However, no evidence indicates large numbers of people migrated from the Tularosa Basin. Other known structures in La Junta depart from the El Paso construction model with jacal rather than adobe walls, built side by side rather than with common walls, and constructed in pits. People in the Tularosa Basin built pithouses and pueblos using a centuries-old template. If they moved to La Junta in large numbers it seems reasonable they would construct structures using their existing technologies. Instead, following Mallouf's (1990, 1999) interpretation, I argue that except for the small Millington-site pueblo, other structures were built, maintained, and rebuilt by people indigenous to La Junta—the hunter-gatherers who had been mobile residents of the region for a long time.

The argument that few people from the Jornada migrated is supported by the limited number of vessels recovered from La Junta. I examined all El Paso ware from La Junta in collections at the Texas Archaeological Research Laboratory, University of Texas at Austin, and at Sul Ross State University in Alpine, Texas. Sherds of this ware recovered from sites throughout the basin and along the river moving north toward the Jornada are few in number. Excavated pithouses have several hundred sherds, perhaps representing 2–5 vessels (see table 10.2).[4] Non-structural sites have 50 sherds or fewer, suggesting a single vessel. There is also little evidence that the Jornada people sought to replicate their wares in La Junta. One of 51 El Paso sherds in the INAA study may have been made in La Junta (Kenmotsu 2013); the remainder were all manufactured in the Western Jornada. Eventually, all vessels were broken; after AD 1450 they could not be replaced because they were no longer manufactured. Had the influx of people been substantial, either more pots would be present or locally made examples found. At present, then, the data indicate migration of only a single household from the Tularosa Basin.

Some researchers may question a single family moving far from their homeland. Migration studies, however, indicate moving to foreign soils is not done haphazardly and is unlikely to occur on a first visit (Clark 2001; Dykeman and Roebuck 2008; Frose et al. 2008; Ives 1990; Lyons 2003). Long-term studies of Ancestral Puebloans and Athapaskan movements illustrate migration is accomplished by small groups moving into areas where they have established alliances and are familiar with the landscape and local residents (Clark 2001; Lyons 2003; Matson and Magne 2007). It is probable that the occupants who built Structure 2 had been to La Junta previously, establishing an alliance with local people. Perhaps they journeyed down the Rio Grande multiple times to cement close ties. Hunter-gatherers from the basin may have traveled to the Jornada as well.

When the alliance was sufficiently strong, they brought their family and constructed a home. The structure's blueprint built far from their homeland suggests the intent to stay; brief trading visits would not merit such a substantial structure. The reasons people from the Tularosa Basin came to this basin may have been several. As horticulturalists, perhaps they recognized the basin's suitability for cultivation of domesticated crops. While there are risks in floodplain farming, these people understood such risks; water was a scarce commodity among the playas and alluvial fans in the Tularosa Basin (see Abbott et al. 2009:2-46 to 2-49).

The data indicate aggregation took place in La Junta (see Mallouf 1999:81–85 for another view). Prior to AD 1200, the archaeological record indicates small family encampments were the norm in the basin (Cloud 2004). After AD 1200, pithouse communities consisting of at least several households appear to have become the new norm and, by the sixteenth century, these communities were relatively sizable, although more radiocarbon dates are needed to determine the sequence of construction and periods of abandonment. In 1535, five villages in the basin were described as "populous" (Nuñez Alvar 1992:285). Forty-five years later, the Spanish described an eight-room "pueblo" at one settlement that was said to house 300 people (see table 10.3) (Gallegos 1871; Hammond and Rey 1929:75). A year later 600 people were reported at Loma Alta and other villages were described as heavily occupied (Hammond and Rey 1929:61). Throughout the eighteenth century, where numbers are reported, the population at individual villages ranged from 71 to 550. While not all Spanish population estimates are reliable, I guardedly accept these. None were made by priests trying to improve baptismal numbers. Estimates are also fairly consistent despite decades between visits. In part, the population size likely related to the local environment. The Río Conchos replenishes the Rio Grande at La Junta and this, in turn, promotes growth of flora (including cultivated crops) and fauna attractive to humans (Kelley and Kelley 1990). Indeed, Gilman (1987:545) notes the densest populations in pithouse communities "have access to large, rich, and fairly predictable food resources." Thus, historical documents combined with excavations (Kelley 1986) indicate that once village construction began in La Junta, it continued and populations grew through 1683.

La Junta settlements also clustered. Guadalupe, buried under modern Ojinaga, was on a high terrace. From it could be seen San Francisco de la Junta, Millington, and Aranzazu (see figure 10.1). With one exception, the other villages are within relatively easy walking distance of these three. Polvo is the most distant, located 20 km from the villages that clustered around the confluence of the two rivers.

La Junta's aggregation and settlement clustering, however, do not appear to have resulted from significant immigration from the Western Jornada. Instead, following Gilman's (1987) model, they represent successful adoption of farming by hunter-gatherers in an environment with adequate water and rich in resources. With access to domesticates through their interaction with the Jornada and Casas Grandes regions, perhaps enhanced by the migration of one household to La Junta, residents who had long occupied the region began building pithouses and raising crops in the area where the Rio Grande is replenished by the Rio Conchos.

Agricultural Intensity

The level of agricultural commitment in the district is examined through lithic assemblages, rock art, mortuary practices, ceramics, and stable isotopes. Individually, these offer hints about agricultural intensity but alone are insufficient to support firm conclusions; together, however, they imply La Junta's limited commitment to cultigens. The first evidence consistent with limited agricultural intensity is the nature of the assemblages (table 10.2), which provides inferences about agricultural intensity. Several studies note the increased usage of course-grained (ryolite, basalt, limestone, quartzite) over fine-grained raw materials (chert, obsidian, and chalcedony) as groups become more agriculturally dependent (Carmichael 1986:185; Miller 1990:152–153; Nelson 1984:228; Gilman 1997:70; see also Lynch and Rocek, chapter 7, this volume). The preference for course-grained lithic materials is the result of reduced mobility and the need to process woody plants. Over 1,900 lithics were recovered from Madera Quemada Pueblo in the Tularosa Basin, most of course-grained raw materials (Miller and Graves 2009:564–569). In contrast, as shown in table 10.2, the proportion of fine-grained lithic raw materials in La Junta assemblages at Millington and Polvo greatly exceeds course-grained materials, suggesting higher levels of mobility among residents at these villages than at Madera Quemada. One-handed manos are considered another proxy measure for low agricultural dependence (Hard, Mauldin, and Raymond 1996). Manos with identifiable form from La Junta (16 from Polvo, two from Millington, and six from Loma Seca) are all one handed (Cloud et al. 1994:84; Cloud and Piehl 2008:142; Shackelford 1951:61). The only three metates with identifiable form recovered from La Junta excavations are basin metates (Shackelford 1951:60). Of the 92 manos with identifiable form recovered at Madera Quemada, 82% are one-handed but 18% are two-handed; among metates, basin forms predominate with 79%, but the remaining 21% of identifiable metates are trough-and-slab forms (Miller and Graves 2009:566), suggesting more-intense processing of cultigens. The distinction in lithic assemblages, then, suggests greater agricultural intensity at Western Jornada pueblos than in La Junta.

As another line of evidence supporting limited agricultural intensity, the iconography in La Junta differs from the Western Jornada. Rock art in the region around La Junta reflects hunter-gatherer imagery with abstract figures, quadrupeds, and anthropomorphs (Roberts 2010). This contrasts with the Jornada rock-art style with its goggle-eyed figures and images "coaxing the rain" that flourished during the Pueblo IV period in the Jornada (Loendorf and White 2012:200). Absence of the Jornada style, like the lack of incentive to emulate the El Paso Polychrome vessels containing the same imagery, argues continuation of a hunter-gatherer cosmology.

Burial data also support the continuation of hunter-gatherer traditions and a limited commitment to agriculture. Piehl (2009) analyzed the mortuary practices and skeletal remains of 123 internments in a portion of the Texas Trans-Pecos, including 23 dating from AD 1200–1683 from sites in La Junta (15 from Millington, two from Loma Alta, five from Polvo, and one from 41PS1005). The only offerings at these burials are loose-cobble cairns placed above the burial place (Piehl 2009:26–39). A number of the other burials elsewhere in the Trans-Pecos dating to the Archaic were also marked in this manner, indicating that the tradition had some antiquity. Interestingly, cairn-burial capping is also found in the Tularosa Basin burials dating to AD 1000–1150, prior to the intensification of agriculture there (Miller 1990).

Distinctive ceramics widely traded, another trait of the Pueblo IV period (Adams and Duff 2004:5; Lekson et al. 2004:54), are not found in La Junta. Prior to AD 1450 El Paso ware made in the Tularosa Basin predominates but is not abundant. Locally made plainwares begin after that date, but, as noted, they may not have been abundantly produced until after the establishment of missions in 1683. Gilman (1997:158) notes that when crop cultivation in pithouse settlements is minimal, the need for vessels is reduced. As agricultural endeavors intensify, the need for more and different containers grows. Thus, limited ceramic inventories in La Junta may reflect a limited commitment to agriculture.

When local ceramics were produced, there is no evidence they were widely traded. In part, this probably reflects abandonment of the Western Jornada and Casas Grandes regions after 1450. I suspect it also relates to mutualistic ties of these groups with others. Documents indicate their closest ties were to hunter-gatherers involved in many rebellions in southern Chihuahua during the sixteenth and seventeenth centuries (Kenmotsu 1994:381–442). Those allies wanted information about new alliances, locations of Spanish troops, and other relevant news, not fragile pots. As Johnson (1989) argues, information is the most frequently exchanged product.

Finally, the assumption of limited commitment to agriculture fits with recent stable isotope analysis on La Junta burials that indicate diets in which maize contributed less than 25%, suggesting occupants did more hunting-gathering than crop production (Cloud and Piehl 2008:109; Piehl 2009:84–87). Unfortunately, the sample is quite small ($n = 6$ that date from AD 1200 to 1683), and they were all from the Millington site. Moreover, these findings are somewhat at odds with the skeletal analyses of the 23 La Junta burials mentioned above. In that analysis, the prominence of skeletal porosity (80%) is high and the individuals with caries (50%) is elevated over burials of individuals outside of La Junta or those dating to earlier periods. Both findings are consistent with a more sedentary lifestyle and agriculture. However, as with the stable isotope study, sample sizes are small, indicating a need for additional research.

In sum, the pithouses, lithic assemblages dominated by fine-grained materials and one-handed manos, rock-art iconography and mortuary practices reflecting hunter-gatherer cosmology, small ceramic inventories until perhaps 1683, production of ceramics for only local use after AD 1450, and burial isotopic data hinting at limited corn consumption—all combine to indicate limited commitment to agriculture. La Juntans supplemented hunter-gatherer subsistence without adopting wholesale the agricultural intensity found in the Jornada or elsewhere in the Pueblo IV period.

INTEGRATION

As villages formed and grew, the La Juntans needed means to blend hunter-gatherer and semisedentary organizational needs. Evidence suggests several mechanisms operated in La Junta. In cases like La Junta with somewhat densely packed villages and egalitarian organization, one option is fission when consensus seems fragile or unlikely (Johnson 1989:379). Spanish accounts provide indirect support for this process, including Cabeza de Vaca's (Nuñez Alvar 1992) statement about villagers away hunting bison, suggesting settlement fluidity was a mechanism to address potential fissioning. In addition, the diarists all agree that La Juntans spoke multiple languages (AHP 1645Aa, 1645Ab; Gallegos 1871; Hammond and Rey 1929, 1966). Asking natives how they acquired their fluency, de Escandón (1930:394) was told "individuals go for a period of time to the nations of their friends to learn their language." Their fluency in other languages suggests residents of La Junta spent significant time outside the basin.

Another option is participation in communal ritual functions to mediate and integrate a growing population (Adams and Duff 2004:4–5; Johnson 1989:379; Miller and Graves 2009:361–369; among others). Kelley (1949; 1986:73, 84; also Shackelford 1955) identified religious and ritually important spaces in the earliest village settlements. Altars were erected in the El Paso pueblo at Millington and in some pithouses of that period, suggesting a shared cosmology operated in the La Junta phase. Pithouses generally lack altars after AD 1450 (Kelley 1986:82), but one was present in a circular pit structure at Millington dating after AD 1450, suggesting the tradition continued. Plazas, serving as shared communal spaces, have been archaeologically identified in

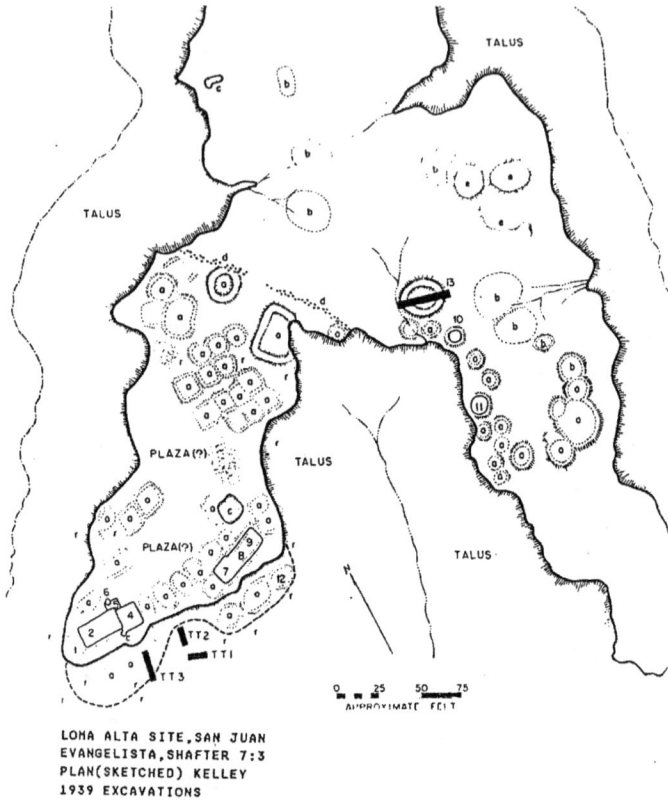

LOMA ALTA SITE, SAN JUAN
EVANGELISTA, SHAFTER 7:3
PLAN(SKETCHED) KELLEY
1939 EXCAVATIONS

FIGURE 10.3. *Map of Loma Alta site showing presence of several plazas (after Kelley and Kelley 1990).*

La Junta. The earliest plaza, dating before AD 1450, is at Loma Seca (Kelley 1951:115), suggesting a need for integrative space early in the sequence. Several probable plazas were mapped at Loma Alta (figure 10.3) (Kelley 1986:80). Spanish visitors describe plazas at Loma Alta, San Francisco, and Guadalupe (AGN 1748; Ayer 1714; Hammond and Rey 1929). Given the number of people estimated to have resided in these villages (see table 10.3), plazas appear to have served to integrate residents in the villages.

LAND TENURE

The villages contain evidence of continual or repeated occupation, representing *persistent sites* as defined by Schriever (2012), with examples of both usufruct (where households or groups retain rights to resources only as long as they actively use them) and heritable land tenure (where rights are retained even when not actively used). Schriever distinguishes between these types of land tenure by arguing that isolated pithouses in villages represent usufruct land tenure. Households without inherited rights to resources would not seek to build in previously occupied areas of a village that might "contain burials, . . . the abode of a witch, or [be] associated with a sickness" (Schriever 2012:415). Hence, usufruct land tenure would be represented by isolated residential pithouses with no overlapping occupation. In La Junta, isolated pit structures have been identified at Millington, Loma Alta, and Polvo throughout the chronological sequence (table 10.3, see figure 10.2a). These hint that some households were new arrivals permitted temporary access to resources, but only while they actively used the resources.

In contrast, heritable land tenure is represented by reuse of the same locality as a previously occupied structure (Schriever 2012:416). Table 10.4 indicates this type of multigenerational land tenure operated in La Junta. At Millington several structures postdating AD 1450 were superimposed over earlier pithouses. Interestingly, Structure 2, the El Paso–phase pueblo, is also superimposed with two later structures (see figure 10.2a). Superposition of structures has also been reported at Loma Alta and Polvo both before and after AD 1450 (see figure 10.2e). Together, these data support a conclusion that heritable land tenure existed, with families returning to persistent sites, specifically to the place they or their ancestors had built earlier homes. Structure 2's reoccupation at Millington suggests that while the El Paso construction template was not adopted in La Junta, the people who lived in the structure intermarried with local residents and they or their descendants returned to reoccupy that place within the larger site. Heritable land tenure is also implied by Spanish documents reporting villages occupied in 1581 were occupied in 1582, 1645, and in the mid-eighteenth century (AGN 1689–1788, 1747a, 1747b, 1747c; AGI 1750; AHP 1645Aa; Hammond and Rey 1929).

It appears, then, that in the period from AD 1200 to 1750, heritable land tenure developed in La Junta as it had elsewhere. Schriever (2012:417) argues that usufruct tenure can morph to heritable land tenure relatively quickly in agricultural societies as children "would simply continue the yearly tasks required to maintain usufruct rights when the parental tenure holder was no longer able. Considering their established ties to the land . . . it seems unlikely that the children's claims would be denied." With heritable rights, households asserted their relationships with their ancestors and through those relationships accessed the resources associated with each community.

TABLE 10.4. Isolated versus superimposed pithouses in La Junta

ISOLATED PITHOUSES

Site Name (Reference)	Structure No.	Age (AD)*
Loma Alta (Kelley 1986:82)	House Group II (structures 7, 8, 9)	Post-1450
Millington (Kelley 1985:157)	1	1200–1450
Millington (Kelley and Kelley 1990)	10	1200–1450
Millington (Kelley and Kelley 1990)	13	1200–1450
Millington (Kelley and Kelley 1990)	14, 15	1200–1450
Millington (Kelley and Kelley 1990)	16	1200–1450
Millington (Kelley and Kelley 1990)	20	1200–1450
Polvo (Kelley 1949; Mallouf 1990)	1	1282–1405 (Beta 29991)[†] 1262–1387 (Beta 29992)[†]

SUPERIMPOSED PITHOUSES

Site Name (Reference)	Structure No.	Age (AD)*	Superimposed Structure	Age (AD)
Loma Alta (Kelley 1986:74–83)	5	1200–1450	House Group 1 (structures 3, 4); Structure 6	Post-1450
Millington (Kelley 1985:150)	2	1250–1450	5, 17	Post-1450
Millington (Kelley 1985:157)	11, 23, 25, 28	1200–1450	9	Post-1450
Millington (Kelley 1985:157)	Number not given	1200–1450	15	Post-1450
Millington (Kelley and Kelley 1990)	21	1200–1450	22	Post-1450
Millington (Kelley and Kelley 1990)	24	1200–1450	7	Post-1450

continued on next page

TABLE 10.4—*continued*

Site Name (Reference)	Structure No.	Age (AD)*	Superimposed Structure	Age (AD)
Polvo (Shackelford 1951)	2, 3	1200–1450	4, 7	Post-1450
Polvo (Shackelford 1951)	5	1200–1450	2, 3	1200–1450
Polvo (Shackelford 1951)	6	1200–1450	3	1200–1450
Polvo (Cloud et al. 1994:58–61)	Feature 3a	1200–1350	Feature 3b	1200–1350
Polvo (Cloud et al. 1994:58–61)	Feature 3b	1200–1350	Feature 3c	1308–1358 (Arizona 7598)[†]

* Dates approximate unless dated via radiocarbon.
[†] Date from radiocarbon assay.

DISCUSSION AND SUMMARY

This chapter has examined the development of pithouse communities in La Junta during a period when significant changes were taking place to the north. This was the Pueblo IV period, when some villages grew due to immigration while others were abandoned. These larger villages resulted in economic and sociopolitical reorganization. Those changes have been archaeologically identified in the Western Jornada. A decades-long debate has ensued about whether La Junta's pithouse communities were the result of immigration from the Tularosa Basin (Kelley 1986) or from indigenous development (Lehmer 1948). Using Gilman's (1987, 1997) ethnographic data on pithouse communities, I argue the development of agriculture and villages in La Junta did not result from a colony of migrants from the Tularosa Basin portion of the Jornada. In fact, the present evidence can only demonstrate a single household from the Tularosa Basin migrated to La Junta. Instead, the selective adoption of part-time farming to supplement hunting and gathering and the establishment and maintenance of pithouse villages clustered within this basin rich in resources and water appears to have developed under the three factors promoting pithouse use: (1) a cool season, (2) a biseasonal settlement pattern, and (3) reliance on stored food while inhabiting the pithouses (Gilman 1987:541).

The people of La Junta were likely influenced in the adoption of agriculture by their interaction with the Jornada and groups to the west in the Casas Grandes region. The dominance of El Paso ceramics over those from the

Casas Grandes region and the El Paso–phase pueblo at Millington suggest that Jornada influences were stronger, but additional studies are needed to confirm this suggestion.

Although successfully adding agricultural products to their subsistence base, the data indicate that agricultural intensity in La Junta was less than that practiced in the Tularosa Basin or elsewhere in the Southern Pueblo IV districts. Lithic assemblages are dominated by fine-grained cherts and chalcedonies and one-handed manos—proxy indicators of mobile hunter-gatherers (Carmichael 1986; Miller 1990; Nelson 1984; Gilman 1997). Rock art in the region reflects a hunter-gatherer, not horticulturalist, cosmology (Loendorf and White 2012; Roberts 2010), as does burial furniture that was restricted to small cobble cairns (Piehl 2009). The limited inventory of ceramics from AD 1200 to 1683 suggests residents lacked a need for a large number of vessels. Isotopes from burials in La Junta hint corn consumption was only about 25% of diets. Together, these factors suggest that the commitment to agriculture in La Junta was limited and was consistent with biseasonal settlement patterns.

Despite a limited commitment to agriculture, the archaeological evidence of increasing pithouse size, in addition to Spanish reports of up to 600 people in some villages, indicate that the villages were relatively large, and required mechanisms to integrate multiple households. Altars suggest some forms of communal ritual operated to integrate the villages. Plazas may have served to structure and mediate interaction and communal activities (see Adams and Duff 2004).

By AD 1450 the Pueblo IV developments in the Jornada and Casas Grandes regions ceased, yet the villages in La Junta were built and rebuilt over earlier components into the historic era. The reconstruction indicates these represent persistent sites and imply that a heritable land tenure system, where people think of themselves as tied to a particular place and retaining access to resources across generations, operated in La Junta. Historical documents, describing villagers who recalled earlier expeditionary forces, reinforce the conclusion that families maintained long tenure at their villages and access to the resources and land surrounding them. The presence of isolated pithouses suggests some households represented new arrivals or migrants with less-firm ties to the land and the basin, and their presence suggests that La Juntans remained open to visitors or migrants.

ACKNOWLEDGMENTS

This chapter has benefited from the assistance and comments of Tom Rocek, Myles Miller, Robert Mallouf, Tim Graves, and Andy Cloud. Darrell Creel helped me develop a proposal to carry out the initial INAA study, and, with the assistance of Laura Nightengale and Matt Peeples, helped make the study a reality. Mary Bones at Sul Ross State University graciously allowed access to their collections. I would also like to acknowledge the comments and support of the late J. Charles Kelley and also thank two anonymous reviewers for their thoughtful comments. Sandra Hannum of Prewitt & Associates, Inc. prepared all the figures.

NOTES

1. See Miller and Burt (2007) and Whalen (1994b:130–140) for similar conclusions about agricultural dependence, mobility, and pit-structure use in the Jornada.

2. The southern part of the basin also contains evidence of what are called Cielo Complex sites on high pediments (Mallouf 1990, 1995, 1999). Radiocarbon dated AD 1250–1680, Cielo sites are also found outside the basin in the Texas Big Bend and Mexico (Mallouf 1999:65). Those in La Junta are often less than 2 km from the villages. Their structures are aboveground, stacked-stone enclosures with internal diameters of ca. 2.7–3.4 m and a single narrow entryway (Mallouf 1990:12). Sites can contain several dozen enclosures. The same assemblages found in the villages are present, but without ceramics (Mallouf 1990:10–13). While intriguing and probably representing the remains of hunter-gatherers as Mallouf (1999) argues, these are not further considered here because of space limitations.

3. Robert Mallouf (personal communication 2013) supports another hypothesis: contacts with the Tularosa Basin were solely through long-distance trade. Future work should seek to explore both hypotheses.

4. Reconstructed El Paso Polychrome vessels commonly have 500 or more sherds (Miller and Graves 2009:350).

11

*The Jornada Mogollon
South of the Río Bravo*

RAFAEL CRUZ ANTILLÓN,
TIMOTHY D. MAXWELL, AND
A. C. MACWILLIAMS

The Southern Jornada Mogollon (SJM) area as defined by Donald Lehmer (1948) included much of northern Chihuahua (see figures 1.1, 1.2). Although approximately 40% of Lehmer's entire SJM area falls south of the Mexico–United States border, it has not provided one percent of what is known about the SJM.

Addressing the SJM in Chihuahua is inescapably a study in interaction between two groups: the Jornada Mogollon and the Casas Grandes culture. Awareness that the Casas Grandes and Jornada areas in nearby portions of southern New Mexico and Texas are difficult to delineate and that populations must have been well acquainted with each other extends back at least to the writings of Donald Brand (1933) and E. B. Sayles (1936a). In actuality, there also was considerable Mimbres involvement in northern Chihuahua until the twelfth century AD, as Brand and Sayles understood, bringing a third group into the mix.

In trying to synthesize what little archaeology there is that has involved the SJM in Chihuahua, several key points emerged that provide the organizational basis for this chapter: (1) Lehmer provided a generally accurate assessment of the extent of the SJM within Chihuahua; (2) the full post-Archaic SJM sequence defined by Lehmer is widespread in northern Chihuahua; (3) SJM sites in Chihuahua have both similarities with sites north of the international border and some distinctive qualities; (4) the SJM and Casas Grandes areas overlap across a

DOI: 10.5876/9781607327950.c011

204

large portion of northern Chihuahua, indicating a large interaction zone; (5) relations between the two groups probably involved substantial exchange and cooperation; and (6) there was considerable sharing of ideology between the SJM and Casas Grandes.

SOURCES OF INFORMATION

Only sporadic archaeology has occurred in northern Chihuahua outside of the Casas Grandes area. This situation creates an extreme data imbalance when compared to the Tularosa Basin, where long-standing CRM programs at federal defense installations provide data from thousands of Western Jornada sites (see Rocek, chapter 2 and figure 2.1, this volume). Pioneering, and still germane, information about northern Chihuahua does come from the vast surveys that Donald Brand (1933, 1943) and E. B. Sayles (1936a) undertook in what was then terra incognita to archaeologists. In subsequent decades, Rex Gerald excavated two SJM sites in northern Chihuahua that were later reported by O'Laughlin (1999, 2001b), Di Peso et al. (1974 et al.) created a somewhat enigmatic map of site locations in northern Chihuahua (discussed by Whalen and Pitezel 2015:108–110), several accounts of rock art were published (Davis 1978, 1980; Mendiola Galván 1998, 2006; P. Schaafsma 1997), and there are ongoing investigations by Cruz Antillón (1996), Cruz Antillón and Maxwell (1999), and Cruz Antillón and colleagues (Cruz Antillón et al. 2004).

Much of the existing site information from northern Chihuahua comes from the efforts of an avocational archaeologist, the late Alan L. Phelps. As a longtime member of the El Paso Archaeological Society, Phelps had approximately one-dozen publications in *The Artifact*, including a 1998 monograph reporting four decades of unpermitted collecting in northern Chihuahua at roughly 400 sites. Phelps created records for these sites in northern Chihuahua, the majority of which are within the SJM area as demarcated by Lehmer. To his credit, Phelps ultimately returned most of what he had collected to the Instituto Nacional de Antropología y Historia (INAH) regional office in Chihuahua. He also provided INAH with copies of his original site records and maps, which have copious information not included in his monograph. From these sources, we have developed a database of 387 sites that provides much of the information used to address the six key points identified at the start of this chapter. The information is not consistent, as Phelps's recording practices morphed over the years. Moreover, by all indications, no aspect of his coverage and collecting was systematic. With few exceptions, the collections are solely from the surface, meaning that original contexts and associations

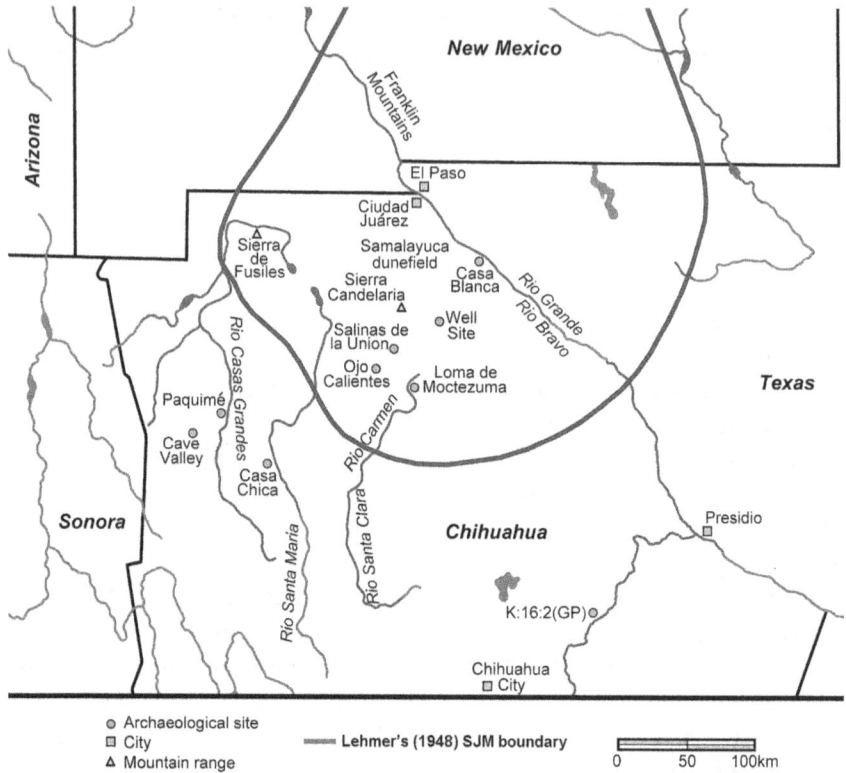

FIGURE 11.1. *Map of the SJM and Casas Grandes areas.*

are unknown, which is a major concern, as many of the sites clearly have multiple components. Hence, we see the information from these sites as approximations, valuable for interpretation and discussion in the spirit of proposing ideas more than for expounding conclusions.

GEOGRAPHY

The landscape of northern Chihuahua looms important in discussing SJM archaeology. The Western Jornada, as defined in chapter 1 of this volume, centers on the Tularosa Basin and Hueco Bolsón (figures 1.2 and 11.1). The Hueco Bolsón extends southeast into Chihuahua. Much of the central area of northern Chihuahua is within the adjacent Mesilla Bolsón, which presents a geographic setting comparable to the Hueco Bolsón.

Tertiary northwest-trending volcanic mountain ranges define these basins, as do the flanking alluvial fans that often attracted people. The Tularosa Basin is divided by a major river—the Rio Grande to Americans and the Río Bravo to Mexicans. Topography within the basins is deceptively complex on either side of this perennial river. For example, there are many fault-trough playas and local topographic differences caused by ongoing basin-fill faulting (Buck 1996). Consequently, small playas within the basins are numerous on both sides of the international border and consistently attracted settlement. And, as Brand recognized (1933:Appendix I:15), the basin-and-range country abounds in springs.

There are also some distinctive features in northern Chihuahua. These include the vast Samalayuca dunefield, isolated mountain ranges such as the Sierra Candelaria, and three rivers that, for the most part, drain northward (figure 11.1). As well, the wider region under consideration is largely within the "true Chihuahua desert" (Schmidt 1979), though the river valleys and mountains in particular do provide some distinctive landforms and biomes.

KEY POINTS ABOUT THE SJM IN CHIHUAHUA

In the following, we discuss key points regarding the distinctive features of the SJM in Chihuahua, its development, and its similarities, differences, and inferred relationships to adjacent areas (particularly with the Western Jornada and Casas Grandes regions). We conclude with a discussion of the implications of these patterns, as well as avenues for future study.

Donald Lehmer Provided a Generally Accurate Assessment of Where the SJM Extends within Chihuahua

Full recognition that there was a SJM presence south of the Río Bravo has its roots in the surveys by Brand (1933) and Sayles (1936a), both of whom encountered El Paso "tradewares" during surveys. These surveys occurred in an era when dominant interest focused on Mimbres and Middle Gila River "influences" on the Casas Grandes area, taken to include northern Chihuahua about as far east as the Ciudad Juárez–El Paso area (e.g., Gladwin and Gladwin 1934; Kidder 1924) and likewise, on Mesoamerican influence (Alessio-Robles 1929; Noguera 1930). Both of these perspectives have merit but the very important presence of nearer neighbors was difficult to bring into focus prior to Lehmer's explication of the Jornada Mogollon.

The extent of SJM sites within Chihuahua as understood by Lehmer is included in figure 11.1. This is an area of approximately 30,000 km^2. Lehmer

(1948:71) explained that "the boundary in Chihuahua is based mainly on Brand's work. Sayles shows a much greater extension to the south and east, but I believe this to be the limit of El Paso Polychrome as a consistent intrusive in this direction."

Brand (1933) provided an assessment of where El Paso pottery occurred in northern Chihuahua, based on his extensive survey and recording of about 400 sites, primarily in northwestern Chihuahua. From a selection of 78 sites in Chihuahua for which Brand (1933:plate 1) reported sherd types and counts, 50 included El Paso Polychrome. Brand (1943) noted that El Paso Polychrome was abundant in the downstream (northern- and easternmost) area of the Casas Grandes drainage. The production span of El Paso Polychrome is between ca. AD 1150 and 1450 (Miller 2005a). However, Sayles's (1935) extension to the southeast was not unfounded. Remaining artifacts from Sayles's Chihuahua survey include several El Paso Polychrome sherds from CHIH K16:2(GP), which is located on the Río Conchos, roughly equidistant between Chihuahua City and Presidio, Texas. The sherds are curated in the Arizona State Museum collections in Tucson, Arizona.

His synthesizing "Gran Chichimeca" vision notwithstanding, Di Peso had surprisingly little to say about the SJM in Chihuahua in his writings. One of Di Peso's (1981) few direct references to the SJM speculated that the Doña Ana phase (see Rocek and Kenmotsu, chapter 1, this volume; and figure 11.2) may have been populated from the south based on a red-on-brown pottery tradition in common with the Viejo period.

Site distributions based on the results of Phelps (1998) and the investigations of Cruz Antillón (n.d.a, n.d.b) are moderately more expansive than Lehmer's assessment of the extent of SJM occupation within Chihuahua. There also was a SJM presence that followed the Río Bravo and in far eastern Chihuahua around the confluence of the Río Conchos and Río Bravo (i.e., La Junta, see discussions in Kenmotsu, chapter 10, this volume). J. Charles Kelley (n.d.) traveled the Río Conchos, proceeding upstream from the confluence in 1951. He did not find SJM pottery far away from the confluence area. Although not found in the southern Casas Grandes area west of the Santa Clara valley (Kelley et al. 1999:71), El Paso Polychrome did get as far as southwestern Coahuila (Heartfield 1975).

The Full SJM Post-Archaic Sequence Is Widespread in Northern Chihuahua

That the Ceramic-period Mesilla–Doña Ana–El Paso SJM sequence as defined by Lehmer (1948) exists in northern Chihuahua has never been

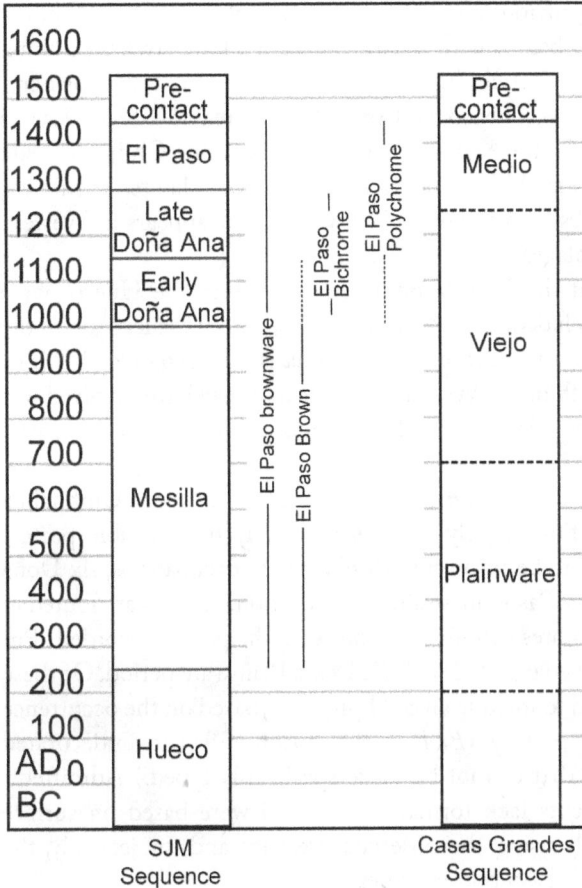

FIGURE II.2.
Southern Jornada Mogollon (left) and Casas Grandes (right) chronologies (after Di Peso et al. 1974; Miller 2005a; Stewart et al. 2004; Whalen and Minnis 2001a).

questioned (figure 11.2). Lehmer (1948) designated the preceding Late Archaic interval as the Hueco phase, which was intended to account for the Late Archaic period and earliest years of agriculture. Lehmer did not have the data to provide a focused description of the Hueco phase. The relevant points about this interval, more generically referred to as the *Late Archaic period* in this chapter, are that components and sites are present in northern Chihuahua and are generally similar to loosely contemporary sites known from the Western Jornada and environs (Cruz Antillón n.d.b.). The most conspicuous elements of these sites are remnants of roasting pits and flaked stone. Phelps (1998, and his site cards) identified several scattered sites that he considered Hueco phase/Late Archaic.

P. Schaafsma (1997) provides an overview of rock art in northern Chihuahua that chronologically begins with identification of a Late Archaic Chihuahua Polychrome Abstract style. The style occurs over central (northern) Chihuahua, southern New Mexico, and the El Paso area of Texas. Designs include the depiction of Late Archaic Shumla points at one Chihuahua site and atlatls at another site. Miller and Kenmotsu (2004; chapter 3, this volume) also report that obsidian acquired from Chihuahua appears in Western Jornada Archaic assemblages.

Lehmer believed that the Mesilla phase emerged from the Hueco phase, northern Chihuahua included. On limited evidence, during the lead-up to the Mesilla phase, occupation in northern Chihuahua is not recognizably different than that to the north in the Western Jornada and may have involved one substantially affiliated population or at least groups of people who were very much in contact.

Beginning with the Mesilla phase, an SJM presence in northern Chihuahua presents a clearer situation, largely because of readily recognizable pottery. Phelps reported 19 sites to be primarily Mesilla-phase occupations, six Doña Ana phase sites, and 46 El Paso–phase sites. An additional 11 sites attributed to the Viejo period or Mimbres contain SJM pottery. Phelps also recorded "Pre-Viejo" sites that he believed equated with Di Peso's Plainware period. Of these sites, 12 were determined to include an SJM presence, based on the occurrence of El Paso Brownware pottery. (*El Paso Brownware* refers to undecorated El Paso pottery sherds that cannot be more specifically typed.) Admittedly, Phelps's phase assessments lack formal criteria and were based on surface observations—essentially using the observed presence and, subjectively, the relative abundances of El Paso pottery types.

The Mesilla and Doña Ana sites reported by Phelps occur in north-central Chihuahua east of the Río Santa María. Of the 46 sites that Phelps categorized as having primarily El Paso–phase occupations, 10 are located farther west than the extent of earlier SJM sites, in the downstream reaches of the Río Casas Grandes. This is an outcome needing replication and considerably more supporting data before leading to firm conclusions about possible El Paso–phase expansion toward the west. Notably, none of 381 Casas Grandes area sites closer to Paquimé recorded by Whalen and Minnis (2001a) were considered SJM.

An important implication of long-term SJM presence in northern Chihuahua is correspondingly long-term proximity to Casas Grandes groups. The SJM chronology, built from the large Western Jornada radiocarbon database (Miller 2005a), and the Casas Grandes sequence are compared in figure 11.2.

Di Peso's (Di Peso et al. 1974) Plainware period, the temporal counterpart of the first centuries of the Mesilla phase, remains enigmatic for want of known, investigated sites. Both SJM and Casas Grandes populations followed the same chain of events at the broadest scale—from pithouses to surface rooms to roomblocks, increasing use of maize, and elaborations in material culture. Of course, many differences emerge at more specific resolution. Determining if these trends have different timelines when comparing these regions is difficult at the imprecise resolution of radiocarbon dating. Perhaps figure 11.2 exposes the possibility that Medio-period roomblocks marginally preceded SJM counterparts. To summarize this section, SJM groups resided in northern Chihuahua throughout the Ceramic period, and likely shared Late Archaic antecedents.

SJM Sites in Chihuahua Have Similarities with SJM Sites North of the International Border and Some Distinctive Qualities

Northern Chihuahua contains sites that are by all reasonable criteria SJM sites. Phelps (1998, and his site cards) recorded 68 sites for which he considered the principal occupation to be SJM. With few exceptions, Phelps noted site settings. Most of the 19 sites that he assigned to the Mesilla phase are in interdunal exposures. There are too few Doña Ana sites to infer a distributional pattern. El Paso–phase sites are in an array of settings, including at least six that are along rivers. It is unrealistic to fully compare these limited, non-systematic results to the wealth of knowledge about SJM site distributions in the Western Jornada, though what stands out as one difference is the unsurprising occupation of river valleys in northern Chihuahua—the Río del Carmen, Río Santa Mária, and Río Casas Grandes east of Cerro de Fusiles.

Below we relate excavation data to support the assessment that "classic" SJM El Paso phase sites exist within Chihuahua. The Well site, located at the south edge of the Samalayuca dunefield (figure 11.1), was recorded and excavated by Rex Gerald in the early 1960s; Tom O'Laughlin (1999) subsequently published the findings. The site was one of five pueblos found within a 5-km radius, potentially all of which are El Paso–phase sites. Architecture at the Well site was typical of the El Paso phase, with some deviations. For example, O'Laughlin (1999:146) noted the site's freestanding walls that helped enclose plazas—a Casas Grandes architectural feature. The rooms are oriented close to cardinal directions (O'Laughlin 1999:figure 1), which is standard for Medio-period roomblocks, whereas El Paso–phase roomblocks are more likely to be rotated up to roughly 13° counterclockwise from cardinal directions (Miller and Graves 2009:101). About 90% of the excavated pottery is El Paso Polychrome. The roughly 10% Casas Grandes pottery is correctly considered high for a typical El Paso–phase site, though explicable given the site's location (O'Laughlin 1999). Roughly one-quarter of the Playas Red and Playas Red textured pottery at the site have distinctive El Paso paste with large inclusions. O'Laughlin recognized that this site was built incrementally, yet occupied only briefly, as there was little evidence of repair or remodeling. He concluded that "although the Well site is located on the southern periphery of the Jornada Mogollon region [i.e., the Western Jornada in this volume], the architecture, ceramics, lithics, and other artifacts manifest the essential characteristics of the El Paso phase" (O'Laughlin 1999:158).

Casa Blanca also was investigated by Rex Gerald, with Tom Harlan's help, during the summer of 1962. Again, O'Laughlin (2001b) reported the site excavations. This site is located 62 km southeast of El Paso within Chihuahua (figure 11.1). Three components were identified. The deepest component included three square pithouses, the middle component two "partially subterranean" small rectangular pit-rooms, and the uppermost component had contiguous surface rooms. The pithouses were similar to each other, each having perimeter posts, hearths located toward the south, and by inference, south-facing entrances. These structures probably remain from seasonal or otherwise short-term El Paso–phase occupation according to O'Laughlin. The deepest architecture is typically but not exclusively associated with, the Late Doña Ana phase (Miller and Kenmotsu 2004).

The final component included either 16 or 17 El Paso–phase surface rooms. Weathering made resolving the overall layout of the rooms difficult. The rooms had adobe walls, adobe plaster floors, and basin plaster hearths. In addition, trash deposits and storage pits were recorded at the site. Some screwbean and corn samples along with a small amount of animal bones were recovered from Casa Blanca (O'Laughlin 2001b).

Most of the almost 5,800 sherds recovered from Casa Blanca were late forms of El Paso Polychrome. A total of nine Casas Grandes pottery types were recognized and comprise about 3–4% of the sherd assemblage. As with the Well site, a few sherds had Playas Red textured designs on paste and temper like El Paso Polychrome. The four projectile points found at Casa Blanca include one that O'Laughlin identifies as Late Archaic and three similar to Toyah points, which are recurrent discoveries in El Paso–phase sites. Shell, fossil coral, and turquoise jewelry also were recovered. Of the eight pieces of turquoise, four are either unworked or debris. The El Paso–phase occupation of Casa Blanca probably began in the thirteenth century and ended in the following century (O'Laughlin 2001b).

A third excavated site that indicates SJM residency in Chihuahua (rather than simply artifact transport) is Loma de Moctezuma, near the town of Villa Ahumada (figure 11.1). This site, located on the Río del Carmen floodplain, has attracted the interest of archaeologists going back to Brand (1933:Appendix III:68). He noted abundant El Paso and Casas Grandes pottery, including plenty of Villa Ahumada Polychrome at the site. Loma de Moctezuma has two conspicuous mounds that are remnants of roomblocks. Excavations by Cruz Antillón, Maxwell, and colleagues partially exposed a large plaza in the adobe architecture. Unlike the Well site and Casa Blanca, Loma de Moctezuma clearly had a lengthy and complex occupation history. Evidence of at least four construction episodes, artifacts of multiple ages, and dense assemblages indicate substantial site use (Cruz Antillón and Maxwell 2017).

Cruz Antillón and Maxwell (1999:table 2.1) report abundant El Paso Polychrome from Loma de Moctezuma excavations, particularly in the upper strata. From a total of 4,782 excavated sherds, they report 1,760 El Paso–series sherds and only 123 decorated Casas Grandes sherds (Cruz Antillón and Maxwell 2017:table 9.1). The excavation assemblage also included over a thousand pieces of turquoise, most of it "production waste" (Cruz Antillón and Maxwell 2017:164). Subsistence data indicate lagomorph and *maize gordo* consumption, the latter of which is unsurprising, given the site location adjacent to an arable floodplain (Cruz Antillón et al., 2004:167). Cruz Antillón and colleagues (2004:167) conclude that "the Villa Ahumada site may have been occupied by people with primary cultural affiliations to the Jornada Branch of the Mogollon."

Another site, Casa Chica, located on the Río Santa María about 40 km southeast of Paquimé, provides an intriguing example of SJM characteristics deep inside what is typically considered the Casas Grandes region (figure 11.1). The site has a small adobe roomblock in which three rooms were excavated (Cruz Antillón et al. 2004). Key results from Casa Chica include recognizing a resemblance to El Paso–phase architecture in layout and orientation, with such design features as walls set into narrow trenches and the absence of T-shaped doorways (Cruz Antillón et al. 2004:171). The roomblock orientation is approximately 10° counterclockwise from cardinal directions. There was no evidence for remodeling, again implying short-term occupation. By far the most abundant polychrome type from the modest ceramic assemblage is El Paso Polychrome at 14.6% of the total ceramic assemblage of 3,667 sherds (Cruz Antillón et al. 2004:table 9.1:172). The most abundant of the Casas Grandes polychromes is Villa Ahumada (4%).

Most famously, the 17,068 pieces of El Paso Polychrome pottery excavated in Paquimé by Di Peso and colleagues (Di Peso et al. 1974:8:156) also bear on the issue of SJM similarities and distinctiveness relative to Casas Grandes. Of course Paquimé is a Medio-period site (possibly with an underlying Viejo-period component). All of the El Paso pottery found there is a small percentage of the total ceramic assemblage, yet it was a lot of pottery, carried in from a considerable distance. Burgett (2006) demonstrated that samples of El Paso polychrome from Paquimé and Loma de Moctezuma have inclusions from the Franklin Mountains at El Paso, Texas.

Aside from specific sites, there are other similarities to SJM sites north and south of the border. Miller and Kenmotsu (2004:figure 7.25) plotted the sum of roasting-pit frequencies through time for sites in the Hueco Bolsón within the Western Jornada, indicating that they were consistently in use throughout the Formative period (see also Miller and Montgomery, chapter 12, this volume). Again, based on information from Phelps (1998, and his site cards), Formative-period roasting features are abundant in northern Chihuahua (table 11.1). Many of Phelps's (1998) site descriptions and site cards convey the characteristics of sites abundant in the Tularosa Basin: interdunal artifact scatters with protruding rock piles left from small roasting pits, black stains from roasting features, and, recurrently, traces of small structures.

The SJM and Casas Grandes Areas Overlap across a Large Portion of Northern Chihuahua, Creating a Large Interaction Zone

The preceding discussion leaves no doubt that there was a sizable area of SJM–Casas Grandes overlap. Imposing a dividing line between these groups would not accurately project the archaeological evidence. Precise chronology is lacking, yet it is central to understanding if the overlap was merely geographic or involved considerable social interaction. With few exceptions, ages of the relevant sites are known only to the broad resolution of phases or periods.

Nonetheless, using distributions of architecture and ceramics, some nuanced suggestions about three potential general patterns of interaction between SJM and Casas Grandes people seem plausible, at least in some instances. One pattern may have been centuries of ebb-and-flow of different groups, leaving only one group residing in any location at a given time. As a prevailing, multicentury pattern, this seems unlikely, given the many dual assemblages. A second pattern could have been SJM and Casas Grandes populations sharing territory but living independently and not

TABLE 11.1. Features in Chihuahua sites of the SJM

Phase/period*	Hearths/ roasting pits	Possible or definite architecture	Darkened soil
El Paso (46)	28	22	4
Doña Ana (6)	5	0	0
Mesilla (15)	8	0	1
Hueco/Archaic (5)	2	0	0
Total (72)	43	22	5

* Total sites defined by Phelps (1998) in parentheses.

appreciably interacting—perhaps limiting involvement to little more than some exchange. Brand (1933) recorded the site of Ojo Caliente de Santo Domingo, about 40 km northwest of Loma de Moctezuma, where a modest sample of polychromes was dominated by El Paso sherds. Yet, about 25 km to the northeast of this site, the site of Salinas de la Unión had almost no El Paso Polychrome but abundant Casas Grandes polychromes. Unfortunately, precise ages of these sites are not known and their contemporaneity remains unresolved. Perhaps this arrangement prevailed in some moments and places, though most archaeological evidence does not support such social distancing as a prevailing practice.

A third possible pattern is close involvement between SJM and Casas Grandes populations in northern Chihuahua: that is having Casas Grandes and SJM people living nearby or among each other and being very much engaged with each other. This idea traces back to Brand (1933:84), who suggested that marginal sites—those on the edge of the Casas Grandes area— "were occupied at the same time by people of two or more cultures." Brand based this idea on the existence of sherd assemblages not dominated by any one ceramic tradition. Phelps recorded almost 200 sites with both SJM and Casas Grandes pottery, and for that matter, many also containing Mimbres pottery. Of the 71 sites Phelps ascribed to the Mesilla, Doña Ana, or El Paso phases (as primary occupations), he reported that 30 sites from all phases also have appreciable Viejo- or Medio-period materials. Ever so tentatively, this tally provides reason to believe that, within the overlap area, SJM and Casas Grandes grew up together. Most tellingly, the aforementioned El Paso Polychrome pottery in Paquimé leaves no doubt about considerable contemporaneous activity involving SJM and Casas Grandes people after ca. AD 1200.

All three variations of how SJM and Casas Grandes people may have lived in a zone of overlap could have some validity. However, the preponderance of evidence points toward substantial interaction, minimally through trading, and perhaps coexistence within frontier communities.

RELATIONSHIPS BETWEEN THE TWO GROUPS PROBABLY INVOLVED SUBSTANTIAL EXCHANGE AND COOPERATION

As remarked earlier in this chapter, there are several environmental differences south of the Río Bravo, including perennial rivers terminating in vast lakebeds in northern Chihuahua. Notable resource differences exist when comparing the northern Hueco Bolsón and the southern Mesilla Bolsón, including perennial flowing water and floodplain farmland in Chihuahua and proximity to turquoise in the north.

These and other differences may have propelled trade between SJM and Casas Grandes people. The materials most often considered in discussing trade are salt, pottery, turquoise, and marine shell. As noted, Di Peso wrote little about the SJM but in the mercantile Puebloan world that he envisioned, trade between Casas Grandes and the SJM loomed important. Di Peso (1974:2:624) explained the abundant El Paso Polychrome found in Paquimé as trade vessels used to carry something "light and bulky" perhaps bearing in mind that El Paso Polychrome is not particularly sturdy pottery. Yet, Di Peso et al. (1974:8:141) and Burgett (2006:158) proposed that the vessels may have arrived at Paquimé containing salt, which is neither light nor bulky.

The ceramics themselves provide some interesting information about the SJM within Chihuahua and hint at some complexity in trade relations. As indicated, SJM ceramics are widespread in northern Chihuahua. Casas Grandes ceramics also frequently appear in Western Jornada sites, invariably in trace quantities. In a study of non-local ceramics from Western Jornada sites, Bullock et al. (2005:13) concluded that Casas Grandes ceramics are often present on Mesilla-phase sites in the region. Viejo sherds also came from three of Phelps's Mesilla-phase sites in Chihuahua. Yet, no SJM pottery was reported among the 338 non-local sherds excavated at the Viejo-period Convento site (Di Peso et al. 1974:8:131).

Bullock et al. (2005:13) note a dropoff of Casas Grandes pottery in Doña Ana–phase site assemblages, followed by a resurgence—specifically of Medio-period polychromes—during the El Paso phase. Conversely, Miller and Kenmotsu (2004:237) describe the Doña Ana phases as times of increased interaction. Nonetheless, the key point is simply that Casas Grandes ceramics are frequently present in SJM sites. To refer yet again to the imprecise yet highly informative Phelps data, we see that SJM ceramics are widespread in

TABLE 11.2. Frequencies of sites with El Paso series and Chupadero pottery recorded by Phelps (in any quantity)

Number of sites	El Paso Brownwares	El Paso Bichrome	El Paso Polychrome	Chupadero Black-on-white
317*	217	10	133	79

* There are 70 sites that lack pottery or for which information about pottery types is incomplete or absent. A total of 226 (of 317) sites are reported to have at least some SJM pottery.

northern Chihuahua (table 14.2). Chupadero Black-on-white sherds are also widely distributed, generally in co-occurrence with El Paso Polychrome.

Asymmetries may also have existed involving El Paso–phase and Medio-period ceramics. Villa Ahumada Polychrome is a Medio-period pottery type not linked to specialized production. It is most abundant toward the east within the Casas Grandes area and appears in many El Paso–phase SJM sites, though how frequently has not been explored in detail. In contrast, several researchers have concluded that at least Ramos Polychrome was the work of Paquimé craft specialists (Di Peso et al. 1974; Phillips 2012; Sprehn 2003). This type also seems to have a low-density, widespread distribution in El Paso–phase sites throughout the SJM area. Part of what remains unknown is if there were processes for the transfer of Ramos Polychrome independent from other Casas Grandes types, such as Villa Ahumada Polychrome into the hands of SJM people. El Paso Polychrome often appears in Casas Grandes sites, particularly north and east of the Casas Grandes Valley. El Paso Polychrome was distributed throughout much of excavated Paquimé, unlike, for example, Salado Polychrome, which apparently was hoarded within the site (Di Peso et al. 1974:8:156).

As noted above, the production area of El Paso pottery evidently was limited to the Western Jornada area (Burgett 2006; Hill 1990:36). Evidence from both sides of the border shows that pottery moved freely but not necessarily under conditions of simple reciprocity. We doubt that this flow can be attributed to one process, but rather it reveals an enduring process of interwoven exchange, relocation, and perhaps gift-giving. Co-occurrence of SJM and Casas Grandes pottery at both regional and site scales may also indicate identity signaling and complementary roles in a generally cooperative, "bicultural" context.

Turquoise and marine shell each have interesting occurrence patterns in northern Chihuahua. Phelps found marine shell, in any quantity, in 168 of 387 sites (43.4% presence) (table 11.3). In total, six genera of marine shell are identified in Phelps's records. For most of these 168 sites, counts are unreported, though it

TABLE 11.3. Occurrences of marine shell and turquoise in reportedly SJM sites recorded by Phelps

Phase/period	Shell disc beads	Olivella beads	Other shell	Total sites with shell	Total sites with turquoise	Turquoise and shell
El Paso (46)	32	22	10	35	16	15
Doña Ana (6)	2	2	0	3	0	0
Mesilla (15)	3	6	1	6	1	1
Hueco/Archaic (5)	0	0	2	2	0	0
Total (72)	35	30	13	46	17	16

is evident that there are many finds of only one or a few shell objects—typically beads. The largest reported numbers are 2,800 shell beads from a site on the upper Río Casas Grandes and by estimation, thousands of beads and pendants from a primarily Doña Ana–phase cache and site located about 60 km southwest of El Paso. Most of the marine-shell artifacts are disc beads (144 sites) and *Olivella* beads (84 sites; 72 of these sites have both). Of the 46 sites ascribed primarily to the El Paso phase, 35 (76%) had some quantity of shell.

Turquoise in any quantity was found in 46 of 387 (11.9%) of the sites recorded by Phelps (table 11.3). He was very general about quantities and it is unclear if much turquoise came from any of these sites. Phelps does describe a mix of unfinished pieces and turquoise jewelry such as beads and pendants. Maxwell and Cruz Antillón (2008; Cruz Antillón and Maxwell 2017) recovered over 2,500 pieces of turquoise from the site of Laguna Patos, located about 10 km north of Loma de Moctezuma. The turquoise from Laguna Patos is almost entirely raw stone and manufacturing waste. Laguna Patos also contained stone drills, polishers, small points, and abraders used for working turquoise. This undated site, which probably is from the late Ceramic period, also had shell beads. Maxwell and Cruz Antillón (2008) report a sizable proportion of unfinished turquoise from Loma de Moctezuma along with finished turquoise jewelry, including numerous beads. The authors propose that turquoise was traded from these eastern workshops to residents of Paquimé. Cruz Antillón and Maxwell (2017) identify the Orogrande mining district, located in the Jarilla Mountains almost 200 km north-northeast of Laguna Patos, as a candidate source of the turquoise.

Separately describing marine shell and turquoise occurrences presents basic information. Considering these materials together is more instructive. Of Phelps's 47 sites with turquoise, 41 also contained marine shell. None of the six sites yielding turquoise without shell had more than three pieces of turquoise. Despite likely shortcomings of how collection and recording transpired, a strong tendency is evident—turquoise often occurs with marine shell on sites in northern Chihuahua east of Paquimé. Phelps was hit-and-miss about recording site sizes, though co-occurrence does not appear to be a large-site phenomenon. The smallest sites with both turquoise and marine shell are reportedly 1,000 m² or less, but some large sites are also in this group.

A second strong tendency is that sites with both marine shell and turquoise usually have either El Paso–phase or Medio-period, or possibly both, components (table 11.3). There are 33 primarily Medio-period or El Paso–phase sites where Phelps found both materials. Adding the previously discussed Loma de Moctezuma, Laguna Patos, Well site, and Casa Blanca amplifies this pattern of turquoise and marine shell co-occurrence.

Paquimé is sometimes described as an end-user for marine shell and turquoise (Cruz Antillón and Maxwell 2017; VanPool et al. 2005:29). Close to 5,900 pieces of turquoise were found at Paquimé, the great majority finished objects (Di Peso et al. 1974). This total is minuscule when compared to the several million pieces of shell excavated from Paquimé (Di Peso et al. 1974). If the marine shell recorded in sites east of Paquimé has Pacific (and Sea of Cortez) origins, it conceivably passed through Paquimé before being taken north and east into the overlap area and throughout the El Paso–phase SJM region. The formidable quantities of shell found in Paquimé encourage the view that ownership was restrictive. Consistent with this possibility, Whalen and Minnis (2001a) did not find much shell in Medio-period sites within 60 km of Paquimé. On the other hand, marine shell has turned up in many Medio-period sites farther from Paquimé, as exemplified by Phelps's results.

Three emphatically tentative conclusions are presented from these results. First, on a presence–absence basis, marine shell occurs in many Formative-period sites of all affiliations, ages, and sizes. Second, both shell and turquoise occur more frequently in El Paso–phase sites than in earlier SJM sites. Lastly, turquoise usually appears on sites with marine shell.

Referring to the last observation, co-occurrence has any number of possible explanations. In a trade-oriented interpretation of Paquimé's hoards, the widespread if quantitatively modest distribution of marine shell at outlying sites points to the release of shell in return for other goods arriving from the northeast, with turquoise, salt, and pottery being leading candidates, as suggested by Wilcox et al. (2008:159).

It is logical, if unverified, to think that the shell and turquoise were passing in opposite directions. If true, it follows that people at Paquimé who kept vast quantities of shell were willing to let some out the door. The suspected reciprocal is turquoise. Indubitably many other items, including pottery, loomed important in what must have been an intertwined system of goods exchange, gift-giving, and offerings. How this involved SJM people is unclear beyond their certain role as consumers of some items. The large overlap area and the pottery distributions imply generally cooperative relations with Casas Grandes people, making it easier to suspect that at least select SJM individuals would be received at Paquimé.

There Was Considerable Ideological Sharing between the SJM and Casas Grandes

Much of the evidence for shared SJM–Casas Grandes ideology comes from rock art and decorated pottery. Several researchers have identified regional rock art–pottery similarities (e.g., Davis 1978, 1980; Gamboa Carrera 1992; Mathiowetz 2011). P. Schaafsma (1997) defined several rock-art traditions, drawing on observations from 10 sites in northern Chihuahua, and incorporated the results into some pan-regional discussion. The late Ceramic-period Jornada and Paquimé styles are defined as contemporaneous regional expressions of a "seemingly similar ideographic tradition" (P. Schaafsma 1997:20).

Masking, horned-serpent-related ideology, human heads, and a rain cult are recurrent in the Jornada style. This style also includes the well-known large-eyed anthropomorphs, horned serpents, and Paquimé-style rectangular "cartouches." The Samalayuca rock-art site (figure 1.1), considered an example of the Jornada style, includes stepped and interlocking designs that also appear on El Paso–phase pottery and the large-eyed anthropomorphs typical of Jornada style rock art (P. Schaafsma 1997:10). P. Schaafsma (1997) cautiously traces the origins of these Jornada style designs to Mesoamerica. The style dates from about AD 1000 to 1450.[1]

The Paquimé style includes the designs noted for the Jornada style, plus various animal and geometric depictions. Designs that also appear on Medio-period pottery include triangles ending in scrolls, and parrot representations. The distributions of Paquimé-style rock art and Medio-period sites may be isomorphic (P. Schaafsma 1997:21). In summary, Polly Schaafsma (1997, 1998, 2001) took the major step of considering what meaning could be associated with SJM or SJM-influenced rock art in Chihuahua. She offers several arguments in support of shared designs and meaning in rock art between the Casas Grandes and SJM regions and people and concludes that, "together with the Río Grande style in the north . . . the Paquimé and Jornada styles comprise a visual art tradition that documents a similar cosmology and belief system" (P. Schaafsma 1998:42).

Design similarities between the two pottery traditions are also noted. For example, Moulard (2005:92) likens Medio-period Corralitos Polychrome to El Paso Polychrome. In overall appearance, similarities stand out, but consistent differences in rim forms and vessel thickness are evidence of convergence from two distinct traditions. More generally, Jackson and Thompson (2005:2) refer to likenesses in vessel form in El Paso Polychrome and Medio-period pottery. Clearly, there was not a shared SJM–Casas Grandes ceramic tradition, as Miller (2018b) emphasizes; in fact, they were two decidedly distinct traditions. Still, what is represented on the pottery does provide indirect evidence for ideological commonalities.

Although sizeable SJM El Paso–phase pueblos exist, there is not a known El Paso–phase site that stands far above all others in scale, elaboration, hoarding, or abundance of public architecture. No El Paso–phase site evokes Paquimé. Admittedly, there is no requirement for such a community to have existed in the SJM region. Consider some of the most often proposed reasons for Paquimé's uniqueness and ascendancy: a trade center, an ideological-pilgrimage-ritual center, and home for an elite. As suggested by J. Charles Kelley (1990), it is possible that Paquimé was the SJM ideological center, at least in the thirteenth and fourteenth centuries. Supporting evidence for this proposition includes evidence for close social and economic interaction through the Formative period over a vast area.

DISCUSSION

Much of the discussion about the SJM in Chihuahua has inescapably dwelled on the area's involvement with Casas Grandes. Several authors have substantially incorporated the SJM within a broader Casas Grandes sphere, following Di Peso (Di Peso et al. 1974). C. Schaafsma (1997:387) suggested a unified culture throughout the Chihuahuan desert. LeBlanc and Whalen (1980) concluded that the Animas, Black Mountain, and El Paso phases are all regional variants of Casas Grandes sites. Wilcox (1995:291) referred to a Paquimé macroeconomy that included Loma de Moctezuma. Moulard (2005:92) speculated that "the region where El Paso Polychrome was produced probably was part of the Paquimé macroeconomy by the fourteenth century."

Throughout this chapter we have called attention to overlap, integration, and coexistence between the SJM in northern Chihuahua and the Casas Grandes area, beginning no later than the Mesilla phase and a postulated

Plainware period (see figure 11.2). This emphasis is based on evidence for a vast overlapping area centuries in duration and material markers for considerable involvement between groups. This does not mean that SJM people in Chihuahua and Western Jornada elsewhere were simply part of an extensive, multigroup Casas Grandes macro anything. The SJM and Western Jornada were distinctive entities with their own complexities as the chapters in this volume collectively demonstrate (a point also made by Rocek in chapter 2). The SJM sites within Chihuahua had more to do with Casas Grandes, in part by virtue of proximity, but are nonetheless distinguishable as SJM sites. Even with considerable commingling, distinct identities are irrefutable.

Jackson and Thompson (2005:3) compare El Paso and Medio pottery and reasonably ask, "Why doesn't El Paso Polychrome look more like Casas Grandes polychrome?" Available archaeological evidence shows that there was a longstanding SJM presence in much of northern Chihuahua. Widespread overlap and involvement with Casas Grandes groups is evident. There was more than ample opportunity for syncretisms and innovations, resulting in a distinctive archaeological pattern, as occurred in the Animas Valley (Douglas 2007), for example.

The persistence of distinct identities within northern Chihuahua is puzzling although far from unanswerable. Two speculative points are offered to address this issue. SJM people in Chihuahua may have been too few, too dispersed, and too mobile for the emergence of sizable, established communities and cohabitation with Casas Grandes people, with the notable exception of Loma de Moctezuma. The brief occupations implied by the small pueblos at Casa Blanca, Casa Chica, and the Well site indirectly supports this possibility. Second, maintaining established identities may have been a basis for retaining understood roles in trade relationships, and more broadly may have defined the terms through which SJM people were received as pilgrims, guests, or even residents in Paquimé.

Brand, Sayles, and Lehmer envisioned people, objects, and information readily moving about in the northern Chihuahua and into the Hueco Bolsón. They leaned toward trade as an explanation for what they observed in sites that had both Casas Grandes and SJM pottery. With the luxury of substantially more information, a much more complex and nuanced truth is evident. The southwest portion of the SJM region was complexly overlapped with Casas Grandes. This situation, opening the way to such substantial Casas Grandes involvement, did not recognizably redefine or overwhelm the characteristics that enable archaeologists to recognize the SJM in northern Chihuahua or Western Jornada elsewhere.

ACKNOWLEDGMENTS

We thank the volume editors, Tom Rocek and Nancy Kenmotsu, for the opportunity to participate in this project. Our gratitude also goes out to the late Jane H. Kelley, who offered many insights for this chapter and to Alan Phelps for making several decades of information available to us and other archaeologists. We also appreciate the truly helpful comments of two anonymous reviewers.

NOTE

1 . Recent work in the Western Jornada has begun to push the origin of the Jornada style far earlier than previously thought (Creel 1997; Loendorf et al. 2013; Miller et al. 2012). Radiocarbon dates on *Pahos* (prayer sticks), painted *tablitas*, and hafted projectile points recovered from Ceremonial Cave (41EP19) range from at least 500 BC to AD 970, possibly earlier (Creel 1997; Miller et al. 2012:177, table 7.2). These dates preceed the advent of El Paso Polychrome designs and suggest that the Jornada style comes from a greater antiquity "with deep structural relationships to broader pan-Southwestern and Mesoamerican belief systems" (Miller et al. 2013:212).

12

Plant-Baking Facilities and Social Complexity

A Perspective from the Western Jornada and Southeastern New Mexico

MYLES R. MILLER
AND JOHN MONTGOMERY

Earth-oven plant-baking facilities and the accumulations of burned rock formed during their use have been a topic of interest since the earliest archaeological, ethnographic, and ethnohistoric explorations of the Western Jornada region of southern New Mexico and far west Texas. As early as 1582, Diego Perez de Luxan, chronicler of the Espejo expedition, mentioned the use of *maquey* (agave) and yucca by the indigenous tribes (presumably ancestral Suma) encountered to the southeast and southwest of present-day El Paso, Texas (Bolton 1916; Hammond and Rey 1966; Kenmotsu 1994), including fermented *mescal* made from the liquid extracted from agave hearts baked in earth ovens (Bandelier 1890; Gerald 1973, 1974; Griffen 1979). Several ethnographic and ethnobotanical studies describe the use of earth ovens to bake agave, yucca, and sotol by the Mescalero Apache of southern New Mexico (Basehart 1960, 1973, 1974; Castetter and Opler 1936; Castetter et al. 1938). Along with rockshelters, pueblos, and pithouse villages, burned-rock middens were among the first types of sites investigated by professional and avocational archaeologists in the region (Greer 1967, 1968a, 1968b; Jackson 1937; Mera 1938; Sayles 1935, 1936a). Indeed the first two archaeological radiocarbon dates reported from the entire Jornada region were obtained from a burned rock midden at the Pow Wow site in El Paso County (Greer 1968a; Valastro et al. 1968).

Plant-baking facilities, commonly referred to as burned-rock middens, mescal pits, or roasting pits,

DOI: 10.5876/9781607327950.c012

224

are among the most common types of prehistoric features in the Jornada region. Studies of plant remains recovered from the pits have identified over 30 species (Miller et al. 2011), but the pits were used mainly for slowly baking the hearts or palms of Agavaceae and Liliaceae family succulents (*Agave neomexicana, Agave lechuguilla, Yucca baccata, Dasylirion wheeleri*) and the fruits, buds, or pads of several genera and species of the Cactaceae family (*Cylindropuntia, Platyopuntia, Mammillaria, Echinocereus, Echinocactus*). The baking pits were used from the Middle Archaic period through the Protohistoric period of the Jornada chronological sequence (Miller et al. 2013). Major changes in settlement-subsistence practices, technology, demography, and social organization took place throughout the Jornada region and the greater Southwest across these time intervals, and while certain technologies appeared and disappeared, the use of plant-baking facilities remained a constant feature of indigenous lifeways. Earth ovens were constructed and used by mobile hunter-gatherer groups during the Archaic period and early part of the Formative period, and by horticulturalists residing at pithouse and pueblo settlements during the latter part of the Formative period. They were used and reused during seasonal subsistence rounds, as special facilities for communal feasts, or as part of logistically organized processing features for baked and fermented agave and succulents. Burned-rock middens have been found in the valleys, slopes, canyons, foothills, and alluvial fans of virtually every mountain range of southern New Mexico and Trans-Pecos Texas.

The excavation of 77 plant-baking facilities and associated burned-rock discard middens in the Sacramento Mountains of south-central New Mexico (figure 12.1) provided what is perhaps the largest and most intensively documented sample of such features in the US Southwest (Miller, Graves, and Landreth 2012; Miller, Graves, Frederick, and Landreth 2012; Miller et al. 2011, 2013; Sale et al. 2012; Vierra and Ward 2012; Ward and Vierra 2011). Conducted over a period of four years, the excavations revealed that these facilities had important economic, social, and ritual functions beyond providing food and subsistence, one of the most significant being the probable fermentation of liquid extracted from baked Agavaceae plants to produce mescal.

Approximately 130 km to the southeast of the Sacramento Mountains, another sample of burned-rock features was investigated along the Black River, a permanent water source draining the southern flanks of the Guadalupe Mountains (figure 12.2). Black River is one of the few permanent water sources in the southeastern New Mexico region of the Chihuahuan Desert physiographic zone. Situated within the Mountain Slope ecological zone, the region is a microcosm of the broader regional and interregional studies of the

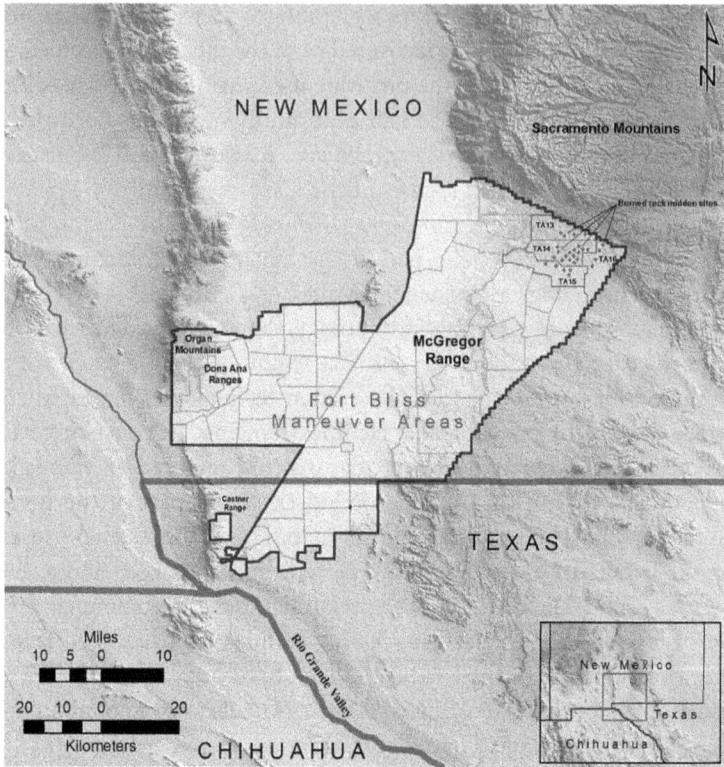

FIGURE 12.1. *Location of the burned-rock midden excavations in the southern foothills of the Sacramento Mountains on McGregor Range of Fort Bliss, south-central New Mexico.*

Jornada's Eastern Extension (in this volume see Boggess et al., chapter 8, and Railey, chapter 13). As suggested by these studies, the archaeological record of the southeastern Jornada region indicates a complex and changing patchwork of cultural activities.

Much of the Black River project region is administered by the Bureau of Land Management (BLM). In support of preservation and interpretive needs of the BLM, Eastern New Mexico University (ENMU) students and staff performed two seasons of survey in the Black River Recreation Area and limited testing to a few sites that had the greatest potential for chronometric dating. Using close-interval pedestrian survey techniques, ENMU examined 1,047 acres, adding 29 prehistoric archaeological sites to the 13 previously recorded sites within the area. This work revealed a landscape dominated by

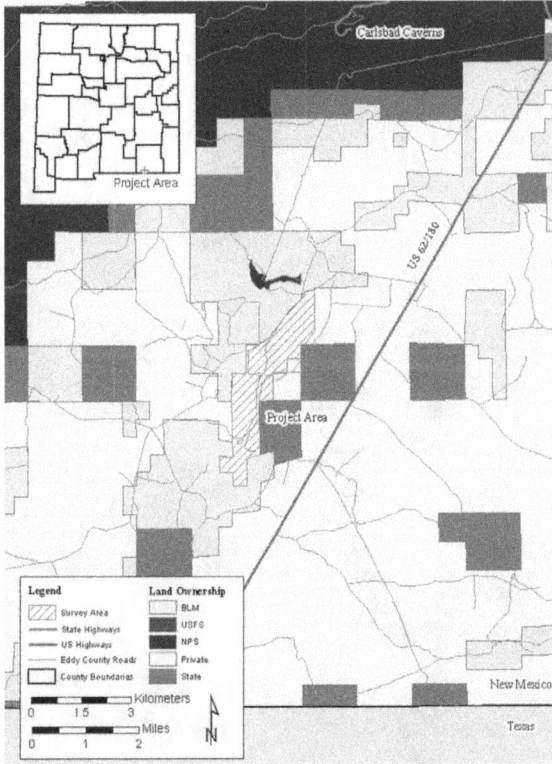

FIGURE 12.2. *Black River project area in the Jornada's Eastern Extension.*

burned-rock features (also known as *fire-cracked rock* or *thermal features*). The survey adopted a landscape-oriented approach wherein the feature was the primary unit of observation and recording. In the end, ENMU field school personnel recorded over 800 burned-rock features (figure 12.3). The sheer number and density of burned-rock features was unexpected, and the study of this large, complicated data set within a small yet interesting landscape focused on both traditional concerns of feature morphology, size, and location as well as how to connect the observed variation among the features to several archaeological questions of current relevance in southeastern New Mexico (Railey 2016).

Prior to these studies, the prevailing view was that the agave and other plant foods baked in the pits were of secondary importance to prehistoric subsistence economies, serving mainly to supplement or buffer agricultural harvests or to

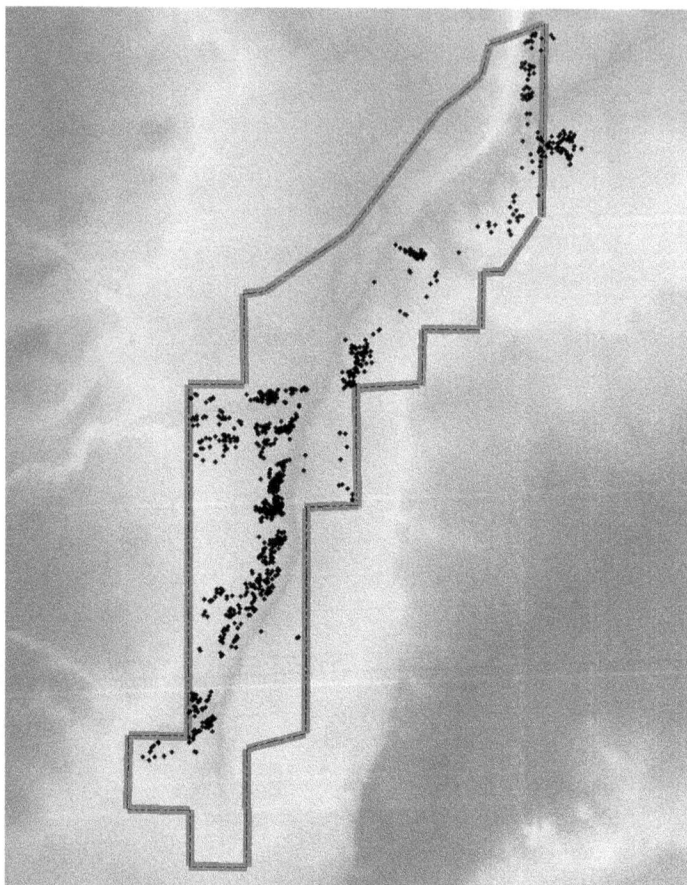

FIGURE 12.3. *Black River Special Management Area, showing burned rock features.*

survive periods of famine (e.g., Anderies et al. 2008; Minnis 1991). The value of baked agave as a famine resource in the Trans-Pecos region is attested to by Bartlett's statement: "The engineers attached to the [United States-Mexican Boundary Survey] Commission told me that the entire Mexican population at Presidio del Norte, consisting of a thousand souls, had no other food for more than six months" (Bartlett 1854:I:291). Given that agave, yucca, and sotol survive even prolonged drought conditions, it is not surprising that they were an important resource during periods of famine among groups residing in the Chihuahuan Desert. While the importance of agave and succulents during periods of shortage or famine cannot be discounted, the issue is that from this perspective agave and yucca are seen as minor or secondary resources, particularly among horticultural and agricultural groups. This viewpoint has been a pervasive influence because archaeologists are often predisposed to interpret the exploitation of Agavaceae[1] and other succulents within diet-breadth models, risk-reduction models, and other tenets of optimal-foraging theory. Such models tend to obscure or minimize the significant roles that agave baking and agave-baking pits played in political economies, social production, and community organization of prehistoric and historic societies in the US Southwest and northern Chihuahua.

COMPONENTS OF BURNED-ROCK MIDDENS

The term *burned-rock midden* is somewhat misleading because it refers to just one component of what was actually a complex of features and refuse-disposal areas that were integral components of plant-baking facilities. These facilities should more appropriately be called *plant-baking complexes* or *earth-oven complexes*, but the term *burned-rock midden* is entrenched in the literature (Black and Thoms 2014). The components of plant-baking facilities include (1) the burned-rock discard midden, (2) the central pit area, (3) rock-lined or unlined baking pits within the central pit area, and (4) various ancillary features such as soil borrow pits, processing areas, pits, and perhaps other types of storage or cooking facilities (figure 12.4).

The burned-rock discard midden is the most prominent and visible attribute of plant-baking complexes and is usually the focus of archaeological excavation. Discard middens consist of accumulations of burned rock, wood charcoal, and soil that were used to cap the centrally located baking pits during the cooking process and were then removed and piled around the perimeter of the pit when it was opened and cleaned out. Some morphological variation is apparent among the shapes of the discard middens that include rings, crescents, amorphous mounds, and diffuse scatters. Being midden formations, the contents of these features are not limited to discarded rock, soil, and charcoal, but also contain tools used to prepare the plants for cooking or for additional processing after baking.

The second component of the Jornada burned-rock midden is what may be termed the *central pit area*. This is analogous to what Black and Creel (1997) refer to as *center-focused middens*; they note that the main focus of production and processing activities—the actual plant-baking pits or ovens—were in the center of the burned-rock midden. The burned-rock discard midden

FIGURE 12.4. *Components of plant-baking facilities. Upper panel, typical circular burned-rock discard midden on the surface; lower left, central pit area with baking pit and portion of soil borrow pit; lower right, rock-lined baking pits.*

that has often been the main focus of archaeological attention in the Jornada and elsewhere throughout New Mexico and Texas is actually a secondary and peripheral (in both the literal/physical and metaphorical senses of the term) component of the facility.

Regardless of the size, density, and shape of the discard midden, each plant-baking complex has a central pit area and, in most instances, one or more rock-lined or unlined baking pits are present in this area. The baking pits, also termed *earth ovens* or *roasting pits*, were the primary focus and productive component of plant-baking facilities and the facility where the actual baking of plants took place. In other words, the baking pits were the raison d'être for the midden. Two forms of baking pits—rock-lined pits and unlined pits—were observed among the sample of plant-baking facilities in the southern Sacramento Mountains. Rock-lined pits are by far the most common baking facility, representing over 85% of the pits in that sample.

Central pit areas often have other features, the most common being soil borrow pits where dirt used to cap the baking pits was excavated. One form is a shallow, circular or semicircular depression positioned outside the perimeter of the central baking pit or beneath the inner margin of the burned-rock discard ring. The second form of borrow area is a series of small, irregular pits located below the discard midden. Pounding stones and other work areas also are present in the central pit areas.

While these fundamental components are present among plant-baking pits, they are often manifested in various shapes and dimensions. Based on a synthesis of survey and excavation data from southeastern New Mexico, Railey (2016; see also Railey et al. 2009) identified a prominent research hurdle concerning archaeological features: an overabundance of terms for burned-rock features and a corresponding lack of systematic recording. Meaningful distinctions are important here, and the ENMU survey of the Black River attempted to develop a consistent and interpretable typology based on the initial work of Greer (1967), Hogan (2006), and Schuelke (2008). Burned-rock discard middens were identified as having accretional depth, primary context, and clearly defined boundaries. Two types of middens were defined and used as a working model in the Black River survey: *ring middens*, which have a central depression, and *linear middens*, which lack a circular shape.

Dimensions of burned-rock discard middens associated with plant-baking facilities are quite variable. The sample of features in the Sacramento Mountains ranged from 4.1 to 95.0 m^2 in size, with an average of 41.1 m^2 (Miller et al. 2011). The average areas of nine midden circles and two linear middens recorded in the Black River survey area are 222.9 m^2 and 107.0 m^2, respectively. The reasons for the larger dimensions of the middens in the Black River area is uncertain, but likely relates to different social and subsistence functions in the two regions. A wide range of variation among burned-rock discard middens is present across both regions, including small, single-use accumulations of rock around a baking pit to massive middens thought to have been used for communal feasting events (Miller 2018a; Miller, Graves, and Landreth 2012; Graves et al. 2012). In this regard, it is noteworthy that the midden features recorded during the ENMU surveys were associated with a local ecotone near the intersection of the Black River and Slaughter Canyon. This local environment hosts a dense and diverse vegetation community, including walnut trees, a pattern that contrasts significantly with surrounding environments dominated by acacia and broom snakeweed. This ecotone may have served as a propitious location for communal gatherings involving bulk processing of agave and other leaf succulents.

SUBSISTENCE FUNCTION OF PLANT-BAKING FACILITIES

Extensive sampling of the fills of plant-baking pits and burned-rock discard middens in the southern Sacramento Mountains for macrobotanical and pollen samples revealed a variety of subsistence foods. A summary of plant-taxa ubiquity from flotation and pollen samples (Miller et al. 2013:table 7.2) confirmed that one of the primary functions of the baking pits was to process agave or yucca (39% ubiquity). Cholla buds (17% ubiquity) and cactus fruits or perhaps cactus pads (12% ubiquity) were common. Prickly pear and *Echinocactus* seeds were also common and, as with cholla, pollen from these plant species or families was identified in numerous baking pits.

Of particular importance was the fact that Agavaceae remains were observed in numerous flotation samples. Plant recovery includes 78 specimens of Agavaceae plants, including fibers and fiber bundles, caudex fragments, tissue, and even a fragment of a heart. Recovery of agave fibers or monocot fragments was particularly common in burned-rock discard mounds (Vierra and Ward 2012; Ward and Vierra 2011).

Although not as extensive in number and scope, the subsistence studies conducted as part of the ENMU investigations of the Black River area provided both new and corroborative data. Fill samples from large (169 m² and 186 m², respectively), circular midden features at LA 160727 (Mesilla phase) and LA 160741 (El Paso phase) were examined for phytoliths and macrofloral remains (Puseman et al. 2010) and a pollen sample from LA 160727 was analyzed. In addition, fire-cracked rocks from the features were tested for the presence of organic residues, especially lipids, using Fourier Transform Infrared Spectroscopy (FTIR). The phytolith, pollen, and macrofloral records from these features indicate the features were used to process hedgehog cactus, prickly pear, and other cacti fruits as well as leaf succulents. An unusual and unprecedented identification was that of a starchy root plant, possibly from a member of the Commelinaceae family such as wild potato (*Solanum jamesii*). Purslane seeds may have been parched on ceramic plates placed over the heated stones. Charred monocot stem fragments, charred unidentified stem fragments, and a very high abundance of bulliform phytoliths suggest use of green grasses and other plants as a buffering vegetation layer when cooking foods. A variety of wood and shrub charcoal types were noted. The FTIR record from fire-cracked rocks suggests that maize, acorn, and cacti were processed, though it should be noted that the match with *Zea mays* is unsupported by any other evidence and is likely a false identification or a detection of grass remains. Other FTIR results suggest that calcium-oxalate-rich foods such as cacti and leaf succulents were processed. However, the results of FTIR analyses have been questioned based on a series of highly inconsistent results of controlled samples submitted from plant-baking facilities in the Sacramento Mountains (Miller et al. 2013).

LIMESTONE ROCK UTILIZATION AND THE LABOR DIMENSION

The structured deposits and arrangements of features in burned-rock middens equate with patterned human action and behavior. Middens are not random accumulations, but were formed through a sequence of construction, use, maintenance, and abandonment of plant-baking pits. They are purposively constructed facilities, the location, construction, and use of which were designed on the basis of several interrelated ecological and social factors. As such, midden structure can provide important clues to their history of use and their functional role within prehistoric settlement and social organization.

Archaeological investigations of the burned-rock middens in the southern Sacramento Mountains were designed to place these features in the larger picture of economic, demographic, and social developments of the Western Jornada Mogollon and it is illuminating to take stock of just how many features were constructed and how much burned rock was used in their construction. One of the data collection and analysis efforts at these sites involved compiling and reviewing quantitative data on the limestone rock used in the construction and operation of prehistoric plant-baking facilities. Each facility was mapped and the area of the burned-rock discard midden was recorded. Two 1-m-wide cross-trenches were excavated through the discard midden and central pit area, providing samples ranging from 10% to 50% of the total midden area. Burned limestone recovered by hand excavation of the midden matrix and during screening was weighed and counted. This method allowed for the total weight and count of rock composing each burned-rock discard midden to be estimated.

Consistent data are available for 66 of the 77 middens at 28 sites[2] (data are presented in Miller et al. 2013). The 66 plant-baking facilities and discard middens contain an estimated 179,525 kg (179.5 metric tons) or 394,955 pounds (197

US tons) of rock that had to be transported from alluvial and colluvial gravel deposits or bedrock exposures. In terms of rock counts, the 66 features contain an estimated 1,461,075 whole and fractured rocks. The count of whole cobbles that were originally collected and transported to the features was probably one-fifth or less of this total, which is still a rather substantial count of 292,215 cobbles.

Envisioning an even broader scale, consider that the 66 middens are just a fraction of the hundreds of sites and thousands of burned-rock midden features in the Sacramento Mountains foothills. Much of the southern foothills have been surveyed using the Transect Recording Unit (TRU) method that requires complete coverage of every 15-m-by-15-m grid square across large survey parcels (see discussion by Railey and Turnbow in chapter 5, this volume). The TRU survey method provides excellent, high-resolution data on site distributions across the landscape. Estimates of the total number of sites and middens in certain segments of the southern Sacramento Mountains can be made using these survey data.

For example, 532 prehistoric sites have been recorded in a 16-km-by-22.5-km area encompassing Wildcat Canyon, McAfee Canyon, El Paso Canyon, the Sacramento River, and the alluvial-fan piedmont along the southwestern foothills (figure 12.5). Most sites have 10 or more burned-rock middens within their boundaries (Ernst and Swanson 2009; Komulainen et al. 2009; MacWilliams et al. 2009; Renn et al. 2010; Stowe et al. 2009). Several sites, particularly those along the lower floodplains or broad terraces bordering El Paso and Wildcat Canyons, are virtual landscapes of 70 or more midden facilities (figure 12.6). Generally, sites at higher elevations have an average of 10 middens while those at lower elevations average 20 middens. Adjusting the average BRM counts for elevation, a conservative estimate is that 7,800 burned-rock-midden features are present along the canyons, valleys, and alluvial fans within the 362 km² area of the southern foothills.

Burned-rock weight and count data are available for the sample of 66 burned-rock middens cited above. The distributions and central tendencies of weight and count data are skewed, due to the presence of two very large middens of Middle Archaic age. The degree of skewness has been somewhat reduced and measures of central tendency and dispersion revised by removing these two features from the calculations. The median rock weight for the remaining 64 middens is 1,173 kg and the mean is 2,114 kg. The median and mean burned-rock counts are 10,502 and 18,896, respectively. Given that the distributions of rock weight and counts are still skewed, the median values may be a more reasonable indicator of central tendencies of the distributions. As with the conservative estimate of the number of middens in the foothills,

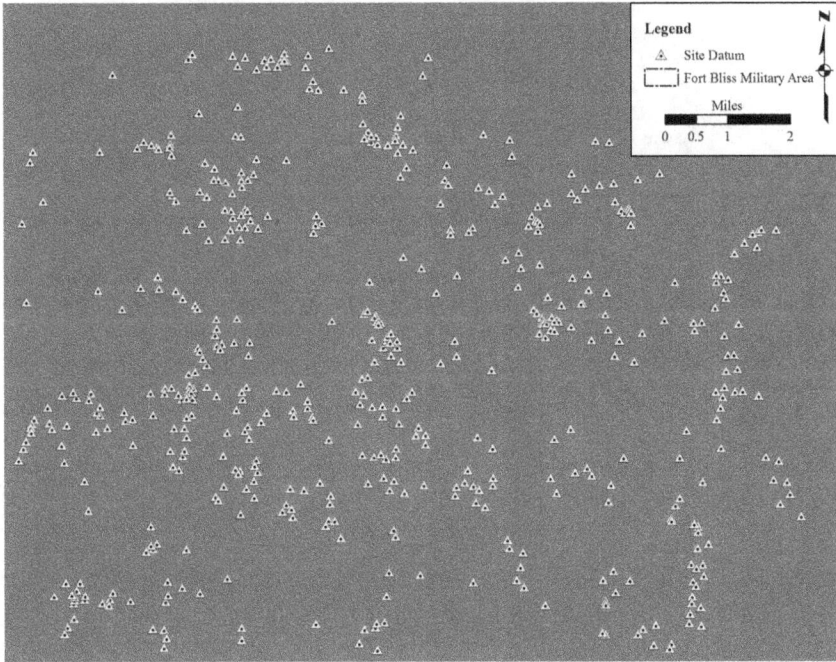

FIGURE 12.5. *Site distributions within the 16-km-by-22.5-km region of southern foothills subsuming Wildcat, El Paso, and McAfee Canyons and the Sacramento River. The figure displays the datum points for 532 prehistoric sites recorded during the past decade of intensive transect-recording unit surveys.*

the use of the median weight and count values in these calculations is conservative and, if anything, these two assumptions actually underestimate the total weight and count values.

If we adopt the median weight value of 1,173 kg, take one-fifth of the median count value (2,100) to reflect whole instead of fractured cobbles, and accept the estimate of 7,800 burned-rock middens in the 362 km² area of the southern Sacramento Mountains, we arrive at the following estimates: an estimated 16.4 million rocks weighing an estimated 9.2 million kilograms were gathered from alluvial and colluvial deposits and bedrock outcrops and transported to construct plant-baking facilities in the 16-km-by-22.5-km region of the southern foothills. An estimated 75% of the baking facilities were constructed between AD 600 and 1300. Based on this proportion, approximately 300,000 kg of rock was collected to build 250 baking pits during each generation of settlement within this small area.

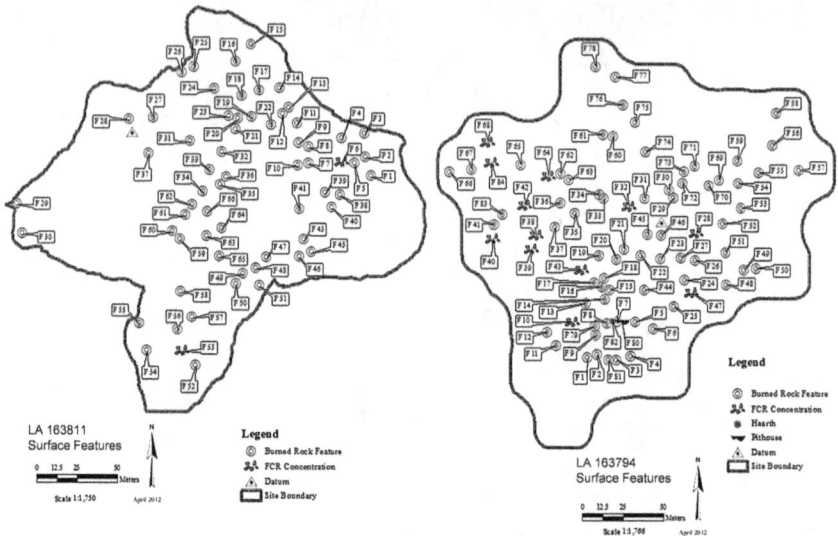

FIGURE 12.6. *Surface map of (left) LA 163811 and (right) LA 163794 along El Paso Canyon, showing landscapes of over 70 burned-rock middens at each location (from Miller, Graves, Frederick, and Landreth 2012).*

So just how many numbers and tons of rock cobbles were gathered to bake agave, succulents, cholla, datil, and other foods in the Jornada region? Looking beyond the study area on the edge of the Highlands, the amount is staggering because these estimates do not take into account the remaining massifs of the Sierra Blanca/Capitan/Sacramento Mountains to the north and east of the southern foothills. The estimates also do not take into account any of the burned-rock middens in the Guadalupe, Organ, Franklin, Hueco, Jarilla, San Andres, Diablo, Eagle, Quitman, and Delaware Mountains and the alluvial fans and valleys around these ranges, nor do they account for the mountain ranges south of the US-Mexico border. Between the mountain ranges, hundreds and perhaps thousands of small baking pits with 100 kg or less of rock have been documented in the surveyed portions of the Tularosa Basin and many more are present in unsurveyed areas of the basin.

If, for the sake of heuristic argument, we assume a conservative estimate of a total of 50,000 middens throughout the Western Jornada and adjacent highlands, the baseline estimate is that 105 million cobbles weighing 58 million kilograms were collected. These estimates are for expository purposes (the actual totals are probably higher) and clearly underscore the labor investment in plant-baking facilities that took place across the western and highland Jornada region.

Furthermore, these estimates do not take into account the time, energy, organization, and caloric investment to harvest, transport, and prepare the cacti and other plants, nor do they consider the time and effort required to gather the fuel wood needed to heat the pits. If we use Dering's (1999:665) experimental estimate that 224 kg of wood was needed to heat a typical baking pit, then somewhere around 14,784 kg of fuel wood would have been needed for the 66 baking pits of the sample—and that is only for a single heating/baking event and does not factor in that most pits were used several times. Multiply this total by several orders of magnitude for the southern foothills and the greater Jornada region and the efforts required to harvest fuel wood are indeed staggering. If the conservative estimate of 50,000 middens is used, approximately 11,200,000 kg of wood was needed to heat those baking pits—and that accounts for only a single use.

BEYOND BAKING: FIBER PRODUCTION AND FERMENTATION

The quantitative estimates of burned-rock weights and counts and fuel-wood quantities would have been manifested in labor costs, caloric investments and return rates, and organizational needs in the past. Accordingly, these values suggest a much different perspective regarding intensification of plant baking and everything else that entails and raise the question of why such a labor-intensive food preparation technology was adopted. What purpose did all this labor serve? The use of Agavaceae to buffer poor agricultural harvests is one possible explanation, as is the fuel-conserving nature of cookstone technology. Cookstones capture, retain, and radiate heat for long periods of time, allowing for complex carbohydrate and sugars to be broken down and rendered edible and palatable (Wandsnider 1997). This is especially critical in desert environments where fuel quantities are limited and sources are scattered, isolated, and do not regenerate rapidly. Cookstones serve to "trap and hold flame heat" (Thoms 2008:445) and this fuel-conserving property of cookstones would have been useful in the Chihuahua Desert setting where fuel sources were limited. Another factor in the expansion of plant-baking facilities may have involved the increasing use of Agavaceae and other cacti as a buffering mechanism against crop failure and famine. Sauer (1941, 1963) first argued that prehispanic populations inhabiting arid lands along the northern periphery of Mesoamerica had to develop a drought-resistant subsistence strategy. The Mesoamerican subsistence base of maize, beans, and squash was highly susceptible to drought conditions that would result in reduced yields; cultivation of agave could have provided a buffering mechanism that would lessen the effects of recurrent droughts in the arid north. In a simulation study, Anderies et al. (2008) demonstrate that supplementing maize agriculture through investments in agave cultivation could, under favorable and consistent rainfall conditions typical of the central Mexican highlands, reduce by as much as 95% the probability of famine resulting from agricultural failure. It is noteworthy, however, that in situations of highly variable and patchy rainfall typical of the northern Chihuahuan Desert, agave cultivation may not have had any appreciable effect on famine reduction—something to consider when approaching the problem of agave exploitation and cultivation in the Jornada region.

While these aspects of plant-baking pits were undoubtedly important, we argue that social factors are at least as important, or perhaps more important. A critical and overlooked factor is that plant-baking facilities had several important functions beyond food and subsistence—including technological, economic, ritual, and social dimensions. Studies of pit baking tend to focus only on the subsistence aspects of agave and yucca, ignoring the critical non-food uses that were important components of prehistoric economies. Fiber production was undoubtedly a major component of Agavaceae baking. Only two major sources of fibers existed in the prehistoric southern Southwest: Agavaceae and cotton. Inventories of perishable items from dry caves in the region show extensive use of Agavaceae fibers for clothing, shoes, baskets, nets, traps and snares, and whatever items required string and thread (Cosgrove 1947; MacNeish 1993; O'Laughlin 1977). Through ethnographic and actualistic research, Parsons and Parsons (1990:361) demonstrate that, using stone tools, fibers can effectively be removed from the hard flesh of maguey (agave) leaves only after the leaves have been softened by some combination of baking and being left to rot for a few days. The leaves are then mashed on flat rocks and fibers are stripped from the mashed flesh using tools such as scraper planes. Maps of modern maguey (*Agave americana*) and lechuguilla (*Agave lechuguilla*) fiber-extraction workshops in highland Mexico illustrated in Parsons and Parsons (1990:193–207) show flat cobble pounding stones anvils in the central pit areas identical to those found in Jornada plant baking facilities (figure 12.7). The presence of scraper planes and pounding stones confirms that fibers were extracted from the leaves of Agavaceae plants within these middens (Bernard-Shaw 1990; Deaver and Prasciunas 2012; Osborne 1965), and the recovery of a pouch of woven Agavaceae fibers from a room floor at Sacramento Pueblo (Miller and Graves 2012) confirms that fiber production continued through the Pueblo period in the foothills of the Sacramento Mountains.

FIGURE 12.7. *(Left, top and bottom) Pounding stones in the central pit areas of Jornada plant-baking facilities. (Right) Baked agave leaves being mashed on a pounding stone (reprinted with permission from Maguey Utilization in Highland Central Mexico by Jeffrey R. Parsons and Mary H. Parsons. Anthropological Papers No. 82, University of Michigan Museum of Anthropology, Ann Arbor, Michigan. 1990:plate 88).*

Of the potential uses of pit baking and Agavaceae consumption, perhaps the most significant, yet most often overlooked, function of pit baking of Agavaceae plants was the extraction of liquid to produce fermented drinks. Agave fermentation and consumption of fermented mescal was witnessed by the first Spanish missionaries who journeyed across northern Mexico, west Texas, and southern New Mexico during the late sixteenth and seventeenths centuries (Bandelier 1890; Beals 1932; Bruman 2000; Gerald 1974; Griffen 1979; Pennington 1963). Identical practices, documented in contemporary ethnographies of indigenous societies of the Southwest and northern Mexico, include the widespread consumption of fermented agave and yucca drinks (Bruman 2000; Castetter et al. 1938; Waddell 1980). Accounts by ethnographers and ethnobotanists describe the use of earth-oven baking pits for ritual and ceremonies, often involving fermented beverages (Basehart 1960, 1973, 1974; Bell and Castetter 1941; Bennett and Zingg 1935; Castetter and Opler 1936; Crist 1940; Lumholtz 1902; Reagan 1930).

Much of the focus in the northern Chihuahuan Desert has been concerned with the production and consumption of *tesgüino* among the contemporary Tarahumara (Bye et al. 1975; Kennedy 1963; Pennington 1963; Zingg 2001). Often overlooked is the fact that *tesgüino* is a term that refers to other fermented drinks, and includes several fermented agave and cacti drinks in addition to the more commonly used corn liquor. Baked agave hearts were pounded on hollow stones, the flesh or pulp was then placed on a lattice of plants over the hollow and the liquid was allowed to drip into the hollow. The liquid was then removed and placed in a ceramic jar to ferment. Other accounts describe the liquid being squeezed directly into a ceramic container from the baked and mashed flesh (Bye et al. 1975). In a similar fashion, the Mescalero Apache collected liquid squeezed from the mashed flesh of baked agave and sotol hearts and let it ferment in ceramic vessels (Basehart 1960; Buskirk 1986; Castetter et al. 1938).

Given the ubiquity of accounts of agave, yucca, and cactus fruit fermentation in the ethnographic and ethnohistoric literature, it is likely that portions of the Agavaceae and other plants baked in the prehistoric burned-rock middens of the Jornada were occasionally, if not regularly, used for production of fermented drinks. The baked flesh would have been mashed on the pounding stones found in the central pit areas and the liquid collected in ceramic vessels for fermentation.

Most alcohols, including fermented mescal, are moderately to strongly acidic. Ceramic vessels used for fermentation often show evidence of etching and pitting of interior surfaces through contact with the acidic liquid (Arthur 2003; Skibo 1992). In fact, fermented saguaro fruit liquid was used by the Hohokam to etch designs on marine shell (Ezell 1937; Haury 1937; Pomeroy 1959), a testament to the acidity of fermented cacti beverages (noting, however, that calcium carbonate is a base and reacts strongly to acid). A particular class of ceramic container at the Postclassic center of La Quemada in north-central Mexico often had etched interior surfaces that are thought to have resulted from the use of the vessels to store and serve *pulque* (Anderies et al. 2008). It should also be noted that corrosion of ceramic interiors could arise from intense boiling of water and other contents; however, in such cases the corrosion tends to occur where the vessel was in contact with an exterior heat source and interior liquid, not throughout the entire interior, as often occurs through contact with acidic liquids.

Similar patterns of etched and pitted interiors should be present on El Paso Brownware vessels, if such vessels were used for fermentation.[3] Indeed, such evidence exists in the form of several large and thick El Paso Brownware jar sherds with heavily pitted and etched interior surfaces recovered from sites in the southern Sacramento Mountains. Several of the sherds were recovered from Room 1, the communal room of the northern roomblock of Sacramento Pueblo (Miller and Graves 2012) and additional examples were recovered from a house structure adjacent to a plant-baking pit at LA 117092 (Miller et al. 2013). It is important to note that such ceramic evidence is seldom found in direct association with burned-rock middens. Instead, the remains of fermentation vessels are recovered from habitation sites where the liquid extracted from baked Agavaceae plants would have been transported for fermentation and consumption.

THE EXPANSION AND INTENSIFICATION OF PIT-BAKING FACILITIES

The evidence for fermentation must be considered within the context of the labor estimates discussed earlier. Why was so much labor invested in the construction of plant-baking facilities, the harvesting of plants and wood, and the time-consuming baking and fermentation processes? A broader historical context regarding temporal patterns and settlement contexts is required to address these questions. Chronological age trends and patterns of use intensity were defined for the 77 features in the Western Jornada, as well as others excavated throughout the region. Examination of 174 radiocarbon dates determined that the majority of plant-baking facilities were constructed and used (and reused) during the Mesilla (AD 500–1000), Early Doña Ana (AD 1000–1150), and Late Doña Ana (AD 1150–1300) phases, with the peak of use occurring during the Early Doña Ana and Late Doña Ana phases.

Radiocarbon dates from four burned-rock middens and ceramic and projectile-point chronological data recorded during the ENMU survey of the Black River area matches the general temporal trends observed in the Sacramento Mountains. The dates from three features range from AD 650 to 1350 (figure 12.8), although Feature 3 yielded a date that calibrates to several intervals between AD 1500 and 1800. Ceramic sherds found on the surfaces of these features include Lincoln Black-on-red, El Paso Brownware, and Chupadero Black-on-white. Overall, the ceramic artifacts from the Black River survey area represent the indigenous Jornada and El Paso Brownware traditions, as well as the geographically far-ranging Chupadero Black-on-white. The known manufacturing dates for the majority of the identified sherds fall within a range between AD 500 and 1450 (Hogan 2006; Roney 1985b), although Chupadero Black-on-white was produced in the Salinas

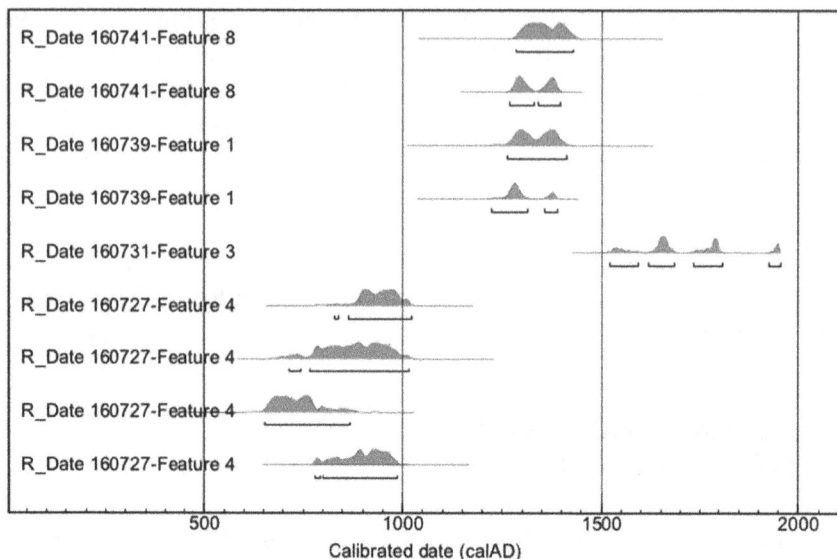

FIGURE 12.8. *Calibrated radiocarbon age estimates from four burned-rock features in the Black River survey area.*

region for another two centuries. Fourteen projectile points collected from midden features were typed using regional typologies (Hogan 2006; Katz and Katz 1985; Leslie 1978; Roney 1985b; Sebastian and Larralde 1989). The majority were produced between AD 850 and 1500.

Several proxy estimates of use intensity were examined (Miller et al. 2011, 2013). Rock-fracture rates provide a proxy for use intensity because increasingly intensive use and reuse of the facilities results in greater degrees of rock fracturing. Artifact densities in the burned-rock discard middens and central pit areas also reflect use intensity of the features and related habitation sites. Examination of these use-intensity variables along a time vector revealed the intriguing finding that while the construction of plant-baking facilities and formation of midden deposits occurred at increasing rates through time, the facilities were used less intensively. Mesilla-phase middens had high rock-fracture rates, indicating intensive use, and had greater artifact densities associated with occupations of longer duration. Middens formed during the subsequent Early Doña Ana phase had significantly less fracturing, indicating lesser degrees of use intensity and less-frequent reuse. Fracturing rates and midden-use intensity continued to decline during the Late Doña Ana phase and possibly through the El Paso phase. Middens of these periods also had significantly lower artifact densities, which suggests their use was organized on a logistical basis from residential base camps at pithouse and pueblo settlements some distance from the midden features.

To frame these conclusions in another manner, during the Early and Late Doña Ana phases, it is inferred that the construction and use of cookstone technology and plant baking pits was intensified. This intensification was manifested by the expansion of facilities, or more middens, across broader swaths of the landscape rather than by more-intensive, focused use of fewer individual middens in fewer, select locations. This is a critical issue, occurring as it does during a period of subsistence, settlement, and demographic changes throughout the Jornada region (see Miller and Kenmotsu, chapter 3, this volume).

It is our impression that a large part of this was due to limiting factors of the environment. Some stresses, such as pressures on the slow reproductive capabilities of agave populations, are difficult to measure with the available archaeological data. One form of resource stress that can be estimated is the effect on fuel-wood availability. In semiarid regions such as the Jornada, the fuel-wood requirements of plant-baking facilities combined with low biomass-recovery rates would have resulted in a rapid depletion of fuel sources in the vicinity of the baking pits. A limited amount of fuel is available from the surrounding desert, even resorting to the use of brush, shrubs, and dead cacti, and thus the fuel-wood requirements of even a small processing site would have rapidly exceeded the carrying capacity of the local environment.

To further explore the effects of wood depletion, radiocarbon age estimates from the plant-baking facilities (see Miller et al. 2013:table 6.1) were tabulated by elevation. Exploratory data analysis identified visible discontinuities among distributions of age and elevation values at circa 1000 AD and at 5,600 feet (figure 12.9). As shown in figure 12.9a, burned-rock middens dating before AD 1000 tend to be located along the lower outwash canyons, alluvial fans, and southern alluvial slopes of the foothills at elevations between 5,100 and 5,800 feet, with 50% (the interquartile range) of the features positioned between 5,360 and 5,590 feet. Middens dating after AD 1000 were often located in higher-elevation landforms, with 50% (the interquartile range) of the features positioned between 5,570 and 5,900 feet. As illustrated in figure 12.9b, there is a general separation of middens located above and below 5,600 feet at circa 1000 BP (1000 AD). A more striking illustration of this pattern is figure 12.9c, where the summed radiocarbon probability distributions for plant-baking facilities positioned above and below 5,600 feet are plotted. Elevations below 5,600 feet show a marked decrease in the numbers and proportions of plant-baking facilities after AD 1000. In contrast, the majority of the summed radiocarbon distribution for features at elevations above 5,600 feet occurs after AD 1000.

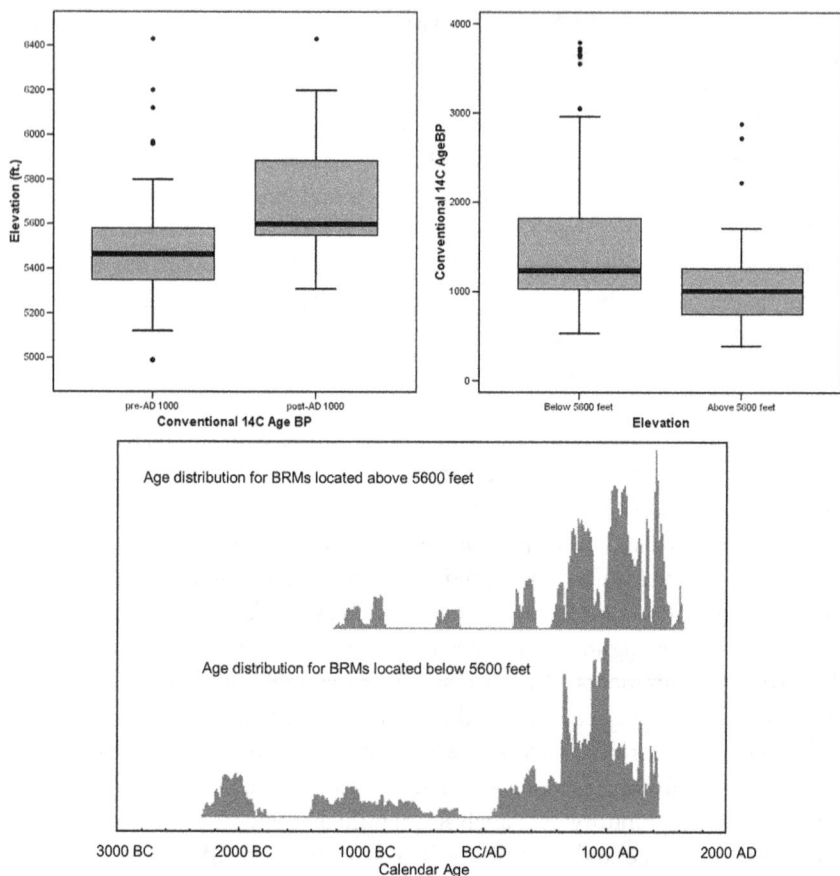

FIGURE 12.9. *Changing elevations of burned-rock middens in the southern Sacramento Mountains. Median boxplots illustrating the relationships between elevation and the ages of BRMs: (a) distributions of radiocarbon ages BP by elevation; (b) distribution of elevations by radiocarbon age; (c) summed probability distributions for radiocarbon age estimates from BRMs arranged by elevations above and below 5,600 ft.*

FERMENTATION AND FEASTING

Some degree of unsustainable practices is evident in the archaeological record of Agavaceae and cacti exploitation during the Formative period in the Western Jornada. The widespread movement of groups and construction of baking pits would have created conflicts and ecological stresses. While we can identify proxy measures of environmental and ecological stress, measuring social stress is a different matter. Yet there are ways to approach the problem. The insights gained from the use histories of burned-rock middens serve as illuminating background for studies of landscape use and social organization. The age trends, formation processes, and elevation shifts of plant-baking facilities suggest that agave plant communities and the wood resources needed to heat the baking pits were being overexploited and stressed during the Early Doña Ana and Late Doña Ana phases of the Formative period. These factors, when combined with the demographic and settlement pressures of the period, resulted in the construction and use of an increasing number of plant-baking pits across broader swaths of the landscape, and on an increasingly logistical basis, particularly during the pueblo interval of AD 1300–1450 (the El Paso phase). The economic, political, social, and ritual structures would have changed and evolved under such circumstances. These social contexts of burned-rock midden use—including ownership of the plant-baking facilities, land tenure of the surrounding resource base of plant communities and fuel supplies, and the distribution and consumption of the processed plant foods (especially fermented mescal)—merit greater attention. The production and distribution of mescal for feasting could have provided a means of ameliorating social conflicts and provided avenues for exploitation by community leaders and individuals or households of status.

Production and consumption of fermented drinks among the Tarahumara provides a useful ethnographic analogy for the role of feasting with fermented beverages in social interaction. Consumption of *tesgüino* (mainly corn-based alcohol but also fermented mescal) plays a fundamental role in social production among the Tarahumara and the beer-drinking ceremony—the *tesgüinada*—is an indispensable component of ritual and social action (Kennedy 1963; Merrill 1978; Pennington 1963; Zingg 2001). Almost all social events and ceremonies involve consumption of *tesgüino*. Cooperative endeavors are rewarded with *tesgüinadas*, social gatherings and meetings are initiated or closed with a *tesgüinada*, and all ritual ceremonies involved *tesgüino* consumption. In fact, Kennedy (1963:635) states that "it is no exaggeration to estimate that the average Tarahumara spends at least 100 days per year directly concerned with tesguino and much of this time under its influence or aftereffects."

Tesgüinadas are most commonly held for communal labor or curing ceremonies. Building houses, corrals, or fences, clearing agricultural fields, producing hay and fodder, and other cooperative endeavors are compensated by the production and distribution of *tesgüino*. *Tesgüinadas* are also held for life-passage events such as births, puberty ceremonies, marriage, and death and are a fundamental component of ritual practice. The ceremonies require significant outlays in terms of labor and corn, and thus serve to establish and maintain social status. What little social differentiation exists among the Tarahumara is based in part on possession of animals and fields, but mostly on ability to sponsor *tesgüinadas*.

One of the more noteworthy aspects of this type of commensal feasting is that the communal labor and ritual feasting serve to integrate disparate social groups residing at some distance from each other. Kennedy (1963:625) terms this the *tesgüino network*. Each household participates in *tesgüinadas* with other households, who in turn participate in the ceremonies with other households. This creates a distinctive structural form of relationships:

> The set of people defined by reciprocal tesguino invitation form the meaningful "community" for any particular individual. The important point about this type of structure is its centrifugal character caused by the fact that the meaningful community shifts its locus from household to household. This brings about a general netlike system of household-centered, overlapping interaction systems, stretching across the region. (Kennedy 1963:625)

As with most ethnographic analogies, the Tarahumara model may be not be entirely applicable or appropriate to the prehistoric Jornada, but the importance of fermented Agavaceae and corn beverages in feasting and social production should not be underestimated or understated. Similar social networks may have evolved throughout the Jornada in response to the demographic and resource stresses described above, and the distribution and consumption of mescal would have served to integrate communities and reduce conflicts over land and resources.

Evidence of large-scale agave pit baking is known at Paquimé and other settlements in the Casas Grandes region (Di Peso 1974; Sayles 1936a; Whalen and Minnis 2000, 2001a, 2009). At the edge of the Jornada, Speth (2004b) describes a large baking pit in the plaza of Henderson pueblo. It is very likely that the processing of Agavaceae in the baking pits at Paquimé and Henderson Pueblo was predominantly for the production of mescal liquor. The location of the baking facility within one of the central plazas of Henderson Pueblo indicates that such production involved communal or suprahousehold organization.

While other facilities of similar size and intensity have not yet been identified among Formative-period Jornada villages, there is substantial evidence for intensification, as seen in the use of hundreds of smaller baking pits throughout the entire region, and it is reasonable to infer that fermented Agavaceae was produced at these facilities. Perhaps agave fermentation was partially supplanted by corn beer during the El Paso–phase puebloan interval. The construction and use of plant-baking pits declines during the pueblo interval (Miller et al. 2011) and it is during this time that large El Paso Polychrome ollas appear, and the similarities between these ollas and Tarahumara *tesgüino* fermentation jars have been noted (Jackson and Thompson 2005; Shafer et al. 1999). Requiring a smaller fuel load, the production of corn beer may have reduced the stress on fuel wood seen in the record of agave pit baking.

Social networks and systems of land tenure were likely much more formalized during the Pueblo period than during the preceding Formative phases. It is suggested here, however, that the roots of such tenure arrangements can be found in the social and political responses to demographic pressures leading to intensified and expanded exploitation of the commons during the Early and Late Doña Ana phases, including the fermentation, sharing, and consumption of mescal. The production of agave and fermented mescal may have provided another path to leadership and inequality in the Jornada region, and taking an even wider view of this concept, it is suggested that the study of plant-baking facilities may reveal alternative pathways leading to the establishment and maintenance of low-level social hierarchies in the prehistoric Southwest.

Rather than a representing a uniform and mundane adaptive strategy, the studies presented in this chapter provide a more complex picture of plant-baking facilities and burned-rock middens across the western and eastern segments of the Jornada Mogollon region. The Sacramento Mountains and Black River study areas present a rich, dynamic, and complex tradition of resource utilization, technological adaptation, and social organization—a tradition that unfortunately is often masked by what, on a superficial examination, seems to be a monotonous and unchanging archaeological record of identical scatters of fire-cracked rock.

ACKNOWLEDGMENTS

Miller wishes to extend his appreciation to Tom Rocek and Jim Railey for the invitation to participate in the 2010 SAA symposium and the subsequent invitation to add thisessay to the volume. The excavation and study of the plant-baking facilities could not have been possible without the support and funding provided by the Conservation Branch, Environmental Division, of Fort Bliss Military Reservation. Brian Knight, chief, and archaeologists Sue Sitton and Chris Lowry supported and encouraged the field and analytical work. The analyses and interpretations presented in this chapter are built upon the dedicated and detailed fieldwork of the supervisors and crew members and upon Tim Graves's unparalleled expertise in teasing out the subtleties of burned-rock middens. Kevin Vaughn produced the GIS figures. An intellectual debt is owed to Steve Black, Darrell Creel, Alston Thoms, and to dozens of ethnographers, ethnobotanists, and ethnohistorians cited within the chapter. Montgomery would also like to acknowledge the Bureau of Land Management, Carlsbad Field Office, for their support of two years of field schools on the Black River. Erin Brown, Antonio De Cunzo, Sarah Millaward, Josh Pfarr, and Katherine Schuelke provided strong project support, both in the field and with data analysis. Finally, we both thank two anonymous reviewers for their useful comments and we thank Tom Rocek and Nancy Kenmotsu for their patience, editorial guidance, and support for this chapter.

NOTES

1. The family-level term "Agavaceae" is used here to encompass the genera *Agave* and *Yucca* and the species composing these genera.

2. Prior to the implementation of standard excavation methods for plant-baking pits, burned-rock counts and weights were not recorded by all investigators working in the southern Sacramento Mountains.

3. An amusing and relevant anecdote sheds some light on this matter. Phil Dering, my colleague and project paleobotanist for the investigations of plant-baking facilities in the Sacramento Mountains, once left a plastic garbage bag containing experimentally baked agave hearts on the floor of his laboratory. Returning to the lab after five days, he found that the mass of baked flesh had fermented and the liquid had dissolved the plastic bag and etched the tile floor. If fermenting agave liquid will etch high-fired ceramic floor tiles, then it is reasonable to assume that the interior fabric of El Paso Brownware vessels would have been affected in a similar manner.

13

Far southeastern New Mexico covers most of the Jornada Mogollon's Eastern Extension (see Leslie 1979 and figure 1.2), and constitutes a vast swath of the broader Jornada region. As such, fleshing out details of this area's Native American past is critical to understanding developments across the Jornada Mogollon region as a whole. Yet the details of prehistory in far southeastern New Mexico remain murky compared to the Western Jornada, particularly the basin lowlands. This is mainly the result of (1) a much lower number (and the typically small scale) of professional excavations, (2) a general lack of detailed, research-oriented studies, and (3) a tendency to view long-term prehistory in the Eastern Extension in rather static terms. This state of underdevelopment has prevailed in spite of several decades of sustained archaeological investigations in far southeastern New Mexico. Most of this has been survey-level work but also includes an appreciable and rapidly growing number of excavations. Yet most of the resulting information has remained buried in the gray literature, leaving our understanding of the region somewhat muddled, and many researchers rely on decades-old notions that assume a long-term persistence of highly mobile, hunter-gatherer lifeways.

This situation is taking a positive turn, however, thanks primarily to efforts spurred by the Bureau of Land Management's (BLM's) Carlsbad Field Office (CFO). The CFO manages a large expanse in far southeastern New Mexico (hereafter *the CFO region*),

Jornada's Other Half

Radiocarbon Dates, Climate Change, and Long-Term Trends in Far Southeastern New Mexico

JIM A. RAILEY

DOI: 10.5876/9781607327950.c013

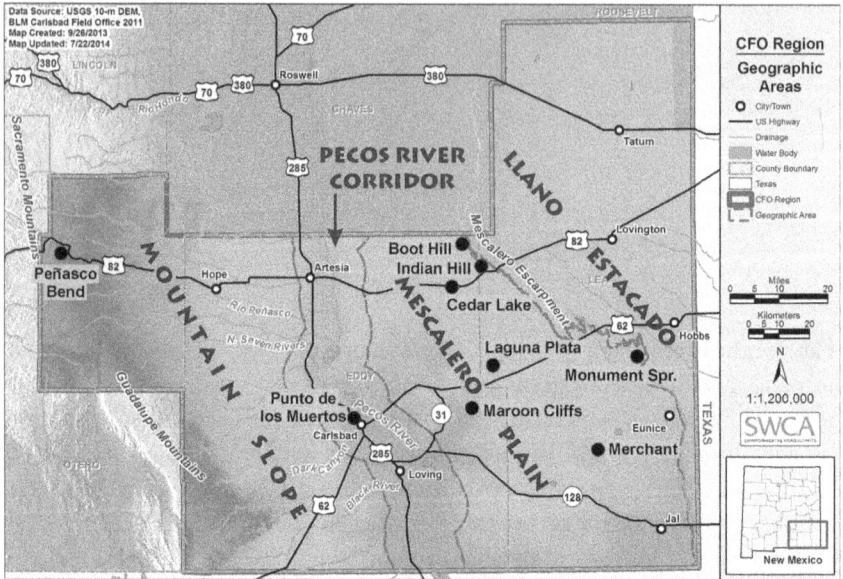

FIGURE 13.1. *Map of the CFO region, showing geographic subdivisions, sites, and locations mentioned in the text.*

and is the focus of this chapter (figure 13.1). For analysis purposes the CFO region is divided into the four geographic areas shown in figure 13.1: the Pecos River Corridor (defined here by a 10-km buffer along the river), Mescalero Plain (the area between the river corridor and Llano Estacado), Mountain Slope (the CFO region west of the river corridor), and Llano Estacado.

Recent BLM-sponsored efforts include syntheses of existing archaeological data from the CFO region (Railey 2013, 2016; Railey et al. 2009, 2011). Although current evidence suggests a persistence of highly mobile, hunter-gatherer lifeways through most of the first millennium AD, the record also reveals dynamic, long-term trends, and hardly suggests an unchanging world of mobile hunter-gatherers in the second millennium AD. While still riddled with many critical data gaps, the archaeological record suggests that the second millennium witnessed reduced forager mobility and investment in substantial house structures, food production, regional interaction spheres, and sociopolitical evolution, all occurring within a context of fluctuating climatic changes. With a focus on the CFO region, this chapter does not encompass important and better-known prehistoric developments documented to the north, in the Roswell area and Sierra Blanca/Capitan/Sacramento Highlands (e.g., Campbell and Railey 2008; Kelley 1984, 1991; Newlander and Speth 2009; Railey 2010, 2016; Railey et al. 2016; Rocek 1995, 2007b; Rocek and Rautman 2012; Speth 1979, 1983, 1984, 2004, 2005; Speth and Newlander 2012; Speth and Parry 1978, 1980; Wiseman 1981a, 1985a, 1996b, 2002, 2013; Zamora and Oakes 2000; see also Lynch and Rocek, chapter 7, this volume). Still, developments to the north are important touchstones for understanding what happened in the CFO region during later prehistoric times.

SOUTHEASTERN NEW MEXICO AND THE "NEO-ARCHAIC" PROBLEM

Several researchers have argued that native people in the CFO region relied on hunting and gathering all the way through to historic times. For example, Leslie (1979:179) stated emphatically that Jornada Mogollon peoples in the Eastern Extension "never practiced agriculture." Leslie's was a bold statement, given that there was virtually no archaeobotanical evidence from the region at that time. But the idea seems to have stuck, and there became a widespread notion that much of the Eastern Extension remained the domain of "Neo-Archaic" hunter-gatherers, distinguished from hunter-gatherers of the Archaic proper only by the addition of ceramics and the bow and arrow (Lord and Reynolds 1985; Phippen et al. 2000:34; Roney 1985a; Sebastian and Larralde 1989:47). This is a fair characterization for at least most of the Early Formative period (ca. AD 500–1100), when ceramics and the bow and arrow came into use yet mobile foraging apparently persisted over much of the CFO region. But even in cases with evidence for substantial agricultural dependence (i.e., high maize ubiquity, large storage pits, and/or substantial pit structures) in southeastern New Mexico, there is still a curious tendency to downplay the role of farming and emphasize the hunter-gatherer component of the subsistence economy (e.g., Wiseman 1996a:205; 2002; 2013; see also Condon and Vasquez, chapter 4, this volume). The term *Neo-Archaic* does not appear much in the recent and current literature from the region, but the notion it embodies seems to enjoy an inertia that continues to steer the thoughts and interpretations of archaeologists working in the area. For example, in a recent excavation report Condon (2010:293) concluded that "adaptations east of the Pecos River continue relatively unaltered until at least AD 1400/1450." But as this chapter illustrates, substantial evolutionary and historical changes did occur in the CFO region, especially during the Late Formative period (ca. AD 1100–1450).

RADIOCARBON DATES

The notion of prehistoric far southeastern New Mexico as a timeless world of conservative foragers has persisted, in part, because there is little direct subsistence evidence from the CFO region. Moreover, professionally excavated house structures are rare, and to date there has been little serious consideration of evidence pertaining to settlement and mobility trends through time. But what we do have in abundance are radiocarbon dates. As of this writing (July 2016) there were in excess of 1,288 archaeological radiocarbon dates (from 421 sites) that were reported with their two-sigma calibrations (or could be calibrated as such), from sites whose locations are known (Boeke 2013; Boggess and Zink 2013:table 5.1; Cummings and Kováčik 2013; Railey 2013, 2016) (figure 13.2). The number of dates per site ranges one to 94 (average = 3.1; standard deviation = 5.7).

Roughly two-thirds of the 1,288 radiocarbon dates for the CFO region are from the Mescalero Plain (n = 841, or 65.3%o), followed by the Pecos River Corridor (n = 340, or 26.4%), the Mountain Slope (n = 94, or 7.3%), and the Llano Estacado (n = 13, or 1.0%). The reason for these disparities is simple: within the CFO region, most oil-and-gas and other resource-development projects occur in the Mescalero Plain, and thus most of the archaeology driven by regulatory compliance has occurred here. More recently, BLM-promoted research has also concentrated in the Mescalero Plain portion of the CFO region.

The frequency graphs for the three areas of the CFO region that have yielded numerous dates are shown in figure 13.2, and figure 13.3 shows the sites from which these dates derive. The graphs are based on the two-sigma calibrations of each date, and all dates presented in this chapter are also expressed as their two-sigma, calibrated ranges. A simulation analysis revealed that variations in the calibration curve have no discernible effect on the radiocarbon frequency trend lines for the CFO region, with the exception of the early first millennium B.C., wherein short calibration time spans appear to slightly exaggerate radiocarbon frequencies. However, sample size varies among the area's subdivisions. Given the differences in the numbers of dates, the trend lines for the Pecos River Corridor and (especially) Mountain Slope are perhaps more affected by sample size than the one for the Mescalero Plain. With this caveat in mind, the dates were examined along with other archaeological evidence from the CFO region and neighboring areas, data on climate change, and existing knowledge of hunter-gather mobility (e.g., Kelly 1995). Led by the radiocarbon data, we can now discern substantial changes over time, and begin to advance some explanations to account for these changes.

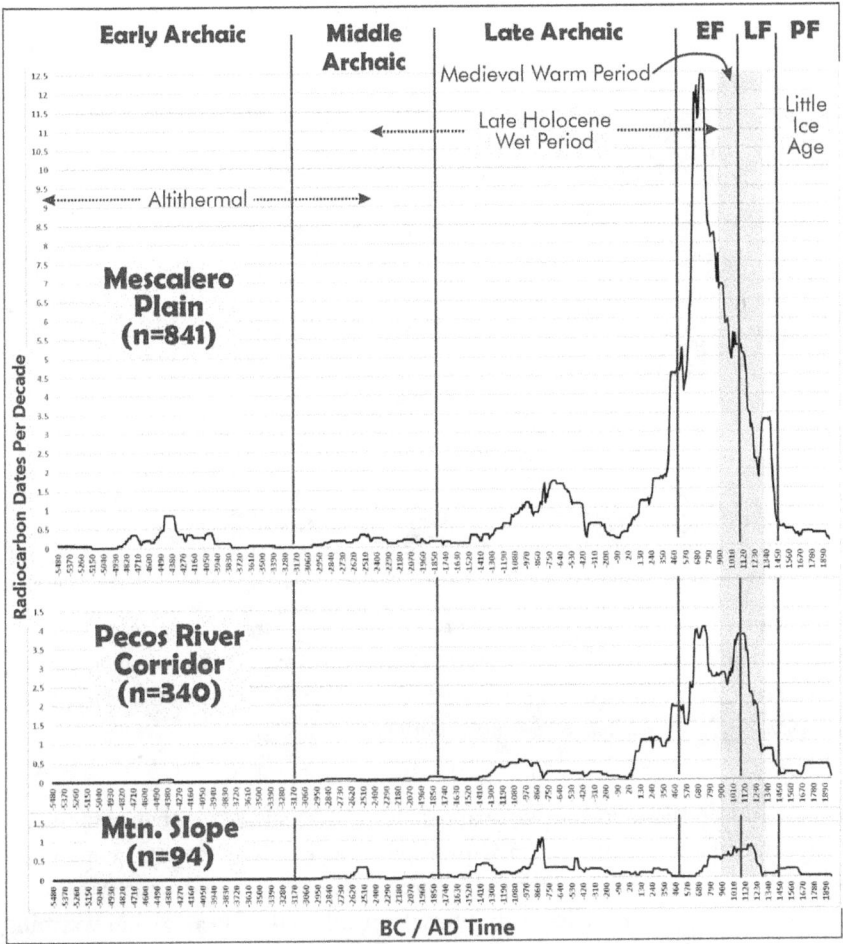

FIGURE 13.2. *Frequency graphs for radiocarbon dates for the CFO region, by geographic subdivision, with archaeological periods and important climatic intervals. The graphs sum the per-decade fractions of the dates' two-sigma, calibrated ranges. EF = Early Formative. LF = Late Formative. PF = Post-Formative/Historic.*

PRECERAMIC AND EARLY FORMATIVE FORAGERS TO AD 900

Following a complete absence of Paleoindian radiocarbon dates in the CFO region, the frequency of dates remains low throughout the Early Archaic (ca. 6500–3200 BC) and Middle Archaic (ca. 3200–1800 BC) periods. Although destruction of charcoal-bearing features from erosion over time may partially account for the paucity of dates from these ancient periods, very low population

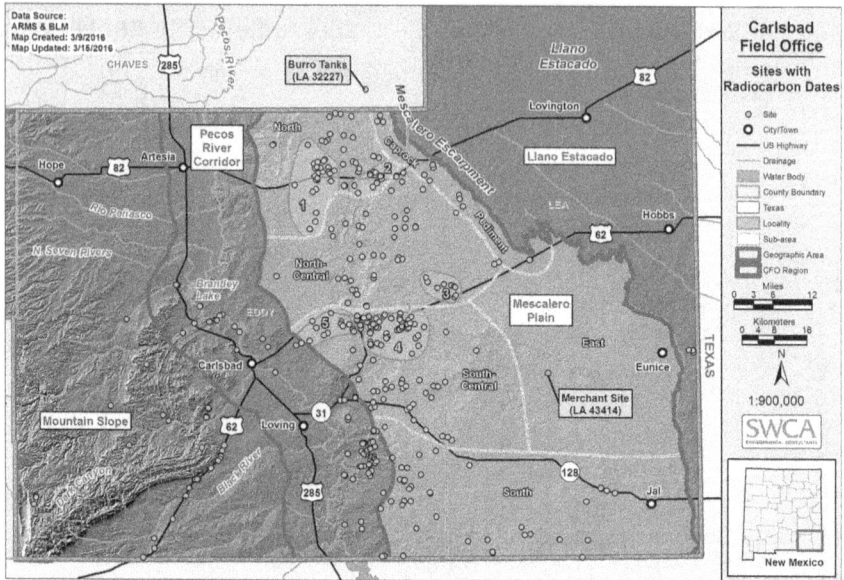

FIGURE 13.3. *Distribution of sites with radiocarbon dates in the CFO region, with subareas and localities within the Mescalero Plain demarcated. Localities are numbered as follows: (1) Bear Grass Draw; (2) Cedar Lake; (3) Lagunas Plata and Gatuna; (4) Maroon Cliffs; (5) Quahada Ridge and Tower Hill.*

levels and densities in the Early and Middle Archaic are probably the more important factors here (*contra* Cummings and Kováčik 2013:27). Population growth and land use were probably suppressed (especially in the Mescalero Plain) during the so-called Altithermal, an interval of near-global warming (Antevs 1948, 1953, 1955; Grayson 1993; Haynes 1975; Hester 1972; Holliday 1989; Johnson and Holliday 1986, 2004:290–291; Meltzer 1991). Overall dry conditions limited foraging options, people probably stuck close to still-wet streams and oases, and some even resorted to digging water wells (Evans 1951; Green 1962; Hester 1972; Meltzer 1991; Meltzer and Collins 1987; Warnica 1966)—a seemingly drastic move that earlier Clovis people had also opted for at Blackwater Draw (Haynes et al. 1999).

Beginning in the Late Archaic period (ca. 1800 BC–AD 500), the frequency of radiocarbon dates in the CFO region begins to increase substantially, as do the numbers of diagnostic projectile points and sites containing them (Railey 2013). Following a decline in dates in the second half of the first millennium BC, the growth trend continues into the Early Formative period, with a dramatic frequency spike in the Mescalero Plain and Pecos Corridor that tops out in the eighth century AD. In contrast, the number of dates in the Mountain Slope area declines over most of this same period, with a sharp increase beginning in the eighth century.

Taken as a whole, these patterns are consistent with a large body of evidence from the Southwest and Southern Plains, suggesting substantial population growth beginning no later than Late Archaic times, and much more ubiquitous use of the landscape than in the earlier Archaic periods (e.g., Berry and Berry 1986; Carmichael 1986; Mallouf 1985, 2005:219; Miller and Kenmotsu 2004:230–232; Walth and Railey 2011:352–366). These trends were made possible by the overall cooler and moister conditions of the Late Holocene Wet Period, which followed the Altithermal and lasted into the first millennium AD (Berry and Berry 1986:312–314; Blum et al. 1994; Cordell and McBrinn 2012:125; Grissino-Mayer et al. 1997; Hall 1990, 2010; Hall and Penner 2013; Hogan 1983, 1994; Johnson and Holliday 2004:291–292; Mallouf 2005; Mason et al. 2004; Mehringer 1967; Mehringer et al. 1966; Oldfield and Schoenwetter 1975; Petersen 1981; Polyak and Asmerom 2001; Smith 2002; Smith and McFaul 1997; Toney and Anderson 2006; Toomey 1993; Toomey et al. 1993; Wendland and Bryson 1974). Although some of these same sources indicate climatic fluctuations in at least some parts of the Southwest during the Late Holocene Wet Period, for the most part conditions were much less harsh than in the preceding Altithermal, and during the Medieval Warm Period that followed (see below). In fact, the tree-ring and stalagmite data indicate the ninth century AD was perhaps the wettest century of the Early Formative period in southern New Mexico (Grissino-Mayer et al. 1997; Polyak and Asmerom 2001).

The archaeological record of the CFO region appears consistent with these broader trends. Not only do site components, dates, and diagnostic artifacts increase sharply during the Late Archaic and Early Formative, but they are also distributed widely across the landscape, including within the Mescalero Plain. At the same time, evidence suggests that at least most of the CFO region (including all of the Mescalero Plain) was inhabited by highly mobile hunter-gatherers, who left behind mostly artifact scatters that lack substantial accumulations of anthropogenic sediments. Moreover, in the CFO region there are almost no structure remains documented for the Late Archaic period. The few known examples from the Early Formative suggest rather expedient, wickiup-like brush huts set in shallow basins (Jones et al. 2010; Railey 2013; Zamora 2000), housing typical of highly mobile hunter-gatherers (Binford 1990; Diehl 1992; Kelly 1995:139–140).

The improved climatic conditions following the Altithermal probably led to higher groundwater levels and a resurgence of springs, playa lakes, wet meadows, and other reliable sources of surface water. If so, then it follows that Late Archaic and Early Formative hunter-gatherers (especially those in the Mescalero Plain) were no longer "tethered" to scarce and dispersed water sources. The more widespread availability of surface water, along with an associated increased biomass and resource abundance, meant that hunter-gatherers could spread across the landscape and forage more efficiently than before. They could do this by moving their camps frequently, among a much wider range of potential locations than were available during drier periods. On average, this strategy would have decreased the distance and time involved in daily foraging trips, translating into greater caloric returns per energy expended (Kelly 1995:111–148). The archaeological result would be higher numbers, and a more ubiquitous distribution of, preserved camp remains (such as artifact scatters and cooking pits), relative to previous periods. This is precisely what we see for the Late Archaic and most of the Early Formative in the CFO region, especially the Mescalero Plain.

Population growth would also have affected mobility and foraging behavior among hunter-gatherers in the CFO region, even without any changes in environmental conditions or sociopolitical organization. Both theoretical models and empirical evidence suggest that the basic, closely-knit group size among highly mobile hunter-gatherers averages 25 persons, or five to six nuclear families (Birdsell 1968; Braun 1991; Johnson 1982, 1989; Johnson and Earle 1987:19, 320; Kelly 1995:210–213; Williams 1981). Larger aggregations of mobile hunter-gatherers, at varying scales, occurred seasonally and/or periodically for specific subsistence, social, or ceremonial reasons (see Hamilton et al. 2007; Johnson and Earle 1987:28–61; Kelly 1995:213–221), but the 25-person average basic group size is fairly constant cross-culturally (and a basic building block of larger, more complex societies [Johnson 1982, 1989]). Hunter-gatherers are also notoriously conservative, and "do not make rapid changes in their adaptive strategies" (Vierra 1990:61). Accordingly, assuming there was no major overhaul in sociopolitical organization, it follows that the basic group size remained unchanged. Thus, an expectable outcome of population growth is that hunter-gatherers fissioned into larger numbers of similarly sized groups with smaller foraging territories (Kelly 1995:151–152). This condition, in turn, could have led to several other potential outcomes: (1) more-intensive foraging within shrinking territories, potentially involving a broader spectrum of low-ranking food resources and decreased energetic efficiency; (2) the introduction of maize and farming into the subsistence economy, to increase the carrying capacity of a group's territory; (3) an expansion of social networks to help even out fluctuating disparities in resource productivity between group territories, which archaeologically might be signaled by the appearance of ornaments and prestige goods of exotic materials; (4) intensified territoriality, including symbolic representation of group territorial claims; and (5) intergroup conflict as competition over available resources intensified.

For the Late Archaic and Early Formative periods in the CFO region, the record is at best mixed with respect to these expected indicators of population growth and packing. The sharp increase in site components and more ubiquitous distribution of site components relative to earlier periods, is consistent with more widespread use of the landscape under rather favorable climatic conditions and population growth. But direct subsistence evidence is rare. West of the Pecos River, expanded use of lower-ranking food resources is suggested by the sharp increase in the number of dated burned-rock middens (Jones et al. 2010; cf. Dering 1999; Miller and Montgomery, chapter 12, this volume). Despite the identification of maize residues and microfloral remains in the Late Archaic and Early Formative (e.g., Brown and Brown 2011; Condon, Hermann, et al. 2008; Yost and Scott-Cummings 2011), there is almost no macrobotanical evidence at present that farming was added to the subsistence economy anywhere in the CFO region before Late Formative times. There is one instance of charred maize associated with an Early Formative radiocarbon date at a site in the Guadalupe Mountains (Kemrer 1998). But whether this is the tip of an iceberg or simply a stray ice cube remains unknown. Given recent discoveries in the Hondo Valley to the north (Campbell and Railey 2008; see Railey and Turnbow, chapter 5, this volume), it would not be surprising if archaeologists eventually find evidence of maize-based farming in the Late Archaic or (especially) Early Formative of the Mountain Slope area of the CFO region. Perhaps the continued decline in radiocarbon dates in the Mountain Slope area up to ca. AD 600 is an indicator of reduced mobility coupled with an increased reliance on farming, for the same reason that the abundance of dates elsewhere suggests high mobility and extensive land use among foragers. But given the dearth of direct subsistence evidence, this scenario remains purely hypothetical. Moreover, the Rio Hondo's is the largest drainage on the eastern slope of the Sierra Blanca-Sacramento-Guadalupe mountain range, heads at a higher elevation (which translates into lots of runoff from spring snowmelt), and enjoys heavier precipitation in its upper reach than any of the other drainages to the south. Thus, of all the valleys along the eastern slope, early farmers in southeastern New Mexico would have found the best conditions for preindustrial agriculture in the Rio Hondo drainage.

There is also no widespread evidence for intensified, extralocal exchange (i.e., items of exotic materials), territoriality, and conflict for the Late Archaic and Early Formative periods. There is one possible exception, however, and that is the Late Archaic site of Punto de los Muertos (LA 116471) (Wiseman 2003a, 2003b). Located on a prominent bluff edge along the Pecos River just outside Carlsbad (see figure 13.1), this important site was badly looted prior to professional excavation. It consisted of some sort of stone structure built from tons of the local limestone, and contained the remains of several burials with grave goods (including numerous shell beads and other ornaments), along with some habitation debris that may have been transported up from another site below the bluff. Although its precise structural character and function remain unknown, the considerable effort that went into the construction (and maintenance?) of this facility underscores its importance as a symbolic monument on the landscape.

The fact that Punto de los Muertos lies along the Pecos River is very likely no accident. Regardless of prevailing climatic conditions and population levels, lands along the Pecos were probably among the hottest of properties throughout the span of human occupation in the CFO region. If so, then we should expect some of the earliest evidence of territoriality to occur along the river corridor. One potential outcome of population growth, packing, and increased competition is the formation of territorially based descent groups (see Renfrew 1976). Such claims are sometimes validated by the construction of monuments containing the remains of deceased ancestors, and become particularly instrumental as territorial markers (Campbell 1959:125–129; Charles 1985; Charles and Buikstra 1983; Goldstein 1976; Hodder 1982:104; Saxe 1970; Saxe and Gall 1977). Such a scenario may help explain the unusual site of Punto de los Muertos, and if so then it was probably a territorial marker for a local group of hunter-gatherers, symbolizing their claims to critical (and spatially circumscribed) resources along the Pecos River.

Punto de los Muertos is a rare example of what may have been a formal mortuary facility, and as such appears unique in the region. However, given that it was originally recorded as a burned-rock midden, there may be many similar mortuary sites along the Pecos that have not been recognized as such. The closest documented sites similar to Punto de los Muertos lie far to the east, in the vicinity of Abilene, Texas (Forrester 1951; Morrow 1936; Ray 1931, 1932, 1933, 1936, 1937, 1939, 1946). At any rate, Punto de los Muertos was constructed during what appear to have been rather prosperous times for hunter-gatherers in the CFO region.

THE MEDIEVAL WARM PERIOD (AD 900–1300)

The onset of the Medieval Warm Period ushered in dry conditions that reversed the apparent good fortunes that people in the region had enjoyed since the end of the Altithermal, and heavily impacted human groups across much of western North America (Jones et al. 1999). Climatic data for areas in or near the CFO region are consistent in showing a distinct drying trend beginning ca. AD 900. The southern New Mexico tree-ring sequence (Grissino-Mayer et al. 1997) records a slightly dry interval at AD 920–940, followed by the most severe, long-term drought in the sequence at AD 940–1040. Likewise, in the western and southern parts of the Great Plains, pollen and other evidence indicate a marked drying trend beginning about AD 900 (e.g., Hall 1982; Wandsnider 1999:10). This climatic shift corresponds to a dramatic plunge in the number of radiocarbon dates in the CFO region, especially in the Mescalero Plain. As seen in figure 13.2, the decline following the Early Formative frequency peak actually commences prior to AD 900, for the both the Mescalero Plain and the Pecos Corridor. However, if the frequency graphs are affected by old wood, then the actual peak use of these areas may have begun to decline closer to onset of the tenth-century drought.

This severe and sustained drought appears to have had drastic effects on the area's mobile hunter-gatherers, especially those with foraging territories in the Mescalero Plain. The region's biomass must have plummeted, and many water sources would have dried up. Under these deteriorating conditions, hunter-gatherers in the Mescalero Plain could no longer maintain their efficient, blanketed use of the landscape. Given what we know about ethnographic hunter-gatherers in desert environments (see Kelly 1995), the deteriorating conditions potentially had four effects on the region's human populations at this time: (1) reduced fertility and/or increased mortality, resulting in a reduction of the region's population; (2) more-restricted residential mobility as hunter-gatherers once again became "tethered" to fewer and more dispersed water sources; (3) gravitation to surviving water sources within the Mescalero Plain (including such areas as Maroon Cliffs and the Caprock Pediment along base of the Mescalero Escarpment); and (4) migration to better-watered areas outside the Mescalero Plain, such as the Pecos River Corridor and Mountain Slope area.

Whether or not regional population levels fell is an open question, but the archaeological evidence strongly indicates much more spatially restricted foraging across the Mescalero Plain, and possibly migration to the other areas. The much lower frequency of cooking pits and other contexts with chronometrically datable materials suggests that there were far fewer campsites established across the desert lowlands, hence the sharp reduction in radio-carbon dates in the Mescalero Plain following the Early Formative frequency peak. Over the same period, however, the number of dates in the Mountain Slope area rises notably, peaking at roughly AD 1000–1200. Moreover, in the Pecos Corridor there is a secondary spike in dates during the eleventh and twelfth centuries. These patterns indeed seem to suggest that many people migrated out of the Mescalero Plain, with at least some moving toward the Pecos River and Mountain Slope areas.

In the Mescalero Plain, radiocarbon evidence suggests locally variable human responses to the Medieval Warm Period, with some areas serving as refugia while others seem to have been depopulated or even abandoned. For analysis purposes, the Mescalero Plain is divided here into five subareas (see figure 13.3; one Late Formative site, Merchant, lies outside these subdivisions and is not considered in this comparison). The frequency graphs for these five subareas are shown in figure 13.4, and table 13.1 shows the magnitude of frequency reduction between each subarea's peak during the seventh through ninth centuries (prior to the tenth-century drought) and AD 1100 (the approximate mid-point of the Medieval Warm Period). Note that the North and North-central areas show dramatic declines in the number of dates, while the decline is much less severe in the South-central area. The South area shows the largest decline at AD 1100, but then rebounds during the twelfth and thirteenth centuries. The Caprock Pediment shows the least precipitous drop; its two highest frequencies actually fall later in time than any of the other Mescalero Plain subareas, with one of those occurring in the tenth century. However, there are comparatively few radiocarbon dates from the Caprock Pediment, and this tempers the potential significance of this area's distinctive trend line.

Zooming in even further, figure 13.5 shows the frequency graphs for five more-specific locations within the Mescalero Plain, with their magnitude of frequency reduction shown in table 13.2. These are examined as they demarcate more-or-less distinct and localized physiographic areas with comparatively large numbers of radiocarbon dates. They were also selected as they relate to the hypothesis that people gravitated toward surviving water sources during the Medieval Warm Period, and include several playa depressions (Cedar Lake, Lagunas Plata, and immediately adjacent Gatuna), a prominent drainage (Bear Grass Draw), a sub-escarpment area with substantial Late Formative occupation (Maroon Cliffs), and a mostly upland area between Maroon Cliffs and the Pecos River Corridor (Quahada Ridge and Tower Hill). Note that Cedar Lake shows by far the most precipitous frequency plunge between its

TABLE 13.1. Radiocarbon frequency falloffs for five subareas within the Mescalero Plain portion of the CFO region

Mescalero Plain, Subarea	Radiocarbon Dates (AD) per Decade		Magnitude of Frequency Reduction
	7th–9th Centuries Maximum	*1100*	
Caprock Pediment	0.37	0.23	1.6
North	3.52	0.99	3.6
North-central	1.46	0.48	3.0
South-central	6.65	3.37	2.0
South	1.20	0.23	5.2

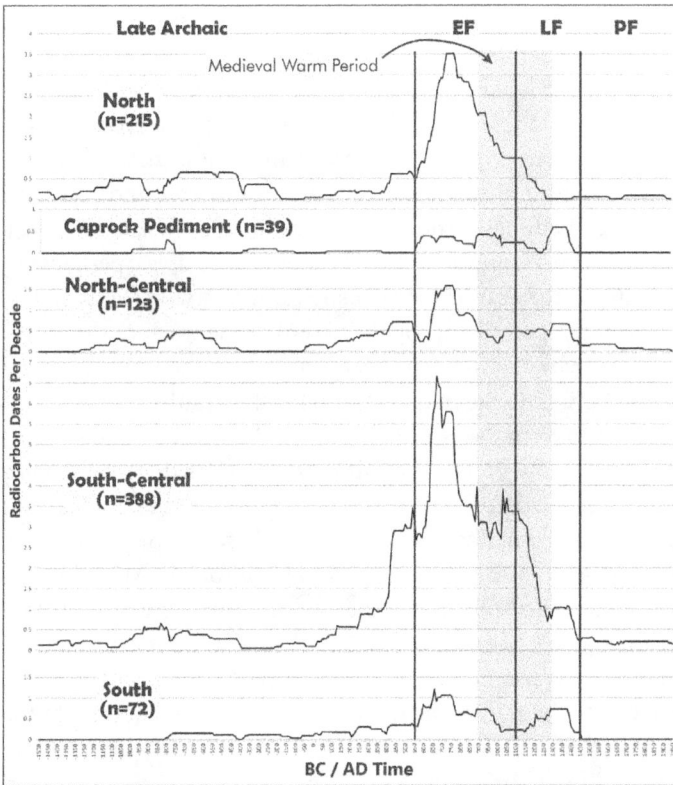

FIGURE 13.4. *Radiocarbon frequency graphs for subareas within the Mescalero Plain. The graphs sum the per-decade fractions of the dates' two-sigma, calibrated ranges, from 1500 BC onward. EF = Early Formative. LF = Late Formative. PF = Post-Formative/Historic.*

peak and AD 1100, and is much greater than the drop within the larger North subarea in which it lies. In contrast, the frequency falloff for Maroon Cliffs is the least severe, and is less than the larger South-central subarea (although note Maroon Cliffs' distinctive frequency canyon that bottoms out at AD 1020, which equates to a nearly fivefold decrease from its frequency peak). In between are Bear Grass Draw and Lagunas Plata and Gatuna, where the frequency declines are less than those for the subareas of which they are a part (North and North-central, respectively), while Quahada Ridge/Tower Hill shows a slightly larger decrease compared to the South-central area as a whole.

In addition to the apparent exodus of some people to the Pecos Corridor and further to the west during the Medieval Warm Period, these patterns suggest some relocations of human groups within the Mescalero Plain. Specifically, it appears that groups gravitated toward the areas below the Mescalero Escarpment and Maroon Cliffs, where springs probably continued to issue during the Medieval Warm Period and, if so, these areas served as important refugia at this time. The sharp reduction in radiocarbon dates in the northern portions of the Mescalero Plain suggests many people here may have moved over (or their movements were restricted more closely) to the nearby Caprock Pediment. The decline in dates at Quahada Ridge and Tower Hill suggests some people abandoned these upland areas, perhaps in favor of Maroon Cliffs to the east or the Pecos River to the west. Maroon Cliffs itself may have been temporarily depopulated during the worst of the tenth-century drought, judging by the frequency canyon that bottoms out at AD 1020, mentioned above (and note the frequency dip for the South-central subarea at this same time, which of course is heavily influenced by the large date sample from Maroon Cliffs). Some groups may also have gravitated toward Lagunas Plata and Gatuna (and perhaps also to the two nearby lagunas, Tonto and Toston, although there are no radiocarbon dates from these two playa basins). The sinks and upper canyons in the southwestern portion of the Mescalero Plain may also have offered surviving water sources to human groups (and/or perhaps resources that people based in the nearby Pecos Corridor continued to use during the Medieval Warm Period). If so this could explain the comparatively mild reduction in dates here from the frequency peak to the postdrought time frame.

In contrast, Cedar Lake appears to have been severely depopulated during and after the Medieval Warm Period. This calls for an explanation, since the data suggest that playa depressions, in general, offered surviving oases during the worst of the tenth-century drought and its aftermath. It is conceivable that hydrological conditions varied between different playas and sub-escarpment areas in the wake of the tenth-century drought. Most or all freshwater springs

TABLE 13.2. Radiocarbon frequency falloffs for selected localities within the Mescalero Plain portion of the CFO region

Mescalero Plain, Selected Localities	Radiocarbon Dates (AD) per Decade		Magnitude of Frequency Reduction
	7th–9th Centuries Maximum	1100	
Bear Grass Draw	1.11	0.37	3.0
Cedar Lake	1.26	0.23	5.5
Lagunas Plata and Gatuna	0.58	0.22	2.6
Maroon Cliffs	2.81	1.65	1.7
Quahada Ridge/Tower Hill	1.33	0.48	2.8

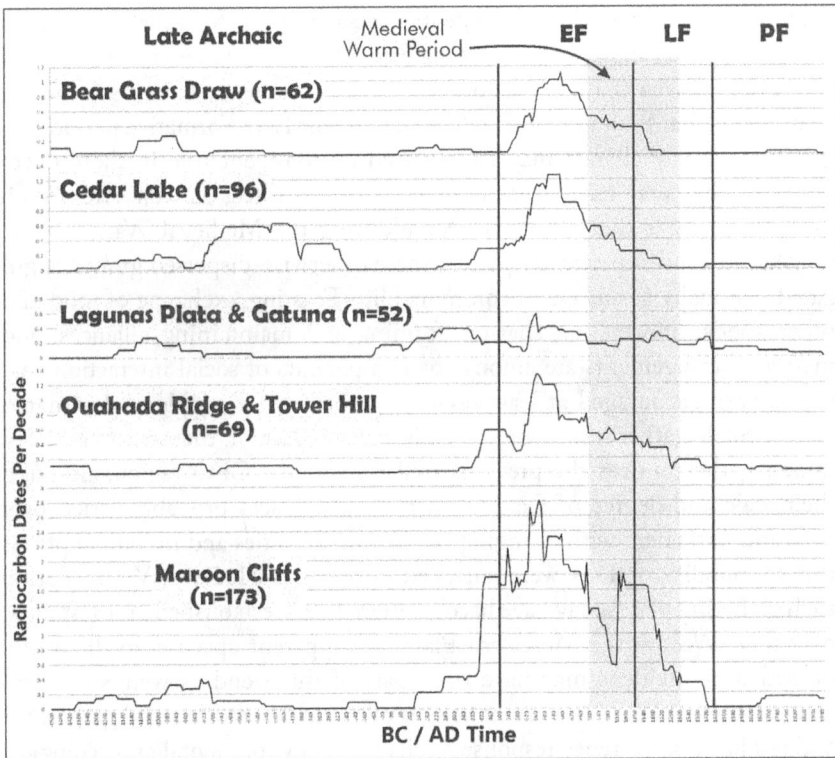

FIGURE 13.5. *Radiocarbon frequency graphs for selected localities within the Mescalero Plain (see figure 13.3). The graphs sum the per-decade fractions of the dates' two-sigma, calibrated ranges, from 1500 BC onward. EF = Early Formative. LF = Late Formative. PF = Post-Formative/Historic.*

around Cedar Lake may have dried up at this time, while at least some along the Mescalero Escarpment, Maroon Cliffs, and Lagunas Plata and Gatuna continued to issue. Moreover, if whatever water remained in Cedar Lake became salinized, then this may also have driven people from this area.

Taken together, the data suggest that people responded to the severe drought conditions by withdrawing to surviving oases in the Mescalero Plain, and to the Pecos River and highlands to the west. In the Mountain Slope area, most of the dates are from burned-rock middens, so the numbers may also indicate an upswing in the use of these sites and the exploitation of low-rank, high-cost food resources processed at them (see Dering 1999). Although precipitation levels apparently increased again during the eleventh century and into the early 1100s (Grissino-Mayer et al. 1997; Polyak and Asmerom 2001), the damage apparently was already done in terms of impacts to available resources (food and water) and reduced carrying capacity. The response to the period of severe drought may have helped prompt some fundamental changes in human adaptations that took hold during the subsequent Late Formative period.

While climate change may have played a prominent role in these developments, they may have been hastened by social forces as well. Areas such as Maroon Cliffs that attracted people during the Medieval Warm Period may have included particular places where otherwise-dispersed groups aggregated seasonally to engage in communal life. Feasting, exchange of food and other goods, information sharing, forming and maintaining alliances, and marriage arrangements are among the components of social interaction that would have encouraged at least seasonal gatherings of people at designated places. Such gatherings were probably always part of the social fabric of hunter-gatherers over the previous millennia in the CFO region, although their scale and degree of fixation on particular places probably varied over time and in tandem with changing population densities and mobility options. But as mobility options were curtailed during the Medieval Warm Period, such gathering places may have become more firmly established and sustained over time. West of the Mescalero Plain, the apparent upswing in the use of burned-rock middens may have been part of this trend as well; such sites are now seen as being important venues of group ceremonies and gatherings and not just a subsistence response to changing environmental and ecological conditions (see in this volume Miller and Kenmotsu, chapter 3, and Miller and Montgomery, chapter 12). Even with climatic amelioration following the drought at the start of the Medieval Warm Period, radiocarbon dates suggests people did not return to their free-range, highly mobile lifeway across most of the CFO region. Thus it seems likely that social forces assumed a role at least equally important to climate change in the apparent trend toward reduced mobility at this time. As such, seasonal aggregation centers may have set the stage for more-settled village life.

At least two sites in and near the CFO region contain evidence of intensive, "village"-like occupations in the AD 1100–1300 time frame. These are Burro Tanks (LA 32227; Bandy 2011) and the Maroon Cliffs site (LA 33085; Church et al. 2012:89–93; Speth 1984:19; Stowe and Condon 2012). Both are large, sprawling, multicomponent sites, but in portions of each are loci with dense artifact concentrations, anthropogenic midden deposits, and ceramics dating mostly between AD 1075 and 1300.

Another site, LA 20241 contains an 8-m-diameter feature described as a "carbon-stained trash midden," recorded during a survey (Husby and Pappas 2005). This site contains decorated ceramics (Chupadero Black-on-white, El Paso Bichrome, unspecified corrugated, and Mimbres Black-on-white), and what appears to be a side-notched arrow point spatially associated with the midden feature. The BLM obtained a radiocarbon date of AD 1175–1264 (Cummings and Kováčik 2013), although apparently not from the reported midden feature. This site is perched atop the edge of side canyon near the Pecos River, and its midden feature may mark the location of an isolated, comparatively sedentary household dating from the Medieval Warm Period. A potentially similar site is LA 171925, in the Maroon Cliffs area (Brown and Brown 2014). This site contains a 6-m-diameter stained midden, and has produced a radiocarbon date of AD 1277–1390 (Cummings and Kováčik 2013) along with an unnotched arrow point (although ceramics included only a few plain sherds and no decorated wares are reported). These sites may be evidence that the beginnings of settled life in far southeastern New Mexico involved scattered households as much or more than nucleated settlements. At any rate, the comparative degree of sedentism and concentrated occupation at these pre–AD 1300 sites appear to evidence a marked change in mobility and settlement patterns at this time, and set the stage for the subsequent period.

LATE FORMATIVE VILLAGES IN THE LITTLE ICE AGE (AD 1300–1450)

By AD 1300, a pattern of substantially occupied "villages" appears to have been well established across much of the CFO region, from the Mountain Slope area in the west to near the Texas state line in the east. This was part of a widespread pattern of village formation across the southern High Plains and Jornada Mogollon region in the early to mid-second millennium AD

(Brooks 2004; Campbell 1976; Collins 1966, 1968; Drass 1998; Drass and Flynn 1990; Jelinek 1967; Kalasz et al. 1999:195–198; Kelley 1984; Lintz 1984, 1986, 1991; Lutes 1959; Miller and Kenmotsu 2004; Speth 2004, 2005; Speth and Newlander 2012; Wendorf 1960; Wiseman 1981a, 1985a, 2002; Zamora and Oakes 2000). Most of what we know about Late Formative "village" sites in the CFO region comes from premodern excavations (Corley and Leslie 1960; Jennings 1940; Lea County Archaeological Society [LCAS] 1971; Leslie 1965b, 1968, 1979), along with subsequent excavations that were more systematic but mostly smaller-scale efforts (Brown 2010; Brown 2011; Haskell 1977; Miller et al. 2016; Stowe and Condon 2012). More recent survey work and systematic surface recording have also documented remains from sites that hosted substantial occupations during the Late Formative, including ones that were dug earlier by the LCAS (e.g., Bandy 2011; Church et al. 2012; Hunt 1989; Lone Mountain Archaeological Services [LMAS] 2001; Railey 2016). As discussed above, some of these "villages" may have been rather dispersed arrangements of households, but settlement layout remains unclear because so few systematic excavations have occurred at Late Formative sites in the CFO region.

Late Formative village sites tend to occur in areas where springs, precipitation runoff, or playa lakes apparently offered reliable sources of surface water and at least limited riparian environments and associated resources. In the Mountain Slope area, the larger river valleys appear to have hosted intensively occupied residential sites, judging from Jennings's (1940) discoveries at Peñasco Bend. Interestingly, similar sites have yet to be clearly documented along the Pecos River Corridor, although LA 20241 (discussed above) may be evidence that Late Formative settlement near the river consisted mostly of small, scattered households. If so, many such sites have escaped archaeological detection thus far, perhaps because they are obscured by debris from multicomponent occupation.

Late Formative villages in the region tend to have substantial midden deposits, and excavations at some of these sites have uncovered the remains of house structures. These range from rather shallow pithouses at Laguna Plata (Brown 2010; LCAS 1971), to what appear to have been much more substantial structures at several sites. At least one of the rooms excavated by Jennings (1940) at Peñasco Bend had four interior support posts arranged in a square around a central, collared hearth. This configuration is common to special-purpose rooms within linear pueblos of the El Paso phase in the Western Jornada lowlands (e.g., Bentley 1993:figure 9; Brook 1966, 1980; Miller and Graves 2009:135–136; O'Laughlin 1985:figure 1, 2001a; Railey et al. 2002:142–143). At the Merchant site, Leslie (1965b:25) uncovered what appear to be roomblocks and several pithouses, including an exceptionally large pit structure. Leslie also reported a large, deep pithouse at Monument Spring (Leslie 1968:80–81). A large survey by LMAS (2001) documented several possible roomblocks at sites near Merchant, and recent investigations at Merchant itself have clarified the patterning of structure remains at this important site, which consist of roomblocks and two probable civic-ceremonial pit structures (Miller et al. 2016:385–387). Given that most other roomblocks are reported from poorly controlled excavations and survey data only, their correct identification may be somewhat in doubt. Still, considering that roomblocks occur in the El Paso phase (Miller and Kenmotsu 2004) and in west Texas (Brooks 2004; Collins 1966, 1968), it should not be surprising if they occur in the CFO region as well.

These developments occurred during the Little Ice Age, under climatic conditions that fluctuated frequently between wet periods and drought (Grissino-Mayer et al. 1997; Johnson and Holliday 2004:292; Polyak and Asmerom 2001). Although there is a slight frequency rebound during the fourteenth century in the Mescalero Plain, this "village" period corresponds to a continued, precipitous drop in the number of radiocarbon dates across the CFO region (see figure 13.2). As with the Medieval Warm Period, however, there is local variation among radiocarbon trend lines within the Mescalero Plain. While there are essentially no dates for this period in the North subarea, along the nearby Caprock Pediment, the radiocarbon trend line actually attains its highest peak in the fourteenth century (see figure 13.4). Again, this trend line should be viewed with some caution, given the small sample size on which it is based, but it is potentially consistent with the reported concentration of Late Formative sites below the Mescalero Escarpment (see Leslie 1979:figure 3). At Lagunas Plata and Gatuna, there is bump in the number of dates that peaks in the late fourteenth century (see figure 13.5), and this includes dates from the Late Formative occupation at the Laguna Plata site (Brown 2010). At Maroon Cliffs the number of dates for the period declines dramatically from the preceding Medieval Warm Period, when this area apparently served as a critical oasis; the reasons for this decline in dates at Maroon Cliffs after AD 1300 remain unclear. In the Quahada Ridge/Tower Hill area to the west, the frequency of radiocarbon dates also declines in the Late Formative period, although the trend line suggests some post–AD 1300 activity here as well. To the east, recent investigations at Merchant have produced a new crop of radiocarbon dates, which confirm a main occupation at this site in the AD 1300–1450 interval (Cummings and Kováčik 2013; Miller et al. 2016).

In the southern portion of the Mescalero Plain, there is a distinct bump in the number of dates for the AD 1300–1450 interval. Although the sample size is small, the trend line suggests comparatively sustained occupation and activity into the Late Formative period, and possibly also a partial return to (or continuation of) high mobility and more spatially ubiquitous use of the landscape here compared to areas to the north. If so, then this may indicate that late prehistoric peoples in the far southern periphery of the CFO region continued to pursue a highly mobile, foraging-based lifeway, like that of contemporary groups farther to the south in the lower Pecos region of Texas (see Hamilton 2001; Turpin 2004).

At any rate, with the possible exception of the southern periphery of the CFO region, the apparent proliferation of "villages" during the Little Ice Age may signal a continuation of changes in settlement patterns and land use that occurred during the Medieval Warm Period. If so, the net effects of reduced mobility, more constrained and logistical use of the landscape, and concentration of the region's population into fewer sites (at oases) continued into the AD 1300–1450 time frame. A key question is whether the data also evidence reduced regional population levels, or if changes in settlement patterns and land use alone can account for the drop in radiocarbon dates—perhaps even in the face of regional population *growth*. But regional demographic trends remain unknown at this time. Regardless, the continued drop in radiocarbon dates across the region indicates that the highly mobile, broad-spectrum, foraging lifeway was never reestablished in the CFO region, with the possible exception of the southern periphery (where it may have simply persisted from earlier times). Instead, more sedentary villagers "dug in" at oases where water apparently remained available through both wet and dry periods.

To what extent these developments were, or were not, supported by maize-based farming remains an open question to some extent. At least some sites suggest a mix of farming and wild-plant use, similar to what was documented in the Roswell area to the north (Speth and LeDuc 2007:46). For example, in the Mountain Slope area, maize-based farming certainly appears to have been important at Peñasco Bend, where Jennings (1940) reported an abundance of maize, along with charred mesquite beans (suggesting processing and consumption of mesquite pods, as the beans themselves are rock-hard and inedible). Farther to the east, evidence for maize-based farming has taken a decisive turn in recent years. The LCAS did not report maize from their early excavations at Late Formative sites in the eastern part of the CFO region (with the exception of Indian Hill, where a later survey found charred maize exposed on the surface [see Hunt 1989]), but their excavations were not geared toward recovery of plant remains. No maize macrobotanical remains were recovered during recent (albeit spatially limited) excavations at Laguna

Plata (Brown 2010), Boot Hill (Brown 2011), or Maroon Cliffs (Stowe and Condon 2012), all of which hosted substantial Late Formative occupations. But even more recent investigations at the Merchant site have produced abundant evidence of maize, including charred kernels and cupules, phytoliths, and pollen, indicating maize was an important component of the diet, and was both grown and consumed at this site (Cummings and Kováčik 2013; Miller et al. 2016). Maize microbotanical materials and residues are more commonly reported for likely or confirmed Late Formative contexts from recent excavations in both the Pecos River Corridor and Mescalero Plains (e.g., Boggess 2009, 2011; Brown 2011; Condon, Kuehn, et al. 2008), but the absence of associated macrobotanical maize at these same sites leaves the significance of these findings unclear.

Another important subsistence trend that inhabitants of these Late Formative villages were caught up in was an increased emphasis on bison hunting. Following a regional hiatus that began in AD 500, there was a resurgence of bison across southeastern New Mexico and elsewhere in the Southern Plains after circa AD 1250 (Baugh 1986; Bozell 1995; Brooks 2004; Collins 1968, 1971; Creel 1991; Dillehay 1974; Drass and Flynn 1990; Greer 1976; Hughes 1989; Jelinek 1967; Speth 1979, 1983, 1984, 2004; Speth and Parry 1978, 1980; Spielmann 1983, 1991; Staley 1996). At some point during the Late Formative time frame, people on the southern High Plains began killing bison beyond what was required for their own subsistence and other resource needs, and traded hides, dried meat, and perhaps other products to the more settled farmers to the west (Creel 1991; Speth 2004a, 2005; Speth and Newlander 2012; Spielmann 1983, 1991).

To what extent Late Formative villagers in the CFO region were involved in this regional interaction sphere is unknown. Large quantities of bison bone in the LCAS's backdirt piles at the Merchant site have been documented and recovered (Miller et al. 2016; Speth 1984:11), and bison bone exposed by an arroyo has been reported for the Indian Hill site (Smith 1970). At Laguna Plata, bison accounted for only 3.4% of the animal-bone fragments identifiable to at least the level of genus (Gray 1977), far lower than at the Henderson site in the Roswell area (Speth 2004). Still, at Henderson the vast majority of bison bones occurred in just one locus (in and around a large earth oven), and they were rare elsewhere within the site. Thus, it is possible that the much lower percentage of bison bones in the Laguna Plata assemblage is due to sampling biases, rather than an actual indicator of relative reliance on bison.

Bison hunting on the southern High Plains may have been a response to profound changes in the Pueblo world to the west. The abandonment of the

Four Corners region by AD 1300 involved a huge influx of people into the Rio Grande valley of central and northern New Mexico (Cordell and McBrinn 2012:268–270; Jones et al. 1999:148; Newlander and Speth 2009; Speth 2004, 2005), where large pueblos (some containing more than a thousand rooms) were constructed in the Classic period (AD 1300–1600). Depletion of game and other resources in the vicinity of these megavillages may have encouraged Pueblo peoples to establish symbiotic trading arrangements with Plains groups (see Creel 1991).

As for far southeastern New Mexico, at present we can only guess as to the role played by Late Formative peoples in the Pueblo-Plains interaction sphere. The El Paso phase and Paquimé (AD 1250/1300–1450) were in full swing to the west and southwest, and Creel (1991:41) reports that the bison-based exchange system extended all the way down to present-day Chihuahua. Occasional bison remains are present in El Paso–phase sites (Miller and Kenmotsu 2004:250), and it appears that bison were disproportionately consumed at higher rank-order sites within the Casas Grandes realm (McCarthy et al. 2013). It seems likely that bison hides (which would not show up in the faunal record) were traded to the Western Jornada and Casas Grandes regions. Late Formative villagers in far southeastern New Mexico were well positioned as likely suppliers of bison products to the Western Jornada Mogollon and settled groups further to the south. But it still remains an open question to what extent, if any, Late Formative villagers in the CFO region developed an export economy fueled by bison products. Moreover, Spielmann (1983) argues that, prior to AD 1450, Pueblo-Plains interaction was limited mostly to gift exchange involving small numbers of items.

POST-FORMATIVE NOMADS (AD 1450-HISTORIC)

Beginning around AD 1450, people all over the southern High Plains abandoned their villages and shifted to a nomadic lifeway centered more squarely on bison hunting (Baugh 1986; Bozell 1995; Brooks 2004; Collins 1968, 1971; Creel 1991; Dillehay 1974; Drass and Flynn 1990; Greer 1976; Hughes 1989; Jelinek 1967; Speth 1979, 1983, 1984, 2004; Speth and Parry 1978, 1980; Spielmann 1991). People on the southern High Plains may have concluded that a more full-time focus on bison hunting made more sense economically than the mixed, village-farming-and-bison-hunting strategy of the Late Formative period. High demand for bison products by the pueblos continued, and Spielmann (1983) argues that if the Plains folks could get whatever else they needed from the pueblos, then this dramatic shift in lifeways may have been a simple "business decision." Spielmann (1983) cites evidence for an increased volume of Pueblo-Plains trade after AD 1450, with much more bulk trade of utilitarian goods in addition to continued gift exchange.

But to the west, not all of the pueblo societies were still there. The El Paso phase and Casas Grandes sites had been abandoned, and as a result any previous demand for bison products from these areas probably disappeared as well. Thus post-Formative groups in the CFO region may have lost their most important links in the regional system. To the north, Pecos Pueblo and the Salinas villages became major entrepôts for Pueblo-Plains trade, and the Plains sites with Pueblo goods from the post–AD 1450 period are mostly north of the CFO region (see Spielmann 1983). Some bison hunting continued into post-Formative times in the CFO region, as evidenced by an isolated bison kill that produced radiocarbon dates ranging from AD 1445 to 1625 (Staley 1996). Similar dates were obtained from the Garnsey Bison Kill site just north of the CFO region (Speth 1979, 1983; Speth and Parry 1978, 1980). Still, given the disappearance of the El Paso phase, Paquimé, and the pueblos in the former Mimbres area, the Pueblo-Plains interaction sphere's center of gravity probably moved to the north. To stay in the game, many people in the CFO region may have moved northward as well.

This scenario finds potential support in the continued decline in radiocarbon dates in the CFO region during the post-Formative period, which may be explained by several factors. Population levels probably declined, as was happening throughout the Southwest at this time (Lekson 2008:197). Any population decline in far southeastern New Mexico was perhaps attributable to both increased mortality—perhaps including intergroup conflict (see Wiseman 1997)—and migration to neighboring regions. Moreover, even though high mobility was once again the norm, the subsistence practices of whatever people remained in the region probably did not include the broad-spectrum foraging typical of their ancient predecessors from the Late Archaic and Early Formative periods. As a result, people were not digging as many cooking pits across the landscape and, hence, compared to the Late Archaic and Early Formative, there were still far fewer of these "time capsules" dug and left for archaeologists to collect charcoal for radiocarbon dating.

CONCLUSION

For a long time far southeastern New Mexico has been the poorest-known and least-understood part of the Jornada Mogollon world. This is so despite a vigorous level of archaeological activity over the past several decades. Many archaeologists working in the area still seem wedded to a notion that little changed here over the long course of prehistory. But this idea is more in line with decades-old thinking about the region than with current (and even some old) evidence. This thinking has been allowed to persist because (1) most of the work has occurred at hunter-gatherer sites, which are ubiquitous on the landscape; (2) there have been no large-scale, systematic excavations at Late Formative villages (in part because these sites are prohibitively expensive to impact under today's regulatory environment); (3) beyond the gray literature the vast majority of the still-accumulating evidence does not get out much; and (4) many of the known Late Formative village sites have been severely looted and for most their remaining data potential is unknown.

But the recent syntheses, sponsored by the BLM, have managed to pull disparate pieces of information together, including more than a thousand radiocarbon dates. Moreover, recent investigations—most notably at the Merchant site (Miller et al. 2016)—are providing new evidence that is reshaping our understanding of prehistory in the CFO region. The current compendium of evidence suggests several salient trends, which in many ways mirror those in the better-known Western Jornada Mogollon (see figure 1.2). First, a highly mobile, hunter-gatherer lifeway persists through the first millennium AD. Second, after what appear to be very low population levels through the Middle Archaic period, rapid population growth appears to ensue during the Late Archaic and into the Early Formative, under improved environmental conditions. Third, the increasing number of radiocarbon dates in the Late Archaic and Early Formative periods—including the eighth-century AD frequency peak—appear to owe as much to high mobility and ubiquitous use of the landscape as to population growth. Fourth, during the first half of the second millennium AD, many if not most people across far southeastern New Mexico settled into "villages" and practiced maize-based farming. Fifth, a resurgence of bison hunting occurred during this period of village life beginning around AD 1200–1300, which probably drew many people in far southeastern New Mexico into the Pueblo-Plains interaction sphere. Finally, around AD 1450 village life was abandoned across the present-day CFO region, in favor of a nomadic lifeway focused more squarely on bison hunting, and this was part of a broader shift across the southern High Plains. Many people may also have left the CFO region for better bison-hunting areas to the north, where they would have been better positioned to continue participating in trade with Pueblo communities that survived after AD 1450.

In sum, current evidence suggests Native Americans in far southeastern New Mexico experienced substantial changes in demography, subsistence, settlement, and economic and sociopolitical organization over time. Even during the long span of time during which the region was occupied by mobile foragers, there were still important changes in demography and land use, which in part appear linked to climate change. During the Late Formative and post-Formative time frames, evidence suggests much more fundamental changes. Many of these changes are in step with broader trends and historical developments in some of the surrounding regions. Prehistoric people in the CFO region became linked into regional networks extending far into the Southwest and southern High Plains, and rolled with the changes happening in this wider world. This new understanding upends the customary, static view of far southeastern New Mexico's prehistory, but many details of the trends suggested here need to be pursued through more research-oriented investigations. This should include extensive investigations at Late Formative village sites, whose individual histories for the most part remain deep in the shadows. At any rate, despite decades of intensive archaeological investigations, there are many remaining mysteries about the prehistory of far southeastern New Mexico, and this region retains a much richer research potential than is generally recognized.

14

Some Potential Ethnic Entities within the Jornada Mogollon Region

REGGE N. WISEMAN

The archaeological entity known as the Jornada branch of the Mogollon culture was first defined by Donald J. Lehmer (1948), based on the excavated archaeological remains found in the greater El Paso area (the Western Jornada Region), including the Hueco and Tularosa Basins as far north as the town of Alamogordo in south-central New Mexico (see figure 1.2). Then, on the basis of limited survey and observations of private collections, he extended the limits of the Jornada Mogollon to encompass areas to the south, west, north, and east, including the south-central chain of mountains composed of the southern Jicarillas, Capitans, Sierra Blanca, Sacramentos, and Guadalupes in New Mexico and Texas (the Sierra Blanca/Capitan/Sacramento Highlands). Somewhat later, Corley (1965) proposed that southeastern New Mexico lying east of the Pecos River be included within the Jornada Mogollon designation (the Eastern Extension); his reasoning included the presence of structures and pottery that at least partly mimicked the houses and pottery of the Jornada Mogollon to the west. At this same time, structures were unknown in adjacent parts of Texas (excepting the Antelope Creek remains of the Texas Panhandle). Thus, a Southwestern and especially a Jornada Mogollon derivation/affiliation for the southeastern New Mexico remains seemed very reasonable.

As these things often work out, new data created new problems. Subsequent work in the southeastern

DOI: 10.5876/9781607327950.c014

quadrant of New Mexico (including the Eastern Extension) has added much new information about the archaeology to be found between the eastern edges of the Hueco and Tularosa Basins and the Pecos River valley. Structures have been excavated, and we have gathered some tantalizing information about materials and manufacturing locales of Jornada Mogollon pottery (Hill, chapter 9, this volume). Not surprisingly, many of these details have exposed differences across the region, raising serious questions about the assumption of cultural homogeneity implied by the term *Jornada Mogollon*. In short, the differences are sufficiently great to make untenable the proposition that a single culture covered the entirety of southeastern New Mexico. Some of these differences may relate to different ethnicities or social differences, while others appear to be the result of differing subsistence strategies. Differences in subsistence strategies may or may not signal differences in ethnicities. A reevaluation of the cultural systematics is clearly required and is currently underway (Wiseman in prep.)

Over the past several years, while contemplating just such a reevaluation, I have been struck by some of the differences that have been documented by various workers in the field. Some rather sharp distinctions can be made in structure types and layouts, pottery assemblages, and certain minor artifact categories. Furthermore, these distinctions might be attributable to actual social differences that might qualify as ethnic markers, whether or not intended by the prehistoric peoples themselves.

The past 20-plus years have seen a resurgence of interest in identifying ethnic or socially distinct entities ("social identity") among archaeological remains of the American Southwest (Bauman 2004; Cordell 2008; Jenkins 1996, 1997; Preucel 2005). These attempts have attained varying degrees of success in both theoretical and practical studies (Adams 2002:249; Baker and Durand 2003; Bernardini 2005; Clark 2001; Davis and Winkler 1956; Haury 1958; Lindsay 1987; Lyons 2003; Neuzil 2005; Roney 1996; Stone 2003; Wiseman 2007, 2010).

The position taken here is the Social Constructionist model of social identity outlined by Lyons and Clark (2008:194–195) following Jenkins (1996, 1997). To them, ethnicity, "is internalized during childhood, . . . is centrally concerned with culture but . . . also rooted in social interaction, . . . is primary but not primordial, . . . is not necessarily fixed and unchanging, . . . can be salient and durable, . . . is not what someone has but is what one does, . . . may be imposed by outsiders, . . . is simultaneously collective and individual, . . . has cultural differences that do not necessarily equate with group boundaries, but . . . are the raw materials from which such boundaries are constructed, and is denoted by groups that choose relevant . . . symbols based on the context of their interaction and their histories" (Wiseman 2010:165).

Humans signal social identity in a variety of ways. Unfortunately, many of these ways do not always preserve archaeologically. Some of the more common types of signaling biologic, socioeconomic, and political membership involve hair styles, clothing, and footgear styles, face and/or body painting and tattooing, language, and certain items of paraphernalia. Regarding paraphernalia, ethnicity can be expressed in the way that the items are constructed, decorated, used, and whether or not they are consciously "displayed." Unfortunately, some of these (such as body paint or tattooing) rarely preserve and others (such as styles of clothing and footwear) are recovered only at sites with exceptional preservation. Usually archaeologists have only durable remains with which to work. The most common among these are projectile points, pottery, and structures (Grosboll 1987; Wiessner 1983). If one has a sufficiently large and varied database, then intra- and intersite patterning, subsistence information, rock art, and other aspects may be useful as well (Bernardini 2005; Santley et al. 1987). As with all lines of archaeological inquiry, the more threads of evidence that can be brought to bear on a problem, the better.

In my experience with the three main categories of durable material (projectile points, pottery, and structures), structures *in some cases* have what I consider to be the most reliable potential for displaying social identity. This is because the planning and construction of the more substantial structures are usually fairly detailed and time consuming compared to the manufacture of projectile points and pots. But, this does not mean that all structures of all peoples necessarily connote social identity. Candidate structures that do have such connotations are found here and there throughout the American Southwest and Southern Plains in certain time periods and specific archaeological cultures. They are quite distinctive in various details relative to those that came before or afterward, and they also differ from those of contemporary cultures in surrounding regions. Two of the best examples are the habitations of the Gallina culture of north-central New Mexico (AD 1050/1100 to 1250/1300) and those of the Antelope Creek phase of the Southern Plains (AD 1000–1500). In a recent study (Wiseman 2007), I make the case for the Gallina house forms as having reflected the Gallinas' sense of their universe and their place in it. As such, the house signaled a place of belonging, security, and a sense of well-being to the inhabitants. To non-Gallina visitors, it signaled that they had entered a "world" different from their own.

Projectile points and pottery, on the other hand, seem less secure in their potential for signaling social identity simply because they are portable, are readily acquired ("exchanged") through a variety of means for a variety of reasons, and they can be easily copied in whole or in part by members of other social groups. That is, while projectile points and pots can signal social identity, *they do not necessarily signal that identity in every context* in which they are found by archaeologists.

In this chapter, I present a case for the delineation of social identity or "ethnicity" as reflected among the prehistoric archaeological remains of certain regions within the so-called Jornada Mogollon culture area as currently defined in its broadest sense (see figure 1.2). The data and inferences focus on five facets of the remains: (1) the habitation structures, (2) the socioreligious structures, (3) the dominant utility ware in each pottery assemblage, (4) freshwater mussel-shell ornaments, and (5) so-called gaming pieces or dice made of bone. These five categories are not necessarily the only ones that might convey information about social identity within the Jornada Mogollon, but they are some of the more obvious ones that have come to attention over the years.

SOCIAL DIFFERENTIATION WITHIN THE JORNADA MOGOLLON

Although it is possible that social differentiation within the Jornada Mogollon started earlier than AD 1200, we do not yet possess sufficient data from the early pottery-period sites in some areas with which to systematically investigate the phenomenon. Thus, for the purposes of this study I concentrate on the period following AD 1200.

The areas for which we have the best data lie within the territory originally defined by Lehmer (1948) as the Jornada branch. For our purposes here, that means the Tularosa and Hueco Basins in south-central New Mexico and far west Texas (the Western Jornada Region) and the chain of mountains comprising the Jicarillas, Capitans, Sierra Blanca, and Sacramentos (the Sierra Blanca/Capitan/Sacramento Highlands) that border the eastern sides of that basin (figure 14.1). At the time that Lehmer encompassed the archaeological remains within these physiographic features within the Jornada Mogollon territory, his criteria were based on excavations in the basins around El Paso and Alamogordo. Then, on the basis of similarities in pottery assemblages and surface characteristics, he extrapolated the Jornada Mogollon concept to the nearby Sierra Blanca/Capitan/Sacramento Highlands. Subsequent work in the basins and the highlands has greatly expanded our hard data for the entire region (Kelley 1984).

The study area for this essay is broken down into three subregions: within the Western Jornada, (1) the Tularosa and Hueco Basins around greater El Paso; within the Sierra Blanca/Capitan/Sacramento Highlands, (2) the southern and (3) northern Sierra Blanca (Kelley 1984). The next few paragraphs

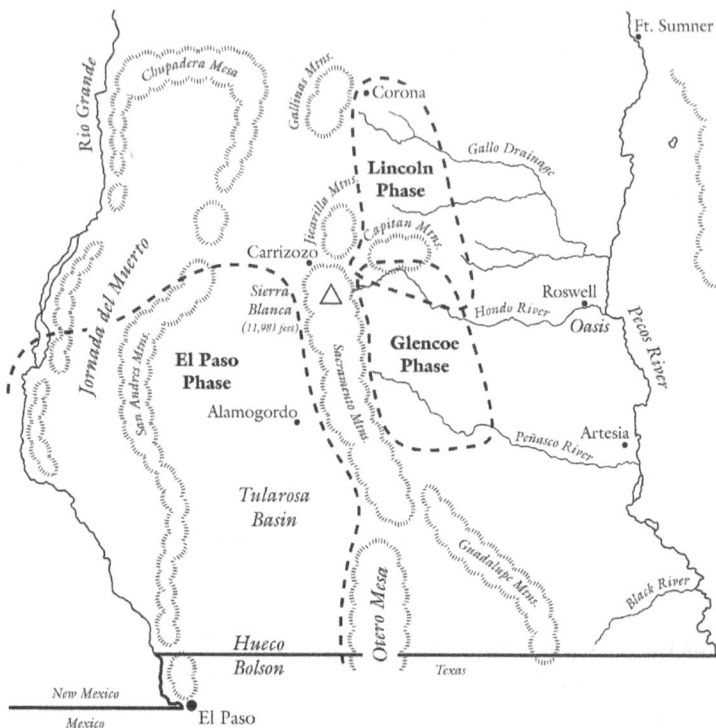

FIGURE 14.1. *Map of study area within the greater Jornada Mogollon, showing part of the original Jornada Mogollon territory as defined by Lehmer (1948) and the southern (Glencoe) and northern Sierra Blanca (Lincoln phase) territories as defined by Kelley (1984; see also Rocek and Kenmotsu, chapter 1, this volume). Adapted and modified from Kelley (1984:figure 9, p. 46).*

briefly characterize the major cultural attributes of each of these areas. Since subsistence practices were similar in each subregion, though definitely not identical, this aspect is not described here. For the record, corn, and perhaps beans and squash, were grown in all three, and the collection of wild plant and animal species was also important but in large part reflected species available in the respective regions.

The remaining subregions usually included within the Jornada Mogollon branch (culture) area—the Guadalupe mountains (Applegarth 1976; Katz and Katz 1985), the Roswell area or "oasis" (Kelley 1984; Speth 2004; Wiseman 2002), the Middle Pecos valley (Jelinek 1967), and southeastern New Mexico lying east of the Pecos River (the "Eastern Extension" of Corley [1965] and

Leslie [1979])—are omitted from consideration because of space limitations (see Rocek and Kemmotsu, chapter 1, this volume).

For the Jicarilla, Capitan, and Sierra Blanca Mountains, Jane Kelley (1984) defined two sets of phases that are geographically distinct except where they overlap along the Rio Bonito drainage (see Rocek and Kenmotsu, chapter 1, this volume). Here, they are designated as the *southern Sierra Blanca* and the *northern Sierra Blanca* areas or subregions. Although Kelley (1984) does not dwell on the point, she suggests that the differences between the northern and southern areas probably represent ethnic differences.

The Glencoe phase (see Rocek and Kenmotsu, chapter 1) is arrayed along the eastern slopes of the Sierra Blanca from the Rio Peñasco on the south to the Rio Bonito (the upstream major tributary of the Hondo, figure 14.1) on the north. By Late Glencoe–subphase times (AD 1250–1400), the southern areas appear to have been abandoned, with the population either concentrating in the northern valleys of the Ruidoso and Bonito streams, or perhaps leaving the region altogether. Glencoe sites of all periods have two salient aspects—(1) the people always lived in pithouses (figure 14.2), and (2) plain Jornada Brown pottery was by far their most important pottery. Late-dating villages consist of both individual and grouped, square-to-rectangular pithouses that vary widely in size; when grouped, the pithouses are often aligned in rows reminiscent of pueblo roomblocks in plan view. That is, the rooms share the earthen balks created between adjacent house pits, but the constructed upper walls apparently sloped inward on each structure and were not shared by adjacent houses. In addition to Jornada Brown pottery, Glencoe people made and used other types such as Three Rivers Red-on-terracotta. We have no direct evidence that they made Chupadero Black-on-white pottery, but they did trade for fairly large numbers of these pots (for instance, at the Bonnell site [Kelley 1984]) with their Corona/Lincoln-phase neighbors to the north. They also imported small numbers of types from a variety of distant lands.

Two other categories of artifacts are noticeably present on Late Glencoe sites, especially the larger ones. The first of these artifacts are both simple and fancy pendants and manufacturing debris created from freshwater-mussel shells (figure 14.3). The mussel shells, which presumably would have been procured from the nearby Pecos River or the lower parts of its tributaries (such as the Hondo and Spring Rivers), are not to be confused with any of a variety of marine shells traded in from coastal areas. It should be noted here that Brook (1965) assumes that the freshwater-shell pendants recovered in small numbers from El Paso-phase sites (see below) in the Western Jornada Mogollon originated at Casas Grandes (or Paquimé) in northern Chihuahua state, Mexico.

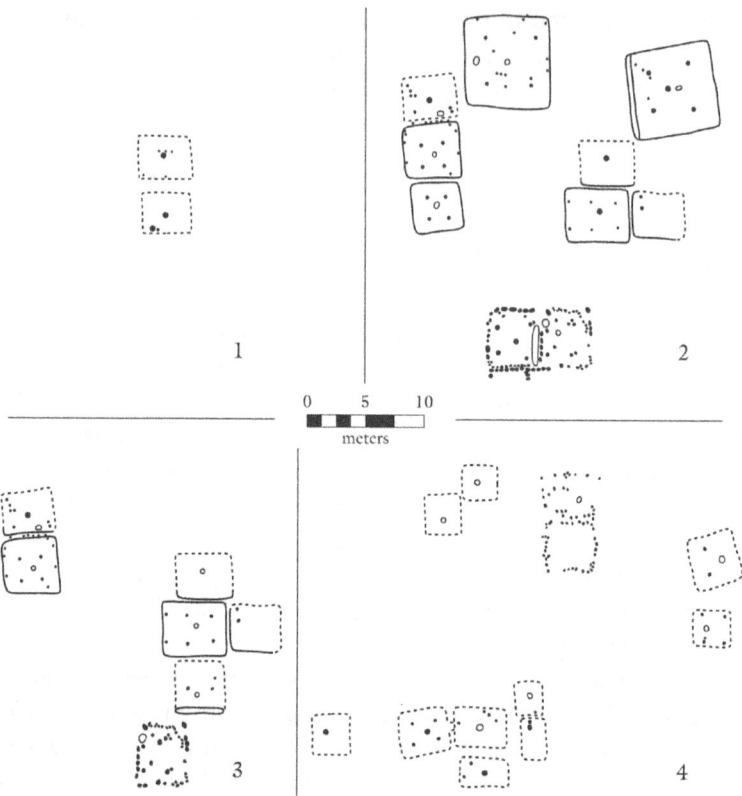

FIGURE 14.2. *Example of a Late Glencoe–phase village: Bonnell site, shows the four occupations as reconstructed by Kelley (1984:452–453). Adapted and modified from Kelley (1984:Map 9).*

However, the origin point or points of freshwater shells for these artifacts will ultimately need to be determined with certainty, probably through analysis by scientific instruments.

The second artifact category, gaming pieces ("dice"), comes in two basic shapes: elongate oval and round. They are made of turtle plastron segments and tabular cortical fragments of large-mammal long bones. The oblong pieces are the most common (figure 14.4). When supposed "sets" of gaming pieces are recovered archaeologically, the number of pieces usually varies from six to 10 in number and are usually composed of mostly oblong pieces, plus one or two round pieces.

The frequencies of both of these types of items—mussel-shell pendants (and manufacture debris) and bone dice—suggest that they were made in the

FIGURE 14.3. *Mussel-shell ornaments from various Late Glencoe–phase villages. Adapted from Kelley (1984:figures 31, 36, 38, 43, 47, and 57); Farwell et al. (1992:figure 37); and Urban (2000:figures 91, 94, 95, 96, and report cover).*

larger Glencoe villages such as the Bonnell site (Kelley 1984) and were occasionally traded to villagers in the surrounding regions (table 14.1).

The Lincoln phase is the final one in the northern Sierra Blanca during the Jornada Mogollon sequence. As defined by Kelley (1984), Lincoln pueblos range from the Rio Bonito on the south side of the Capitan Mountains (where they overlap in territory with Glencoe sites) to the Gallo and Bonito Canyons east of the Gallinas Mountains in north-central Lincoln County on the north (but see suggested reclassification of the northern pueblos in Wiseman [in prep.]). Like El Paso–phase pueblos (see Rocek, chapter 2, this volume), Lincoln-phase pueblos are composed of groupings or blocks of contiguous, square-to-rectangular surface rooms (figure 14.5). The rooms differ from El Paso–phase pueblo rooms (see below) in that they are generally small and fairly uniform in size and shape. Numbers of rooms per roomblock vary from a few to as many as a hundred or more. Large pueblos were often built around open spaces called *plazas*. Communal/religious activities took place in large, deep, square-to-rectangular pit rooms *that are separate from the roomblocks*. Pottery assemblages are dominated by Corona Corrugated and smaller amounts of Chupadero Black-on-white. Chupadero was a manufacturing

TABLE 14.1. Semi-quantitative accounting of freshwater mussel-shell ornaments and bone gaming pieces in late prehistoric sites in the Western Jornada, Southern Sierra Blanca, and Northern Sierra Blanca regions*

	Western Jornada (El Paso Phase)	Southern Sierra Blanca Subregion (Middle/Late Glencoe Subphases)	Northern Sierra Blanca Subregion (Lincoln Phase)
Number of excavated/tested houses	115	48	33
Freshwater-mussel ornaments recovered (number/number per room)	> 30/unknown	34/0.26	4/0.12
Bone gaming pieces (number/number per room)	0/0	61/1.27	2/0.06

* Sierra Blanca sites include only those in the mountains, not sites at Roswell (e.g., Fox Place, Rocky Arroyo, Henderson, Bloom Mound). House counts include pithouses, pueblo rooms, and socioreligious structures. References consulted for this table: Western Jornada: Brook 1965, 1966, 1967, 1978, 1980a, 1980b, 1984; Browning et al. 1993; Bussey et al. 1976; Cosgrove and Cosgrove 1965; L. Davis 1967; Foster and Bradley 1984; Gerald 1988; Green 1968, 1969; Hammack 1961; Hedrick 1967; Hunter 1988; Miller 2008; Moore 1947; O'Laughlin 1999; Scarborough 1985; Schultz 1967. Southern and Northern Sierra Blanca subregions: Farwell et. al. 1992; Kelley 1984; Wiseman 1975; Wiseman et al. 1971; Wiseman et al. 1976; Zamora and Oakes 2000.

specialty of at least some Lincoln-phase villages (Creel et al. 2002; Clark 2006). Other regional types such as Three Rivers Red-on-terracotta and Lincoln Black-on-red are commonly recovered in small numbers at Lincoln-phase sites. And, as is usually the case for late sites in south-central New Mexico, pottery types imported from across the Southwest are present in very small numbers. Mussel-shell pendants and turtle/mammal-bone gaming pieces occur occasionally as individual pieces but are nowhere as common as in the larger Glencoe villages.

Miller and Kenmotsu (2004; see also Rocek, chapter 2, this volume) present the most succinct synthesis of the prehistory of the Tularosa and Hueco Basins in terms of the architecture, pottery, subsistence, and other aspects of the Jornada Mogollon culture. Drawn from dozens of excavated sites, Miller renders a convincing, detailed sequence of architectural development, starting with individual pithouses and developing through individual and small surface pueblos. He ends with medium and large pueblos, some having as many as a hundred or more rooms in buildings arranged in single or multiple roomblocks (figure 14.6). This last period is the El Paso phase. For our purposes here, two aspects of El Paso–phase pueblos should be noted—the square-to-rectangular rooms vary greatly in size. And, every pueblo has at

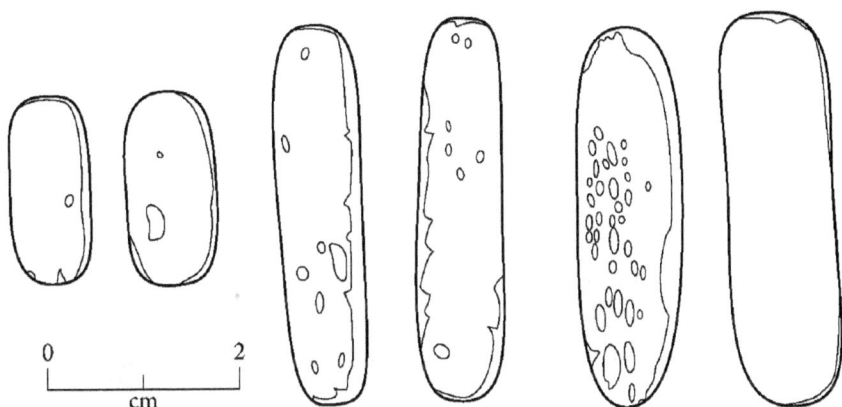

FIGURE 14.4. *Gaming pieces or "dice" from various Late Glencoe–phase villages. Adapted from Kelley (1984:Plate 59).*

least one extraordinarily large, nearly square room incorporated *within* the roomblock; most archaeologists believe these large rooms served a communal/religious function (Miller and Kenmotsu 2004:244). The pottery assemblage comprises mainly (> 80%) El Paso Polychrome, a painted ware that was used for cooking, storage, serving, and ritual. A few sherds each of various intrusive pottery types are usually present as well. Mussel-shell pendants occur with some frequency in El Paso–phase villages, but gaming pieces/dice, apparently, are absent altogether.

Table 14.2 lists the salient features of the three study regions (phases) and highlights the differences among them. To me, these differences are sufficient for suggesting that they warrant two tentative assumptions: (1) the material culture of the three phases are too dissimilar to permit classification under the single designation *Jornada Mogollon*, and (2) the people responsible for each phase, judging especially from the architecture, may have been socially or ethnically distinct from one another as outlined earlier (see also Wiseman 2007).

In summary, three of the ethnic expressions as currently conceived within the Jornada-Mogollon are:

- In the southern Sierra Blanca/Capitan/Sacramento Highlands (eastern slopes of Sierra Blanca) in the Late Glencoe phase: the pithouses occur either at random or aligned in quasi-pueblo style; the placement of socio-religious rooms is in the same manner as the habitations (i.e., either at random or in alignment with habitations); the pottery assemblage is composed

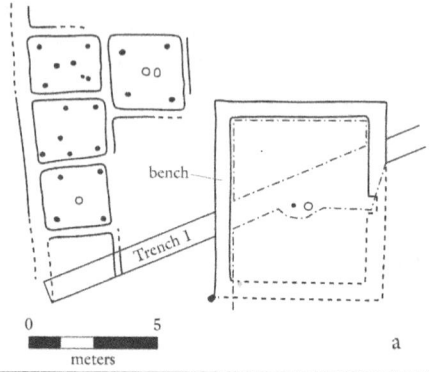

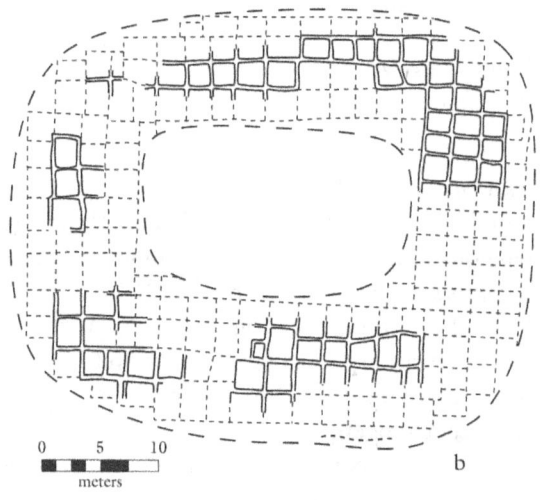

FIGURE 14.5. *Examples of Lincoln-phase villages: (a) Block Lookout site; (b) Hiner Site 1, Mound 1. Adapted from Kelley (1984:Maps 3 and 8). Map 3 modified for use here.*

largely of plain-surfaced Jornada Brown jars and bowls; personal adornment was with shiny pendants and spangles(?) made of freshwater-mussel shell; in some of the larger villages, fragments of freshwater-mussel shell represents wastage generated by freshwater-shell-ornament manufacture; and there was a propensity on the part of the inhabitants for gambling and/or playing games involving bone "dice."

- In the Lincoln phase of the northern Sierra Blanca (more precisely in the Capitan and Jicarilla Mountains and the eastern foothills of the Gallinas Mountains of the Sierra Blanca/Capitan Highlands), there are: linear or plaza pueblo buildings with uniformly small rooms; subterranean structures located in plazas used as socioreligious rooms; cooking vessels of textured Corona Corrugated jars and some bowls; service vessels of Chupadero

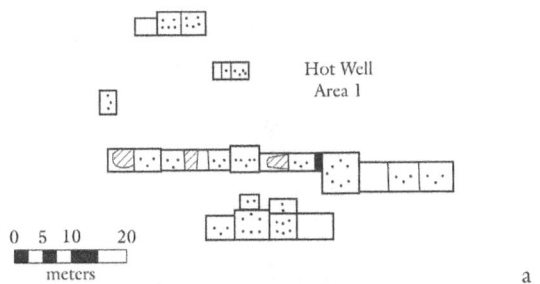

Hot Well
Area 1

0 5 10   20
meters

a

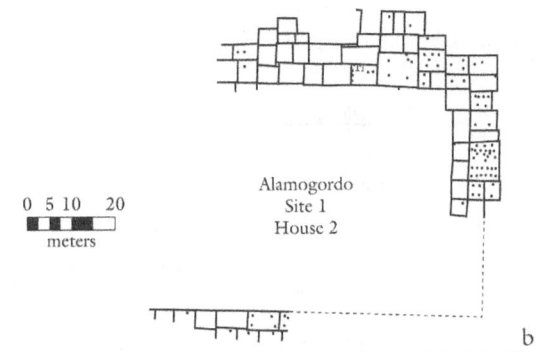

Alamogordo
Site 1
House 2

0 5 10   20
meters

b

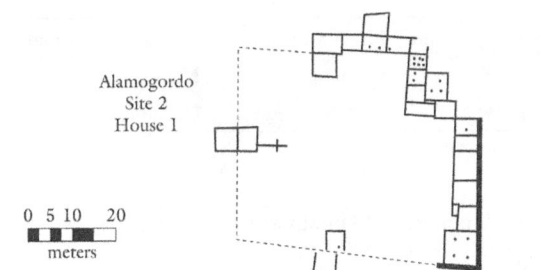

Alamogordo
Site 2
House 1

Alamogordo
Site 2
House 1

0 5 10   20
meters

c

FIGURE 14.6. *Examples of El Paso–phase villages: (a) Hot Well, Area 1; (b) Alamogordo Site 1, House 2; (c) Alamogordo Site 2, House 1. Adapted from Lehmer (1948:figures 23, 24) and Miller and Graves (2009:figure 3.5).*

Black-on-white; personal adornment mainly of marine shells and stones with only occasional pendants of freshwater-mussel shell; and gambling/gaming activities and paraphernalia characteristic of Glencoe peoples are known but not widely practiced.

- In the Tularosa and Hueco Basins (Western Jornada) El Paso phase, there are: linear or plaza pueblo buildings composed of large rooms that are highly variable in size and largely arranged in roomblocks; socioreligious rooms incorporated within the roomblocks; pottery consisting mostly of El Paso Polychrome bowls and jars; personal adornment with marine shells, stone,

TABLE 14.2. Salient characteristics of late prehistoric sites in the lowland and highland sectors of Lehmer's Jornada Mogollon

Cultural Attribute	Western Jornada	Late Glencoe	Lincoln
Layout	Linear and/or enclosed plaza roomblocks	Scattered and/or aligned structures	Linear and/or enclosed plaza roomblocks
Number of rooms per site	6–100+?	1–25	10–100+?
Room arrangement	Disorderly	Random or orderly (aligned)	Orderly
Room shape	Rectangular; odd shaped	Rectangular	Square to rectangular
Room size (m²)	3–25	6–25	3–9
Communal/religious			
Structure types	Surface room	Pit room	Pit room
Placement	Within pueblo	Scattered	Separate from pueblo
Shape	Square to rectangular	Slightly rectangular	Square to rectangular
Room size (m²)	30–72	± 36	36–57
Artifacts			
Primary pottery	El Paso Polychrome	Jornada Brown	Corona Corrugated
Mussel debris	Uncommon	Common	None
Mussel ornaments	Uncommon	Common	Uncommon

and occasional freshwater-shell pendants. Gambling/gaming activities involving bone "dice" not evident.

The attributes just summarized are readily identifiable in archaeological sites in the three areas of the Jornada summarized here. I conclude that they are sufficiently distinctive to argue that they call into question the inclusion of all three under the single classification "Jornada Mogollon." I also conclude that the attributes are sufficiently different in each case to suggest that they represent characteristics of ethnically distinct groups.

ACKNOWLEDGMENTS

The author would like to thank Tom Rocek and Nancy Kenmotsu for providing helpful comments on an earlier draft of this chapter.

References

Abbott, J. T., T. Church, S. Hall, M. R. Miller, E. Perez, and M. Goetz. 2009. "Natural Environment." In *Significance and Research Standards for Prehistoric Sites at Fort Bliss: A Design for the Evaluation, Treatment and Management of Cultural Resources,* ed. M. R. Miller, N. A. Kenmotsu, and M. Landreth, 2–1 to 2–55. Environmental Division, Historic and Natural Resources Report 05–16. Fort Bliss, TX: Garrison Command.

Abbott, J. T., S. A. Hall, and M. R. Miller. 2009. "Paleoenvironments and Paleoenvironmental Research." In *Significance and Research Standards for Prehistoric Archaeological Sites at Fort Bliss: A Design for the Evaluation, Management, and Treatment of Cultural Resources,* ed. M. R. Miller, N. A. Kenmotsu, and M. Landreth, 7–1 to 7–32. Environmental Division, Historic and Natural Resources Report 05-16. Fort Bliss, TX: Garrison Command.

Abbott, J. T., R. Mauldin, P. E. Patterson, W. N. Trierweiler, R. J. Hard, C. R. Lintz, and C. L. Tennis. 1996. *Significance Standards for Prehistoric Archaeological Sites at Fort Bliss: A Design for Further Research and the Management of Cultural Resources.* Austin: US Army Corps of Engineers, Fort Worth District, and TRC Mariah Associates.

Adams, E. Charles. 1991. *The Origin and Development of the Pueblo Katsina Cult.* Tucson: University of Arizona Press.

Adams, E. Charles. 2002. *Homol'ovi: An Ancient Hopi Settlement Cluster.* Tucson: University of Arizona Press.

Adams, E. Charles, and Andrew I. Duff. 2004. "Settlement Clusters and the Pueblo IV Period." In *The Protohistoric*

DOI: 10.5876/9781607327950.c015

Pueblo World A.D. 1275–1600, ed. E. Charles Adams and Andrew I. Duff, 3–17. Tucson: University of Arizona Press.

Adams, Karen R. 2004. *Archaeobotanical Analysis: Principles and Methods.* http://www .crowcanyon.org/plantmethods.

Adler, Michael A. 2002. "The Ancestral Pueblo Community as Structure and Strategy." In *Seeking the Center Place: Archaeological and Ancient Communities in the Mesa Verde Region*, ed. M. D. Varien and R. H. Wilshusen, 25–40. Salt Lake City: University of Utah Press.

Akins, Nancy J. 2003. *Salt Creek: Data Recovery at Seven Prehistoric Sites along U.S. 285 in Chaves and De Baca Counties, New Mexico.* Archaeology Notes 298. Santa Fe: Museum of New Mexico, Office of Archaeological Studies.

Alessio-Robles, Carmen. 1929. *La Region Arqueologica de Casas Grandes, Chihuahua.* México, DF: Imprenta Nuñez, Re. Salvador 26.

Allen, M. S., and E. E. Foord. 1991. "Geological Geochemical and Isotopic Characteristics of the Lincoln County Porphyry Belt, New Mexico: Implications for Regional Tectonics and Mineral Deposits." In *Geology of the Sierra Blanca, Sacramento and Capitan Ranges, New Mexico*, ed. J. M. Baker, B. S. Kues, G. S. Austin, and S. G. Lucas, 79–114. Socorro: New Mexico Geological Society.

Allen, M. S., and V. T. McLemore. 1991. "The Geology and Petrogenesis of the Capitan Pluton, New Mexico." In *Geology of the Sierra Blanca, Sacramento and Capitan Ranges, New Mexico*, ed. J. M. Baker, B. S. Kues, G. S. Austin, and S. G. Lucas, 115–125. Socorro: New Mexico Geological Society.

Alvarado, Luis A. 2008. "Instrumental Neutron Activation Analysis of Corrugated Wares and Brownwares from the Texas Southern Plains and Southeastern New Mexico." Master's thesis, Department of Anthropology, Texas State University, San Marcos.

Anderies, John M., Ben A. Nelson, and Ann B. Kinzig. 2008. "Analyzing the Impact of Agave Cultivation on Famine Risk in Arid Pre-Hispanic Northern Mexico." *Human Ecology* 36(3):409–422. https://doi.org/10.1007/s10745-008 -9162-9.

Andersson, J. Gunnar. 1973. *Children of the Yellow Earth: Studies in Prehistoric China.* Cambridge, MA: MIT Press. (Reprint of original 1934 publication.)

Andrefsky, William, Jr. 1994. "Raw Material Availability and the Organization of Technology." *American Antiquity* 59(01):21–34. https://doi.org/10.2307/3085499.

Anschuetz, Kurt F., and Richard H. Wilshusen. 2010. "Ensouled Places: Ethnogenesis and the Making of the Din'etah and Tewa Basin Landscapes." In *Movement, Connectivity, and Landscape Change in the Ancient Southwest*, ed. M. C. Nelson and C. Strawhacker, 321–344. Boulder: University of Colorado Press.

Anyon, Roger, and Steven A. LeBlanc. 1984. *The Galaz Ruin: A Prehistoric Mimbres Village in Southwestern New Mexico*. Albuquerque: Maxwell Museum of Anthropology and University of New Mexico Press.

AGI (Archivo General de las Indias). 1750. "Testimonio de los autos del reconocimiento fechos Río abajo del Norte desde el expresado río hasta las Misiones de la Junta de dho río y el de Conchos, por el Capitán del Real Presidio de El Passo Don Alonso Victores Rubín de Celis. Transcript on file, Center for American History, University of Texas at Austin." Audiencia de Guadalajara, 67–3-30.

AGI (Archivo General de las Indias). 1751. "Testimonio de los autos fechos en el orden al derrotero de compaña executado por el Capitán Comandante del real presidio del Paso Don Juan de Ydoyaga." Transcript on file, Center for American History, University of Texas at Austin. Audiencia de Guadalajara, 67–3-30.

AGN (Archivo General de la Nación). 1689–1788. "Historia 298." Copias del Padre Talamantes 1689–1778. Autos sobre el Derroteo y Viaje al Río de las Nueces. Microfilm files, Nettie Benson Library, University of Texas at Austin.

AGN (Archivo General de la Nación). 1747a. "Historia 52." Informe y Testimonio del Viaje de Don Fermín de Vidaurre a la Junta de los Rios del Norte y Conchos.

AGN (Archivo General de la Nación). 1747b. "Historia 52." Carta Certificada de la Llegada de Rábago y Terán a ésta mi Misión por Fray Francisco Sanches. Transcript on file, Center for American History, University of Texas at Austin.

AGN (Archivo General de la Nación). 1747c. *"Copia del Diario de la Campaña Executaba de Orden del Exmo." Señor Conde de Rebilla Gigedo en el año 1747 por el Governador de Coahuila Don Pedro de Rávago y Terán para el Reconocimiento de las Márgenes del Río Grande del Norte. Audiencia de Guadalajara, 104–6-15. Transcript on file.* Center for American History, University of Texas at Austin.

AGN (Archivo General de la Nación). 1748. "Historia 52." Testimonio de las Dilixencias y Derrotero Practicado en Virtud de Superior Horden, sobre el Descubrimiento y Tránsito de las Juntas de los Rios de Conchos y Grande del Norte. Transcript on file, Center for American History, University of Texas at Austin.

AHP (Archivo del Hidalgo de Parral). 1645Aa. "Autos para Acordar lo Conveniente a la Seguridad y al Recibimiento de los Indios que se Mandaron Traer de Tierra Adentro para la Cosecha de Trigo." Microfilm on file Nettie Lee Benson Latin American Library, the University of Texas at Austin, frames 105–109.

AHP (Archivo del Hidalgo de Parral). 1645Ab. "Expediente formado con motivo de la paz de los indios Tobosos por el Maestro Francisco Montaño de la Cueva." Microfilm on file Nettie Lee Benson Latin American Library, the University of Texas at Austin, frames 227–283.

Antevs, Ernst. 1948. "Climatic Changes and Pre-White Man." *University of Utah Bulletin* 38:168–191.

Antevs, Ernst. 1953. "Climatic History and the Antiquity of Man in California." *University of California Archaeological Survey Reports* 16:23–31.

Antevs, Ernst. 1955. "Geologic-Climatic Dating in the West." *American Antiquity* 20(4):317–335. https://doi.org/10.2307/277066.

Applegarth, Susan. 1976. "Prehistoric Utilization of the Environment of the Eastern Slopes of the Guadalupe Mountains, Southeastern New Mexico." PhD dissertation, University of Wisconsin, Madison, WI.

Arnold, Dean E. 1988. *Ceramic Theory and Cultural Process.* Cambridge, UK: Cambridge University Press.

Arntzen, Kristen K., and John D. Speth. 2004. "Seasonality of Catfish Procurement at the Henderson Site." In *Life on the Periphery: Economic Change in Late Prehistoric Southeastern New Mexico*, ed. John D. Speth, 320–328. Museum of Anthropology Memoirs No. 37. Ann Arbor: University of Michigan.

Arthur, John W. 2003. "Brewing Beer: Status, Wealth and Ceramic Use Alteration among the Gamo of Southwestern Ethiopia." *World Archaeology* 34(3):516–528. https://doi.org/10.1080/0043824021000026486.

Austin, Daniel F. 2004. *Florida Ethnobotany.* Boca Raton, FL: CRC Pres. https://doi.org/10.1201/9780203491881.

Ayer. 1714. "Notícia de las Misiones de la Junta de los Rios por Trasviña Retis." Manuscripts collected by E. Ayer, on file at the Newberry Library, Chicago.

Baker, Larry L., and Stephen R. Durand, eds. 2003. *Prehistory of the Middle Rio Puerco Valley, Sandoval County, New Mexico.* Special Publication 3. Albuquerque: Archaeological Society of New Mexico.

Baldwin, Stuart J. 1987. "Room Size Patterns: A Quantitative Method for Approaching Ethnic Identification in Architecture." In *Ethnicity and Culture: Proceedings of the 18th Annual Chacmool Conference*, ed. Reginald Auger, Margaret Glass, Scott McEachern, and Peter McCartney, 163–174. Calgary, BC: University of Calgary, Archaeological Association.

Bancroft, Hubert H. 1890. *Antiquities of California.* San Francisco, CA: History Company.

Bandelier, Adolph F. 1890. *Final Report of Investigations among the Indians of the Southwest United States Carried on Mainly in the Years from 1880 to 1885, Part I.* Papers of the Archaeological Institute of America, American Series III. Cambridge, MA: Archaeological Institute of America.

Bandelier, Adolph F. 1892. *Final Report of Investigations among the Indians of the Southwestern United States, Carried on Mainly in the Years from 1880 to 1885, Part II.*

Papers of the Archaeological Institute of America, American Series 4. Cambridge, MA: Archaeological Institute of America.

Bandy, Matthew S. 2011. *A Class III Transect-Recording-Unit Survey and Geophysical Prospection at the Burro Tanks Site (LA 32227), Chavez County, New Mexico*. Albuquerque, NM: SWCA Environmental Consultants.

Bartlett, John R. 1854. *Personal Narrative of Explorations and Incidents in Texas, New Mexico, California, Sonora, and Chihuahua connected with the United States and Mexico Boundary Commission during the Years 1850, '51, '52, and '53*. New York: D Appleton and Company. https://doi.org/10.5962/bhl.title.125597.

Basehart, Harry W. 1960. *Mescalero Apache Subsistence Patterns and Socio-Political Organization: The Mescalero-Chiricahua Land Claims Project*. United States Indian Claims Commission Reports. New York: Garland Publishing Company.

Basehart, Harry W. 1973. "Mescalero Apache Subsistence Patterns." In *Technical Manual 1973 Survey of the Tularosa Basin*. Tularosa, NM: Human Systems Research.

Basehart, Harry W. 1974. *Mescalero Apache Subsistence Patterns and Sociopolitical Organization*. American Indian Ethnohistory, Indians of the Southwest, vol. 12, *Apache Indians*. New York: Garland.

Baugh, Susan T. 1986. "Late Prehistoric Bison Distributions in Oklahoma." In *Current Trends in Southern Plains Archaeology*, ed. Timothy G. Baugh, 83–96. Memoir 21. Lincoln, NE: Plains Anthropological Society.

Bauman, Timothy. 2004. "Defining Ethnicity." *SAA Archaeological Record* (September):12–14.

Beals, Ralph L. 1932. "The Comparative Ethnology of Northern Mexico before 1750." *Iberoamericana (Madrid, Spain)* 2:93–226.

Becker, Kenneth M., and Jeffrey H. Altschul. 2003. *Historic Contexts for Prehistoric and Protohistoric Trails and Related Features at Yuma Proving Grounds, Arizona*. Command Technology Directorate. Yuma Proving Grounds, AZ: Environmental Sciences Division.

Bell, W. H., and E. F. Castetter. 1941. "The Utilization of Yucca, Sotol and Beargrass by the Aborigines in the American Southwest." *University of New Mexico Bulletin* 372, Ethnobiological Studies in the American Southwest 7, Biological Series, 4(5). Albuquerque: University of New Mexico Press.

Bennett, Wendell C., and Robert M. Zingg. 1935. *The Tarahumara: An Indian Tribe of Northern Mexico*. Chicago, IL: University of Chicago Press.

Bentley, Mark T. 1993. "Hot Well Village and Reservoir: A Preliminary Overview." *Artifact* 31(2):1–32.

Bernardini, Wesley. 2005. *Hopi Oral Tradition and the Archaeology of Identity*. Tucson: University of Arizona Press.

Bernard-Shaw, Mary. 1990. "Experimental Agave Fiber Extraction." In *Rincon Phase Seasonal Occupation in the Northern Tucson Basin*, ed. Mary Bernard-Shaw and F. Huntington, 181–196. Center for Desert Archaeology Technical Report 90–92. Tucson, AZ: Desert Archaeology.

Berry, Claudia F., and Michael S. Berry. 1986. "Chronological and Conceptual Models of the Southwestern Archaic." In *Anthropology of the Desert West*, ed. Carol Condie and Don Fowler, 254–327. Salt Lake City: University of Utah Press.

Binford, Lewis R. 1965. "Archaeological Systematics and the Study of Culture Process." *American Antiquity* 31(2):203–210. https://doi.org/10.2307/2693985.

Binford, Lewis R. 1990. "Mobility, Housing, and Environment: A Comparative Study." *Journal of Anthropological Research* 46(2):119–152. https://doi.org/10.1086/jar .46.2.3630069.

Birdsell, Joseph. 1968. "Some Predictions for the Pleistocene Based on Equilibrium Systems for Recent Hunter-Gatherers." In *Man the Hunter*, ed. Richard B. Lee and Irven DeVore, 229–240. Chicago, IL: Aldine.

Bishop, R. L., R. I. Rands, and G. R. Holley. 1982. "Ceramics Compositional Analysis in Archaeological Perspective." In *Advances in Archaeological Method and Theory*, vol. 5. ed. M. B. Schiffer, 275–330. New York: Academic Press. https://doi.org/10 .1016/B978-0-12-003105-4.50012-1.

Black, Stephen L., and Darrell Creel. 1997. "The Central Texas Burned Rock Midden Reconsidered." In *Hot Rock Cooking on the Greater Edwards Plateau: Four Burned Rock Midden Sites in West Central Texas*, by S. L. Black, L. W. Ellis, D. G. Creel, and G. T. Goode, 269–305. TARL Studies in Archeology 22, University of Texas at Austin and Report No. 2. Austin: Archeological Studies Program, Texas Department of Transportation.

Black, Stephen L., and Alston V. Thoms. 2014. "Hunter-Gatherer Earth Ovens in the Archaeological Record: Fundamental Concepts." *American Antiquity* 79(02):204–226. https://doi.org/10.7183/0002-7316.79.2.204.

Blitz, John H. 1993. *Ancient Chiefdoms of the Tombigbee*. Tuscaloosa: University of Alabama Press.

Blomster, Jeffrey P. 1998. "Context, Cult, and Early Formative Period Public Ritual in the Misteca Alta." *Ancient Mesoamerica* 9(02):309–326. https://doi.org/10.1017 /S0956536100002017.

Blum, M. D., R. S. Toomey, III, and S. Valastro, Jr. 1994. "Fluvial Response to Late Quaternary Climatic and Environmental Change, Edwards Plateau, Texas." *Palaeogeography, Palaeoclimatology, Palaeoecology* 108(1–2):1–21. https://doi.org/10.1016 /0031-0182(94)90019-1.

Boeke, Bruce. 2013. "Population Density and Movement Reflected in AMS Dates from the Permian Basin." *Permian Quarterly* 1(3):8–14.

Boggess, Douglas H. M. 2009. *Data Recovery at LA 99434 on Quehada Ridge, Eddy County, New Mexico*. LMAS Report no. 904-14. Albuquerque, NM: Lone Mountain Archaeological Services.

Boggess, Douglas H. M. 2010. *Archaeological Treatment of Three Sites for Proposed Solar Ponds at the West Mine, Intrepid Potash-NM, LLC, Eddy County, New Mexico*. LMAS Report No. 1195. Albuquerque, NM: Lone Mountain Archaeological Services.

Boggess, Douglas H. M. 2011. *Data Recovery at 14 Sites for the Intrepid–BLM Land Exchange, Eddy County, New Mexico*. LMAS Report No. 1077. Albuquerque, NM: Lone Mountain Archaeological Services.

Boggess, Douglas H. M., and Andrew Zink. 2013. *Dunes and Deflation: Excavations at LA 124525 and LA 161918 at the Intrepid Potash East Mine, Eddy County, New Mexico*. Albuquerque, NM: Lone Mountain Archaeological Services.

Bogucki, Peter. 1999. *The Origins of Human Society*. Malden, MA: Blackwell.

Bohrer, Vorsila L. 1981. "Former Dietary Patterns of People as Determined from Archaic-Age Plant Remains from Fresnal Shelter, South-Central New Mexico." In *Archaeological Essays in Honor of Mark Wimberly*, ed. Michael S. Foster. *The Artifact* 19(3–4):41–50.

Bohrer, Vorsila L. 2006. "Flotation Analysis from High Rolls Cave." In *High Rolls Cave: Insectos, Burritos, y Frajos: Archaic Subsistence in Southern New Mexico*, ed. Stephen C. Lentz, 183–221. Archaeological Notes No. 125. Santa Fe: Office of Archaeological Studies, Museum of New Mexico.

Bolton, Herbert E. 1916. *Spanish Exploration in the Southwest, 1542–1706*. New York: Charles Scribner's Sons. https://doi.org/10.5479/sil.261021.39088005888821.

Borck, Lewis, Barbara J. Mills, Matthew A. Peeples, and Jeffery J. Clark. 2015. "Are Social Networks Survival Networks? An Example from the Late Pre-Hispanic US Southwest." *Journal of Archaeological Method and Theory* 22(1):33–57. https://doi.org /10.1007/s10816-014-9236-5.

Borhegyi, S. F. 1965. "Archaeological Synthesis of the Guatemalan Highlands." In *Handbook of Middle American Indians*, ed. R. Wauchope and Gordon R. Willey, 2:3–58. Austin: University of Texas Press.

Bowden, Jocelyn J. 1962. "The Magoffin Salt War." *Password* 7:95–121. El Paso, TX: El Paso County Historical Society.

Boyd, Doug K. 1997. *Caprock Canyonlands Archeology: A Synthesis of the Late Prehistory and History of Lake Alan Henry and the Texas Panhandle-Plains*. vol. 2. Austin, TX: Prewitt and Associates.

Bozarth, Steven. 2000. "Microfossil Evidence of Agriculture and Wild Plant Utilization." In *A Highway through Time: Archaeological Investigations along NM 90*, ed. Christopher A. Turnbow, 565–580. New Mexico State Highway and Transportation Department, Technical Report 2000–3. Albuquerque, NM: TRC.

Bozell, John R. 1995. "Culture, Environment, and Bison Populations on the Late Prehistoric and Early Historic Central Plains." *Plains Anthropologist* 40(152): 45–163. https://doi.org/10.1080/2052546.1995.11931769.

Bradley, Ronna J., and Jerry M. Hoffer. 1985. "Playas Red: A Preliminary Study of Origins and Variability in the Jornada Mogollon." In Proceedings of the Third Jornada Mogollon Conference, ed. Michael S. Foster and Thomas C. O'Laughlin. *The Artifact* 23(1–2):161–178.

Brand, Donald D. 1933. "The Historical Geography of Northwest Chihuahua." PhD dissertation, University of California, Berkeley.

Brand, Donald D. 1943. "The Chihuahua Culture Area." *New Mexico Anthropologist* 6–7(3):115–158. https://doi.org/10.1086/newmexianthr.6_7.3.4291266.

Braun, David P. 1980. "Experimental Interpretation of Ceramic Vessel Use on the Basis of Rim and Neck Formal Attributes." In *The Navajo Project: Archaeological Investigations, Page to Phoenix 500 kV Southern Transmission Line*, ed. D. C. Fiero, R. W. Munson, M. T. McClain, S. W. Wilson, and A. H. Zier, 171–221. Research Paper 11. Flagstaff: Museum of Northern Arizona.

Braun, David P. 1991. "Are There Cross-Cultural Regularities in Tribal Social Practices?" In *Between Bands and States*, ed. Susan A. Gregg, 423–444. Occasional Paper 9, Center for Archaeological Investigations. Carbondale: Southern Illinois University at Carbondale.

Breternitz, David A. 1957. "A Brief Archaeological Survey of the Lower Gila River." *Kiva* 22(2–3):1–13. https://doi.org/10.1080/00231940.1957.11757552.

Brewington, R. L., and H. J. Shafer. 1999. "The Ceramic Assemblages of Ojasen and Gobernadora." In *Archaeology of the Ojasen (41EP289) and Gobernadora (41EP321) Sites, El Paso County, Texas*, ed. H. J. Shafer, J. E. Dockall, and R. L. Brewington, 149–198. Reports of Investigations No. 2. Archeology Studies Program Report No. 13. College Station: Center for Ecological Anthropology, Texas A&M University; Austin: Environmental Affairs Division, Texas Department of Transportation.

Bright, Jason R., and Andrew Ugan. 1999. "Ceramics and Mobility: Assessing the Role of Foraging Behavior and Its Implications for Culture-History." *Utah Archaeology* 12:17–30.

Brook, Vernon R. 1965. "Cultural Traits of the El Paso Phase of the Mogollon." *Transactions of the First Regional Archeological Symposium for Southeastern New Mexico and Western Texas*. Bulletin No. 1:18–22.

Brook, Vernon R. 1966. "The McGregor Site (32:106:16:4; E.P.A.S. 4)." *Artifact* 4(4):3–22.

Brook, Vernon R. 1980. "The Sabina Mountain Site." *Transactions of the 15th Regional Archeological Symposium for Southeastern New Mexico and Western Texas*, 15–86. El Paso, TX: El Paso Archaeological Society.

Brooks, Robert L. 2004. "From Stone Slab Architecture to Abandonment: A Revisionist View of the Antelope Creek Phase." In *Prehistory of Texas*, ed. Timothy K. Perttula, 331–344. College Station: Texas A&M University Press.

Browman, David L. 1976. "Demographic Correlations of the Wari Conquest of Junin." *American Antiquity* 41(4):465–477. https://doi.org/10.2307/279012.

Brown, Gary M. 1998. *Archeological Data Recovery in the Tailings Pond Enlargement Area at the Continental Mine, Grant County, New Mexico.* Farmington, NM: Western Cultural Resource Management.

Brown, Kenneth L., ed. 2010. *The Laguna Plata Site Revisited: Current Testing and Analysis of New and Existing Assemblages at LA 5148, Lea County, New Mexico.* Albuquerque, NM: TRC.

Brown, Kenneth L., and Marie E. Brown. 2014. *A Class I and Class III Cultural Resource Survey of 1,553.43 Acres for the Southwestern Public Service Company's 41-Mile Long Potash Junction to Roadrunner Substations 345 kV Transmission Line, Eddy and Lea Counties, New Mexico.* Albuquerque, NM: TRC.

Brown, Marie E., ed. 2011. *The Boot Hill Site (LA 32229): An Oasis in the Desert, Eddy County, New Mexico.* Albuquerque, NM: TRC.

Brown, Marie E., and Kenneth L. Brown. 2011. *Data Recovery Report for a Transmission Line: Seven Rivers Interchange to Pecos Interchange to Potash Junction Interchange, Eddy County, New Mexico.* Albuquerque, NM: TRC.

Brown, Patricia E., and Connie L. Stone. 1982. *Granite Reef: A Study in Desert Archaeology.* Anthropological Research Papers No. 28. Tempe: Arizona State University.

Browning, Cody, M. Sale, D. T. Kirkpatrick, and K. W. Laumbach. 1993. *MOTR Site: Excavation at Site LA 72859, an El Paso Phase Structure on Fort Bliss, Otero County, New Mexico.* Report 89–27. Las Cruces, NM: Human Systems Research.

Bruman, Henry J. 2000. *Alcohol in Ancient Mexico.* Salt Lake City: University of Utah Press.

Buck, Brenda J. 1996. *Late Quaternary Landscape Evolution, Paleoclimate, and Geoarchaeology, Southern New Mexico and West Texas.* PhD dissertation, Department of Agronomy, New Mexico State University. Las Cruces, NM.

Buffington, L. C., and C. H. Herbel. 1965. "Vegetational Changes on a Semidesert Grassland Range from 1858 to 1963." *Ecological Monographs* 35(2):139–164. https://doi.org/10.2307/1948415.

Bullock, Peter Y., Gary A. Hebler, James E. Bowman, and Charles S. Carrig. 2005. "Knowing thy Neighbors: Cross-cultural Contacts of the Jornada Mogollon." In *Archaeology between the Borders: Papers from the 13th Biennial Jornada Mogollon Conference*, ed. Marc Thompson, Jason Jurgena and Lora Jackson, 9–24. El Paso, TX: El Paso Museum of Archaeology.

Bureau of Land Management (BLM). 2013. "Introduction to the Permian Basin Memorandum of Agreement." *Permian Quarterly* 1(1):2–3.

Bureau of Land Management (BLM). 2016. "Introduction to the Permian Basin Programmatic Agreement." *Permian Quarterly* 4(1):2.

Burgett, Jessica Prue. 2006. "El Paso Polychrome in the Casas Grandes Region, Chihuahua, Mexico: Ceramic Exchange Between Paquime and the Jornada Mogollon." PhD dissertation, Pennsylvania State University, University Park.

Burgett, Jessica Prue. 2007. "Just Like That, but Different: El Paso Polychrome in the Casas Grandes Region, Chihuahua, Mexico." In *Viva la Jornada! Papers from the 14th Biennial Jornada Mogollon Conference*, ed. Jason Jurgena, Lora Jackson, and Marc Thompson, 53–59. El Paso, TX: El Paso Museum of Archaeology.

Buskirk, Winfred. 1986. *The Western Apache: Living with the Land before 1950*. Norman: University of Oklahoma Press.

Bussey, Stanley D., Richard Kelly, and Judith Southward. 1976. *LA 4921 Three Rivers, Otero County, New Mexico: A Project of Excavation, Stabilization, and Interpretation of a Prehistoric Village*. Cultural Resources Management Division Report No. 69. Las Cruces: New Mexico State University.

Bye, Robert A., Jr. Don Burgess, and Albino Mares Trias. 1975. "Ethnobotany of the Western Tarahumara of Chihuahua, Mexico. Volume I: Notes on the Genus *Agave*." *Botanical Museum Leaflets* 24(5):85–112. Cambridge, MA: Harvard University Press.

Camarena-Garcés, David, Megan Bruckse, Ignacio Ibarra, Michael S. Droz, Paul Lukowski, and Elia Perez. 2011. *Survey of 2,475 Acres and National Register of Historic Places Eligibility Assessment of Archeological Sites for Orogrande Camp Upgrade, Otero County, New Mexico*. Fort Bliss Cultural Resources Report 1032. Fort Bliss, TX: Environmental Division—Conservation Branch. TRC Report Number 179058–0000. El Paso, TX: TRC Environmental.

Cameron, Catherine M., and Andrew I. Duff. 2008. "History and Process in Village Formation: Context and Contrasts from the Northern Southwest." *American Antiquity* 73(1):29–57. https://doi.org/10.1017/S0002731600041275.

Camilli, Eileen L., Luann Wandsnider, and James I. Ebert. 1988. *Distributional Survey and Excavation of Archaeological Landscapes in the Vicinity of El Paso, Texas*. Las Cruces District, NM: Bureau of Land Management.

Campbell, Joseph. 1959. *The Masks of God: Primitive Mythology*. New York: Penguin Books.

Campbell, Kirsten, and Jim A. Railey, eds. 2008. *Archaeology of the Hondo Valley, Lincoln County, New Mexico: Archaeological Investigations along US 70 from Ruidoso Downs to Riverside*. New Mexico Department of Transportation, Cultural Resource Technical Series 2006–1. Albuquerque, NM: SWCA Environmental Consultants and Parsons Brinckerhoff.

Campbell, Robert G. 1976. *The Panhandle Aspect of the Chaquaqua Plateau*. Graduate Studies, No. 11. Lubbock: Texas Tech University.

Capone, Patricia. 2002. "Petrographic Analysis of Chupadero Black-on-White." Manuscript on file, Harvard University, Peabody Museum, Boston.

Carmichael, David L. 1981. "Non-residential Occupation of the Prehistoric Southern Tularosa Basin, New Mexico." In *Archaeological Essays in Honor of Mark Wimberly*, ed. Michael S. Foster. *The Artifact* 19(3/4):51–68. El Paso, TX: El Paso Archaeological Society.

Carmichael, David L. 1985. "Pithouse to Pueblo Transition in the Jornada Mogollon: A Reappraisal." In *Proceedings of the Third Jornada-Mogollon Conference*, ed. Michael S. Foster and Thomas C. O'Laughlin. *The Artifact* 23(1/2):109–118. El Paso, TX: El Paso Archaeological Society.

Carmichael, David L. 1986. Archaeological Survey in the Southern Tularosa Basin of New Mexico. Historic and Natural Resources Report No. 3. Publications in Anthropology No. 10, El Paso Centennial Museum, University of Texas at El Paso. Fort Bliss, TX: Environmental Division.

Castetter, Edward Franklin. 1935. "The Ethnobiology of the Chiricahua and Mescalero Apache." *University of New Mexico Bulletin* 297, Ethnobiological Studies in the American Southwest 3, Biological Series 4(5). Albuquerque: University of New Mexico Press.

Castetter, Edward F., Willis H. Bell, and Alvin R. Grove. 1938. "The Early Utilization and Distribution of Agave in the American Southwest." *University of New Mexico Bulletin* 335, Ethnobiological Studies in the American Southwest 6, Biological Series 5(4). Albuquerque: University of New Mexico Press.

Castetter, Edward F., and Morris E. Opler. 1936. "The Ethnobiology of the Chiricahua and Mescalero Apache: The Use of Plants for Foods, Beverages, and Narcotics." *University of New Mexico Bulletin* 297, Ethnobiological Studies in the American Southwest 3, Biological Series 4(5). Albuquerque: University of New Mexico Press.

Chapman, Richard, and Peggy Gerow. 2006. "Standards and Guidelines for Testing and Data Recovery." In *Southeastern New Mexico Regional Research Design and*

Resource Management Strategy, by Patrick Hogan, 6–1 to 6–21. Santa Fe: Historic Preservation Division, Department of Cultural Affairs.

Charles, Douglas K. 1985. "Corporate Symbols: An Interpretive Prehistory of Indian Burial Mounds in West Central Illinois." PhD dissertation, Northwestern University, Evanston, IL.

Charles, Douglas K., and Jane E. Buikstra. 1983. "Archaic Mortuary Sites in the Central Mississippi Drainage: Distribution, Structure, and Behavioral Implications." In *Archaic Hunters and Gatherers in the American Midwest,* ed. James L. Phillips and James A. Brown, 117–145. New York: Academic Press.

Church, Tim, Raymond Mauldin, Myles R. Miller, Phil Dering, Peter C. Condon, and Mike Quigg. 2009. "Subsistence and Subsistence Economy." In *Significance and Research Standards for Prehistoric Sites at Fort Bliss: A Design for the Evaluation, Management, and Treatment of Cultural Resources,* ed. Myles R. Miller, Nancy A. Kenmotsu, and Melinda R. Landreth, 8–1 to 8–68. Fort Bliss Garrison Command, Historic and Natural Resources Report No. 05–16. Fort Bliss, TX.

Church, Tim, Beth McCormack, Victoria Menchaca, Teresa Cordura, Cathy Travis, and Douglas H. M. Boggess. 2012. *Looking Over the Edge: A High-Resolution Survey of the 17,945 Acre Maroon Cliffs Special Management Area, Carlsbad District, Bureau of Land Management.* Albuquerque, NM: Lone Mountain Archaeological Services.

Church, T., M. Sale, and S. Ruth. 2002. *Coping with a Dynamic Environment: Prehistoric Subsistence in the Central Hueco Bolson, New Mexico. Evaluation of 586 Sites in Maneuver Areas 5A and 5B, Dona Ana Range, Fort Bliss, New Mexico.* Report No. 508. Albuquerque, NM: Lone Mountain Archaeological Services.

Clark, J. J. 2001. *Tracking Prehistoric Migrations: Pueblo Settlers among the Tonto Basin Hohokam.* Anthropological Papers of the University of Arizona, Number 65. Tucson: The University of Arizona Press.

Clark, Tiffany C. 2006. "Production, Exchange, and Social Identity: A Study of Chupadero Black-on-white Pottery (New Mexico)." PhD dissertation, Arizona State University, Tempe.

Clifton, Don. 1995. *Data Recovery at Site LA 104607, Eddy County, New Mexico.* Report 119. Pep, NM: Don Clifton.

Cloud, W. A. 2004. *Arroyo de la Presa Site: A Stratified Late Prehistoric Campsite along the Rio Grande, Presidio County, Trans-Pecos Texas.* Archeological Studies Program Report 56. Austin: Texas Department of Transportation.

Cloud, W. A., R. J. Mallouf, P. A. Mercado-Allinger, C. A. Hoyt, N. A. Kenmotsu, J. M. Sanchez, and E. R. Madrid. 1994. *Archeological Testing at the Polvo Site (41PS21), Presidio County, Texas.* Office of the State Archeologist Report 39. Austin: Texas Historical Commission.

Cloud, William A., and Jennifer Piehl. 2008. *The Millington Site: Archaeological and Human Osteological Investigations, Presidio County, Texas.* Papers of the Trans-Pecos Archaeological Program, No. 4. Alpine: Center for Big Bend Studies, Sul Ross State University.

Collins, Michael B. 1966. "The Andrews Lake Sites: Evidence of Semi-Sedentary Prehistoric Occupation in Andrews County, Texas." *Transactions of the Second Regional Archaeological Symposium for Southeastern New Mexico and Western Texas.* Hobbs, NM.

Collins, Michael B. 1968. "The Andrews Lake Locality: New Archaeological Data from the Southwestern Llano Estacado, Texas." Master's thesis, University of Texas, Austin.

Collins, Michael B. 1971. "A Review of Llano Estacado Archaeology and Ethnohistory." *Plains Anthropologist* 16:85–104.

Colton, Harold S. 1964. "Principal Hopi Trails." *Plateau* 36:91–94.

Condon, Peter C. 2010. "Conclusions." In *The Laguna Plata Site Revisited: Current Testing and Analysis of New and Existing Assemblages at LA 5148, Lea County, New Mexico*, ed. Kenneth L. Brown, 259–300. Albuquerque, NM: TRC.

Condon, Peter C., and Robert Hall, G. Smith, Willi Hermann, Lillian Ponce, and Howard Higgins. 2006. *A Data Recovery of Ten Prehistoric Sites in the Hueco Mountain Area, Maneuver Area 2C and 2D, Fort Bliss Military Installation, El Paso, Texas.* Fort Bliss, TX: Directorate of Environment, Conservation Division.

Condon, Peter C., and Robert Hall, G. Smith, Willi Hermann, Lillian Ponce, and Howard Higgins. 2007. *A Data Recovery of Five Prehistoric Sites in the Hueco Mountain Area, Maneuver Area 2C and 2D, Fort Bliss Military Installation, El Paso, Texas.* Fort Bliss, TX: Directorate of Environment, Conservation Division.

Condon, P. C., W. Hermann, L. Ponce, J. Vasquez, S. Sampson, G. D. Smith, S. N. Cervera, and L. Sierra. 2008. *Assessing Organizational Strategies during the Late Mesilla Phase (A.D. 600 to 1100): A Data Recovery of Four Prehistoric Sites along the Organ Mountain Alluvial Fans, Doña Ana Firing Complex, Range 48, Fort Bliss Military Installation, Doña Ana County, New Mexico.* Vol 1. Fort Bliss, TX: Directorate of Public Works, Conservation Division.

Condon, P. C., W. Hermann, G. D. Smith, L. M. Ponce, and H. Higgins. 2006. *The Data Recovery of 41EP1039, 41EP46, and 41EP1050, Three Prehistoric Sites, Maneuver Area 1, Limited Use Area 1B South, El Paso County, Texas.* Fort Bliss, TX: Directorate of Environment, Conservation Division.

Condon, Peter C., M. E. Hroncich, B. G. Bury, W. Hermann, D. D. Kuehn, J. A. Jacobson, L. Scott-Cummings, E. Hickey, and K. Puseman. 2010. *Cultural Coalescence and Economic Diversity in the Formative Period: A Data Recovery of 14*

Prehistoric Sites Adjacent to U.S. Highway Loop 375, Maneuver Area 1B, Fort Bliss Military Installation, El Paso County, Texas. Fort Bliss Cultural Resource Report No. 0745. Fort Bliss, TX: Directorate of Environment-Conservation Division.

Condon, P. C., R. Klein, G. D. Smith, M. Yduarte, L. M. Ponce, T. G. Baugh, V. Vargas, M. Malainey, and R. Holloway. 2005. *A Mitigation of Five Prehistoric Sites in the Hueco Mountain Project Area, UTM Blocks 8528, 8628, and 8629, on Fort Bliss Military Reservation, El Paso, Texas.* Fort Bliss, TX: Directorate of Environment, Conservation Division.

Condon, Peter C., David Kuehn, Linda Scott Cummings, Maria Hroncich, Lilian M. Ponce, Nancy Komulainen, and Willi Hermann. 2008. *Archaeological Testing and Data Recovery Recommendations for 16 Prehistoric Sites, Bear Grass Draw, Eddy County, New Mexico.* El Paso, TX: TRC Environmental.

Condon, P. C., and M. J. Swanson. 2012. *Testing and Mitigation of Three Archaeological Sites along Proposed Tank Trails, Fort Bliss Military Reservation, Otero County, New Mexico.* Fort Bliss Cultural Resource Report No. 1011. Fort Bliss, TX: Directorate of Public Works, Environmental Division, and Fort Bliss Garrison Command.

Cordell, Linda S. 1984. *Prehistory of the Southwest.* Orlando: Academic Press.

Cordell, Linda S. 1997. *Archaeology of the Southwest.* 2nd ed. San Diego: Academic Press.

Cordell, Linda S. 2008. "Exploring Social Identities through Archaeological Data from the Southwest." In *Archaeology without Borders: Contact, Commerce, and Change in the U.S. Southwest and Northwestern Mexico,* ed. Laurie D. Webster, M. E. McBrinn, and E. Gamboa Carrera, 145–154. Boulder: University Press of Colorado.

Cordell, Linda S., David E. Doyel, and Keith W. Kintigh. 1994. "Processes of Aggregation in the Prehistoric Southwest." In *Themes in Southwest Prehistory,* ed. George J. Gumerman, 109–134. Santa Fe, NM: School of American Research Press.

Cordell, Linda S., and Maxine E. McBrinn. 2012. *Archaeology of the Southwest.* 3rd ed. Walnut Creek, CA: Left Coast Press.

Corley, John. 1965. "Proposed Eastern Extension of the Jornada Branch of the Mogollon Culture." In *Transactions of the First Archeological Symposium for Southeastern New Mexico and Western Texas,* 30–36. Bulletin 1. Hobbs, NM: Lea County Archeology Society.

Corley, John A., and Robert H. Leslie. 1960. *The Boot Hill Site L.C.A.S B-5: A Preliminary Report.* Hobbs, NM: Lea County Archaeological Society.

Cosgrove, C. B. 1947. "Caves of the Upper Gila and Hueco Areas in New Mexico and Texas." *Papers of the Peabody Museum of American Archaeology and Ethnology* 15(1). Cambridge, MA: Harvard University.

Creel, Darrell. 1991. "Bison Hides in Late Prehistoric Exchange in the Southern Plains." *American Antiquity* 56(1):40–49. https://doi.org/10.2307/280971.

Creel, Darrell. 1997. "Ceremonial Cave: An Overview of Investigations and Contents." Appendix A in *The Hueco Mountain Cave and Rock Shelter Survey: A Phase I Baseline Inventory in Maneuver Area 2D on Fort Bliss, Texas*, by F. A. Almarez and J. D. Leach, 75–88. Archaeological Technical Reports No. 10. El Paso: Anthropology Research Center, University of Texas at El Paso.

Creel, Darrell. 2006a. "Variability in Classic Mimbres Room Suites: Implications for Household Organization and Social Differences." In *Mimbres Society*, ed. V. S. Powell-Martí and P. A. Gilman, 45–65. Tucson: University of Arizona Press.

Creel, Darrell. 2006b. *Excavations at the Old Town Ruin, Luna County, New Mexico, 1989–2003. Cultural Resources Series No. 16.* vol. 1. Santa Fe: New Mexico Bureau of Land Management, New Mexico State Office.

Creel, Darrell. 2013. "The Mimbres Vessel Sourcing Project." Paper presented at the annual meeting of the Archaeological Society of New Mexico, May 4, 2013, Albuquerque, NM.

Creel, Darrell, Tiffany Clark, and Hector Neff. 2002. "Production and Long Distance Movement of Chupadero Black-on-white Pottery in New Mexico and Texas." In *Geochemical Evidence for Long Distance Exchange*, ed. Michael Glascock, 109–132. Westport: Bergin and Garvey Publishers.

Crist, Raymond E. 1940. "Some Geographic Aspects of the Manufacture of Mezcal." *Scientific Monthly* 50:234–236.

Cruz Antillón, Rafael. 1996. "Recientes Investigaciones Arqueológicas en Villa Ahumada, Chihuahua." In *Prehistory of the Borderlands*, ed. John Carpenter and Guadalupe Sanchez, 1–9. Arizona State Museum Archaeological Series 186. Tucson: Arizona State Museum.

Cruz Antillón, Rafael. n.d.a. "El Periodo Medio o Formativo Tardío (A.D. 1250–1400 A.D.)." Unpublished manuscript in possession of the author. Chihuahua, Mexico: Centro INAH Chihuahua.

Cruz Antillón, Rafael. n.d.b. "La Región Fronteriza de Villa Ahumada." Unpublished manuscript in possession of the author. Chihuahua, Mexico: Centro INAH Chihuahua.

Cruz Antillón, R., R. Leonard, T. D. Maxwell, T. L. Van Pool, M. J. Harmon, C. S. Van Pool, D. A. Hyndman, and S. S. Brandwine. 2004. "Galeana, Villa Ahumada, and Casa Chica, Diverse Sites in the Casas Grandes Region." In *Surveying the Archaeology of Northwest Mexico*, ed. G. E. Newell and E. Galluga, 149–175. Salt Lake City: University of Utah Press.

Cruz Antillón, Rafael, and Timothy D. Maxwell. 1999. "The Villa Ahumada Site." In *The Casas Grandes World*, ed. Curtis F. Schaafsma and Carroll L. Riley, 43–53. Salt Lake City: University of Utah Press.

Cruz Antillón, Rafael, and Timothy D. Maxwell. 2017. "The Villa Ahumada Region." In *Not So Far from Paquimé: Essays on the Archaeology of Chihuahua*, ed. Jane Holden Kelley and David A. Phillips Jr., 153–165. Salt Lake City: University of Utah Press.

Cummings, Linda Scott, and Peter Kováčik. 2013. *Macrofloral, Phytolith, and Starch Analyses, and AMS Radiocarbon Dating for the Permian Basin MOA, New Mexico.* PaleoResearch Institute Technical Report 12–050. Golden, CO: PaleoResearch Institute.

Cummings, Linda Scott, Chad Yost, Kathryn Puseman, and Melissa K. Logan. 2011. "Appendix E: Pollen, Phytolith, Organic Residue (FTIR), and AMS Radiocarbon Analyses." In *Data Recovery at 14 Sites for the Intrepid–BLM Land Exchange, Eddy County, New Mexico*, prepared by Douglas H. M. Boggess, LMAS Report No. 1077. Albuquerque, NM: Lone Mountain Archaeological Services.

Currid, John D., and Avi Navon. 1989. "Iron Age Pits and the Lahav (Tell Halif) Gran Storage Project." *Bulletin of the American Schools of Oriental Research* 273(273):67–78. https://doi.org/10.2307/1356774.

Dahlin, Eleanor Sherlock. 2003. "INAA and Distribution Patterns of Classic Mimbres Black-on-white Vessels during the Classic Period." Master's thesis, Texas A&M University, College Station.

Darling, J. Andrew. 2006. *Pima Song and the Archaeology of Space.* Sacaton, AZ: Cultural Resources Management Program, Gila River Indian Community.

Darling, J. Andrew. 2009. "O'odham Trails and the Archaeology of Space." In *Landscapes of Movement: Trails, Paths, and Roads in Anthropological Perspective*, ed. J. E. Snead, C. L. Erickson, and A. J. Darling, 61–83. Philadelphia: University of Pennsylvania Press.

Darling, J. Andrew, and B. Sunday Eiselt. 2003. "Trails Research in the Gila Bend." In *Trails, Rock Features and Homesteading in the Gila Bend Area: A Report on the State Route 85, Gila Bend to Buckeye, Archaeological Project*, ed. J. C. Czarzasty, K. Peterson and G. E. Rice, 199–227. Anthropological Field Studies No. 43. Tempe: Office of Cultural Resource Management, Arizona State University.

Davis, Emma Lou, and J. H. Winkler. 1956. "A Late Mesa Verde Site in the Rio Puerco Valley." *El Palacio* 66:92–100.

Davis, John V. 1978. "Prehistoric Art of Cave Valley." *Transactions of the 13th Regional Symposium for Southeastern New Mexico and Western Texas*, 39–59. Lamesa, TX.

Davis, John V. 1980. "The Candelaria Style: An Identifiable Rock Art Tradition of Northern Chihuahua." *Artifact* 18(2):43–55.

Davis, Leslie. 1967. "Recent Excavations at Hot Well Site (EPAS 3)." *Transactions of the 3rd Regional Archeological Symposium for Southeastern New Mexico and Western Texas*, 23–32. Lubbock, TX: South Plains Archeological Society.

Davis, Owen K., Tom Minckley, Tom Moutoux, Tim Jull, and Bob Kalin. 2002. "The Transformation of Sonoran Desert Wetlands Following the Historic Decrease in Burning." *Journal of Arid Environments* 50(3):393–412. https://doi.org/10.1006/jare .2001.0914.

Deaver, William L., and Mary M. Prasciunas. 2012. *Archaeology of an Agave Field: Data Recovery for the Tucson Electric Power Tortolita to North Loop Transmission Line Project, Pinal and Pima Counties, Arizona*. Cultural Resources Report 2012–36. Tucson, AZ: West Land Resources.

DeBoer, Warren. 1988. "Subterranean Storage and the Organization of Surplus: The View from Eastern North America." *Southeastern Archaeology* 7(1):1–20.

Deen, Roy D. 1974. "Geology and Mineralization of the Precambrian Rocks of the Northern Franklin Mountains, El Paso County, Texas." Master's thesis, Department of Geology, University of Texas at El Paso.

Del Bene, Terry, Allen Rorex, and Linda Brett. 1986. *Report on Excavations at LA 30949 and 30951*. Agency for Conservation Archaeology Report MD82.1. Portales: Eastern New Mexico University.

Dering, J. Phil. 1999. "Earth Oven Plant Processing in Archaic Period Economies: An Example from a Semi-arid Savannah in South-Central North America." *American Antiquity* 64(4):659–674. https://doi.org/10.2307/2694211.

Dering, J. Phil. 2005. "Ecological Factors Affecting the Late Archaic Economy of the Lower Pecos River Region." In *The Late Archaic across the Borderlands: From Foraging to Farming*, ed. Bradley J. Vierra, 247–258. Austin: University of Texas.

Dering, J. Phil. 2007. "Appendix D: Plant Remains from 41EP3175, 41EP3259, 41EP3266, and 41EP3326." In *Excavations at El Arenal and Other Late Archaic and Early Formative Period Sites in the Hueco Mountain Project Area of Fort Bliss, Texas*, ed. Myles R. Miller, [D]1–14. Directorate of Environment, Historic and Natural Resources Report No. 02–12. Fort Bliss, TX.

Dering, J. Phil. 2014. "Appendix B: Macrofloral, Starch Grain, and XRF Results." In *Archaeological Data Recovery at Five Sites in the Tobin Well Expansion Area on Fort Bliss, El Paso County, Texas: Investigations into Mesilla and Dona Ana Phase Residential Settlements in the Hueco Bolson*, by P. Condon, and M. Swanson. Cultural Resources Report 1326. Fort Bliss, TX: Directorate of Public Works, Environmental Division, Garrison Command, El Paso, Texas.

Dering, J. P., H. J. Shafer, and R. P. Lyle, eds. 2001. *The El Paso Loop 375 Archaeological Project: Phase II Testing and Phase II Mitigation*. Archeological Studies Program

Report No. 28, Texas Department of Transportation, Environmental Affairs Division, Austin and Reports of Investigations No. 3. College Station: Center for Ecological Archaeology, Texas A&M University.

Dibble, Harold L. 1991. "Local Raw Material Exploitation and its Effects on Lower and Middle Paleolithic Assemblage Variability." In *Raw Material Economics among Prehistoric Hunter-Gatherers*, ed. A. Montet-White and S. Holen, 33–48. Publications in Anthropology 19. Lawrence: University of Kansas.

Dick, Herbert W. 1965. *Bat Cave.* Monograph No. 27. Santa Fe, NM: School of American Research.

Diehl, Michael W. 1992. "Architecture as Material Correlate of Mobility Strategies: Some Implications for Archaeological Interpretation." *Behavior Science Research* 26(1–4):1–35. https://doi.org/10.1177/106939719202600101.

Diehl, Michael W. 2003. "Prehistoric Subsistence Strategies and the Macrobotanical Assemblage." In *Hohokam Farming on the Salt River Floodplain*, ed. T. Kathleen Henderson, 211–230. Anthropological Papers No. 42. Anthropological Papers No. 9. Tucson, AZ: Center for Desert Archaeology; Phoenix: Pueblo Grande Museum.

Diehl, Michael W., and Owen K. Davis. 2016. "The Short, Unhappy Use Lives of Early Agricultural Period 'Storage' Pits at the Las Capas Site, Southern Arizona." *American Antiquity* 81(2):333–344. https://doi.org/10.7183/0002-7316.81.2.333.

Dillehay, Tom D. 1974. "Late Quaternary Bison Population Changes on the Southern Plains." *Plains Anthropologist* 19(65):180–196. https://doi.org/10.1080/2052546.1974.11908675.

Di Peso, C. Charles. 1974. *Casas Grandes: A Fallen Trading Center of the Gran Chichimeca.* Publication 9, vol. 1–3. Dragoon, AZ: Amerind Foundation.

Di Peso, C. Charles. 1981. *The Rio Grande as Seen from Casas Grandes.* Papers of the Archaeological Society of New Mexico 6:23–41. Albuquerque, NM: Archaeological Society of New Mexico.

Di Peso, Charles C., John B. Rinaldo, and Gloria J. Fenner. 1974. *Casas Grandes: A Fallen Trading Center of the Gran Chichimeca.* Publication 9, vol. 4–8. Dragoon, AZ: Amerind Foundation.

Doleman, William H. 2005. "Environmental Constraints on Forager Mobility and the Use of Cultigens in Southeastern Arizona and Southern New Mexico." In *The Late Archaic: Across the Borderlands, From Foraging to Farming*, ed. Bradley J. Vierra, 113–140. Austin: University of Texas Press.

Douglas, John E. 2007. "Making and Breaking Boundaries in the Hinterlands: The Social and Settlement Dynamics of Southeastern Arizona and Southwestern New Mexico." In *Hinterlands and Regional Dynamics in the Ancient Southwest*, ed. Alan P. Sullivan, III, and James M. Bayman, 97–108. Tucson: University of Arizona Press.

Drass, Richard R. 1998. "The Southern Plains Villagers." In *Archaeology of the Great Plains*, ed. Raymond Wood, 415–455. Lawrence: University Press of Kansas.

Drass, Richard R., and Peggy Flynn. 1990. "Temporal and Geographic Variation in Subsistence Practices for Plains Villagers in the Southern Plains." *Plains Anthropologist* 35(128):175–190. https://doi.org/10.1080/2052546.1990.11909567.

Dudd, S. N., and R. P. Evershed. 1998. "Direct Demonstration of Milk as an Element of Archaeological Economies." *Science* 282(5393):1478–1481. https://doi.org/10.1126/science.282.5393.1478.

Dykeman, D., and P. Roebuck. 2008. "Navajo Emergence in Dinetah: Social Imaginary and Archaeology." Paper presented at the 73rd Annual Meeting of the Society of American Archaeology, Vancouver, BC.

Ebert, James I. 1992. *Distributional Archaeology*. Albuquerque: University of New Mexico Press.

Eckert, Suzanne E., and Linda S. Cordell. 2004. "Pueblo IV Community Formation in the Central Rio Grande Valley." In *The Protohistoric Pueblo World, A.D. 1275–1600*, ed. E. Charles Adams and Andrew I. Duff, 35–42. Tucson: The University of Arizona Press.

Eerkens, Jelmer W. 2003. "Residential Mobility and Pottery Use in the Western Great Basin." *Current Anthropology* 44(5):728–738. https://doi.org/10.1086/379262.

Eichhorn, Barbara, Katharina Neumann, and Aline Garnier. 2010. "Seed Phytoliths in West African *Commelinaceae* and their Potential for Paleoecological Studies." *Palaeogeography, Palaeoclimatology, Palaeoecology* 298(3-4):300–310. https://doi.org/10.1016/j.palaeo.2010.10.004.

Ellis, Linda. 1997. "Hot Rock Technology." In *Hot Rock Cooking on the Greater Edwards Plateau: Four Burned Rock Midden Sites in West Central Texas*, by S. L. Black, L. W. Ellis, D. G. Creel, and G. T. Goode, 43–48. TARL Studies in Archeology 22; Report No. 2. Austin: Archeological Studies Program, Texas Department of Transportation, and University of Texas at Austin.

Emslie, Steven D., John D. Speth, and Regge N. Wiseman. 1992. "Two Prehistoric Puebloan Avifaunas from the Pecos Valley, Southeastern New Mexico." *Journal of Ethnobiology* 12(1):83–115.

Ernst, Moira, and Matthew Swanson. 2009. *Archaeological Survey and NRHP Evaluation of 10,181 Acres on McGregor Range Training Areas 14, 15, and 16, Fort Bliss Military Reservation, Otero County, New Mexico*. Historic and Natural Resources Report No. 08–29. Fort Bliss, TX: Environmental Division.

Ernst, Moira, and Matthew Swanson. 2012. *Archaeological Survey and NRHP Evaluation of 5,120 Acres in Training Area 6C, Dona Ana Range, Fort Bliss Military Reservation, Doña Ana and Otero Counties, New Mexico*. Cultural Resources Report No.

11–08. Fort Bliss, TX: Directorate of Public Works, Environmental Division, Fort Bliss Garrison Command.

de Escandón, José. 1930. *Estado General de las Fundaciones Hechas por José de Escandón en la Colonia de Nuevo Santander*. Tomo II. *Publicaciones del Archivo General de la Nación XV*. México: Secretaria de Gobernación, Tallares de la Nación.

Espejo, Antonio. 1871. "Relación del Viaje, que yo, Antonio Espejo, ciudadano de la ciudad de México, natural de la ciudad de Cordoba, hize con Catorce Soldados y un Relijioso de la Orden de San Francisco." In *Colección de Documentos Inéditos Relativos al Descubrimiento, Conquista y Organización de las Antiguas Posesiones españolas de Améria y Oceanía*, vol. 15. ed. Joaquin F. Pacheco and Francisco Cardenas, 101–126. Madrid: M. Bernaldo de Quirós.

Evans, Glen. 1951. "Prehistoric Wells in Eastern New Mexico." *American Antiquity* 17(1-Part1):1–9. https://doi.org/10.2307/277350.

Evershed, R. P. 1993. "Biomolecular Archaeology and Lipids." *World Archaeology* 25(1):74–93. https://doi.org/10.1080/00438243.1993.9980229.

Evershed, R. P. 2000. "Biomolecular Analysis by Organic Mass Spectrometry." In *Modern Analytical Methods in Art and Archaeology*, vol. 155. ed. E. Ciliberto and G. Spoto, 177–239. New York: Chemical Analysis. John Wiley & Sons.

Evershed, R. P., S. N. Dudd, M. J. Lockheart, and S. Jim. 2001. "Lipids in Archaeology." In *Handbook of Archaeological Sciences*, ed. D. R. Brothwell and A. M. Pollard, 331–349. New York: John Wiley & Sons.

Evershed, R. P., H. R. Mottram, S. N. Dudd, S. Charters, A. W. Stott, G. J. Lawrence, A. M. Gibson, A. Conner, P. W. Blinkhorn, and V. Reeves. 1997. "New Criteria for the Identification of Animal Fats Preserved in Archaeological Pottery." *Naturwissenschaften* 84(9):402–406. https://doi.org/10.1007/s001140050417.

Ezell, Paul. 1937. "Shell Work of the Prehistoric Southwest." *Kiva* 3(3):9–12. https://doi.org/10.1080/00231940.1937.11757801.

Faden, Robert B. 2000. "Commelinaceae." In *Flora of North America North of Mexico*, ed. Flora of North America Editorial Committee, vol. 22, 170–197. New York: Oxford University Press.

Farwell, Robin E. 1981. "Potlids, Plates and Pukis." *Pottery Southwest* 8(3):1–4.

Farwell, Robin E., Yvonne R. Oakes, and Regge N. Wiseman. 1992. *Investigations into the Prehistory and History of the Upper Rio Bonito, Lincoln County, Southeastern New Mexico*. Laboratory of Anthropology Notes 297. Santa Fe: Office of Archaeological Studies, Museum of New Mexico.

Fenneman, N. M. 1931. *Physiography of the Western United States*. New York: McGraw-Hill.

Ferdon, Edwin N., Jr. 1946. *An Archeological Excavation of Hermit's Cave, New Mexico.* Monograph 10. Santa Fe, NM: School of American Research.

Ferguson, Jeffrey R., and Michael D. Glascock. 2007. *Instrumental Neutron Activation Analysis of Mimbres Pottery from Three Sites in Southwestern New Mexico.* Columbia, MO: Archaeometry Laboratory, Research Reactor Center, University of Missouri.

Ferguson, T. J., G. Lennis Berlin, and J. Leigh Kuwanwisiwma. 2009. "*Kukhepya*: Searching for Hopi Trails." In *Landscapes of Movement: Trails, Paths, and Roads in Anthropological Perspective*, ed. J. E. Snead, C. L. Erickson, and A. J. Darling, 20–41. Philadelphia: University of Pennsylvania Press.

Fish, Paul R., Suzanne K. Fish, and John H. Madsen. 2006. *Prehistory and Early History of the Malpai Borderlands: Archaeological Synthesis and Recommendations.* General Technical Report RMRS-GTR-176. Fort Collins, CO: US Department of Agriculture, Forest Service. https://doi.org/10.2737/RMRS-GTR-176.

Flannery, Kent V. 2009. "The Early Mesoamerican House." In *The Early Mesoamerican Village*, updated edition, ed. Kent V. Flannery, 16–44. Walnut Creek, CA: Left Coast Press.

Flannery, Kent V., and Marcus C. Winter. 1976. "Analyzing Household Activities." In *The Early Mesoamerican Village*, ed. Kent V. Flannery, 34–45. New York: Academic Press.

Ford, Richard I. 1983. "Inter-Indian Exchange in the Southwest." In *Handbook of North American Indians* vol. 10, *Southwest*, edited by Alfonso Ortiz, 711–722. Washington, DC: Smithsonian Institution.

Forenbaher, Stašo, and Preston T. Miracle. 2005. "The Spread of Farming in the Eastern Adriatic." *Antiquity* 79(305):514–528. https://doi.org/10.1017/S0003598X00114474.

Forrester, Robert E., Jr. 1951. "A Series of Eighteen Indian Skeletons Excavated in Shackelford County, Texas." *Bulletin of the Texas Archeological and Paleontological Society* 22:132–143.

Foster, Michael S., and Ronna Jane Bradley. 1984. "La Cabrana: A Preliminary Discussion of a Jornada Mogollon Pueblo." In *Recent Research in Mogollon Archaeology*, ed. S. Upham, F. Plog, D. G. Batcho, and B. F. Kauffman, 193–214. Occasional Papers 10 of the University Museum. Las Cruces: New Mexico State University.

Freeman, Martha D. 1981. "The Historic Resource." In *A Cultural Resource Inventory and Assessment of Dona Ana Range, New Mexico, Part II*, ed. D. W. Skelton, M. D. Freeman, N. Smiley, J. D. Pigott, and D. S. Dibble. Texas Archaeological Survey Research Report No. 69. Austin: The University of Texas at Austin.

Frose, D., C. E. Buck, J. J. Clague, L. J. McColl, and P. G. Hare. 2008. "Rapid Technological Change Following the White River Eruption and Athapaskan

Migration from the Yukon Territory." Paper presented at the 73rd Meeting, Society of American Archaeology, Vancouver, BC.

Gallegos, Hernando. 1871. "Testimonio." In *Colección de Documentos Inéditos Relativos al Descubrimiento, Conquista y Organización de las Antiguas Posesiones Españolas de América y Oceanía*, vol. 15. ed. Joaquin F. Pacheco and Francisco Cárdenas, 88–95. Madrid: M. Mernaldo de Quirós.

Gamboa Carrera, Eduardo P. 1992. "Petrograbados del Desierto de Samalayuca, Chihuahua." *Arqueología* 37:34–42.

Gardner, J. L. 1951. "Vegetation in the Creosotebush Area of the Rio Grande Valley." *Ecological Monographs* 21(4):379–403. https://doi.org/10.2307/1948655.

Garrett, Elizabeth M. 1991. "Preliminary Report of the Petrographic Analysis of 200 Sherds from the Capitan North Areas." In *Mogollon V*, ed. Patrick H. Beckett, 191–196. Las Cruces, NM: COAS Publishing & Research.

Geib, Phil R., and Kimberly Spurr. 2000. "The Basketmaker II–III Transition on the Rainbow Plateau." In *Foundations of Anasazi: The Basketmaker–Pueblo Transition*, ed. Paul F. Reed, 175–200. Salt Lake City: University of Utah Press.

Geib, Phil R., and Kimberly Spurr. 2002. "The Forager to Farmer Transition on the Rainbow Plateau." In *Traditions, Transitions, and Technologies: Themes in Southwestern Archaeology*, ed. Sarah H. Schlanger, 224–244. Boulder: University Press of Colorado.

Gerald, Rex E. 1973. *The Suma Indians of Northern Chihuahua and Western Texas.* Santa Fe, NM: Santa Fe Corral of the Westerners Books.

Gerald, Rex E. 1974. "Aboriginal Use and Occupation by Tigua, Manso, and Suma Indians." In *Apache Indians III*, ed. A. H. Schroeder, 9–212. Santa Fe, NM: Santa Fe Corral of the Westerners Books.

Gerald, Rex E., ed. 1988. "Pickup Pueblo, A Late Prehistoric House Ruin." *The Artifact* 26(2):1–86.

Gilman, Patricia A. 1987. "Architecture as Artifact: Pitstructures and Pueblos in the American Southwest." *American Antiquity* 52(03):538–564. https://doi.org/10.2307/281598.

Gilman, Patricia A. 1997. *Wandering Villagers: Pit Structures, Mobility, and Agriculture in Southeastern Arizona.* Anthropological Research Papers No. 49. Tempe: Arizona State University.

Gilman, Patricia A., and Valli S. Powell-Martí. 2006. "Mimbres Society." In *Mimbres Society*, ed. V. S. Powell-Martí and P. A. Gilman, 1–14. Tucson: University of Arizona Press.

Givens, Douglas R. 1992. *Alfred Vincent Kidder and the Development of Americanist Archaeology.* Albuquerque: University of New Mexico Press.

Gladwin, Winifred, and Harold S. Gladwin. 1934. "A Method for the Designation of Cultures and their Variations." Medallion Papers, No. 15. Globe, AZ: Gila Pueblo.

Goldborer, S. E. 1988. "Botanical Remains from the Conejo Site (FB46)." In "Settlement and Subsistence Patterns during Pithouse Occupations in the Chihuahua Desert." Manuscript on file, Archaeological Program. Fort Bliss, TX: Environmental Management Office.

Goldstein, Lynn G. 1976. "Spatial Structure and Social Organization: Regional Manifestations of Mississippian Society." PhD dissertation, Northwestern University, Evanston, IL.

Gorenflo, Larry J., and Thomas L. Bell. 1991. "Network Analysis and the Study of Past Regional Organization." In *Ancient Road Networks and Settlement Hierarchies in the New World*, ed. C. D. Trombold, 80–98. Cambridge, UK: Cambridge University Press.

Graves, Tim, Juan Arias, and Mark Willis. 2012. *Guadalupe Village (LA 143472): A Burned Rock Midden Site in Southeastern New Mexico and the Use of Innovative and Inexpensive Mapping Techniques.* Carlsbad, NM: Bureau of Land Management, Carlsbad Field Office.

Graves, Tim B., Myles R. Miller, and Melinda Landreth. 2013. *Archaeological Data Recovery at Five Sites in Training Area 4D and 5A and Site Characterizing of One Site in Training Area 7B on Fort Bliss, Otero County, New Mexico.* Cultural Resources Report No. 12–11. Fort Bliss, TX: Directorate of Public Works, Environmental Division, Fort Bliss Garrison Command.

Graves, Tim B., Myles R. Miller, and Melinda Landreth. 2014. *Three Millennia of Village Settlements in the Western Tularosa Basin: Excavations at Four Sites near the Organ Mountains on Fort Bliss, Doña Ana County, New Mexico.* Cultural Resources Report No. 1325. El Paso, TX: Directorate of Public Works, Environmental Division, Fort Bliss Garrison Command, Fort Bliss Texas. QRI/GMI Joint Venture.

Graves, T., M. Miller, and M. Willis. n.d. *"Jornada Mogollon Feature Data Base: Dated Thermal Features, Structures, and Other Features." Database on file with Fort Bliss Environmental Division.* TX: Fort Bliss.

Graves, Tim B., John A. Peterson, and Mark Willis. 1996. "Jornada Mogollon Structure data: A Comparison of Structures in and nearby the Jornada Mogollon." Manuscript on file. El Paso: Department of Sociology and Anthropology, University of Texas.

Graves, Tim B., Christopher A. Turnbow, Timothy G. Baugh, Grant D. Smith, James Railey, Elia Perez, R. M. Reycraft, Sue Sitton, Martha Yduarte, and Richard D. Holmes. 2002. *The Doña Ana Range Survey and Site Evaluations in Limited Use*

Areas A through N, Fort Bliss, Dona Ana and Otero Counties, New Mexico. Vol. 1. El Paso, TX: TRC Mariah Associates.

Gray, W. C. 1977. "Faunal Analysis Feature 1, ENM 10017." In *Caprock Water System Archaeological Project, Lea County, New Mexico*, edited by J. L. Haskell, 303–317. Portales, NM: Agency of Conservation Archaeology, Eastern New Mexico University.

Grayson, Donald K. 1993. *The Desert's Past: A Natural Prehistory of the Great Basin.* Washington, DC: Smithsonian Institution Press.

Green, F. E. 1962. "Additional Notes on Prehistoric Wells at the Clovis Site." *American Antiquity* 28(02):230–234. https://doi.org/10.2307/278382.

Green, John W. 1968. "A Preliminary Report on the Salvage of an El Paso Phase House Ruin (EPAS 53)." *Transactions of the 4th Regional Archeological Symposium for Southeastern New Mexico and Western Texas*, 73–77. Iraan, TX: Iraan Archeological Society.

Green, John W. 1969. "Preliminary Report on Site EPAS-60, an El Paso Phase House Ruin." *Transactions of the 5th Regional Archeological Symposium for Southeastern New Mexico and Western Texas*, 1–12. Portales, NM: El Llano Archaeological Society.

Greenwald, Dawn M. 2008. "Flaked Stones." In *Archaeology of the Hondo Valley; Lincoln County, New Mexico*, ed. Kristen Campbell and Jim A. Railey, 477–536. SWCA Cultural Resources Report No. 2008–417. Albuquerque, NM: SWCA Environmental Consultants.

Greer, John W. 1967. "Midden Circles versus Mescal Pits." *American Antiquity* 32(1):108–109. https://doi.org/10.2307/278786.

Greer, John W. 1968a. "Excavations at a Midden Circle Site in El Paso County, Texas." *Bulletin of the Texas Archeological Society* 39:111–131.

Greer, John W. 1968b. "Notes on Excavated Ring Midden Sites, 1963–1968." *Bulletin of the Texas Archeological Society* 38:39–44.

Greer, John W. 1976. "Notes on Bison in Val Verde County, Texas: Additions to Dillehay." *Plains Anthropologist* 21(73):237–239. https://doi.org/10.1080/2052546.1976.11908756.

Gregory, David A., Fred L. Nials, and J. Brett Hill. 2011. "Early Agricultural Period Settlement Strategies in the Southern Southwest." In *The Latest Research on the Earliest Farmers*, ed. Sarah A. Herr. Archaeology Southwest. www.archaeologysouthwest.org/what-we-do/investigations/earliest-farmers.

Griffen, William B. 1979. *Indian Assimilation in the Franciscan Area of Nueva Vizcaya.* Anthropological Papers No. 33. Tucson: University of Arizona Press.

Grissino-Mayer, H. D., C. H. Baisan, and T. W. Swetnam. 1997. *Year Reconstruction of Annual Precipitation for the Southern Rio Grande Basin.* Fort Bliss, TX: Legacy Program, Natural Resources Division, Directorate of Environment. *A* 1:373.

Griswold, George B. 1959. "Mineral Deposits of Lincoln County, New Mexico." State Bureau of Mines and Mineral Resources Bulletin 67. Socorro: New Mexico Institute of Mining and Technology.

Gronenborg, Detlef. 1997. "An Ancient Storage Pit in the SW Chad Basin, Nigeria." *Journal of Field Archaeology* 24:431–439.

Grosboll, Sue. 1987. "Ethnic Boundaries within the Inca Empire: Evidence from Huanuco, Peru." In *Ethnicity and Culture: Proceedings of the 18th Chacmool Conference*, e. Reginald Auger, M. F. Glass, S. MacEachern, and P. H. McCartney, 115–126. Calgary, AB: University of Calgary Archaeological Association.

Gumerman, George J. 1994. "Patterns and Perturbations in Southwest Prehistory." In *Themes in Southwest Prehistory*, ed. George J. Gumerman, 3–10. Santa Fe, NM: School of American Research Press.

Hall, Stephen A. 1982. "Late Holocene Paleoecology of the Southern Plains." *Quaternary Research* 17(03):391–407. https://doi.org/10.1016/0033-5894(82)90030-8.

Hall, Stephen A. 1990. "Channel Trenching and Climatic Change in the Southern U.S. Great Plains." *Geology* 18(4):342–345. https://doi.org/10.1130/0091-7613(1990)o 18<0342:CTACCI>2.3.CO;2.

Hall, Stephen A. 2002. *Field Guide to the Geoarchaeology of the Mescalero Sands, Southeastern New Mexico*. Santa Fe, NM: Red Rock Geological Enterprises.

Hall, Stephen A. 2010. "New Interpretations of Alluvial and Paleo-vegetation Records from Chaco Canyon, New Mexico." *New Mexico Geological Society Guidebook, 61st Field Conference*, 231–246.

Hall, Stephen A., and William L. Penner. 2013. "Stable Carbon Isotopes, C_3–C_4 Vegetation, and 12,800 Years of Comate Change in Central New Mexico, USA." *Palaeogeography, Palaeoclimatology, Palaeoecology* 369:272–281. https://doi.org/10 .1016/j.palaeo.2012.10.034.

Hamilton, Donny L. 2001. *Prehistory of the Rustler Hills: Granado Cave*. Austin: University of Texas Press.

Hamilton, Marcus J., Bruce T. Milne, Robert S. Walker, Oskar Burger, and James H. Brown. 2007. "The Complex Structure of Hunter-Gatherer Social Networks." *Proceedings of the Royal Society Bulletin* 274(1622):2195–2202. https://doi.org/10.1098 /rspb.2007.0564.

Hammack, Laurens C. 1961. *Missile Range Archaeology*. Laboratory of Anthropology Note 2. Santa Fe: Museum of New Mexico.

Hammond, George P., and Agapito Rey. 1929. *Expedition into New Mexico Made by Antonio de Espejo in 1582–1583, as Revealed in the Journal of Diego Pérez de Luxán, a Member of the Party*. Los Angeles, CA: Quivera Society Publications, Quivera Society. Revised.

Hammond, George P., and Agapito Rey. 1966. *Rediscovery of New Mexico 1580–1594: The Explorations of Chamascado, Espejo, Morlete, and Leyva de Bonilla and Humaña.* Albuquerque, NM: University of New Mexico Press.

Harbour, R. L. 1972. *Geology of the Northern Franklin Mountains, Texas and New Mexico.* vol. 1298. United States Geological Survey Bulletin. Washington, DC: United States Government Printing Office.

Hard, Robert J. 1983a. *Excavations in the Castner Range Archeological District in El Paso, Texas.* Publications in Anthropology No. 11. El Paso: El Paso Centennial Museum, University of Texas.

Hard, Robert J. 1983b. "A Model for Prehistoric Land Use, Ft. Bliss, Texas." In *Proceedings, 1983*, 41–51. New York: American Society for Conservation Archaeology.

Hard, Robert J. 1988. "The Emergence of Farming Economies in the American Southwest." Paper presented at the 53rd Annual Meeting of the Society of American Archaeology, Phoenix, AZ.

Hard, Robert J. 1997. "A Comparative Analysis of Agricultural Dependence in the Northern and Southern Jornada Mogollon Regions." In *Ninth Jornada-Mogollon Conference*, ed. Raymond P. Mauldin, Jeff D. Leach and Susan Ruth, 93–98. Publications in Archaeology No. 12. El Paso, TX.

Hard, Robert J., Jeffrey Durst, and Gerry Raymond. 1996. "Farmers or Foragers? Upland versus Lowland Exploitation on the Eastern Periphery of the Southwest." Paper Presented at *61st Annual Society for American Archaeology*, New Orleans, LA.

Hard, Robert J., Raymond P. Mauldin, and Gerry R. Raymond. 1996. "Mano Size, Stable Carbon Isotope Ratios, and Macrobotanical Remains as Multiple Lines of Evidence of Maize Dependence in the American Southwest." *Journal of Archaeological Method and Theory* 3(3):253–318. https://doi.org/10.1007/BF02229401.

Hard, Robert J., and John R. Roney. 2005. "The Transition to Farming on the Rio Casa Grandes and in the Southern Jornada Mogollon Region." In *The Late Archaic Across the Borderlands*, ed. Bradley J. Vierra, 141–186. Austin: University of Texas Press.

Haskell, J. Loring. 1977. *Caprock Water System Archaeological Project, Lea County, New Mexico.* Portales, NM: Agency for Conservation Archaeology, Eastern New Mexico University.

Haury, Emil W. 1936. *The Mogollon Culture of Southwestern New Mexico.* Medallion No. 19. Globe, AZ: Gila Pueblo.

Haury, Emil W. 1937. "Shell." In *Excavations at Snaketown: Material Culture*, by H. S. Gladwin, E. W. Haury, E. B. Sayles, and N. Gladwin, 135–53. Medallion Papers No. 25. Globe, AZ: Gila Pueblo.

Haury, Emil W. 1958. "Evidence at Point of Pines for Prehistoric Migration from Northeastern Arizona." In *Migrations in New World Culture History*, ed. Raymond H. Thompson, 1–6. Social Science Bulletin 27, Tucson: University of Arizona.

Haury, Emil W. 1962. "The Greater American Southwest." In *Courses toward Urban Life: Some Archaeological Considerations of Cultural Alternatives*, ed. Robert J. Braidwood and Gordon R. Willey, 106–131. Viking Fund Publications in Anthropology 32. New York: Viking Fund.

Hawley, J. W. 1975. "Quaternary History of Doña Ana County Region, South-Central New Mexico." In *New Mexico Geological Society, Guidebook 26th Field Conference*, ed. W. Seager, R. E. Clemons, and J. F. Callender, 139–150. Socorro: New Mexico Geological Society.

Hawley, J. W., and F. E. Kottlowski. 1969. "Quaternary Geology of South-Central New Mexico Border Region." In *Border Stratigraphy Symposium*, New Mexico Bureau of Mines and Mineral Resources. Circular No. 104:52–76.

Hawthorne-Tagg, Lori, and Deni J. Seymour, Robert. J. Hall, R. Martinez, and Susan Ruth. 1998. *Traces of the Trails: The Spanish Salt Trail and Butterfield Trail on Fort Bliss, Doña Ana County New Mexico*. Historic and Natural Resources Report No. 523. Fort Bliss, TX: Fort Bliss Directorate of Environment, Conservation Division.

Hayden, Julian D. 1965. "Fragile Pattern Areas." *American Antiquity* 31(02):272–276. https://doi.org/10.2307/2693998.

Hayden, Julian D. 1967. "A Summary Prehistory and History of the Sierra Pinacate, Sonora." *American Antiquity* 32(03):335–344. https://doi.org/10.2307/2694662.

Hayes, Alden C., Jon Young, and A. H. Warren. 1981. *Excavation of Mound 7, Gran Quivera National Monument, New Mexico*. Publications in Archaeology, vol. 15. Washington, DC: National Park Service.

Haynes, C. Vance, Jr. 1975. "Pleistocene and Recent Stratigraphy." In *Late Pleistocene Environments of the Southern High Plains*, ed. Fred Wendorf and James J. Hester, 57–96. Dallas, TX: Fort Burgwin Research Center, Southern Methodist University.

Haynes, C. Vance, Jr., Dennis Stanford, Margaret Jodry, Joanne Dickenson, John L. Montgomery, Phillip H. Shelley, Irwin Rovner, and George A. Agogino. 1999. "A Clovis Well at the Type Site 11,500 BC: The Oldest Prehistoric Well in America." *Geoarchaeology: An International Journal* 14(5):455–470. https://doi.org/10.1002 /(SICI)1520-6548(199906)14:5<455::AID-GEA6>3.0.CO;2-L.

Heartfield, Lorraine. 1975. "Archaeological Investigations of Four Sites in Southwestern Coahuila, Mexico." *Bulletin of the Texas Archaeological Society* 46:127–177.

Hedrick, Mrs. John A. 1967. "Escondida Survey." *Artifact* 5(2):19–24.

Hegmon, M., M. C. Nelson, R. Anyon, D. Creel, S. A. LeBlanc, and H. J. Shafer. 1999. "Scale and Time-Space Systematics in the Post-A.D. 1100 Mimbres Region in the North American Southwest." *Kiva* 65(2):143–166. https://doi.org/10.1080 /00231940.1999.11758405.

Heizer, Robert F. 1978. "Trade and Trails." In *Handbook of North American Indians*, vol. 8. *California*, ed. R. F. Heizer, 690–693. Washington, DC: Smithsonian Institution.

Herhahn, Cynthia L., and Ann F. Ramenofsky, eds. 2016. *Exploring Cause and Explanation: Historical Ecology, Demography, and Movement in the American Southwest.* Boulder: University Press of Colorado. https://doi.org/10.5876/9781607324737.

Heron, C., and A. M. Pollard. 1988. "The Analysis of Natural Resinous Materials from Roman Amphoras." In *Science and Archaeology Glasgow 1987, Proceedings of a Conference on the Application of Scientific Techniques to Archaeology, Glasgow, 1987*, ed. E. A. Slater and J. O. Tate, 429–447. BAR British Series 196 (ii). Oxford, UK: British Archaeological Reports.

Hester, J. J. 1972. *Blackwater Draw Locality No. 1: A Stratified, Early Man Site in Eastern New Mexico.* Fort Burgwin Research Center 8. Dallas, TX: Southern Methodist University.

Hill, David V. 1988. "Petrographic Analysis of El Paso Polychrome Pottery from Pickup Pueblo." In *Pickup Pueblo: A Late Prehistoric House Ruin in Northeast El Paso*, ed. Rex Gerald. Appendix D. *The Artifact* 26(2):75–78.

Hill, David V. 1990. "Ceramic Production and Settlement Patterns in the Paso del Norte." In *Actas del Segundo Congreso de Historia Regional Comparada*, ed. Ricardo León García, 29–43. Chihuahua, Mexico: Universidad Autónoma de Ciudad Juárez, Ciudad Juárez.

Hill, David V. 2009. "Regional Mobility and the Sources of Undecorated Ceramics Recovered from Southeastern New Mexico and West Texas." Paper presented at the 74th Annual Meeting of the Society for American Archaeology, Atlanta, GA.

Hill, David V. 2011. "Appendix E: Petrographic Analysis of Ceramics." In *Data Recovery at 14 Sites for the Intrepid–BLM Land Exchange, Eddy County, New Mexico*, prepared by Douglas H. M. Boggess, LMAS Report No. 1077. Albuquerque, NM: Lone Mountain Archaeological Services.

Hill, David V. 2012. "Variation in the Production of Ceramics by Athapaskans." In *From the Land of Ever Winter to the American Southwest: Athapaskan Migrations, Mobility and Ethnogenesis*, ed. Deni J. Seymour, 225–240. Salt Lake City: University of Utah Press.

Hill, David V. 2014. "Understanding Sources of Variability of Brownware Ceramics from Southeastern New Mexico." Manuscript on file, Historic Preservation Division, Museum of New Mexico, Santa Fe.

Hill, David V. 2017. "Theoretical and Methodological Approaches to the Study of the Ceramics of Protohistoric Hunter-Gatherers." In *Fierce and Indomitable: The*

Protohistoric Non-Pueblo World, ed. Deni J. Seymour, 154–160. Salt Lake City: University of Utah Press.

Hill, David V., and David P. Staley. 1999. "Pots, Points and Dates: New Information toward Understanding the Archaic/Formative Transition in Southeastern New Mexico." In *Sixty Years of Mogollon Archaeology: Papers from the Ninth Mogollon Conference*, Silver City, NM, ed. S. M. Whittlesly, 157–162. Tucson, AZ: Statistical Research.

Hill, David V., and Gene Wheaton. 2009. "Analysis of Ceramics in the Texas Portion of the AT&T NEXGEN/CORE Project Archaeological Investigations for the AT&T NEXGE/CORE Project: Texas Segment." In *Archaeological Investigations for the AT&T NEXGEN/CORE Project* by G. Wheaton, 941–959. Farmington: Western Cultural Resources Management.

Hill, David V., and Gene Wheaton. 2010. *Analysis of Ceramics from the New Mexico Portion of the AT&T NEXGEN/CORE Fiber Optic Cable Right-of-Way.* Farmington, NM: Western Cultural Resources Management.

Hill, J. Brett, Jeffrey J. Clark, William H. Doelle, and Patrick D. Lyons. 2004. "Prehistoric Demography in the Southwest: Migration, Coalescence, and Hohokam Population Decline." *American Antiquity* 69(4):689–716. https://doi.org/10.2307/4128444.

Hines, M. H., S. A. Tomka, and K. W. Kibler. 1994. *Data Recovery at the Wind Canyon Site, 41HZ119, Hudspeth County, Texas.* Reports of Investigations No. 99. Austin: Prewitt and Associates.

Hitchcock, R. K., and L. E. Bartram, Jr. 1998. "Social Boundaries, Technical Systems, and the Use of Space and Technology in the Kalahari." In *The Archaeology of Social Boundaries*, ed. M. T. Stark, 12–49. Washington, DC: Smithsonian Institution Press.

Hodder, Ian. 1982. *The Present Past: An Introduction to Anthropology for Archaeologists.* New York: Pica Press.

Hodder, Ian. 2012. *Entangled; An Archaeology of the Relationships between Humans and Things.* Chichester, UK: Wiley-Blackwell. https://doi.org/10.1002/9781118241912.

Hogan, Patrick. 1983. "Paleo-Environmental Reconstruction." In *Economy and Interaction along the Lower Chaco River*, ed. Patrick Hogan and Joseph C. Winter, 49–62. Albuquerque: Office of Contract Archaeology and the Maxwell Museum of Anthropology, University of New Mexico.

Hogan, Patrick. 1994. "Foragers to Farmers: The Adoption of Agriculture in the Northern Southwest." In Archaic Hunter-Gatherer Archaeology in the American *Southwest*, ed. B. Vierra, 155–184. Contributions in Anthropology No. 13. Portales, NM: Eastern New Mexico University.

Hogan, Patrick. 2006. *Development of Southeastern New Mexico Regional Research Design and Cultural Resource Management Strategy*. UNM Report No. 185–849. Albuquerque: University of New Mexico.

Holliday, Vance T. 1989. "Middle Holocene Drought on the Southern High Plains." *Quaternary Research* 31(01):74–82. https://doi.org/10.1016/0033-5894(89)90086-0.

Holloway, R. 2012. "Charcoal and Macrobotanical Analyses from Three Archaeological Sites, Geo-Marine Tank Trails, Mitigation Project, Fort Bliss Military Reservation McGregor Range, Otero County, New Mexico." In *Testing and Mitigation of Three Archaeological Sites along Proposed Tank Trails, Fort Bliss Military Reservation, Otero County, New Mexico*. Cultural Resource Report No. 10–11, Appendix B. Fort Bliss, TX: Directorate of Public Works, Fort Bliss Garrison Command, Environmental Division.

Howey, Meghan, and Thomas R. Rocek. 2008. "Ceramic Variability, Subsistence Economies, and Settlement Patterns in the Jornada Mogollon." *Kiva* 74(1):7–32. https://doi.org/10.1179/kiv.2008.74.1.001.

Huckell, Bruce B. 1995. *Of Marshes and Maize: Preceramic Agricultural Settlements in the Cienega Valley, Southeastern Arizona*. Anthropological Papers of the University of Arizona, No. 59. Tucson: University of Arizona.

Huckell, Bruce B. 1996. "The Archaic Prehistory of the North American Southwest." *Journal of World Prehistory* 10(3):305–373.

Huckell, Bruce B., Lisa W. Huckell, and Karl K. Benedict. 2002. "Maize Agriculture and the Rise of Mixed Farming-Foraging Economies in Southeastern Arizona during the Second Millennium B.C." In *Traditions, Transitions, and Technologies: Themes in Southwestern Archaeology*, ed. Sarah H. Schlanger, 137–246. Boulder: University Press of Colorado.

Huckell, Bruce B., Lisa W. Huckell, and Suzanne K. Fish. 1995. *Investigations at Milagro, a Late Preceramic Site in the Eastern Tucson Basin*. Technical report No. 94–5. Tucson, AZ: Center for Desert Archaeology.

Huckell, Lisa W. 2000. "Paleoethnobotany." In *A Highway through Time: Archaeological Investigations Along NM 90*, ed. Christopher A. Turnbow, 509–564. New Mexico State Highway and Transportation Department, Technical Report 2000–3. Albuquerque, NM: TRC.

Hughes, Jack T. 1989. "Prehistoric Cultural Developments on the Texas High Plains." *Bulletin of the Texas Archaeological Society* 60:1–55.

Hunt, James E. 1989. *Archaeological Clearance Report for Dawson Geophysical Company's Seismic Testing Line 89–41, Situated on Public Lands in Lea County, New Mexico*. Carlsbad, NM: Pecos Archaeological Consultants.

Hunter-Anderson, Rosalind L. 1986. *Prehistoric Adaptation in the American Southwest.* New York: Cambridge University Press.

Hunter, Rosemary. 1988. "The Tony Colon Site I." *Fourth Jornada Mogollon Conference (Oct. 1985) Collected Papers,* ed. M. S. Duran and D. T. Kirkpatrick, 137–162. Tularosa, NM: Human Systems Research.

Husby, M., and S. Pappas. 2005. LA 20241. Laboratory of Anthropology Site Form. On file at the Bureau of Land Management, Carlsbad, NM.

Huysecom, E., M. Rasse, L. Lespez, K. Neumann, A. Fahmy, A. Ballouche, S. Ozainne, M. Maggetti, Ch. Tribolo, and S. Soriano. 2009. "The Emergence of Pottery in Africa during the Tenth Millennium Cal BC: New Evidence from Ounjougou (Mali)." *Antiquity* 83(322):905–917. https://doi.org/10.1017/S0003598X00099245.

Ibrahim, Jemilat, Vivian Chioma Ajaegbu, and Henry Omoregie Egharevba. 2010. "Pharmacognostic and Phytochemical Analysis of *Commelina benghalensis* L." *Ethnobotanical Leaflets* 14:610–615.

Ingold, Timothy. 2000. *The Perception of the Environment: Essays in Livelihood, Dwelling, and Skill.* London: Routledge. https://doi.org/10.4324/9780203466025.

Isaksson, Sven. 1999. "Guided by Light: The Swift Characterisation of Ancient Organic Matter by FTIR, IRFingerprinting and Hierarchical Cluster Analysis." *Laborativ Arkeologi* 12:35–43.

Ives, J. W. 1990. *A Theory of Northern Athapaskan Prehistory.* Boulder: Westview Press.

Jackson, A. T. 1937. "Exploration of Certain Sites in Culberson County, Texas." *Bulletin of the Texas Archaeological and Paleontological Society* 9:146–192.

Jackson, Lora, and Marc Thompson. 2005. "Form and Function: A Reassessment of El Paso Polychromes." In *Archaeology between the Borders: Papers from the 13th Biennial Jornada Mogollon Conference,* ed. M. Thompson, J. Jurgena, and L. Jackson, 1–7. El Paso, TX: El Paso Museum of Archaeology.

Jelinek, Arthur J. 1967. *A Prehistoric Sequence in the Middle Pecos Valley, New Mexico.* Anthropological Papers No. 31. Ann Arbor: Museum of Anthropology, University of Michigan.

Jelks, Edward B. 1967. "The Gilbert Site: A Norteno Focus Site in Northeastern Texas." *Bulletin of the Texas Archeological Society* 37.

Jenkins, Richard. 1996. *Social Identity.* London: Routledge. https://doi.org/10.4324/9780203292990.

Jenkins, Richard. 1997. *Rethinking Ethnicity.* London: Sage.

Jennings, Jesse D. 1940. *A Variation on Southwestern Pueblo Culture.* Bulletin No. 10. Laboratory of Anthropology Technical Series. Santa Fe, NM: Laboratory of Anthropology.

Johnson, Allen W., and Timothy Earle. 1987. *The Evolution of Human Societies: From Foraging Group to Agrarian State*. Stanford, CA: Stanford University Press.

Johnson, Eileen, and Vance T. Holliday. 1986. "The Archaic Record at Lubbock Lake." *Plains Anthropologist* 31(114):7–54. https://doi.org/10.1080/2052546.1986.11909334.

Johnson, Eileen, and Vance T. Holliday. 2004. "Archeology and Late Quaternary Environments of the Southern High Plains." In *The Prehistory of Texas*, ed. Timothy K. Perttula, 283–295. College Station: Texas A&M University Press.

Johnson, Francis J., and Patricia H. Johnson. 1957. "An Indian Trail Complex of the Central Colorado Desert: A Preliminary Survey." *University of California Archaeological Survey Reports* 37:22–34. Berkeley: University of California.

Johnson, Gregory A. 1982. "Organizational Structure and Scalar Stress." In *Theory and Explanation in Archaeology: The Southampton Conference*, ed. C. Renfrew, M. J. Rowlands, and B. A. Segraves, 389–421. New York: Academic Press.

Johnson, Gregory A. 1989. "Dynamics of Southwestern Prehistory: Far Outside—Looking." In *In Dynamics of Southwest Prehistory*, ed. Linda S. Cordell and George J. Gumerman, 371–389. Tuscaloosa: University of Alabama Press.

Jones, Joshua G., Timothy M. Kearns, and Janet L. McVickar. 2010. *Archaeological Investigations for the AT&T Nexgen/Core Project: New Mexico Segment*. Farmington, NM: Western Cultural Resource Management.

Jones, Terry L., Gary M. Brown, L. Mark Raab, Janet L. McVickar, W. Geoffrey Spaulding, Douglas J. Kennett, Andrew York, and Phillip L. Walker. 1999. "Environmental Imperatives Reconsidered: Demographic Crises in Western North America during the Medieval Climatic Anomaly." *Current Anthropology* 40(2):137–170. https://doi.org/10.1086/200002.

Jordan, Peter, and Marek Zvelebil. 2009. "Ex Oriente Lux: The Prehistory of Hunter-Gatherer Ceramic Dispersals." In *Ceramics before Farming*, ed. Peter Jordan and Marek Zvelebil, 33–90. Walnut Creek, CA: Left Coast Press.

Kalasz, Stephen M., Christian J. Zier, and Mark Mitchell. 1999. "Late Prehistoric Stage." In *Colorado Prehistory: A Context for the Arkansas Basin*, ed. Christian M. Zier and Stephen M. Kalasz, 141–263. Fort Collins, CO: Centennial Archaeology.

Katz, Susana R., and Paul Katz. 1985. *The Prehistory of the Carlsbad Basin, Southeastern New Mexico: Technical Report of Prehistoric Archaeological Investigations in the Brantley Project Locality*. Amarillo, TX: Bureau of Reclamation, Southwest Regional Office.

Keller, G. R., and W. S. Baldridge. 1999. "The Rio Grande Rift: A Geological and Geographysical Overview." *Rocky Mountain Geology* 34(1):121–130. https://doi.org/10.2113/34.1.121.

Kelley, Jane H. 1984. *The Archaeology of the Sierra Blanca Region of Southeastern New Mexico*. Anthropological Papers No. 74. Ann Arbor: Museum of Anthropology, University of Michigan.

Kelley, Jane H. 1991. "An Overview of the Capitan North Project." In *Mogollon V*, ed. Patrick H. Beckett, 166–176. Las Cruces, NM: COAS Publishing and Research.

Kelley, Jane H., and Joe D. Stewart, A. C. MacWilliams, and Loy C. Neff. 1999. "A West Central Chihuahuan Perspective on Chihuahuan Culture." In *The Casas Grandes World*, ed. Curtis F. Schaafsma and Carroll L. Riley, 63–77. Salt Lake City: The University of Utah Press.

Kelley, J. Charles. n.d. "Second Rio Conchos Expedition—Summer 1951." Unpublished narrative report submitted to the American Association for Advancement of Science, Sponsors.

Kelley, J. Charles. 1939. "Archaeological Notes on the Excavation of a Pithouse near Presidio Texas." *El Palacio* 44:221–234.

Kelley, J. Charles. 1940. "Trans-Pecos." In *Texas Archaeological News: An Occasional Report Issued by the Council of Texas Archeologists*, ed. T. N. Campbell, 1–4. Austin: Council of Texas Archaeologists.

Kelley, J. Charles. 1949. "Archaeological Notes on Two Excavated House Structures in Western Texas." *Bulletin of the Texas Archaeological and Paleontological Society* 20:89–114.

Kelley, J. Charles. 1951. "A Bravo Valley Aspect Component of the Lower Rio Conchos Valley, Chihuahua, Mexico." *American Antiquity* 17(02):114–119. https://doi.org/10.2307/277245.

Kelley, J. Charles. 1952. "The Historic Indian Pueblos of La Junta de los Rios." *New Mexico Historical Review* 27:257–95.

Kelley, J. Charles. 1953. "The Historic Indian Pueblos of La Junta de los Rios." *New Mexico Historical Review* 28:21–51.

Kelley, J. Charles. 1985. "Review of the Architectural Sequence at La Junta de los Rios." In *Proceedings of the Third Jornada Mogollon Conference*, ed. M. S. Foster and T. C. O'Laughlin. *The Artifact* 23(1/2):149–159.

Kelley, J. Charles. 1986. *Jumano and Patarabueye, Relations at La Junta de los Rios*. Anthropological Papers No. 77. Ann Arbor: Museum of Anthropology, University of Michigan.

Kelley, J. Charles. 1990. "The Rio Conchos Drainage: History, Archaeology, Significance." *Journal of Big Bend Studies* 2:29–41.

Kelley, J. Charles, T. N. Campbell, and Donald J. Lehmer. 1940. "The Association of Archaeological Materials with Geological Deposits in the Big Bend Region of Texas." *West Texas Historical and Scientific Society Publication* 10:1–173.

Kelley, J. Charles, and Ellen Abbott Kelley. 1990. *Presidio, Texas (Presidio County) Water Improvement Project, an Archaeological and Archival Survey and Appraisal.* Fort Davis, TX: Blue Mountain Consultants.

Kelley, Vincent C. 1971. *Geology of the Pecos Country, Southeastern New Mexico.* New Mexico Bureau of Mines and Mineral Resources, Memoir 24. Socorro: New Mexico Institute of Mining and Technology.

Kelly, Robert L. 1992. "Mobility/Sedentism: Concepts, Archaeological Measures, and Effects." *Annual Review of Anthropology* 21(1):43–66. https://doi.org/10.1146/annurev.an.21.100192.000355.

Kelly, Robert L. 1995. *The Foraging Spectrum: Diversity in Hunter-Gatherer Lifeways.* Washington, DC: Smithsonian Institution Press.

Kemrer, Meade F. 1998. *Data Recovery at Site LA 103523: A Complex Domestic Area in Eddy County, New Mexico.* Tularosa, NM: Human Systems Research.

Kenmotsu, Nancy A. 1994. "Helping Each Other Out, A Study of the Mutualistic Relations of Small Scale Foragers and Cultivators in Las Junta de Los Rios Region, Texas and Mexico." PhD dissertation, University of Texas at Austin.

Kenmotsu, Nancy A. 2013. "Pottery at La Junta: One View of Regional Interaction along the Rio Grande." *Bulletin of the Texas Archeological Society* 84:5–28.

Kenmotsu, Ray D., and John D. Pigott. 1977. *A Cultural Resource Inventory and Assessment of McGregor Guided Missile Range: Otero County, New Mexico.* Archeological Survey Research Report No. 65, Part 3. Austin: The University of Texas at Austin.

Kennedy, John G. 1963. "Tesguino Complex: The Role of Beer in Tarahumara Culture." *American Anthropologist* 65(3):620–640. https://doi.org/10.1525/aa.1963.65.3.02a00080.

Kidder, Alfred Vincent. 1924. *An Introduction to the Study of Southwestern Archaeology: With a Preliminary Account of the Excavations at Pecos.* Papers of the Southwestern Expedition, No.1(1). Andover, MA: Phillips Academy Department of Archaeology.

Kidder, Alfred Vincent. 1927. "Southwestern Archeological Conference." *Science* 66(1716):489–491. https://doi.org/10.1126/science.66.1716.489.

Kintigh, K. W. 1994. "Chaco, Communal Architecture, and Cibolan Aggregation." In *The Ancient Southwestern Community: Models and Methods for the Study of Prehistoric Social Organization*, ed. W. H. Wills and R. D. Leonard, 131–140. Albuquerque: University of New Mexico Press.

Kludt, Trevor. 2007. *Landform and Settlement*, Part 1, *Farming the Fans.* Historic and Natural Resources Reports 517 & 531, LMAS Report 560-011-013, Fort Bliss, TX: Fort Bliss Garrison Command.

Kludt, Trevor, Tim Church, and David Kuehn. 2007. "'Unseen' Ancient Paths in the Tularosa Basin." In *Viva La Jornada: Papers from the 14th Biennial Jornada Mogollon*

Conference, ed. J. Jurgena, L. Jackson, and M. Thompson, 95–109. El Paso, TX: El Paso Museum of Archaeology.

Kludt, Trevor, Michael Stowe, Tim Church, and Scott Walley. 2007. *Pathfinding on McGregor Range: Archaeological Survey of Approximately 8,000 Acres on Fort Bliss, New Mexico.* Cultural Resources Report No. 04-12, LMAS No. 560-008. Fort Bliss, TX: Directorate of the Environment, Fort Bliss Garrison Command.

Knowles, B. B., and R. A. Kennedy. 1958. "Groundwater Resources of the Hueco Bolson, Northeast of El Paso, Texas." In *West Texas Geological Society Guidebook: Franklin and Hueco Mountains*, ed. L. A. Nelson and B. R. Haig, 55–66. Midland, TX: West Texas Geological Society.

Komulainen, Nancy, Elia Perez, Paul Lukowski, and Peter Condon. 2009. *The NRHP Eligibility Assessment of 40 Sites in the Foothills of the Sacramento Mountains, Fort Bliss Military Installation, Otero County, New Mexico.* Cultural Resources Report 08-40. Fort Bliss, Texas: Fort Bliss Directorate of Public Works, Environmental Division.

Kuhn, Thomas S. 1962. *The Structure of Scientific Revolutions.* Chicago, IL: University of Chicago Press.

Kuzmin, Yaroslav V. 2006. "Chronology of the Earliest Pottery in East Asia: Progress and Pitfalls." *Antiquity* 80(308):362–371. https://doi.org/10.1017/S0003598X0009 3686.

Kyte, Michael. 1988. "A Ceramic Sequence from the Chupadera Arroyo Basin, Central New Mexico." Master's thesis, Eastern New Mexico University, Portales, New Mexico.

Laumbach, Karl, Helen B. Shields, Robert L. Miller, and Delton Estes. 2002. *Data Recovery Report on Sites LA 86735, LA 86736, LA 86737 and LA 120,979 along US Highway 54 Between Tularosa and Carizozo, Otero County, New Mexico.* Human Systems Research Report No. 9946C. Santa Fe, NM: New Mexico State Highway and Transportation Division.

Leach, Jeff D., Frederico A. Almarez, Brenda Buck, and Galen R. Burgett. 1993. "The Hueco Mountains Reservoir: A Preliminary Assessment of an El Paso Phase Water Catchment Basin." *Artifact* 31(2):33–45.

Lea County Archaeological Society. 1971. *The Laguna Plata Site L.C.A.S. C-10-C LA-5148: A Preliminary Report.* Hobbs, NM: Lea County Archaeological Society.

LeBlanc, Stephen A. 1983. *The Mimbres People: Ancient Pueblo Painters of the American Southwest.* New York: Thames and Hudson.

LeBlanc, Stephen A. 1989. "Cultural Dynamics in the Southern Mogollon Area." In *Dynamics of Southwestern Prehistory*, ed. Linda S. Cordell and George J. Gumerman, 179–207. Washington, DC: Smithsonian Institution.

LeBlanc, Steven A., and Michael E. Whalen. 1980. *An Archaeological Synthesis of South-Central and Southwestern New Mexico.* Albuquerque: Office of Contract Archaeology, Department of Anthropology, University of New Mexico.

Leckman, Phillip O. 2010. "Spatial Patterning." In *Results of a 5,000-Acre Cultural Resource Survey in the Southern Maneuver Areas, Fort Bliss Military Reservation, El Paso County, Texas,* ed. A. C. MacWilliams, B. J. Vierra, and K. M. Schmidt, 263–296. Historic and Natural Resources Report 08–51. Fort Bliss, Texas: Fort Bliss Directorate of Public Works, Environmental Division–Conservation Branch.

Leckman, Phillip O., and Christina Chavez. 2013. "Ceramic Trails and Land Use on the Northern McGregor Alluvial Fans." In *Survey and Evaluation of 7.025 Acres on McGregor Range. Fort Bliss Military Reservation, Otero County, New Mexico,* ed. T. M. Mills, C. G. Ward, and B. J. Vierra, 10.1–10.34. Historic and Natural Resources Report No. 12–09. Fort Bliss, Texas: Fort Bliss Directorate of Public Works, Environmental Division.

Lehmer, Donald J. 1948. "The Jornada Branch of the Mogollon." *Social Science Bulletin* 17. *University of Arizona Bulletin* 19(2). Tucson: University of Arizona.

Lekson, Steven H. 1988. "Regional Systematics in the Later Prehistory of Southern New Mexico." In *Fourth Jornada Mogollon Conference (Oct. 1985) Collected Papers,* ed. Meliha S. Duran and Karl W. Laumbach, 1–37. Tularosa, NM: Human Systems Research.

Lekson, Steven H. 2008. *A History of the Ancient Southwest.* Santa Fe, NM: School for Advanced Research.

Lekson, Stephen H., Michael Bletzer, and A. C. MacWilliams. 2004. "Pueblo IV in the Chihuahuan Desert." In *The Protohistoric Pueblo World, A.D. 1275–1600,* ed. E. Charles Adams and Andrew I. Duff, 53–61. Tucson: University of Arizona Press.

Leney, L., and W. Casteel. 1975. "Simplified Procedure for Examining Charcoal Specimens for Identification." *Journal of Archaeological Science* 2(2):153–159. https://doi.org/10.1016/0305-4403(75)90035-7.

Lentz, Stephen C. 2006. *High Rolls Cave: Insectos, Burritos, y Frajos: Archaic Subsistence in Southern New Mexico.* Excavations at LA 114103, Otero County, New Mexico. Archaeology Notes 345. Santa Fe: Office of Archaeological Studies, Museum of New Mexico.

Lentz, Stephen C, Robert D. Dello-Russo, Pamela McBride, Doanld Tatum, Linda Scott Cummings, and Chad L. Yost. 2013. "Evidence for Early Domesticates at LA 159879: An Early Agricultural Site in the Mimbres Bolson Near Deming, Luna County, New Mexico." In *Collected Papers from the 17th Biennial Mogollon Archaeology Conference,* ed. Lonnie C. Ludeman, 19–30. Silver City, NM: Western New Mexico University.

Leonard, R. D. 1989. "Resource Specialization, Population Growth, and Agricultural Production in the American Southwest." *American Antiquity* 54(3):491–503. https://doi.org/10.2307/280777.

Leslie, Robert H. 1965a. "Ochoa Indented Brown Ware. Facts and Artifacts." *Newsletter of the Lea County Archaeological Society* 1(2):5–6.

Leslie, Robert H. 1965b. "The Merchant Site (LCAS E–4)." In *Transactions of the First Regional Archaeological Symposium for Southeastern New Mexico and Western Texas* 23–29.

Leslie, Robert H. 1968. "The Monument Springs Site, LCAS No. D16." *Transactions of the Fourth Regional Archaeological Symposium for Southeastern New Mexico and Western Texas*, 79–83. Iraan, TX: Iraan Archaeological Society.

Leslie, Robert H. 1978. "Projectile Point Types and Sequences of the Eastern Jornada-Mogollon Extreme Southeastern New Mexico." *Transactions of the 13th Regional Archeological Symposium for Southeastern New Mexico and Western Texas*, 81–157. Lamesa, TX: Dawson County Archeological Society.

Leslie, Robert H. 1979. "The Eastern Jornada Mogollon, Extreme Southeastern New Mexico (A Summary)." In *Jornada Mogollon Archaeology*, ed. Patrick H. Beckett and Regge N. Wiseman, 179–199. Las Cruces: Cultural Resource Management Division, New Mexico State University.

Levine, Daisy F. 1997. *Excavation of a Jornada Mogollon Pithouse along US 380, Socorro County, New Mexico.* Archaeology Notes 138. Santa Fe: Office of Archaeological Studies, Museum of New Mexico.

Lightfoot, K. G., and A. Martinez. 1995. "Frontiers and Boundaries in Archaeological Perspective." *Annual Review of Anthropology* 24(1):471–492. https://doi.org/10.1146/annurev.an.24.100195.002351.

Lindsay, Alexander J. 1987. "Anasazi Population Movements to Southeastern Arizona." *American Archaeology* 6:190–198.

Lintz, Christopher. 1984. "The Plains Villagers: Antelope Creek." In *Prehistory of Oklahoma*, ed. Robert E. Bell, 325–346. New York: Academic Press.

Lintz, Christopher. 1986. *Architecture and Community Variability within the Antelope Creek Phase of the Texas Panhandle.* Studies in Oklahoma's Past No. 14. Norman: Oklahoma Archaeological Survey.

Lintz, Christopher. 1991. "Texas Panhandle-Pueblo Interactions from the Thirteenth through the Sixteenth Century." In *Farmers, Hunters, and Colonists: Interaction between the Southwest and the Southern Plains*, ed. K. A. Spielmann, 89–106. Tucson: University of Arizona Press.

Loendorf, Lawrence L., Myles R. Miller, Leonard Kemp, Laurie White, Mark Willis, and Nancy Kenmotsu. 2013. "Rock Art at the Pintada Cave Complex, Red House

Canyon, Fusselman Canyon, and Three Rockshelters on Fort Bliss." Cultural Resources Report No. 11-06. Fort Bliss, TX: Fort Bliss Garrison Command, Environmental Division.

Loendorf, Lawrence L., and Laurie White. 2012. "Coaxing the Rain." In *Picture Cave and Other Rock Art Sites on Fort Bliss*, by Myles R. Miller, Lawrence L. Loendorf, and Leonard Kemp, 200–208. Cultural Resources Report No. 10–36. Fort Bliss, TX: Fort Bliss Garrison Command, Environmental Division.

Lone Mountain Archaeological Services. 2001. *Southwest Lea County 3-D Seismic Survey, Lea County, New Mexico, Tier 1.* Albuquerque, NM: Lone Mountain Archaeological Services.

Lord, Kenneth J., and William E. Reynolds. 1985. *Archaeological Investigations of Three Sites within the Wipp Core Area, Eddy County, New Mexico.* Albuquerque, NM: Chambers Consultants and Planners.

Lukowski, P., E. Perez, J. Vasquez, B. Bury, D. Oseman, R. Ricklis, N. Komulainen-Dillenburg, D. Camarena, S. Simpson, J. Clark, et al. 2001. *Survey of 4,006 Acres and National Register of Historic Places Eligibility Assessment of Archaeological Sites, Maneuver Area 2E, Fort Bliss, El Paso County, Texas, Volume I.* Historic and Natural Resources Report No. 09–29. Fort Bliss, TX: Directorate of Public Works, Environmental Division, Fort Bliss Garrison Command.

Lumholtz, Carl. 1902. *Unknown Mexico: A Record of Five Years' Exploration among the Tribes of the Western Sierra Madre, in the Tierra Caliente of Tepic and Jalisco, and among the Tarascos of Michoacan.* 2 vols. New York: Charles Scribner's Sons.

Lumholtz, Carl. 1912. *New Trails in Mexico.* New York: Charles Scribener's Sons.

Lutes, Eugene. 1959. "A Marginal Prehistoric Culture of Northeastern New Mexico." *El Palacio* 66(2):59–68.

Lyons, Patrick D. 2003. *Ancestral Hopi Migrations.* Anthropological Papers of the University of Arizona, No. 68. Tucson: The University of Arizona Press.

Lyons, Patrick D., and Jeffrey D. Clark. 2008. "Interaction, Enculturation, Social Distance, and Ancient Ethnic Identities." In *Archeology without Borders: Contact, Commerce, and Change in the U.S. Southwest and Northwestern New Mexico*, ed. M. E. McBrinn and Laurie D. Webster, 185–207. Boulder: University Press of Colorado.

Mabry, Jonathan B. 2005. "Changing Knowledge and Ideas about the First Farmers in Southeastern Arizona." In *The Late Archaic scross the Borderland: From Foraging to Farming*, ed. Bradley J. Vierra, 41–83. Austin: University of Texas Press.

Mabry, Jonathan B., and William E. Doolittle. 2008. "Modeling the Early Agricultural Frontier in the Desert Borderlands." In *Archaeology without Borders: Contact, Commerce, and Change in the U.S. Southwest and Northwestern Mexico*, ed. Maxine E. McBrinn and Laurie D. Webster, 55–70. Boulder: University Press of Colorado.

Mabry, Jonathan B., and Douglas L. Schwartz, H. Wocherl, J. J. Clark, G. H. Archer and M. W. Linderman. 1997. *Archaeological Investigations of Early Village Sites in the Middle Santa Cruz Valley: Descriptions of the Santa Cruz Bend, Square Hearth, Stone Pipe, and Canal Sites.* Anthropological Papers 18. Tucson, AZ: Center for Desert Archaeology.

MacNeish, Richard S., ed. 1993. *Preliminary Investigations of the Archaic in the Region of Las Cruces, New Mexico.* Historic and Natural Resources Report No. 9. Fort Bliss, TX: Cultural Resource Management Program, Directorate of the Environment, Army Air Defense Artillery Center. https://doi.org/10.21236 /ADA277994.

MacWilliams, Art C., Bradley J. Vierra, and Kari M. Schmidt. 2009. *Archaeological Mitigations at FB 17 (LA 91017) and FB 9122 (LA 30116) on the Doña Ana Range, Doña Ana County, New Mexico.* Historic and Natural Resources Report No. 07–49. Fort Bliss, TX: Fort Bliss Garrison Command, Directorate of Public Works, Environmental Division, Conservation Branch.

MacWilliams, Art C., Bradley J. Vierra, and Kari M. Schmidt. 2010. *Results of a 5,000-Acre Cultural Resource Survey in the Southern Maneuver Areas, Fort Bliss Military Reservation, El Paso County, Texas.* Historic and Natural Resources Report 08-51. Fort Bliss, TX: Fort Bliss Garrison Command, Directorate of Public Works, Environmental Division, Conservation Branch.

Madrid, Enrique. 1993. *Expedition to La Junta de los Rios, 1747–1748: Captain Commander Joseph de Ydoiaga's Report to the Viceroy of New Spain. Office of the State Archeologist Special Report 33.* Austin: Texas Historical Commission.

Maker, H. J., M. T. Turney, W. B. Gallman, and J. U. Anderson. 1971. *Soil Associations and Land Classification for Irrigation, Lincoln County.* Agricultural Experiment Station Research Report 212. Las Cruces: New Mexico State University.

Malainey, Mary E. 1997. "The Reconstruction and Testing of Subsistence and Settlement Strategies for the Plains, Parkland and Southern Boreal forest." PhD thesis, University of Manitoba, Winnipeg, MB, Canada.

Malainey, Mary E. 2007. "Fatty Acid Analysis of Archaeological Residues: Procedures and Possibilities." In *Theory and Practice of Archaeological Residue Analysis*, ed. H. Barnard and J. W. Eerkens, 77–89. BAR International Series 1650. Oxford, UK: British Archaeological Reports.

Malainey, Mary E. 2011. "Appendix F: Lipid Analysis of Fire-Cracked Rock and Pottery." In *Data Recovery at 14 Sites for the Intrepid–BLM Land Exchange, Eddy County, New Mexico*, ed. Douglas H. M. Boggess. LMAS Report No. 1077. Albuquerque, NM: Lone Mountain Archaeological Services.

Malainey, M. E., K. L. Malisza, R. Przybylski, and G. Monks. 2001. "The Key to Identifying Archaeological Fatty Acid Residues." Paper presented at the 34th Annual Meeting of the Canadian Archaeological Association, Banff, AB, Canada.

Malainey, M. E., R. Przybylski, and G. Monks. 2000a. "The Identification of Archaeological Residues Using Gas Chromatography and Applications to Archaeological Problems in Canada, United States and Africa." Paper presented at the 11th Annual Workshops in Archaeometry, State University of New York at Buffalo.

Malainey, M. E., R. Przybylski, and G. Monks. 2000b. "Refining and Testing the Criteria for Identifying Archaeological Lipid Residues Using Gas Chromatography." Paper presented at the 33rd Annual Meeting of the Canadian Archaeological Association, Ottawa, ON, Canada.

Malainey, M. E., R. Przybylski, and G. Monks. 2000c. "Developing a General Method for Identifying Archaeological Lipid Residues on the Basis of Fatty Acid Composition." Paper presented at the Joint Midwest Archaeological and Plains Anthropological Conference, Minneapolis, MN.

Malainey, M. E., K. L. Malisza, R. Przybylski, and G. Monks. 2000d. "Developing a General Method for Identifying Archaeological Lipid Residues on the Basis of Fatty Acid Composition." Paper presented at the Joint Midwest Archaeological and Plains Anthropological Conference, Minneapolis, Minnesota.

Malainey, M. E., R. Przybylski, and B. L. Sherriff. 1999a. "The Fatty Acid Composition of Native Food Plants and Animals of Western Canada." *Journal of Archaeological Science* 26(1):83–94. https://doi.org/10.1006/jasc.1998.0305.

Malainey, M. E., R. Przybylski, and B. L. Sherriff. 1999b. "The Effects of Thermal and Oxidative Degradation on the Fatty Acid Composition of Food Plants and Animals of Western Canada: Implications for the Identification of Archaeological Vessel Residues." *Journal of Archaeological Science* 26(1):95–103. https://doi.org/10.1006/jasc.1998.0306.

Mallouf, Robert. 1985. "A Synthesis of Eastern Trans-Pecos Prehistory." Master's thesis, University of Texas at Austin.

Mallouf, Robert. 1990. "A Commentary on the Prehistory of Far Northeastern Chihuahua, the La Junta District, and the Cielo Complex." In *Historia General de Chihuahua I: Geologia y Arqueologia*, ed. Arturo Marquez-Alameda, 137–162. Juárez.: Universidad Autónoma de Ciudad Juárez y Gobierno del Estado de Chihuahua, Mexico.

Mallouf, Robert. 1995. "Arroyo de las Burras: Preliminary Findings from the 1992 SRSU Archeological Field School." *Journal of Big Bend Studies* 7:3–39.

Mallouf, Robert. 1999. "Comments on the Prehistory of Far Northeastern Chihuahua, the La Junta District, and the Cielo Complex." *Journal of Big Bend Studies* 11:49–92.

Mallouf, Robert. 2005. "Late Archaic Foragers of Eastern Trans-Pecos Texas and the Big Bend." In *The Late Archaic across the Borderlands*, ed. Bradley J. Vierra, 219–246. Austin: University of Texas Press.

Mannessier, J. 1950. "Silos Metalliques Etanches pour le Stockage des Graines." *Information Documentation Agriculture* 14:n.p.

Marshall, Michael P. 1997. "The Chacoan Roads: A Cosmological Interpretation." In *Anasazi Architecture and American Design*, ed. B. H. Morrow and V. B. Price, 62–74. Albuquerque: University of New Mexico Press.

Martin, A. C., and W. D. Barkley. 1961. *Seed Identification Manual.* Berkeley: University of California Press.

Martin, Paul S., John Beach Rinaldo, and Elaine Ann Bluhm. 1954. "Caves of the Reserve Area." *Fieldiana: Anthropology* 42. Chicago, IL: Chicago Natural History Museum.

Martin, Paul S., John B. Rinaldo, A. Bluhm Elaine, Hugh C. Cutler, and Roger Grange, Jr. 1952. "Mogollon Cultural Continuity and Change: The Stratigraphic Analysis of Tularosa and Cordova Caves." *Fieldiana: Anthropology* 42. Chicago, IL: Chicago Natural History Museum.

Martinek, Dain. 1998. "Oneota Food Storage Technology." La Crosse: University of Wisconsin-La Crosse. *Journal of Undergraduate Studies* 1:89–102.

Mason, J. A., J. B. Swinehart, R. J. Goble, and D. B. Loope. 2004. "Late-Holocene Dune Activity Linked to Hydrological Drought, Nebraska Sand Hill, USA." *Holocene* 14(2):209–217. https://doi.org/10.1191/0959683604hl677rp.

Mathiowetz, Michael Dean. 2011. "The Diurnal Path of the Sun: Ideology and Interregional Interaction in Ancient Northwest Mesoamerica and the American Southwest." PhD dissertation, University of California, Riverside.

Matson, R. G., and M.P.R. Magne. 2007. *Athapaskan Migrations, Archaeology of Eagle Lake, British Columbia.* Tucson: University of Arizona Press.

Mauldin, Raymond P. 1995. "Groping for the Past: Archaeological Patterns across Space and Time in the Southern Southwestern United States." PhD dissertation, University of New Mexico, Albuquerque.

Mauldin, Raymond P., Tim B. Graves, and Mark T. Bentley. 1998. *Small Sites in the Central Hueco Bolson: A Final Report on Project 90–11.* Historic and Natural Resources Report No. 90–11. Fort Bliss, TX: Fort Bliss Garrison Command, Directorate of Environment, Conservation Division.

Mauldin, Raymond P., and Myles R. Miller. 2009. "Previous Research and Cultural Context." In *Significance and Research Standards for Prehistoric Archaeological Sites at Fort Bliss: A Design for the Evaluation, Management, and Treatment of Cultural Resources*, ed. M. R. Miller, N. A. Kenmotsu, and M. Landreth, 3–1 to 3–21. Fort

Bliss, TX: Environmental Division, Historic and Natural Resources Report 05–16, Garrison Command.

Maxwell, Timothy D. 1986. *Archaeological Test Excavations at the Townsend Site (LA 34150), Chaves County, New Mexico. Laboratory of Anthropology Note 344*. Santa Fe, NM: Office of Archaeological Studies.

Maxwell, Timothy D., and Rafael Cruz Antillón. 2008. "Production and Exchange of Turquoise in the Casas Grandes Region: A View from the East." Paper presented at the 73rd Society for American Archaeology Meeting. Vancouver, BC, Canada.

McBride, Pamela J. 2011. "Appendix C: Flotation Results." In *Data Recovery at 14 Sites for the Intrepid–BLM Land Exchange, Eddy County, New Mexico*, by Douglas H. M. Boggess. LMAS Report No. 1077. Albuquerque, NM: Lone Mountain Archaeological Services.

McCarthy, Elizabeth M., Christine VanPool, Gordon Rakita, and Todd VanPool. 2013. "Birds, Bunnies, and Bison: Variation in Faunal Utilization in the Casas Grandes World." In *Collected Papers from the 17th Biennial Mogollon Conference*, ed. Lonnie C. Ludeman, 63–68. Silver City, NM: Friends of Mogollon Archaeology.

McGregor, John C. 1941. *Southwestern Archaeology*. New York: John Wiley & Sons.

McGregor, John C. 1965. *Southwestern Archaeology*. 2nd ed. Urbana: University of Illinois Press.

McGuire, Randall H., and Michael B. Schiffer. 1983. "A Theory of Architectural Design." *Journal of Anthropological Archaeology* 2(3):277–303. https://doi.org/10.1016/0278-4165(83)90002-8.

McNally, Elizabeth. 2002. "Variation in Flaked Stone Tool Assemblages." In *Archaeological Variation within the Middle Rio Bonito*, ed. Phillip H. Shelley and Kristen E. Wenzel, 143–196. Cultural Resources Series No. 14. Santa Fe: New Mexico Bureau of Land Management.

Mehringer, Peter. 1967. "Pollen Analysis of the Tule Springs Area, Nevada." In *Pleistocene Studies in Southern Nevada*, ed. H. M. Wormington and D. Ellis, 130–200. Anthropological Papers No. 13. Carson City: Nevada State Museum.

Mehringer, Peter J., Jr., Paul S. Martin, and C. Vance Haynes. 1966. "Murray Springs, A Mid-Postglacial Pollen Profile from Southern Arizona." University of Arizona Geochronology Laboratories Interim Research Report 13. Tucson: University of Arizona.

Meltzer, David J. 1991. "Altithermal Archaeology and Paleoecology at Mustang Springs on the Southern High Plains of Texas." *American Antiquity* 56(02):236–267. https://doi.org/10.2307/281417.

Meltzer, David J., and Michael B. Collins. 1987. "Prehistoric Water Wells on the Southern High Plains: Clues to Altithermal Climate." *Journal of Field Archaeology* 14(1):9–28.

Mendiola Galván, Francisco. 1998. "A Recent Reconnaissance of Rock Art Sites in Chihuahua and Southern New Mexico." In *Rock Art of the Chihuahuan Desert Borderlands*, ed. Sheron Smith-Savage and Robert J. Mallouf, 9–22. Center for Big Bend Studies Occasional Papers, No. 3. Alpine, TX: Sul Ross State University.

Mendiola Galván, Francisco. 2006. *Espejo de Piedra: Memoria de Luz (El Arte Rupestre en Chihuahua)*. Chihuahua City, México: Grupo Cementos de Chihuahua.

Mera, Harry Percival. 1938. *Reconnaissance and Excavation in Southeastern New Mexico*. Memoirs of the American Anthropological Association No. 51. Washington, DC: American Anthropological Association.

Mera, H. P., and W. S. Stallings, Jr. 1931. *Lincoln Black-on-Red*. Bulletin No. 2. Laboratory of Anthropology Technical Series. Santa Fe, NM: Laboratory of Anthropology.

Merrill, William L. 1978. "Thinking and Drinking: A Raramuri Interpretation." In *The Nature and Status of Ethnobotany*, ed. R. I. Ford, 101–117. Ann Arbor: Museum of Anthropology, University of Michigan.

Miller, Myles R. 1989. *Archeological Excavations at the Gobernadora and Ojasen Sites: Doña Ana Phase Settlement in the Western Hueco Bolson, El Paso County, Texas*. Center for Archaeological Research Report 673. Las Cruces: New Mexico State University.

Miller, Myles R. 1990. *The Transitional Period in the Southern Jornada Mogollon: Archaeological Investigations in the North Hills Subdivision, Northeast El Paso, Texas*. Batcho & Kauffman Associates Research Report No. 1. Las Cruces, NM: Batcho & Kauffman Associates.

Miller, Myles R. 1991. "Transitional Period Ceramic Developments in the Southern Jornada Mogollon A.D.1100–1200." Paper presented at the Seventh Jornada Mogollon Conference, The Wilderness Park Museum, El Paso, TX.

Miller, Myles R. 1995. "Ceramics of the Jornada Mogollon and Trans-Pecos Regions of West Texas." *Bulletin of the Texas Archaeological Society* 66:210–219.

Miller, Myles R. 1996. *The Chronometric and Relative Chronology Project*. Archaeological Technical Report No. 5. El Paso: Anthropological Research Center and Department of Sociology and Anthropology, University of Texas at El Paso.

Miller, Myles R. 2002. "Long Term Adaptive and Demographic Patterns in the Jornada Mogollon Region and Implications for a Broader Understanding of Southwestern Prehistory." Paper presented at the 67th Annual Meeting of the Society for American Archaeology, Denver, Colorado.

Miller, Myles R. 2005a. "Revision of the Jornada Mogollon Ceramic Period Sequence and Alignment with the Greater Southwest." In *Archaeology between the Borders: Papers from the 13th Biennial Jornada Mogollon Conference*, ed.

M. Thompson, J. Jurgena, and L. Jackson, 59–88. El Paso, TX: El Paso Museum of Archaeology.

Miller, Myles R. 2005b. "The Eastern Limits of Southwestern Agriculture: Patterns and Processes Underlying Prehistoric Agricultural Developments in the Jornada Mogollon Region of West Texas and Southern New Mexico." Paper presented at the 46th Annual Meeting of the Society for Economic Botany, Fort Worth, TX.

Miller, Myles R. 2005c. "Peripheral Basins and Ephemeral Polities: INAA of Mimbres Black-on-White Ceramics and Insights into Mimbres and Jornada Mogollon Social Relationships." Paper presented at the 70th Annual Meeting of the Society for American Archaeology, Salt Lake City, UT.

Miller, Myles R. 2007a. "Spatial Point Pattern Analysis of a Transect Recording Unit Dataset from McGregor Range." In *A Cultural Resource Survey of 10,500 Acres, Fort Bliss Military Reservation, Otero County, New Mexico,* by M. Stowe, A. Martinez, and M. R. Miller, 6.1–6.20. Historic and Natural Resources Report No. 05–13. Fort Bliss, TX: Fort Bliss Garrison Command, Directorate of Environment.

Miller, Myles R. 2007b. "Spatial Analysis of TRU-Recorded Ceramic Landscape Distributions in the CACTF Survey Area." In *A Cultural Resource Survey of 11,500 Acres to the Combined Arms Combat Test Facility Part I, Fort Bliss Military Reservation, Otero County, New Mexico,* by M. Stowe, K. Arford, C. Mears, M. Swanson, M. Goetz, and M. Miller. Historic and Natural Resources Report No. 05–35, Fort Bliss, TX: Fort Bliss Garrison Command, Directorate of Environment.

Miller, Myles R. 2009. "Expressions of Jornada Rock Art Iconography across Multiple Media." Paper presented at the 80th Annual Meetings of the Texas Archaeological Society, Del Rio, TX.

Miller, Myles R. 2018a. "Archaic Transitions and Transformations in the Jornada Mogollon Region." In *The Southwest Archaic,* ed. Bradley J. Vierra, 119–144. Salt Lake City: University of Utah Press.

Miller, Myles R. 2018b. "A Millennium of Identity Formation and Maintenance in the Jornada Mogollon Region." In *Social Identity in Frontier and Borderland Communities of the North American Southwest,* ed. Karen G. Harry and Sarah Herr, 239–272. Boulder: University Press of Colorado.

Miller, M. R., and C. Burt. 2007. *Miscellaneous Investigations at the Conejo Site (LA 91044/FB 46) Fort Bliss, Doña Ana County, New Mexico.* Historic and Natural Resources Report 03–17. Fort Bliss, TX: Fort Bliss Garrison Command, Directorate of Environment.

Miller, Myles R., and Tim Church. 2008. "Theoretical Perspectives." In *Significance and Research Standards for Prehistoric Sites at Fort Bliss: A Design for the Evaluation, Management, and Treatment of Cultural Resources,* ed. Miller, Myles R., Nancy A.

Kenmotsu, and Melinda R. Landreth, 4.1–4.15. Historic and Natural Resources Report No. 05–16. Fort Bliss, TX: Fort Bliss Garrison Command, Directorate of Public Works, Environmental Division.

Miller, Myles R., and Jeffrey R. Ferguson. 2010. "An Update on NAA Analysis of Brown Wares, Textured Wares, and Red Wares from Southern New Mexico and Western Texas." Paper presented at the 16th Biennial Mogollon Conference, New Mexico State University, Las Cruces, NM.

Miller, Myles R., and Jeffrey R. Ferguson. 2014. "NAA Classification and Provenance of Brown Ware, Textured Ware, and Red Ware from Southern New Mexico and Western Texas." Manuscript on file. Austin: Missouri University Research Reactor and VersarGMI.

Miller, Myles R., and Tim B. Graves. 2009. *Madera Quemada Pueblo: Archaeological Investigations at a Fourteenth Century Jornada Mogollon Pueblo*. Historic and Natural Resources Report No. 03–12. Fort Bliss, TX: Fort Bliss Garrison Command, Directorate of Public Works, Environmental Division.

Miller, Myles R., and Tim B. Graves. 2012. *Sacramento Pueblo: An El Paso and Late Glencoe Phase Pueblo in the Southern Sacramento Mountains*. Cultural Resources Report No. 10–22. Fort Bliss, TX: Fort Bliss Garrison Command, Directorate of Public Works, Environmental Division.

Miller, Myles R., and Tim B. Graves. 2015a. *Archaeological Testing and Characterization of LA 91406 (FB 415), Training Area 4B, Fort Bliss Military Reservation*. Cultural Resources Report No. 14–14B. Fort Bliss, TX: Fort Bliss Garrison Command, Directorate of Public Works, Environmental Division.

Miller, Myles R., and Tim B. Graves. 2015b. "Reviewing the Jornada Archaic Sequence." Paper presented at the 17th Biennial Jornada Mogollon Conference, El Paso Museum of Archaeology, El Paso, TX.

Miller, Myles R., Tim B. Graves, Moira Ernst, and Michael Stowe. 2011. *Burned Rock Middens of the Southern Sacramento Mountains*. Historic and Natural Resources Report No. 09-28. El Paso, TX: Geo-Marine; Fort Bliss, TX: Fort Bliss Garrison Command, Directorate of Public Works, Environmental Division. GMI Report No. 782EP.

Miller, Myles R., Tim B. Graves, Charles Frederick, and Melinda Landreth. 2012. *Investigations at Four Burned Rock Midden Sites along Wildcat Canyon in the Southern Sacramento Mountains*. Cultural Resources Report No. 11-13. Fort Bliss, TX: Fort Bliss Garrison Command, Directorate of Public Works, Environmental Division. GMI Report No. 803EP. El Paso, TX: Geo-Marine.

Miller, Myles R., Tim B. Graves, and Melinda Landreth. 2012. *Further Investigations of Burned Rock Middens and Associated Settlements: Mitigation of Three Sites* for the IBCT, Fort Bliss, Otero County, New Mexico. Cultural Resources Report No. 10–21. Fort Bliss, TX: Fort Bliss Garrison Command, Directorate of Public Works, Environmental Division.

Miller, Myles R., Tim B. Graves, Melinda Landreth, Charles Frederick, Brittney Gregory, and Tabitha Burgess, J. Phil Dering, Susan J. Smith, Moira Ernst, Michael Stowe, Juan Arias, Mark Sale, Matt Swanson, Leonard Kemp, and Lillian Ponce. 2013. *Investigations of Burned Rock Middens along the Sacramento Mountains Alluvial Fans: Excavation of 18 BRMs at Nine Sites and a Summary of 77 BRM Excavations in the Sacramento Mountains of Fort Bliss, Otero County, New Mexico*. Historic and Natural Resources Report No. 12–05. Fort Bliss, TX: Fort Bliss Garrison Command, Directorate of Public Works, Environmental Division.

Miller, Myles R, Tim B. Graves, and Robert H. Leslie. 2016. *The Merchant Site: A Late Prehistoric Ochoa Phase Settlement in Southeastern New Mexico*. Prepared for the Bureau of Land Management, Carlsbad Field Office. Versar Cultural Resources Report No. 836EP. El Paso: Versar.

Miller, Myles R., Tim B. Graves, and Mark Willis. 2010. "A History of Excavations of El Paso Phase Pueblos by the El Paso Archaeological Society and Other Institutions." *Artifact* 48:1–54.

Miller, Myles R., and Nancy A. Kenmotsu. 2004. "Prehistory of the Jornada Mogollon and Eastern Trans-Pecos Regions of West Texas." In *The Prehistory of Texas*, ed. Timothy K. Perttula, 205–265. College Station: Texas A&M University Press.

Miller, M. R., N. A. Kenmotsu, and M. R. Landreth, eds. 2009. *Significance and Research Standards for Prehistoric Archaeological Sites at Fort Bliss: A Design for the Evaluation, Management, and Treatment of Cultural Resources*. Environmental Division, Historic and Natural Resources Report 05–16. Fort Bliss, TX: Garrison Command.

Miller, Myles R., Lawrence L. Loendorf, and Leonard Kemp. 2012. *Picture Cave and Other Rock Art Sites on Fort Bliss*. Fort Bliss Cultural Resources Report No. 10–36. Fort Bliss, TX: Fort Bliss Garrison Command, Directorate of Public Works, Environmental Division.

Miller, Myles R., and Christopher Lowry. 2006. *Investigations of Burned Rock Features at 41EP2863 in Northeast El Paso, El Paso County, Texas*. Report No. 725EP. El Paso, TX: Texas Veterans Land Board, Austin, and Geo-Marine.

Miller, M. R., and M. S. Shackley. 1997. "New Interpretations of Obsidian Procurement and Movement in West Texas, Southern New Mexico, and Northern Chihuahua." Paper presented at the 69th Meeting of the Texas Archeological Society, Waco, TX.

Mills, Barbara J., Jeffery J. Clark, Matthew A. Peeples, William R. Haas, Jr., John M. Roberts, Jr., Brett Hill, Deborah L. Huntley, Lewis Borck, Ronald L. Breiger, Aaron Clauset, et al. 2013. "The Transformation of Social Networks in the Late Prehispanic U.S. Southwest." *Proceedings of the National Academy of Sciences of the United States of America* 110(15):5785–5790. https://doi.org/10.1073/pnas.1219966110.

Mills, Barbara J., Matthew A. Peeples, W. Randall Haas Jr., Jeffery J. Borck, Lewis Clark, and John M. Roberts Jr. 2015. "Multiscalar Perspectives on Social Networks in the Late Prehispanic Southwest." *American Antiquity* 80(1):3–24. https://doi.org /10.7183/0002-7316.79.4.3.

Minnis, Paul. 1991. "Famine Foods of the Northern American Desert Borderland in Historical Context." *Journal of Ethnobiology* 11(2):213–257.

Moerman, Daniel E. 1999. *Native American Ethnobotany.* Portland, OR: Timberline Press.

Montgomery, F. H. 1977. *Seeds and Fruits of Plants of Eastern Canada and Northeastern United States.* Toronto, ON: University of Toronto Press.

Moore, Mrs. Glen E. 1947. "Twelve Room House Ruin." *Bulletin of the Texas Paleontological and Archaeological Society* 18:94–114.

Moore, Samuel L., Tommy B. Thompson, and Eugene E. Foord. 1991. "Structure and Igneous Rocks of the Ruidoso Region, New Mexico." In *Geology of the Sierra Blanca, Sacramento and Capitan Ranges, New Mexico,* ed. J. M. Baker, B. S. Kues, G. S. Austin, and S. G. Lucas, 137–145. Socorro: New Mexico Geological Society.

Morrow, James G. 1936. "A Prehistoric Cremated Burial of the Abilene Region." *Bulletin of the Texas Archeological and Paleontological Society* 8:17–24.

Moulard, Barbara L. 2005. "Archaism and Emulation in Casas Grandes Painted Pottery." In *Casas Grandes and the Ceramic Art of the Ancient Southwest,* ed. Richard F. Townsend, 67–97. Chicago, IL: Art Institute of Chicago; New Haven and London: Yale University Press.

Musil, A. F. 1963. *Identification of Crop and Weed Seeds.* Agricultural Handbook No. 219. Washington, DC: US Department of Agriculture.

Natker, Leon. 2016. "Chupadero Black-on-white: Communities of Practice and Expression at the Hiner Ruin." *Pottery Southwest* 32(4):8–26.

Neff, Hector, and Donna M. Glowacki. 2002. "Ceramic Source Determination by Instrumental Neutron Activation Analysis in the American Southwest." In *Ceramic Production and Circulation in the Greater Southwest: Source Determination by INAA and Complementary Mineralogical Investigations,* ed. Donna Glowacki and Hector Neff, 1–14. Monograph 44. Los Angeles: The Costen Institute of Archaeology University of California.

Nelson, Margaret. 1984. "Food Selection at Galaz: Inferences from Chipped Stone Analysis." In *The Galaz Ruin A Prehistoric Mimbres Village in Southwestern New Mexico,* by R. Anyon and S. A. LeBlanc, 225–246. Albuquerque: Maxwell Museum of Anthropology, University of New Mexico Press.

Neuzil, Anna A. 2005. "In the Aftermath of Migration: Assessing the Social Consequences of Late 13th and 14th Century Population Movements into Southeastern Arizona." PhD dissertation, University of Arizona, Tucson.

Newlander, Khori, and John D. Speth. 2009. "Interaction Patterns in the Southern Plains as Seen Through Ultraviolet Fluorescence (UVF): Study of Cherts from Late Prehistoric Villages in the Pecos Valley, New Mexico." In *Quince: Papers from the 15th Biennial Jornada Mogollon Conference,* ed. Marc Thompson, 43–60. El Paso, TX: El Paso Museum of Archaeology.

Noguera, Eduardo. 1930. "Ruinas Arqueológicas del Norte de México." *Dirección de Monumentos Prehispánicos,* Publicaciones de la Secretaria de Educación Publica, 5–27. México, DF.

Nuñez Alvar, Cabeza de Vaca. 1992. *Los Naufragios.* Ed. Enrique Pupo-Walker. Madrid, Spain: Nueva Biblioteca de Erudición y Critica.

O'Laughlin, Thomas C. 1977. "Excavations of Two Caves in the Mountain Zone of Fort Bliss Maneuver Area II." In *Settlement Patterns of the Eastern Hueco Bolson,* by M. E. Whalen, 169–189. El Paso Centennial Museum Publications in Anthropology No. 4. El Paso: University of Texas at El Paso.

O'Laughlin, Thomas C. 1980. *The Keystone Dam Site and Other Archaic and Formative Sites in Northwest El Paso, Texas.* El Paso Centennial Museum Publications in Anthropology No. 8. El Paso: University of Texas at El Paso.

O'Laughlin, Thomas C. 1981. "The Roth Site." *Artifact* 19(3/4):133–149.

O'Laughlin, Thomas C. 1985. "Intrasite and Intersite Variability in Architecture: The Pueblo Model." *Artifact* 23(3):19–39.

O'Laughlin, Thomas C. 1999. *Beyond Borders: The Well Site.* Papers of the Archaeological Society of New Mexico 25:143–160. Albuquerque: Archaeological Society of New Mexico.

O'Laughlin, Thomas C. 2001a. "Long Lessons and Big Surprises: Firecracker Pueblo." In *Following Through: Papers in Honor of Phyllis S. Davis,* ed. R. N. Wiseman, T. C. O'Laughlin, and C. T. Snow, 115–131. Papers of the Albuquerque Archaeological Society No. 28. Albuquerque: Archaeological Society of New Mexico.

O'Laughlin, Thomas C. 2001b. "Casa Blanca." *Artifact* 39:1–39.

O'Laughlin, Thomas C. 2002. "Macrobotanical Remains." In *Across the Desert Floor: Cultural Resource Investigations along US 54, Otero County,* ed. Jim A. Railey, 677–685. Santa Fe, NM: New Mexico State Highway and Transportation.

O'Laughlin, Thomas C. 2005. "Hot Well and Sgt. Doyle Pueblos Faunal Remains." In *Archaeological Investigations of the Hot Well and Sgt. Doyle Sites, Fort Bliss, Texas: Late Formative Period Adaptations in the Hueco Bolson,* by C. Lowry, 236–280. Historic and Natural Resources Report No. 94–18. Fort Bliss, TX: Directorate of Environment, Conservation Division, US Army Air Defense Artillery Center and Fort Bliss.

Oldfield, F., and James Schoenwetter. 1975. "Pollen-Analytical Results, Part II." In *Late Pleistocene Environments of the Southern High Plains,* ed. Fred Wendorf and James J. Hester, 149–177. Dallas, TX: Fort Burgwin Research Center, Southern Methodist University.

Orr, B. R., and R. G. Myers. 1986. *Water in Basin-Fill Deposits in the Tularosa Basin, New Mexico.* vol. 85–4219. US Geological Survey Water-Resources Investigations Report Albuquerque: US Geological Survey.

Osborne, Carolyn M. 1965. "The Preparation of Yucca Fibers: An Experimental Study." In *Contributions of the Wetherill Mesa Archeological Project,* ed. D. Osborne, 45–50. Memoir No. 19. Salt Lake City, UT: Society for American Archaeology.

Pailes, Matthew C. 2014. "Social Network Analysis of Early Classic Hohokam Corporate Group Inequality." *American Antiquity* 79(03):465–486. https://doi.org /10.7183/0002-7316.79.3.465.

Pangburn, Jeffrey. 2012. "A Final Report of Investigations on LA 54834." Manuscript on file, Bureau of Land Management, Carlsbad Resource Area Office, Carlsbad.

Parry, William J., and Robert L. Kelly. 1987. "Expedient Core Technology and Sedentism." In *The Organization of Core Technology,* ed. Jay K. Johnson and Carol A. Morrow, 285–304. Boulder, CO: Westview Press.

Parsons, Jeffrey R., and Mary H. Parsons. 1990. *Maguey Utilization in Highland Central Mexico: An Archaeological Ethnography.* Anthropological Papers No. 82. Ann Arbor: Museum of Anthropology, University of Michigan.

Peckham, Stewart. 1976. "Taylor Draw: A Mogollon-Anasazi Hybrid?" In *Collected Papers in Honor of Marjorie Ferguson Lambert,* ed. Albert H. Schroeder. Papers of the Archaeological Society of New Mexico 3:37–68. Albuquerque: Archaeological Society of New Mexico.

Pennington, Campbell W. 1963. *The Tarahumar of Chihuahua: Their Environment and Material Culture.* Salt Lake City: University of Utah Press.

Peregrine, Peter N., and Melvin Ember. 2001. *Human Relations Area Files.* vol. 4. Encyclopedia of Prehistory. New York: Kluwer Academic/Plenum Publishers.

Petersen, Kenneth Lee. 1981. "10,000 Years of Climate Change Reconstructed from Fossil Pollen, La Plata Mountains, Southwestern Colorado." PhD dissertation, Washington State University, Pullman.

Peterson, John A., ed. 2001. *Archaeological Investigations of the Meyer Pithouse Village, Fort Bliss, Texas*. Fort Bliss, TX: Fort Bliss Garrison Command, Directorate of Public Works, Environmental Division.

Phelps, Alan L. 1998. "An Inventory of Prehistoric Native American Sites in Northwestern Chihuahua." *The Artifact* 36(2).

Phillips, David A., Jr. 2012. "The Northwest Mexican Polychrome Traditions." In *Potters and Communities of Practice: Glaze Paint and Polychrome Pottery in the American Southwest, A.D. 1250 to 1700*, ed. Linda S. Cordell and Judith A. Habicht-Mauche, 34–44. Anthropological Papers of the University of Arizona Number 75. Tucson: University of Arizona Press.

Phillips, David A., Jr., and Eduardo Gamboa. 2015. "The End of Paquimé and the Casas Grandes Culture." In *Ancient Paquimé and the Casas Grandes World*, ed. Paul E. Minnis and Michael E. Whalen, 148–171. Tucson: University of Arizona Press. https://doi.org/10.2307/j.ctt183p9cj.11.

Phillips, Shaun M., and Phillip O. Leckman. 2012. "Wandering the Desert: Least Cost Path Modeling for Water Transport Trails in the Jornada Mogollon Region, Fort Bliss, South-Central New Mexico." In *Least Cost Path Analysis of Social Landscapes*, ed. D. A. White and S. L. Surface-Evans, 46–66. Salt Lake City: University of Utah Press.

Phillips, Shaun M., Phillip O. Leckman, and David T. Unruh. 2011. "Ceramic Trails and Land Use." In *Results of a 4,500-Acre Survey and Evaluation in Maneuver Area 2C, Fort Bliss Military Reservation, El Paso County, Texas*, ed. A. C. MacWilliams and B. J. Vierra, 597–626. Historic and Natural Resources Report 10–31. Fort Bliss, TX: Fort Bliss Garrison Command, Directorate of Public Works, Environmental Division.

Phippen, G. R., A. B. Silverberg, C. J. Zier, K. B. Menke, C. L. Wase, G. D. Smith, M. McFaul, G. W. Crawford, T. J. Kludt, D. V. Hill, et al. 2000. *Excavation of Thirteen Archaeological Sites along the D.S.E. El Paso Pipeline, Otero and Chavez Counties, Southeastern New Mexico*. Fort Collins, CO: Centennial Archaeology.

Piehl, Jennifer C. 2009. *Human Osteology and Mortuary Practices in the Eastern Trans-Pecos Region of Texas*. Papers of the Trans-Pecos Archaeological Program No. 5. Alpine, TX: Sul Ross State University, Center for Big Bend Studies.

Pitezel, Todd. 2011. "From Archaeology to Ideology in Northwest Mexico: Cerro de Moctezuma in the Casas Grandes Ritual Landscape." PhD dissertation, University of Arizona, Tucson.

Polyak, Victor J., and Yemane Asmerom. 2001. "Late Holocene Climate and Cultural Changes in the Southwestern United States." *Science* 294(5540):148–151. https://doi.org/10.1126/science.1062771.

Pomeroy, J. Anthony. 1959. "Hohokam Etched Shell." *Kiva* 24(4):12–21. https://doi
.org/10.1080/00231940.1959.11757582.

Popper, V. S. 1988. "Selecting Quantitative Measurements in Paleoethnobotany." In
Current Paleoethnobotany, ed. C. A. Hastorf and V. S. Popper, 53–71. Chicago, IL:
University of Chicago Press.

Preucel, Robert W. 2005. "Ethnicity and Southwestern Archaeology." In *Southwest
Archaeology in the Twentieth Century*, ed. Linda S. Cordell and Don D. Fowler,
174–193. Salt Lake City: University of Utah Press.

Propst, David L. 1999. "Threatened and Endangered Fishes of New Mexico." Technical Report No. 1. Santa Fe: New Mexico Department of Game and Fish.

Puseman, Kathryn, Melissa K. Logan, Chad Yost, and Linda Scott Cummings.
2010. *Phytolith, Organic Residue (FTIR), Macrofloral, and Pollen Analysis of
Samples from Sites LA 160727, LA 160739, and LA 160741 for the Black River
Research Analysis, New Mexico*. Technical Report 10–08. Golden, CO: PaleoResearch Institute.

Quigg, J. M., C. Lintz, S. Smith, and S. Wilcox. 2000. *The Lino Site: A Stratified Late
Archaic Campsite in a Terrace of the San Idelfonzo Creek, Webb County, Southern Texas*.
Technical Report No. 23765. Austin: TRC Mariah Associates. Archaeological
Studies Program Report 20. Austin: Texas Department of Transportation, Envi-
ronmental Affairs Division.

Quigg, J. M., M. E. Malainey, R. Przybylski, and G. Monks. 2001. "No Bones about
It: Using Lipid Analysis of Burned Rock and Groundstone Residues to Examine Late Archaic Subsistence Practices in South Texas." *Plains Anthropologist*
46(177):283–303. https://doi.org/10.1080/2052546.2001.11932035.

Quigg, M., M. Sechrist, and G. Smith. 2002. *Testing and Data Recovery of Burned
Rock Features in Sites on Otero Mesa, New Mexico*. El Paso, TX: TRC Mariah Associ-
ates. Fort Bliss, TX: Fort Bliss Garrison Command, Directorate of Public Works,
Environmental Division.

Rachal, David M. 2013. "Geomorphology of Training Areas (TA) 4D, 5A, and 7B on
Fort Bliss Military Reservation, Dona Ana and Otero Counties, New Mexico."
Appendix B in *Archaeological Data Recovery at Five Sites in Training Area 4D
and 5A and Site Characterizing of One Site In Training Area 7B on Fort Bliss, Otero
County, New Mexico*, by T. B. Graves, M. R. Miller, and M. Landreth, 255–276.
Cultural Resources Report No. 12–11. Fort Bliss, TX: Fort Bliss Garrison Com-
mand, Directorate of Public Works, Environmental Division.

Railey, Jim A. 2008. "Early Intensive Farming in the Hondo Valley, Southern New
Mexico." Poster presented at the 2008 [71st] Annual Pecos Conference, Flagstaff,
AZ.

Railey, Jim A. 2010. "Reduced Mobility or the Bow and Arrow? Another Look at 'Expedient' Technologies and Sedentism." *American Antiquity* 75(2):259–286. https://doi.org/10.7183/0002-7316.75.2.259.

Railey, Jim A. 2016. *Native American Archaeology and Cultural Resources.* vol. I. Permian Basin Research Design 2016–2026. Albuquerque: Bureau of Land Management, Carlsbad Field Office, Carlsbad, New Mexico, and SWCA Environmental Consultants.

Railey, Jim A., ed. 2002. *Across the Desert Floor: Cultural Resources along U.S. 54, Otero County, New Mexico.* New Mexico State Highway and Transportation Department Technical Report 2002–1. Albuquerque, NM: TRC.

Railey, Jim A., ed. 2011. *Archaeology in Far Southeastern New Mexico; Data Recovery at LA 143755, LA 143758, LA 143759, LA 155888, and LA 155893 Along New Mexico Highway 128, Eddy And Lea Counties, New Mexico.* Albuquerque, NM: SWCA Environmental Consultants.

Railey, Jim A., ed. 2013. *The Human Landscape in Southeastern New Mexico: A Class I Overview of Cultural Resources within the Bureau of Land Management's Carlsbad Field Office Region.* Albuquerque, NM: SWCA Environmental Consultants.

Railey, Jim A., ed. 2015. *Red Tank: Archaeological Data Recovery at LA 43257 for the Zia II Natural Gas Pipeline, Eddy County, New Mexico.* Albuquerque, NM: SWCA Environmental Consultants.

Railey, Jim A., Matthew S. Bandy, and Lance Lundquist. 2011. "Radiocarbon Dates, Climate Change, and Settlement-Subsistence Trends in the Permian Basin Study Area, Southeastern New Mexico." In *Patterns in Transition: Papers from the 16th Biennial Jornada Mogollon Conference,* ed. Melinda R. Landreth, 191–232. El Paso, TX: El Paso Museum of Archaeology.

Railey, Jim A., Timothy B. Graves, Richard M. Reycraft, Lori S. Reed, Joell Goff, Jonathan Van Hoose, Lance Lundquist, John C. Acklen, and Gwyneth A. Duncan. 2002. "The Jaca Site (LA 6820)." In *Across the Desert Floor: Cultural Resource Investigations Along US 54, Otero County, New Mexico,* ed. Jim A. Railey, 99–224. New Mexico State Highway and Transportation Department, Technical Series 2002-1. Albuquerque, NM: TRC and Taschek Environmental Consulting.

Railey, Jim, and Patrick O. Mullen. 2006. *Cultural Resources Survey of the Intrepid Potash Land Exchange, Eddy and Lea Counties, New Mexico.* SWCA Report No. 2005–03. Albuquerque, NM: SWCA Environmental Consultants.

Railey, Jim A., Kimberly A. Parker, and Emily Stovel. 2016. *A Class I Overview of Cultural Resources within the Fort Stanton-Snowy River Cave National Conservation Area.* Albuquerque, NM: SWCA Environmental Consultants.

Railey, Jim A., John Rissetto, and Matthew S. Bandy. 2009. *Synthesis of Excavation Data for the Permian Basin Mitigation Program*. Albuquerque, NM: SWCA Environmental Consultants.

Railey, Jim A., and Samantha Ruscavage-Barz. 2008. "Synthesis and Interpretations." In *Archaeology of the Hondo Valley, Lincoln County, New Mexico: Archaeological Investigations along US 70 from Ruidoso Downs to Riverside*, ed. Kirsten Campbell and Jim A. Railey, 721–774. New Mexico Department of Transportation, Cultural Resource Technical Series 2006–1. Albuquerque, NM: SWCA Environmental Consultants and Parsons Brinckerhoff.

Randolph, Daniel, Jr. 2001. "Stone Raw Material Availability and Early Archaic Settlement in the Southeastern United States." *American Antiquity* 66(2):237–265. https://doi.org/10.2307/2694607.

Rapoport, Amos. 1969. *House Form and Culture*. Englewood Cliffs, NJ: Prentice-Hall.

Ray, Cyrus N. 1931. "Recent Archeological Researches in the Abilene Section." *Bulletin of the Texas Archeological and Paleontological Society* 3:76–89.

Ray, Cyrus N. 1932. "Archeological Research in Central West Texas." *Bulletin of the Texas Archeological and Paleontological Society* 4:63–70.

Ray, Cyrus N. 1933. "Multiple Burials in Stone Cist Mounds of the Abilene Region." *Bulletin of the Texas Archeological and Paleontological Society* 5:14–24.

Ray, Cyrus N. 1936. "Some Unusual Cremated Burials Found near Colorado, Texas." *Bulletin of the Texas Archeological and Paleontological Society* 8:9–16.

Ray, Cyrus N. 1937. "More Evidence Concerning Abilene Man." *Bulletin of the Texas Archeological and Paleontological Society* 9:193–217.

Ray, Cyrus N. 1939. "Some Unusual Abilene Region Burials." *Bulletin of the Texas Archeological and Paleontological Society* 11:226–250.

Ray, Cyrus N. 1946. "Two Buried Multiple Stone Cist Structures." *Bulletin of the Texas Archeological and Paleontological Society* 17:18–27.

Rea, Amadeo. 1997. *At the Desert's Green Edge*. Tucson: The University of Arizona Press.

Reagan, Albert B. 1930. "Notes on the Indians of the Fort Apache Region." *Anthropological Papers of the American Museum of Natural History* 31:281–345.

Reina, R. E., and R. M. Hill. 1980. "Lowland Maya Subsistence: Notes from Ethnohistory and Ethnography." *American Antiquity* 45(01):74–79. https://doi.org/10.2307/279660.

Renfrew, Colin. 1975. "Trade as Action at a Distance: Questions of Integration and Communication." In *Ancient Civilization and Trade*, ed. J. Sabloff and C. C. Lamberg-Kalovsky, 3–59. Albuquerque: University of New Mexico Press.

Renfrew, Colin. 1976. "Megaliths, Territories, and Populations." In *Acculturation and Continuity in Atlantic Europe*, ed. Sigfried J. De Laet, 198–220. Brugge, Belgium: De Tempel.

Renfrew, Colin. 1977. "Alternative Models for Exchange and Spatial Distribution." In *Exchange Systems in Prehistory*, ed. T. K. Earle and J. E. Ericson, 71–90. New York: Academic Press. https://doi.org/10.1016/B978-0-12-227650-7.50010-9.

Renn, James C., Jennifer Wiskowski, and Tim Church. 2010. *Work Smart Not Hard: Optimal Subsistence and the Jornada Mogollon–An Archaeological Survey of 9,664 Acres in Training Areas 12, 13, 14, 15, 17, 29, and 33 on McGregor Range, Fort Bliss, Otero County, New Mexico.* Historic and Natural Resources Report No. 08–27. Fort Bliss, TX: Fort Bliss Garrison Command, Directorate of Public Works, Environmental Division.

Reynolds, Peter J. 1974. "Experimental Iron Age Storage Pits: An Interim Report." *Proceedings of the Prehistoric Society* 40:118–131. https://doi.org/10.1017/S0079497X00011348.

Reynolds, Peter J. 1979a. "A General Report of Underground Grain Storage Experiments at the Butser Ancient Farm Project." In *Les Techniques de Conservation des Grains a Long Terme I*, ed. M. Gast and F. Sigaut, 70–80. Paris: Centre National de la Recherche Scientifique.

Reynolds, Peter J. 1979b. *Iron-Age Farm: The Butser Experiment.* London: British Museum.

Richerson, P. J., R. Boyd, and R. L. Bettinger. 2001. "Was Agriculture Impossible During the Pleistocene but Mandatory During the Holocene? A Climate Change Hypothesis." *American Antiquity* 66(3):387–411. https://doi.org/10.2307/2694241.

Roberts, Frank Harold Hanna, Jr. 1935. "A Survey of Southwestern Archaeology." *American Anthropologist New Series* 37(1, pt. 1):1–35. https://doi.org/10.1525/aa.1935.37.1.02a00020.

Roberts, Tim E. 2010. "'Big Bend Bold' Pictographs: Defining a New Rock Image Style in the Big Bend Region of Texas." *Journal of Big Bend Studies* 22:81–108.

Robinson, David G. 2004. "Petrographic Analysis of Prehistoric Ceramics from Two Sites in the La Junta Archeological District, Presidio County, Trans-Pecos Texas." In *Arroyo de la Presa Site: A Stratified Late Prehistoric Campsite along the Rio Grande, Presidio County, Trans-Pecos Texas*, by William A. Cloud, 227–236. Reports in Contract Archeology 9. Alpine, TX: Center for Big Bend Studies, Sul Ross State University.

Robinson, K. R. 1963. "A Note on Storage Pits: Rhodesian Iron Age and Modern Africa." *South African Archaeological Bulletin* 18(70):62–63. https://doi.org/10.2307/3887508.

Rocek, Thomas R. 1990. "Examining the Pithouse to Pueblo Transition: The Dunlap-Salazar Site, LA 41344, in South-Central New Mexico." Paper presented at the 55th Annual Meeting of the Society for American Archaeology, Las Vegas, NV.

Rocek, Thomas R. 1991. "Research at LA 51344, The Dunlap-Salazar Pit House Site, near Lincoln, New Mexico." In *Mogollon V*, ed. Patrick H. Beckett, 106–118. Las Cruces, NM: COA Publishing and Research.

Rocek, Thomas R. 1995. "Sedentarization and Agricultural Dependence: Perspectives from the Pithouse-to-Pueblo Transition in the American Southwest." *American Antiquity* 60(2):218–239. https://doi.org/10.2307/282138.

Rocek, Thomas R. 1997. "Variation in the Settlement-Subsistence Correlation within the Jornada Mogollon." Paper Presented at 62nd Annual Society for American Archaeology, Nashville, TN.

Rocek, Thomas R. 1998. "Subsistence, Settlement, and Social Variability in the Mogollon: Regional Variation in House Size." Paper presented at the 63rd Annual meeting of the Society for American Archaeology, Seattle, WA.

Rocek, Thomas R. 2007a. "Variation in the Settlement-Subsistence Correlation within the Jornada Mogollon." In Exploring Variation in Mogollon Pithouses, ed. Barbara J. Roth and Robert J. Stokes, 61–70. Anthropological Research Papers No. 58. Tempe: Arizona State University.

Rocek, Thomas R. 2007b. "Early Villages or Palimpsest Farmsteads? Chronological Analysis of the Dunlap-Salazar Pithouse Site, Lincoln County, New Mexico." Paper presented at the Annual Meeting of the 72nd annual meeting of the Society for American Archaeology, Austin, TX.

Rocek, Thomas R. 2011. "Housing on the Periphery: Pithouse Change and Variation in Late Prehistoric Southeastern New Mexico." Paper presented at the 76th annual meeting of the Society for American Archaeology, Sacramento, CA.

Rocek, Thomas R. 2013. "The Dunlap-Salazar Site (LA 51344) and the Context of Village Origins in the Jornada Highlands." In *Papers from the 17th Biennial Jornada Mogollon Conference in 2011*, ed. C. VanPool and E. McCarthy, 137–150. El Paso, TX: El Paso Museum of Archaeology.

Rocek, Thomas R., and Alison E. Rautman. 2007. "No Peripheral Vision: A View of the Concepts of 'Heartland' and 'Hinterland' from South-Central New Mexico." In *Hinterlands and Regional Dynamics in the Ancient Southwest*, ed. A. Sullivan and J. Bayman, 125–138. Tucson: University of Arizona Press.

Rocek, Thomas R., and Alison E. Rautman. 2012. "First Millennium Pithouse Village Diversity in Southeastern New Mexico." In *Southwestern Pithouse Communities, A.D. 200–900*, ed. Lisa Young and Sarah Herr, 110–122. Tucson: University of Arizona Press.

Rocek, Thomas R., and John D. Speth. 1986. *The Henderson Site Burials: Glimpses of a Late Prehistoric Population in the Pecos Valley.* Technical Report 18. Ann Arbor: Museum of Anthropology, University of Michigan.

Rogers, Malcolm J. 1939. "Early Lithic Industries of the Lower Basin of the Colorado River and Adjacent Areas." San Diego Museum Papers No. 3. San Diego, CA: Museum of Man.

Rogers, Malcolm J. 1941. "Aboriginal Culture Relations between Southern California and the Southwest." San Diego, CA: Museum of Man. *Bulletin No.* 5(3):1–6.

Rogers, Malcolm J. 1966. *Ancient Hunters of the Far West.* San Diego, CA: Union-Tribune Publishing Company.

Roney, John R. 1985a. "Prehistory of the Guadalupe Mountains." Master's thesis, Eastern New Mexico University, Portales, NM.

Roney, John R. 1985b. "Projectile Points as Chronological Markers in the Guadalupe Mountains, Southeastern New Mexico." In *Views of the Jornada Mogollon,* ed. Colleen Beck, 5–29. Eastern New Mexico University Contributions in Anthropology, Volume 12. Portales, NM: Department of Anthropology and Applied Archaeology.

Roney, John R. 1996. "The Pueblo III Period in the Eastern San Juan Basin and Acoma-Laguna Areas." In *Prehistoric World, A.D. 1150–1350,* ed. Michael A. Adler, 145–169. Tucson: University of Arizona Press.

Runyan, John W., and John A. Hedrick. 1973. "Pottery Types of the SWFAS Area." In *Transactions of the Eighth Regional Archaeological Symposium for Southeastern New Mexico and Western Texas,* 19–45. Hobbs, NM: Lea County Archaeological Society.

Sale, Mark, Myles R. Miller, and Amy Silberberg. 2012. *Pits and Pieces: Mitigation of One Site in the IBCT on Fort Bliss Military Reservation, Otero County, New Mexico.* Cultural Resources Report No. 11–26. Fort Bliss, TX: Fort Bliss Garrison Command, Directorate of Public Works, Environmental Division.

Santley, Robert, C. Yarbrough, and B. Hall. 1987. "Enclaves, Ethnicity, and the Archaeological Record at Matacapan." In *Ethnicity and Culture: Proceedings of the 18th Chacmool Conference,* ed. Reginald Auger, M. F. Glass, S. MacEachern, and P. H. McCartney, 85–100. Alberta, Canada: The University of Calgary Archaeological Association.

Sauer, Carl O. 1941. "The Personality of Mexico." *Geographical Review* 31(3):353–364. https://doi.org/10.2307/210171.

Sauer, Carl O. 1963. *Land and Life: A Selection from the Writing of C. O. Sauer.* Berkeley: University of California Press.

Saxe, Arthur A. 1970. "Social Dimensions of Mortuary Practices." PhD dissertation, University of Michigan, Ann Arbor.

Saxe, Arthur A., and Patricia L. Gall. 1977. "Ecological Determinants of Mortuary Practices: The Temuan of Malaysia." In *Cultural-Ecological Perspectives on Southeast Asia*, ed. William Wood, 74–82. Papers in International Studies, Southeast Asia Series 41. Columbus: Center for International Studies, Ohio State University.

Sayles, Edwin B. 1935. *An Archaeological Survey of Texas*. Medallion Papers, No. 17. Globe, AZ: Gila Pueblo.

Sayles, Edwin B. 1936a. *An Archaeological Survey of Chihuahua, Mexico*. Medallion Papers, No. 22. Globe, AZ: Gila Pueblo.

Sayles, Edwin B. 1936b. *Some Southwestern Pottery Types, Series 4*. Medallion Papers, No. 21. Globe, AZ: Gila Pueblo.

Sayles, Edwin B. 1983. *The Cochise Cultural Sequence in Southeastern Arizona*. Anthropological Papers No. 42. Tucson: University of Arizona.

Scarborough, Vernon L. 1985. "Anapra Pueblo Site: Proceedings of the 3rd Jornada Mogollon Conference." Ed. M. S. Foster and T. C. O'Laughlin. *The Artifact* 23(1/2):129–135.

Scarborough, Vernon L. 1988. "A Water Storage Adaptation in the American Southwest." *Journal of Anthropological Research* 44(1):21–40. https://doi.org/10.1086/jar.44.1.3630123.

Schaafsma, Curtis F. 1997. "The 'El Paso Phase' and its Relationship to the 'Casas Grandes Phenomenon.'" In *Jornada Mogollon Archaeology: Proceedings of the First Jornada Conference*, ed. Patrick H. Beckett and Regge N. Wiseman, 383–388. Las Cruces: New Mexico State University.

Schaafsma, Polly. 1980. *Indian Rock Art of the Southwest*. Santa Fe, NM: School of American Research.

Schaafsma, Polly. 1997. "Ten Rock Art Sites in Chihuahua Mexico." Office of Archaeological Studies Archaeology Notes 171, Santa Fe: Museum of New Mexico.

Schaafsma, Polly. 1998. "The Paquime Rock Art Style, Chihuahua, Mexico." In, *Rock Art of the Chihuahuan Desert Borderlands*, ed. Sheron Smith-Savage and Robert J. Mallouf, 33–44. Center for Big Bend Studies Occasional Papers, No. 3. Alpine, TX: Sul Ross State University.

Schaafsma, Polly. 2001. "Quetzalcoatl and the Horned and Feathered Serpent of the Southwest." In *The Road to Aztlan*, ed. Virginia M. Fields and Victor Zamudio-Taylor, 138–149. Los Angeles, CA: Los Angeles County Museum of Art.

Schaafsma, Polly. 2009. "The Cave in the Kiva: the Kiva Niche and Painted Walls in the Rio Grande Valley." *American Antiquity* 74(04):664–690. https://doi.org/10.1017/S0002731600049003.

Schmidt, Robert H. 1979. "A Climatic Delineation of the 'Real' Chihuahuan Desert." *Journal of Arid Environments* 2(3):243–250.

Schopmeyer, C. S. 1974. *Seeds of Woody Plants*. Agricultural Handbook 450. Washington, DC: US Department of Agriculture.

Schriever, B. A. 2012. "Mobility, Land Tenure, and Social Identity in the San Simon Basin of Southeastern Arizona." *Kiva* 77(4):413–438. https://doi.org/10.1179/kiv.2012.77.4.003.

Schuelke, Katherine J. 2008. "Variation in Burned Rock Features in Southeastern New Mexico: A Siteless Approach Using Statistics and GIS." Master's thesis, Eastern New Mexico University, Portales, NM.

Schultz, Robert E. 1967. "Excavation of a Single Room at Hot Well in the Spring of 1966." *Artifact* 5(4):15–30.

Sebastian, Lynne, and Signa Larralde. 1989. *Living on the Land: 11,000 Years of Human Adaptation in Southeastern New Mexico: An Overview of Cultural Resources in the Roswell District, Bureau of Land Management*. Bureau of Land Management Cultural Resource Series No. 6.

Seebach, J. D. 2007. *Late Prehistory along the Rimrock, Pinto Canyon Ranch*. Papers of the Trans-Pecos Archaeological Program, No. 3. Alpine, TX: Center for Big Bend Studies, Sul Ross State University.

Shackelford, William J. 1951. "Excavations at the Polvo Site in Western Texas." Master's thesis, University of Texas at Austin.

Shackelford, William J. 1955. "Excavations at the Polvo Site in Western Texas." *American Antiquity* 20(03):256–262. https://doi.org/10.2307/277002.

Shackley, M. 1982. "Gas Chromatographic Identification of a Resinous Deposit from a 6th Century Storage Jar and Its Possible Identification." *Journal of Archaeological Science* 9(3):305–306. https://doi.org/10.1016/0305-4403(82)90026-7.

Shafer, Harry J. 2003. *Mimbres Archaeology at the NAN Ranch Ruin*. Albuquerque: University of New Mexico Press.

Shafer, Harry J. 2006. "Extended Families to Corporate Groups: Pithouse to Pueblo Transformation of Mimbres Society." In *Mimbres Society*, ed. V. S. Powell-Martí and P. A. Gilman, 15–31. Tucson: University of Arizona Press.

Shafer, Harry J., and Robbie Brewington. 1995. "Microstylistic Changes in Mimbres Black-on-white Pottery: Examples from the NAN Ranch Ruin, Grant County, New Mexico." *Kiva* 61(1):5–29. https://doi.org/10.1080/00231940.1995.11758291.

Shafer, Harry J., J. E. Dockall, and R. L. Brewington. 1999. *Archaeology of the Ojasen (41EP289) and Gobernadora (41EP321) Sites, El Paso County, Texas*. Center for Ecological Archaeology Report of Investigation No. 2. College Station: Texas A&M University. Archeology Studies Program Report 13. Austin: Texas Department of Transportation.

Shah, Monica. 1998. "Preliminary Petrographic Analysis of Ceramics from the Dunlap-Salazar Site, New Mexico." Manuscript on file, Department of Anthropology, University of Delaware, Newark.

Shelley, Phillip H. 1992. "Archaeology and Paleoecology of the Fort Stanton Reservation near Lincoln, New Mexico." In *Interpreting the Past; Research with Public Participation*, ed. LouAnn Jacobson and June-el Piper, 1–19. Cultural Resources Series No. 10. Santa Fe: Bureau of Land Management, New Mexico State Office.

Shook, E. M. 1951. "The Present Status of Research on the Pre-Classic Horizons in Guatemala." In *The Civilizations of Ancient America*, ed. Sol Tax, 92–100. Chicago, IL: University of Chicago Press.

Sidwell, R. 1946. "Sediments from Alaskite, Capitan Mountain, New Mexico." *Journal of Sedimentary Petrology* 16(3):121–123.

Simms, Steven R., Jason R. Bright, and Andrew Ugan. 1997. "Plain-Ware Ceramics and Residential Mobility: A Case Study from the Great Basin." *Journal of Archaeological Science* 24(9):779–792. https://doi.org/10.1006/jasc.1996.0160.

Skibo, James M. 1992. *Pottery Function: A Use-Alteration Perspective.* New York: Plenum Press. https://doi.org/10.1007/978-1-4899-1179-7.

Smith, Calvin B. 1970. "New Mexico Archaeological Services, Inc. site record: LA 32228." On file at the New Mexico Archaeological Management System, Santa Fe, NM.

Smith, Grant D. 2002. "Geomorphological Investigations." In *Cultural Resource Monitoring for Proposed West Mesa to Person Station Gas Line Project, Bernalillo County, New Mexico*, by D. A. Jones-Bartholomew, John C. Acklen, Grant D. Smith, Stephen W. Yost, Jim A. Railey, and Joan M. Yost, 91–107. TRC Report No. 32166. Albuquerque, NM.

Smith, Geoffrey M., and David C. Harvey. 2018. "Reconstructing Prehistoric Landscape Use at a Regional Scale: A Critical Review of the Lithic Conveyance Zone Concept with a Focus on its Limitations." *Journal of Archaeological Science: Reports* 19:828–835. https://doi.org/10.1016/j.jasrep.2017.05.048.

Smith, Grant D., and M. McFaul. 1997. "Paleoenvironmental and Geoarchaeological Implications of Late Quaternary Sediments and Paleosols: North-Central to Southwestern San Juan Basin, New Mexico." *Geomorphology* 21(2):107–138. https://doi.org/10.1016/S0169-555X(97)00038-X.

Snead, James E. 2002. "Ancestral Pueblo Trails and the Cultural Landscape of the Pajarito Plateau, New Mexico." *Antiquity* 76(293):756–765. https://doi.org/10.1017/S0003598X00091201.

Snead, James E. 2008a. *Ancestral Landscapes of the Pueblo World.* Tucson: University of Arizona Press.

Snead, James E. 2008b. "Ancestral Pueblo Trails of the Pajarito Plateau: A Summary of Recent Research." In *The Land Conveyance and Transfer Data Recovery Project: 7000 Years of Land Use on the Pajarito Plateau,* Volume 4, *Research Design,* ed. B. J. Vierra and K. M. Schmidt, 201–240. Los Alamos, NM: U.S. Department of Energy National Nuclear Security Administration, Los Alamos Site Office, Los Alamos National Laboratories.

Snead, James E., Clark L. Erickson, and Andrew J. Darling. 2009. "Making Human Space: The Archaeology of Trails, Paths, and Roads." In *Landscapes of Movement: Trails, Paths, and Roads in Anthropological Perspective,* ed. J. E. Snead, C. L. Erickson, and A. J. Darling, 1–19. Philadelphia: University of Pennsylvania Press.

Southward, Judith A. 1979. "A Summary of Ceramic Technology, Plant Remains and Shell Identification from LA 4921, Three Rivers, New Mexico." In *Jornada Mogollon Archaeology,* ed. Patrick H. Beckett and Regge N. Wiseman, 91–102. Las Cruces, NM: COAS Publishing and Research.

Speakman, Robert J. 2007. *"Instrumental Neutron Activation Analysis of Pottery Recovered from the AT&T Nexgen/Core Fiber Optic Mitigation Project, Texas." Manuscript on file.* Farmington, NM: Western Cultural Resources Management.

Speakman, Robert J., and Michael D. Glascock. 2005. *Instrumental Neutron Activation Analysis of Pottery from Presidio and Hudspeth Counties, Texas.* Columbia, MO: Archaeometry Laboratory, Missouri University Research Reactor, University of Missouri.

Speth, John D. 1979. "The Garnsey Bison Kill Site, Chaves County, New Mexico." In *Jornada Mogollon Archaeology: Proceedings of the First Jornada Conference,* ed. P. H. Beckett and R. N. Wiseman, 143–158. Santa Fe: New Mexico Historic Preservation Division.

Speth, John D. 1983. *Bison Kills and Bone Counts: Decision Making By Ancient Hunters.* Chicago, IL: University of Chicago Press.

Speth, John D. 1984. *Application for a Federal Permit under the Archaeological Resources Protection Act (to Conduct Excavations at the Maroon Cliffs Site Complex and the Merchant Site).* Ann Arbor: University of Michigan.

Speth, John D. 1988. "Do We Need Concepts Like 'Mogollon,' 'Anasazi,' and 'Hohokam' Today? A Cultural Anthropological Perspective." *Kiva* 53(2):201–204. https://doi.org/10.1080/00231940.1988.11758093.

Speth, John D. 2004a. "Life on the Periphery: Economic and Social Change in Southeastern New Mexico." In *Life on the Periphery: Economic Change in Late Prehistoric Southeastern New Mexico,* ed. J. D. Speth, 420–429. Memoirs No. 37. Ann Arbor: Museum of Anthropology, University of Michigan.

Speth, John D. 2004b. "The Henderson Site." In *Life on the Periphery: Economic Change in Late Prehistoric Southeastern New Mexico*, ed. J. D. Speth, 4–66. Memoirs No. 37. Ann Arbor: Museum of Anthropology, University of Michigan.

Speth, John D. 2005. "The Beginnings of Plains-Pueblo Interaction: An Archaeological Perspective from Southeastern New Mexico". In *Engaged Anthropology: Research Essays on North American Archaeology, Ethnobotany, and Museology (Papers in Honor of Richard I. Ford)*, ed. M. Hegmon and B. S. Eiselt, 129–147. Anthropological Paper 94. Ann Arbor: Museum of Anthropology, University of Michigan.

Speth, John D. 2008. "Following in Jane Kelley's Footsteps: Bloom Mound Revisited." In *Celebrating Jane Holden Kelley and Her Work*, ed. Meade F. Kemrer, 35–47. Special Publication No. 5. Albuquerque: New Mexico Archaeological Council.

Speth, John D. 2018. "A New Look at Old Assumptions: Paleoindian Communal Bison Hunting, Mobility, and Stone Tool Technology." In *The Archaeology of Large-Scale Manipulation of Prey: The Economic and Social Dynamics of Mass Hunting*, ed. Kristen Carlson and Leland Bement, 161–285. Boulder: University Press of Colorado.

Speth, John D., ed. 2004. *Life on the Periphery: Economic Change in Late Prehistoric Southeastern New Mexico*. Memoir 37. Ann Arbor: Museum of Anthropology, University of Michigan.

Speth, John D., and Matthew LeDuc. 2007. "El Paso Polychrome Jars: New Insights from Complete Vessels." In *Viva la Jornada!: Papers from the 14th Biennial Jornada Mogollon Conference*, ed. Jason Jurgena, Lora Jackson, and Marc Thompson, 33–52. El Paso, TX: El Paso Museum of Archaeology.

Speth, John D., and Tatum M. McKay. 2004. "Freshwater Mollusks: A Source of Food or Just Ornaments?" In *Life on the Periphery: Economic Change in Late Prehistoric Southeastern New Mexico*, ed. John D. Speth. Museum of Anthropology Memoir No. 37, Ann Arbor: Museum of Anthropology, University of Michigan.

Speth, John D., and Khori Newlander. 2012. "Plains-Pueblo Interaction: A View from the 'Middle." In *The Toyah Phase of Central Texas: Late Prehistoric Economic and Social Processes*, ed. Nancy A. Kenmotsu and Douglas K. Boyd, 152–180. College Station: Texas A&M Press.

Speth, John D., and William J. Parry. 1978. *Late Prehistoric Bison Procurement in Southeastern New Mexico: The 1977 Season at the Garnsey Site*. Museum of Anthropology Technical Report 8. Ann Arbor: Museum of Anthropology, University of Michigan.

Speth, John D., and William J. Parry. 1980. *Late Prehistoric Bison Procurement in Southeastern New Mexico: The 1987 Season at the Garnsey Site (LA–18399)*. Museum of Anthropology Technical Report 12, Ann Arbor: Museum of Anthropology, University of Michigan.

Speth, John D., Susan L. Scott, and Ralph F. Stearley. 2004. "Fish and Fishing at Henderson." In *Life on the Periphery: Economic Change in Late Prehistoric Southeastern New Mexico*, e. John D. Speth, 305–319. Museum of Anthropology Memoirs No. 37, Ann Arbor: Museum of Anthropology, University of Michigan.

Spielmann, K. A. 1998. "The Pueblo IV Period: History of Research." In *Migration and Reorganization: The Pueblo IV Period in the American Southwest*, ed. K. A. Spielmann, 1–29. Anthropological Research Papers, No. 51. Tempe: Arizona State University.

Spielmann, K. A. 2004. "Clusters Revisited." In *The Protohistoric Pueblo World, A.D. 1275–1600*, ed. E. C. Adams and A. I. Duff, 137–156. Tucson: University of Arizona Press.

Spielmann, Katherine. 1983. "Late Prehistoric Exchange between the Southwest and Southern Plains." *Plains Anthropologist* 28(102):257–272. https://doi.org/10.1080/2052546.1983.11909162.

Spielmann, Katharine, ed. 1991. *Farmers, Hunters, and Colonists: Interaction between the Southwest and Southern Plains*. Tucson: University of Arizona Press.

Sprehn, Maria S. 2003. "Social Complexity and the Specialist Potters of Casas Grandes in Northern Mexico." PhD dissertation, University of New Mexico, Albuquerque.

Staley, David P., ed. 1996. *Archaeological Investigations along the Potash Junction to Cunningham Station Transmission Line, Eddy and Lea Counties, New Mexico*. Mescalero Plain Archaeology, Vol. 2. TRC Mariah Technical Report No. 11034–0030. Albuquerque.

Staley, D. P., K. A. Adams, T. Dolan, J. A. Evaskovich, D. V. Hill, R. G. Holloway, W. B. Hudspeth, and R. B. Roxlau. 1996. *Archaeological Investigations along the Potash Junction to Cunningham Station Transmission Line, Eddy and Lea Counties, New Mexico*. Mescalero Plains Archaeology, vol. 2. Albuquerque, NM: Mariah Associates.

Staller, John E., Robert H. Tykot, and Bruce F. Benz. 2006. *Histories of Maize: Multidisciplinary Approaches to the Prehistory, Linguistics, Biogeography, Domestication, and Evolution of Maize*. Boston, MA: Elsevier Academic Press.

Stewart, Joe D. 1979. "The Formal Definition of Decorative Traditions in the Jornada Area: A Case Study of Lincoln Black-on-Red Designs." In *Jornada Mogollon Archaeology*, ed. Patrick H. Beckett and Regge N. Wiseman, 295–344. Las Cruces, NM: COAS Publishing and Research.

Stewart, Joe D., Jonathan C. Driver, and Jane H. Kelley. 1991. "The Capitan North Project: Chronology." In *Mogollon V*, ed. Patrick H. Beckett, 177–190. Las Cruces, NM: COAS Publishing and Research.

Stewart, Joe D., Philip Fralick, Ronald G. V. Hancock, Jane H. Kelley, and Elizabeth M. Garrett. 1990. "Petrographic Analysis and INAA Geochemistry of Prehistoric

Ceramics from Robinson Pueblo, New Mexico." *Journal of Archaeological Science* 17(6):601–625. https://doi.org/10.1016/0305-4403(90)90043-5.

Stewart, Joe D., and Jane H. Kelley, A. C. MacWilliams, and Paula J. Reimer. 2004. "Archaeological Chronology in West-Central Chihuahua." In *Surveying the Archaeology of Northwest Mexico*, ed. Gillian E. Newell and Emiliano Gallaga, 205–245. Salt Lake City: The University of Utah Press.

Stone, Connie. 1986. *Deceptive Desolation: Prehistory of the Sonoran Desert in West Central Arizona.* Cultural Resource Series No. *1*. Phoenix: Bureau of Land Management, Arizona State Office.

Stone, Tammy. 2003. "Social Identity and Ethnic Interaction in the Western Pueblos of the American Southwest." *Journal of Archaeological Method and Theory* 10(1):31–67. https://doi.org/10.1023/A:1022808529265.

Stowe, Michael A., and Peter C. Condon. 2012. *Archaeological Investigations at LA 33085 and LA 165710 in the Maroon Cliffs Special Management Area, Eddy County, New Mexico.* El Paso, TX: Bureau of Land Management, Carlsbad Field Office, Carlsbad, New Mexico, and Geo-Marine.

Stowe, Michael, Chad Norred, and Amanda Hoiness. 2009. *An Archaeological Survey of 9,872 Acres in Training Areas 13, 14, 15, and 16 on McGregor Range, Fort Bliss Military Reservation, Otero County, New Mexico.* Historic and Natural Resources Report No. 08–25. Fort Bliss, TX: Fort Bliss Garrison Command, Directorate of Public Works, Environmental Division.

Stuart, David E., and Robbin E. Farwell. 1983. "Out of Phase: Late Pithouse Occupation in the Highlands of New Mexico." In *High-Altitude Adaptations in the Southwest*, ed. Joseph C. Winter, 115–158. Cultural Resources Management Report No. 2. Albuquerque, NM: USDA Forest Service.

Sturtevant, E. L. 1919. *Sturtevant's Notes on Edible Plants.* Ed. U. P. Hedrick. Geneva, NY: New York Agricultural Experiment Station. https://doi.org/10.5962/bhl.title.24577.

Swanson, Matthew, and Tim Graves. 2011. *Cultural Resource Survey and Evaluation of 1,065 Acres in the Doña Ana Range, Fort Bliss Military Reservation, Otero County, New Mexico.* Historic and Natural Resources Report No. 10–23. Fort Bliss, TX: Fort Bliss Garrison Command, Directorate of Public Works, Environmental Division.

Swanson, Steve. 2003. "Documenting Prehistoric Communication Networks: A Case Study in the Paquime Polity." *American Antiquity* 68(04):753–767. https://doi.org/10.2307/3557071.

Syms, E. Leigh. 1974. "History of a Refuse Pit: Interpreting Plains Camp Activity at a Microcosmic Level." *Plains Anthropologist* 19(66):306–315. https://doi.org/10.1080/2052546.1974.11908707.

Tagg, Martyn D. 1996. "Early Cultigens from Fresnal Shelter, Southeastern New Mexico." *American Antiquity* 61(2):311–324. https://doi.org/10.2307/282428.

Thoms, Alston V. 2008. "Ancient Savannah Roots of the Carbohydrate Revolution in Southcentral North America." *Plains Anthropologist* 53(205):121–136. https://doi.org/10.1179/pan.2008.008.

Titiev, Mischa. 1937. "A Hopi Salt Expedition." *American Anthropologist* 39(2):244–258. https://doi.org/10.1525/aa.1937.39.2.02a00050.

Toll, M. S. 2006. "Chapter 19: High Rolls Corn." In *High Rolls Cave: Insectos, Burritos, y Frajos: Archaic Subsistence in Southern New Mexico. Excavation at LA 114103, Otero County, New Mexico*, ed. Stephen C. Lentz, Archaeological Notes 34, 223–225. Santa Fe, NM: Office of Archaeological Studies, Department of Cultural Affairs.

Toney, J. L., and R. S. Anderson. 2006. "A Postglacial Palaeoecological Record from the San Juan Mountains of Colorado USA: Fire, Climate and Vegetation History." *Holocene* 16(4):505–517. https://doi.org/10.1191/0959683606hl946rp.

Toomey, R. S., III. 1993. "Late Pleistocene and Holocene Faunal and Environmental Changes at Hall's Cave, Kerr County, Texas." PhD dissertation, University of Texas at Austin, Austin.

Toomey, R. S., III, M. D. Blum, and S. Valastro, Jr. 1993. "Late Quaternary Climate and Environments of the Edwards Plateau, Texas." *Global and Planetary Change* 7(4):299–320. https://doi.org/10.1016/0921-8181(93)90003-7.

Tristam, H. B. 1898. *The Natural History of the Bible*. London: Published by the author.

Turnbow, Christopher A., ed. 2000. *A Highway through Time: Archaeological Investigations along NM 90*. New Mexico Technical Report 2000–3. Albuquerque, NM: TRC.

Turpin, Solveig A. 2004. "The Lower Pecos River Region of Texas and Northern Mexico." In *The Prehistory of Texas*, ed. Timothy K. Perttula, 266–280. College Station: Texas A&M University Press.

Upham, Steadman. 1984. "Adaptive Diversity and Southwestern Abandonment." *Journal of Anthropological Research* 40(2):235–256. https://doi.org/10.1086/jar.40.2.3629574.

Upham, Steadman, and Richard S. MacNeish. 1993. "The Evolution of Maize in the Jornada Region of New Mexico and its Implications for the Southwest." In *Preliminary Investigations of the Archaic in the Region of Las Cruces, New Mexico*, ed. Richard S. MacNeish, 105–116. Historic and Natural Resources Report No. 9. Fort Bliss, TX: Fort Bliss Garrison Command, Directorate of Public Works, Environmental Division.

Upham, Steadman C., Richard S. MacNeish, W. C. Galinat, and C. M. Stevenson. 1987. "Evidence Concerning the Origin of Maiz de Ocho." *American Anthropologist* 89(2):410–419. https://doi.org/10.1525/aa.1987.89.2.02a00090.

US Army. 2010. *Fort Bliss Army Growth and Force Structure Realignment; Final Impact Statement. Fort Bliss.* TX: US Army Garrison.

US Army Corps of Engineers, Tulsa District, and Directorate of Public Works Environmental Division, Fort Bliss. 2016. *Environmental Assessment for the Implementation of the 2017–2021 Integrated Cultural Resources Management Plan; Fort Bliss, Texas and New Mexico.* Draft October 2016. Fort Bliss, TX: US Army Garrison.

Valastro, Jr. Sam, E. Mott Davis, and Craig T. Rightmire. 1968. "University of Texas at Austin Radiocarbon Dates VI." *Radiocarbon* 10(2):384–401. https://doi.org/10.1017/S0033822200010985.

Van Dyke, Ruth M. 2007. *The Chaco Experience: Landscape and Ideology at the Center Place.* Santa Fe, NM: School for Advanced Research Press.

Van Dyke, Ruth M. 2009. "Chaco Reloaded: Discursive Social Memory on the Post-Chacoan Landscape." *Journal of Social Archaeology* 9(2):220–248. https://doi.org/10.1177/1469605309104137.

Van Dyke, Ruth M., Richard Ciolek-Torrello, and Chester W. Shaw, Jr. 1998. "Excavated Features." In *Early Farmers of the Sonoran Desert: Archaeological Investigations at the Houghton Road Site, Tucson, Arizona,* ed. Richard Ciolek-Torrello, 51–87. Technical Series 72. Tucson, AZ: Statistical Research.

VanPool, Christine S., Todd L. VanPool, and Robert D. Leonard. 2005. "The Casas Grandes Core and Periphery." In *Archaeology between the Borders: Papers from the 13th Biennial Jornada Mogollon Conference,* ed. Marc Thompson, Jason Jurgena and Lora Jackson, 25–35. El Paso, TX: El Paso Museum of Archaeology.

Varien, Mark D., and James M. Potter, eds. 2008. *The Social Construction of Communities: Agency, Structure, and Identity in the Prehispanic Southwest.* Lanham, MD: AltaMira Press.

Vierra, Bradley J. 1990. "Archaic Hunter-Gatherer Archaeology in Northwestern New Mexico." In *Perspectives on Southwestern Prehistory,* 57–70. Boulder, CO: Westview Press.

Vierra, Bradley J., and Christine G. Ward. 2012. *Mitigation of Three Archaeological Sites along and near El Paso Draw in the New IBCT Training Area, East McGregor Range, Fort Bliss Military Reservation, Otero County, New Mexico.* Cultural Resources Report No. 11–14. Fort Bliss, TX: Fort Bliss Garrison Command, Directorate of Public Works, Environmental Division.

Vivian, R. Gordon. 1997a. "Chacoan Roads: Morphology." *Kiva* 63(1):7–34. https://doi.org/10.1080/00231940.1997.11758345.

Vivian, R. Gordon. 1997b. "Chacoan Roads: Function." *Kiva* 63(1):35–67. https://doi.org/10.1080/00231940.1997.11758346.

Waddell, Jack O. 1980. "The Use of Intoxicating Beverages among the Native Peoples of the Aboriginal Greater Southwest." In *Drinking Behavior among Southwestern Indians*, ed. Jack O. Waddell and Michael W. Everett, 1–32. Tucson: University of Arizona Press.

Walth, Cherie K., and Jim A. Railey, eds. 2011. *Data Recovery Excavations at Seven Sites along Interstate 25, Sandoval County, New Mexico.* New Mexico Department of Transportation, Cultural Resource Technical Series 2011–1. Albuquerque, NM: SWCA Environmental Consultants.

Wandsnider, LuAnn. 1988. "Experimental Investigation of the Effect of Dune Processes on Archeological Remains." *American Archeology* 7(1):8–29.

Wandsnider, LuAnn. 1997. "The Roasted and the Boiled: Food Composition and Heat Treatment with Special Emphasis on Pit-Hearth Cooking." *Journal of Anthropological Archaeology* 16(1):1–48. https://doi.org/10.1006/jaar.1997.0303.

Wandsnider, LuAnn. Spring 1999. "Late Prehistoric High Plains Foragers: Starving Nomads, Affluent Foragers?" *Great Plains Research* 9:9–39.

Ward, Christine G., and Bradley J. Vierra. 2011. *Mitigation of Three Archaeological Sites in the IBCT Training Area, East McGregor Range, Fort Bliss Military Reservation, Otero County, New Mexico.* Cultural Resources Report No. 10–24. Fort Bliss, TX: Fort Bliss Garrison Command, Directorate of Public Works, Environmental Division.

Warnica, J. W. 1966. "New Discoveries at the Clovis Site." *American Antiquity* 31(03):345–357. https://doi.org/10.2307/2694737.

Warren, A. Helene. 1992. "Temper Analysis of the Pottery of the Rio Bonito Valley." In *Investigations into the Prehistory and History of the Upper Rio Bonito, Lincoln County, Southeastern New Mexico,* by Robin E. Farwell, Yvonne R. Oakes, and Regge N. Wiseman, 195–196. Laboratory of Anthropology Notes 297. Santa Fe: Office of Archaeological Studies, Museum of New Mexico.

Wedel, Waldo R. 1982. "Further Notes in Puebloan-Central Plains Contacts in Light of Archaeology." In *Pathways to Plains Prehistory: Anthropological Perspectives of Plains Natives and Their Pasts,* ed. Don G. Wycoff and Jack L. Hofman, 145–152. Anthropological Society Memoir No.3. Duncan, OK: The Cross Timbers Press.

Wiessner, Polly. 1983. "Style and Social Information in Kalahari San Projectile Points." *American Antiquity* 48(2):253–276. https://doi.org/10.2307/280450.

Wendland, Wayne M., and Reid A. Bryson. 1974. "Dating Climatic Episodes of the Holocene." *Quaternary Research* 4(1):9–24. https://doi.org/10.1016/0033-5894(74)90060-X.

Wendorf, Fred. 1960. "The Archaeology of Northeastern New Mexico." *El Palacio* 67(2):2–12.

Whalen, Michael E. 1977. *Settlement Patterns of the Eastern Hueco Bolson.* Publications in Anthropology Paper No. 4. El Paso: El Paso Centennial Museum, University of Texas at El Paso.

Whalen, Michael E. 1978. *Settlement Patterns of the Western Hueco Bolson.* Publications in Anthropology No. 6. El Paso: El Paso Centennial Museum, University of Texas at El Paso.

Whalen, Michael E. 1981a. "Cultural-Ecological Aspects of the Pithouse-to-Pueblo Transition in a Portion of the Southwest." *American Antiquity* 46(01):75–92. https://doi.org/10.2307/279988.

Whalen, Michael E. 1981b. "An Investigation of Pithouse Village Structure in Western Texas." *Journal of Field Archaeology* 8(3):303–311.

Whalen, Michael E. 1985. "Chronological Studies in the Jornada Area." In *Views of the Jornada Mogollon,* ed. Coleen M. Beck, 136–142. Contributions in Anthropology No. 12. Portales: Eastern New Mexico State University.

Whalen, Michael E. 1994a. "Moving Out of the Archaic on the Edge of the Southwest." *American Antiquity* 59(04):622–638. https://doi.org/10.2307/282337.

Whalen, Michael E. 1994b. *Turquoise Ridge and Late Prehistoric Residential Mobility in the Desert Mogollon Region.* University of Utah Anthropological Papers No. 118. Salt Lake City: University of Utah Press.

Whalen, Michael E., and Paul E. Minnis. 2000. "Leadership at Casas Grandes, Chihuahua, Mexico." In *Alternative Leadership Strategies in Prehispanic Southwest,* ed. B. J. Mills, 168–179. Tucson: The University of Arizona Press.

Whalen, Michael E., and Paul E. Minnis. 2001a. *Casas Grandes and Its Hinterland: Prehistoric Regional Organization in Northwest Mexico.* Tucson: University of Arizona Press.

Whalen, Michael E., and Paul E. Minnis. 2001b. "The Casas Grandes Regional System: A Late Prehistoric Polity in Northwestern Mexico." *Journal of World Prehistory* 15(3):313–364. https://doi.org/10.1023/A:1013187605760.

Whalen, Michael E., and Paul E. Minnis. 2009. *The Neighbors of Casas Grandes: Excavating Medio Period Communities of Northwest Chihuahua, Mexico.* Tucson: University of Arizona Press.

Whalen, Michael E., and Todd Pitezel. 2015. "Settlement Patterns of the Casas Grandes Area." In *Ancient Paquimé and the Casas Grandes World,* ed. Paul E. Minnis and Michael E. Whalen, 103–125. Tucson: University of Arizona Press. https://doi.org/10.2307/j.ctt183p9cj.9.

Wheat, Joe Ben. 1955. *Mogollon Culture Prior to AD 1000.* Memoirs of the Society for American Archaeology 10. Memoirs of the American Anthropological Association 82. Menasha, WI.

Wheaton, Gene. 2013. "Pitstructures or Brush Huts? An Analysis of 20 Recently Discovered Residential Structures in the Jornada Mogollon Area of Southern New Mexico and West Texas." *Kiva* 79(1):55–81. https://doi.org/10.1179/0023194014Z.0000000014.

White, Devin Alan. 2007. "Transportation, Integration, Facilitation: Prehistoric Trail Networks of the Western Papagueria." PhD dissertation, University of Colorado, Boulder.

White, Devin A., and Sarah L. Surface-Evans. 2012. *Least Cost Path Analysis of Social Landscapes*. Salt Lake City: University of Utah Press.

Whitehead, William, and Conor Flynn. 2016. *Plant Utilization in Southeastern New Mexico: Botany, Ethnobotany, and Archaeology*. Prepared for the Bureau of Land Management-Carlsbad Field Office. Albuquerque, NM: SWCA Environmental Consultants.

Wilcox, David. 1995. "A Processual Model of Charles C. Di Peso's Babocomari Site and Related Systems." In *The Gran Chichimeca: Essays on the Archaeology and Ethnohistory of Northern Mesoamerica*, ed. Jonathan E. Reyman, 281–319. Worldwide Archaeology Series 12. London: Avebury.

Wilcox, David. 2002. "A Geoarchaeological Investigation at Upper Bonito I (LA 84319)." In *Archaeological Variation within the Middle Rio Bonito*, ed. Philip H. Shelley and Kristen E. Wenzel, 31–57. Cultural Resources Series No. 14. Santa Fe: Bureau of Land Management, New Mexico State Office.

Wilcox, David R., Phil C. Wiegand, J. Scott Wood, and Jerry B. Howard. 2008. "Ancient Cultural Interplay of the American Southwest in the Mexican Northwest." *Journal of the Southwest* 50(2):103–206. https://doi.org/10.1353/jsw.2008.0016.

Williams, B. J. 1981. "A Critical Review of Models in Sociobiology." *Annual Review of Anthropology* 10(1):163–192. https://doi.org/10.1146/annurev.an.10.100181.001115.

Willis, Mark D., Tim B. Graves, and John A. Peterson. 2002. *H. G. Foster: Archaeological Investigations near Smuggler's Pass*. El Paso, TX: John A. Peterson and Associates.

Wills, Wirt H. 1988a. *Early Prehistoric Agriculture of the American Southwest*. Santa Fe, NM: School of American Research Press.

Wills, Wirt H. 1988b. "Early Agriculture and Sedentism in the American Southwest: Evidence and Interpretations." *Journal of World Prehistory* 2(4):445–488. https://doi.org/10.1007/BF00976198.

Wills, Wirt H. 1992. "Plant Cultivation and the Evolution of Risk-Prone Economies in the Prehistoric American Southwest." In *Transitions to Agriculture in Prehistory*, ed. A. B. Gebauer and T. D. Price, 153–176. Monographs in World Archaeology No. 4. Madison, WI: Prehistory Press.

Wills, Wirt H. 2001. "Pithouse Architecture and the Economics of Household Formation in the Prehistoric American Southwest." *Human Ecology* 29(4):477–500. https://doi.org/10.1023/A:1013198022095.

Wills, Wirt H., and Bruce B. Huckell. 1994. "Economic Implications of Changing Land-Use Patterns in the Late Archaic." In *Themes in Southwestern Prehistory*, ed. George J. Gumerman, 33–52. Santa Fe, NM: School of American Research Advanced Seminar Series.

Wilson, A. K. 1981. "*Commelinaceae*: A Review of the Distribution, Biology, and Control of the Important Weeds belonging to this Family." *Tropical Pest Management* 27(3):405–418. https://doi.org/10.1080/09670878109413812.

Wilson, C. Dean. 1999a. "Ceramic Dating." In *Archaeology of the Mogollon Highlands: Settlement Systems and Adaptations*, Volume 4, *Ceramics, Miscellaneous Artifacts, Bioarchaeology, Bone Tools, and Faunal Analysis*, ed. Yvonne R. Oakes, and Dorothy A. Zamora, 87–130. Archaeology Notes 232. Santa Fe: Museum of New Mexico, Office of Archaeological Studies.

Wilson, C. Dean. 1999b. "Ceramic Analysis." In *Red Lake Tank: The Excavation of Four Sites East of Roswell, New Mexico*, by Peter Y. Bullock 31–40. Archaeology Notes 250. Santa Fe: Museum of New Mexico, Office of Archaeological Studies.

Wilson, C. Dean. 2004. "Pottery Analysis." In *Fallen Pine Shelter: 3,000 Years of Prehistoric Occupation on the Mescalero Apache Reservation*, by Yvonne R. Oakes, 43–61. Archaeology Notes 325. Santa Fe: Office of Archaeological Studies, Museum of New Mexico.

Wilson, Gilbert L. 1987. *Buffalo Bird Woman's Garden: Agriculture of the Hidatsa Indians*. St. Paul: Minnesota Historical Society Press. (Reprint of the original 1917 book published by the University of Minnesota.)

Winham, R. Peter, and F. A. Calabrese. 1998. "The Middle Missouri Tradition." In *Archaeology on the Great Plains*, ed. Raymond Wood, 269–307. Lawrence: University Press of Kansas.

Winter, Marcus C. 2009. "The Archaeological Household Cluster in the Valley of Oaxaca." In *The Early Mesoamerican Village*, ed. Kent V. Flannery, 25–30. Updated ed. Walnut Creek, CA: Left Coast Press.

Wiseman, Regge N. 1975. "Test Excavations at Three Lincoln Phase Pueblos in the Capitan Mountains Region, Southeastern New Mexico." *Awanyu* 3(1):6–36. Albuquerque: Archaeological Society of New Mexico.

Wiseman, Regge N. 1981a. "Further Investigations at the King Ranch Site, Chaves County, New Mexico." In *Archaeological Essays in Honor of Mark Wimberly*, ed. Michael S. Foster. *The Artifact* 19(3/4):169–198.

Wiseman, Regge N. 1981b. "Playas Incised, Sierra Blanca Variety: A New Pottery Type in Jornada Mogollon." *Transactions of the 16th Regional Archeological Symposium for Southeastern New Mexico and Western Texas*, 21–28. Midland, TX: The Midland Archeological Society.

Wiseman, Regge N. 1982. "The Intervening Years: New Information on Chupadero Black-on-white and Corona Corrugated." *Pottery Southwest* 9(4):5–7.

Wiseman, Regge N. 1985a. "Bison, Fish, and Sedentary Occupations: Startling Data from Rocky Arroyo (LA 25277), Chaves County, New Mexico." In *Views of the Jornada Mogollon*, ed. Colleen M. Beck, 30–32. Contributions in Anthropology No. 12. Portales: Eastern New Mexico University.

Wiseman, Regge N. 1985b. "Proposed Changes in Some of the Ceramic Period Taxonomic Sequences of the Jornada Branch of the Mogollon." *Proceedings of the Third Jornada-Mogollon Conference*, ed. Michael S. Foster and Thomas C. O'Laughlin, 9–17. *The Artifact* 23(1/2):9–17.

Wiseman, Regge N. 1986. *An Initial Study of the Origins of Chupadero Black-on-white*. Technical Note No.2. Albuquerque: Albuquerque Archaeological Society.

Wiseman, Regge N. 1988. "The Continuing Saga of the King Ranch Site (LA 26764): Update and Summary of Findings." In *Fourth Jornada Mogollon Conference (Oct. 1985) Collected Papers*, ed. Meliha S. Duran and Karl W. Laumbach, 223–254. Tularosa, NM: Human Systems Research.

Wiseman, Regge N. 1991. *The Bent Project: Archaeological Excavation at the Bent Site (LA 10835), Otero County, Southern New Mexico*. Las Cruces, NM: COAS Publishing & Research.

Wiseman, Regge N. 1996a. "Socioreligious Architecture in the Sierra Blanca/Roswell Regions of Southeastern New Mexico." In *La Jornada: Papers in Honor of William F. Turney*, ed. Meliha S. Duran and David T. Kirkpatrick. Papers of the Archaeological Society of New Mexico 22:205–224.

Wiseman, Regge N. 1996b. *The Land in Between: Archaic and Formative Occupations along the Upper Rio Hondo of Southeastern New Mexico*. Archaeological Notes No. 125. Santa Fe: Museum of New Mexico, Office of Archaeological Studies.

Wiseman, Regge N. 1997. "A Preliminary Look at Evidence for Late Prehistoric Conflict in Southeastern New Mexico." In *Layers of Time: Essays in Honor of Robert H. Weber*, ed. Meliha S. Duran and David T. Kirkpatrick, 135–146. Papers of the Archaeological Society of New Mexico 23. Albuquerque: Archaeological Society of New Mexico.

Wiseman, Regge N. 2000. *Bob Crosby Draw and River Camp: Contemplating Prehistoric Social Boundaries in Southeastern New Mexico*. Archaeology Notes 235. Santa Fe: Museum of New Mexico, Office of Archaeological Studies.

Wiseman, Regge N. 2002. *The Fox Place: A Late Prehistoric Hunter-Gatherer Pithouse Village near Roswell, New Mexico.* Archaeology Notes 234. Santa Fe: Museum of New Mexico, Office of Archaeological Studies.

Wiseman, Regge N. 2003a. "Punto de los Muertos (LA 116471): A Possible Late Archaic Cemetery in the Northern Trans-Pecos of Southeastern New Mexico." Alpine, TX: Center for Big Bend Studies, Sul Ross State University. *Journal of Big Bend Studies* 15:1–26.

Wiseman, Regge N. 2003b. *The Roswell South Project: Excavations in the Sacramento Plain and the Northern Chihuahuan Desert of Southeastern New Mexico.* Archaeology Notes 237. Santa Fe: Museum of New Mexico, Office of Archaeological Studies.

Wiseman, Regge N. 2004. "The Pottery of the Henderson Site, the 1980–1981 Seasons." In *Life on the Periphery, Economic Change in Late Prehistoric Southeastern New Mexico,* ed. John D. Speth, 67–96. University of Michigan Memoirs, No. 37. Ann Arbor: Museum of Anthropology, University of Michigan.

Wiseman, Regge N. 2007. *On the Relationship between the Largo-Gallina and the Jemez.* Papers of the Archaeological Society of New Mexico 33. Ed. R. N. Wiseman, T. C. O'Laughlin, and C. T. Snow, 201–222. Albuquerque: Archaeological Society of New Mexico.

Wiseman, Regge N. 2010. *Mesita Lagunitas: Prelude to Ethnogenesis?* Papers of the Archaeological Society of New Mexico 36, ed. Emily Brown, K. Armstrong, D. N. Brugge, and C. J. Condie, 165–180. Albuquerque.

Wiseman, Regge N. 2013. *The Prehistoric Social Landscape of the Roswell Oasis and the 1980 Excavations at the Rocky Arroyo Site (LA 25277), Chaves County, New Mexico.* Albuquerque: University of New Mexico, Maxwell Museum Technical Series No. 21.

Wiseman, Regge N. 2014. "Introduction to Mera's 'Ceramic Developments in Southern and Southeastern New Mexico.'" In *Since Mera: The Original Eleven Bulletins with Essays and Opinions Derived from Recent Research,* compiled and edited by Emily J. Brown, Regge N. Wiseman, and Rory P. Gauthier, with contributions by Hayward H. Franklin and Theodore R. Frisbie. Special Publication No. 5. Santa Fe: Archaeological Society of New Mexico.

Wiseman, Regge N. 2016a. "Corona Corrugated, Capitan Variety: A New Manufacture Source for Corona Corrugated." *Pottery Southwest* 32(4):2–7.

Wiseman, Regge N. 2016b. *The Abajo de la Cruz Site (LA 10832) and Late Prehistory in Northern Otero County, New Mexico.* Maxwell Museum Technical Series No. 28. Albuquerque: University of New Mexico, Maxwell Museum of Anthropology.

Wiseman, Regge N. 2017. Lincoln Black-on-Red, a Late Prehistoric Pottery from the Northern Sierra Blanca Region in New Mexico with a Report on Petrography by David V. Hill, Ph.D. *Pottery Southwest* 33(3): 2–24.

Wiseman, Regge N. In prep. "Pruning the Jornada Branch." *Changing Perspectives on the Prehistory of Southeastern New Mexico.*

Wiseman, Regge N., David V. Hill, and Dennis McIntosh. 1999. "The Llano Estacado Pottery Project: A Tabulation Report on the Typological Study." *Transactions of the 34th Regional Archaeological Symposium for Southeastern New Mexico and Western Texas*, 15–60. Midland, TX: Midland Archaeological Society.

Wooldridge, Harold G. 1979. "The Bald Eagle Cache: Implications of an Early Exchange System in the Jornada Region of South-Central New Mexico." Master's thesis, The University of Texas at Austin.

Wu, Xiahong, Chi Zhang, Paul Goldberg, David Cohen, Yan Pan, Trina Arpin, and Ofer Bar-Yosef. 2012. "Early Pottery at 20,000 years ago from Xianrendong Cave, China." *Science* 336(6089):1696–1700. https://doi.org/10.1126/science.1218643.

Wyman, Leland C., and Stuart K. Harris. 1941. *Navajo Indian Medical Ethnobotany.* University of New Mexico Bulletin, Anthropological Series 3(5). Albuquerque: University of New Mexico.

Yerkes, Richard W., Attila Gyucha, and William Parkinson. 2009. "A Multiscalar Approach to Modeling the End of the Neolithic on the Great Hungarian Plain Using Calibrated Radiocarbon Dates." *Radiocarbon* 51(3):1071–1109. https://doi.org/10.1017/S0033822200034123.

York, John C., and William A. Dick-Peddie. 1969. "Vegetational Changes in Southern New Mexico during the Past Hundred Years." In *Arid Lands in Perspective*, ed. W. G. McGuiness and B. J. Goldman, 155–166. Tucson: University of Arizona Press.

Yost, Chad. 2010a. *Phytolith Analysis of Historic Garden Soil Samples from the Weir Farm NHS, Wilton, Connecticut.* Manuscript on file with New South Associates, Stone Mountain, Georgia. PRI Technical Report 10–169.

Yost, Chad. 2010b. "Phytolith Analysis of Soil Samples from Site CeEu–4, Fort Cartier-Roberval, Quebec, Canada." Manuscript on file with Commission de la Capitale Nationale du Québec, Canada. PRI Technical Report 10–75.

Yost, Chad. 2012. "Phytolith and Starch Grain Analysis of a Pit Feature from the Armstrong Bay Pit Site (21SL1134), Lake Vermillion State Park, Minnesota." Manuscript on file with Minnesota Department of Natural Resources, Division of Parks and Trails, St. Paul, Minnesota. PRI Technical Report 12-045.

Yost, Chad. 2015. "Phytolith Analysis of Early Agricultural Period Field Sediments at Las Capas, AZ AA:12:111 (ASM)." In *The Anthropogenic Landscape of Las Capas,* an *Early Agricultural Irrigation Community in Southern Arizona*, ed. James M. Vint and Fred L. Nials, 169–199. Anthropological Papers No. 50. Tucson: Archaeology Southwest.

Yost, Chad, and Linda Scott-Cummings. 2010a. "Phytolith Analysis of Stratigraphic Soil Samples from Stone-Lined Features at the Coctaca Site, Jujuy Province, Argentina." Manuscript on file with Alejandra Korstanje, Universidad Nacional de Tucuman, Argentina. PRI Technical Report 10-49.

Yost, Chad, and Linda Scott-Cummings. 2010b. "Phytolith and Pollen Analysis of Pit Features from the Kolomoki Mounds Site (9ER1), Southwestern Georgia." Manuscript on file with University of Southern Florida, Department of Anthropology, Tampa, Florida. PRI Technical Report 09-160.

Yost, Chad, and Linda Scott-Cummings. 2011. "Phytoliths and Starch." In *Archaeology in Far Southeastern New Mexico: Data Recovery at LA 143755, LA 143758, LA 143759, LA 155888, and LA 155893, along New Mexico Highway 128, Eddy and Lea Counties, New Mexico*, ed. Jim A. Railey, 293–299. Albuquerque, NM: SWCA Environmental Consultants.

Zamora, Dorothy. 2000. *Prehistoric Burned Brush Structures and a Quarry Site along the Carlsbad Relief Route, Eddy County, New Mexico*. Archaeology Notes 203. Santa Fe: Museum of New Mexico, Office of Archaeological Studies.

Zamora, Dorothy, and Yvonne R. Oakes, eds. 2000. *The Angus Site: A Late Prehistoric Settlement along the Rio Bonito, Lincoln County, New Mexico*. Archaeology Notes 276. Santa Fe: Museum of New Mexico, Office of Archaeological Studies.

Zingg, Robert. 2001. *Behind the Mexican Mountains*. Ed. H. Campbell, J. Peterson, and D. Carmichael. Austin: University of Texas Press.

Contributors

Douglas H. M. Boggess

Peter C. Condon

Rafael Cruz Antillón

Linda Scott Cummings

Moira Ernst

Tim Graves

David V. Hill

Nancy A. Kenmotsu

Shaun M. Lynch

A. C. MacWilliams

Mary Malainey

Timothy D. Maxwell

Myles R. Miller

John Montgomery

Jim A. Railey

Thomas R. Rocek

Matt Swanson

Christopher A. Turnbow

Javier Vasquez

Regge N. Wiseman

Chad L. Yost

Architecture, 14–17, 53–54, 55(fig.), 124, 160, 203n2, 211–212, 266, 274–277, 282–283; adobe brick, 180, 182; adobe construction, 36, 67, 180, 192, 212–213; adobe floors, 14, 181, 212; diversity of, 27–39; jacal (wattle and daub), 181–182, 188, 192; orientation of room blocks, 211–213; T-shaped doorways, 213. *See also* Pueblo; Ritual, burning
Artesia, New Mexico, 10
Atalayas, 100. *See also* Shrines
Athapaskan, 193. *See also* Apache
Atlatls, 133, 210

Bald Eagle Cache, 110
Bands. *See* Social organization, bands
Basin-and-range, 7. *See also* Environment
Basin-edge, 33, 66, 87–89, 91, 99–100, 118, 193
Basketry, 93, 238
Beads. *See* Turquoise; Shell
Beans. *See* Agriculture
Bear Grass Draw, 152, 154, 260, 262–263
Bias (data bias), 20, 29, 34–35, 37–38, 73, 117–118, 123, 127, 133, 249, 252, 269, 272
Big Bend, Texas, 203n2
Big Burro Mountains, 79, 82
Biological anthropological analysis, 93, 195–197, 202
Birds, 137, 143, 172, 220
Bison, 17–18, 23, 37, 191, 197, 269–272
Black Mountain phase, 221
Black River, 144, 153, 225–228(fig.), 231–232, 241–242, 247–248
Blackwater Draw, New Mexico, 254
Block Lookout site, 15, 284(fig.)
Bloom Mound, xix, 16, 36, 282
Body decoration, 276
Bonito Canyon, 281
Bonnell site, 15, 35, 279–281
Boot Hill site, 269
Bow and arrow, 12–15, 84, 133, 251, 265
Brand, Donald, 204–208, 213, 215, 222
Broadline Red-on-terracotta, 12
Brownware ceramics, 127, 151–152, 154, 161, 165–168, 170; red-slipped (*see* Jornada Brown). *See also individual type names*
Bureau of land management (BLM), 23, 39n1, 138, 150, 152, 226, 248–250, 252, 265, 272. *See also* Carlsbad Field Office (CFO)

Burial, 61, 82, 93, 181, 196–197, 199, 202, 258. *See also* Biological anthropological analysis
Burned-rock middens (BRMs). *See* Earth ovens
Burro Tanks site, 265

Cabeza de Vaca, 185, 191–192, 197
Caches, 82, 110, 151, 153, 218
Cacti and succulents, 17, 45–52, 62, 65, 69, 71–72, 74, 87, 143, 191, 224–248; agave, 21, 45, 48, 52, 109, 116, 144, 150–151, 154, 224–248n1 (*see also* Alcoholic beverages); as fallback for crop failure, 227–229, 237–238; yucca, 45, 47, 48, 69, 71, 74, 148, 224–248
Calcite, 110
Capitan Mountains, 10, 24, 31, 34–35, 163–164, 167, 169, 171, 274, 279–286. *See also* Sierra Blanca/Capitan/Sacramento Highlands
Capitan phase, 12–13, 26
Capitan New Mexico, 143
Capote ceramics, 181
Caprock Pediment, 259–262, 267
Carlsbad Field Office (CFO), 150, 152, 249–273; Programmatic Agreement, 39, 150, 249–250. *See also* Bureau of Land Management
Carlsbad, New Mexico, 138, 160, 167, 258
Carrizo Mountains, 163
Casa Blanca site, 212–213, 219, 222
Casa Chica site, 206(fig.), 213, 222
Casas Grandes, 56, 77, 118, 165, 178–179, 192, 201–202, 204–223, 270–271; ceramics, 212–217, 221–222 (*see also individual type names*); Medio period, 100, 165, 209(fig.), 211, 214–217, 219–222; Paquimé, 19, 100, 210, 213–222, 246, 270–271, 279; Plainware period, 209–211, 221–222; Rio Casas Grandes, 78–79, 86, 92, 208, 210–211, 217–218; Viejo period, 208, 209(fig.), 210, 214–216
Caves, 78, 80, 93, 109, 116, 238. *See also individual site names*
Cedar Lake, 254(fig.), 260, 262–264
Ceramic period. *See* Formative period
Ceramics, 12, 14, 73, 150–151, 158–173, 185, 196, 251, 274–277; compositional analysis, 99, 109, 110, 120, 123n3, 141, 158–173 (*see also* Petrographic Analysis; Instrumental Neutron Activation Analysis); origins, 84,

151, 154, 160–161; pot breaks, 97, 100, 103, 105, 107, 117; red-on-brown in Viejo period, 208; residue analysis, 87, 117, 119–120, 140–141, 143–146, 149, 153–157, 173 (*see also* Earth ovens; Lipid residue analysis); vessel form, 100–101, 110, 123, 221, 247, 284–285; non-local, 12, 56–58, 112, 133, 137–154, 161–162, 179, 193, 216, 279, 282–283 (*see also* Exchange). *See also individual type names*; Alcoholic beverages; Exchange

Ceremonial, 9; features (*see also* Atalayas; Rock art, Shrines), 16, 23; structure (or room), 15–16, 32, 36, 170, 179, 241, 266–267, 277, 281–286

Ceremonial Cave, 114(fig.), 116, 223n1

Ceremony, 16, 115, 239, 245–246, 256, 264. *See also* Alcoholic beverages; Pilgrimage; Ritual; Sacred

Cerro de Fusiles, 206(fig.), 211

Chaco Canyon, 97, 99, 106

Chalcedony, 195, 202

Cheno-ams/Chenopodium, 47, 49, 63, 68–69, 72, 74, 85, 87, 145–148

Chert, 131, 133–134, 137, 184, 195, 202

Chihuahua, 8, 12, 18, 24, 34, 38, 55–57, 63, 79, 86, 100, 165, 204–223, 229, 270, 279. *See also* Casas Grandes; Jornada, southern

Chihuahua City, 208

Chihuahuan Desert, 66, 90, 180, 207, 221, 225, 228, 237–238, 240

Chinati ceramics, 181

Chupadera Mesa, 118, 151. *See also* Salinas pueblos

Chupadero Black-on-white, 12, 118, 138, 151, 164, 168–171, 181, 183, 217, 241, 265, 279, 281–282, 284–285

Cielo Complex, 203n2

Cimiento wall foundations, 16

Climate, 18, 74, 250, 255–256, 258–259, 264, 273. *See also* Altithermal; Holocene; Little Ice Age; Medieval Warm Period

Clothing, 238, 276

Coahuila, 208

Coe Lake, 15

Colorado Plateau, 7

Colorado River, 7

Commelina. *See* Dayflower

Communal activity, 53, 109, 197, 202, 225, 231–232, 245–246, 264, 281. *See also* Ceremonial

structure; Community; Feasting; Labor; Plaza

Communal room. *See* Ceremonial structure

Community, 34, 99, 177–178, 119–120, 177–178, 229, 245–246. *See also* Social organization

Competition, 59–61, 257–258. *See also* Social organization; Stress; Violence

Concepcion phase, 180–181, 184, 185

Conchos ceramics, 181

Conchos phase, 180–181, 184

Conejo site, 80(fig.), 87

Contact period, 19, 55–56, 154, 180–181, 185–186, 194, 196–197, 199, 202, 224

Contiguous rooms. *See* Pueblo

Convento site, 216

Coral, fossil, 212

Corona Corrugated, 12, 138, 281, 284, 286

Corona phase, xxvi, 12–13, 31, 279

Corralitos Polychrome, 221

Corrugated wares, 165–166, 265. *See also individual type names*

Cotton, 238

Creosote Bush, 72, 102

Crosbyton, Texas, 158, 159(fig.)

Cultural Resource Management (CRM), xxxi, 7, 15, 23, 27–29, 37, 39n1, 152, 168, 205, 249, 252, 272

Dayflower, 21, 138, 145–150, 153–154

Debitage, 124–136, 180, 184, 209

Deer and elk, 11, 143, 155

Delaware Mountains (Texas), 236

Demography, 54–59, 62, 186–190, 194, 202, 233, 247, 253–260, 264, 268, 271–273

Dendroclimatology, 54, 253, 255, 257, 259

Di Peso, C. Charles, 208, 214, 216

Diablo Mountains, 236

Doleman, William H., 78–79, 89–91

Domesticated plants. *See* Agriculture

Doña Ana phase, xx, 12–13, 26, 44, 66, 69–70, 72, 106, 147, 208–212, 215–216, 218; Early, 13, 17, 45, 52, 55–59, 241–243, 209(fig.), 245, 247; Late, 13, 17, 45–47, 54–56, 58(fig.), 71, 74, 99, 209(fig.), 212, 241–243, 245, 247

Dropseed grass, 49, 85, 148. *See also* Grass

Drought, 14, 54, 74, 102, 172, 228, 237–238, 254, 259–260, 262, 264, 267

Dunes. *See* Sand dunes

Dunlap-Salazar site, 35, 80(fig.), 85, 124–136

Eagle Mountains, 236

Earth ovens, 16, 43, 168, 224–248, 257–258, 264, 269; fiber production, 237–238; plant-baking facilities, 17, 22, 44–53, 74, 116, 224–248; pounding stones, 231, 238–240; residue analysis, 232, 257; roasting pit, 67, 82, 209, 214–215, 224, 230, 256, 259, 271. *See also* Stone boiling

Eastern Extension: pueblos, 16, 35, 36, 152, 169–170. *See* also Jornada, Eastern Extension; Ochoa phase villages

Economy, 233, 245, 272–273; political, 119, 229, 245–247. *See also* Agriculture; Exchange; Hunting; Paleobotanical analysis; Subsistence patterns

Ecotones, 78–79, 82, 231–232

El Paso Bichrome, 13, 163, 169, 217, 265; Black, 162, 170, 209(fig.); Red, 162, 170

El Paso Brown, 162–163, 168–170, 209(fig.)

El Paso Brownware, 57–58, 61, 99, 109–112, 118, 162–163, 193, 196, 202, 209(fig.), 212–213, 217, 222, 240–241, 248n3; for fermentation, 240–241, 247. *See also* Alcoholic beverages

El Paso Canyon, 234, 236

El Paso phase, xix-xxi, 99, 106, 245–246, 266–267, 270–271, 281–283, 285–286; definition and developmental sequence, 12–13, 15–17, 54–58, 279; occurrence outside the Western Jornada, 177, 179–185, 197, 199, 202, 208–221; sites of, 232 (*see also individual site names*); subsistence, 36, 45, 66, 68–75, 147, 242, 245–246; variation in, 35–36. *See also* Pueblo

El Paso Polychrome, 162–163, 169–170, 179–181, 183, 185, 203n4, 208–209(fig.), 212–217, 221–223n1; function of, 110, 123, 180, 247, 283; lack of, 192, 196; location where made, 13, 162–163, 170, 179

El Paso, Texas, 8, 29, 43, 60, 151, 160, 163, 166–168, 171, 177, 207, 210, 212, 224, 274, 277. *See also* Hueco Bolson; Tularosa Basin

Elevation, 11, 22, 35, 83, 86, 89, 91, 234, 243–245, 257. *See also* Environment

Elk, 143

Environment, 7–10, 33, 102, 256, 264, 272; anthropogenic, 148–150; basin, 8, 54–55, 86–92, 118; basin-and-range, 7, 10, 29, 55, 57, 66, 207; piñon-juniper forest, 10, 83, 88, 90; plains, 10; ponderosa forest, 10, 83; riverine/

riparian, 8, 29, 34, 37–38, 88–91, 138, 266; semiarid, 26, 83, 86, 243; subalpine, 10, 83. *See also* Basin-edge; Climate; Ecotones

Eolian, 102, 105, 150

Ethnicity, 29–32, 35, 37, 60–61, 215, 274–286; Social Constructionist model of, 275

Exchange, 53, 127, 131, 137, 172, 203n3, 215, 258, 276, 281; center or entrepôts, 211, 271; falloff models, 60; networks of, 101, 108, 111–112, 119, 154, 205, 216–222, 264; of pottery, 13, 57–61, 111–112, 152, 162, 179–180, 196, 207, 214, 216, 219–220, 279; shifting patterns of, 65, 269–272. *See also* Hunter-gatherers, interaction with farmers

Feasting, 109, 112, 114, 225, 231, 244–247, 264

Fiddleneck, 70

Fillmore Pass, 114(fig.), 117–118

Firecracker site, 36

Firewood consumption, 33, 52, 71, 74–75, 237, 243, 247

Fish, 21, 37, 83, 138, 143–144, 150, 153, 155, 191

Forager adaptations, 43

Forest Home site, 82. *See also* New Mexico Route 90 sites

Formative period, 5, 12–19, 43–44, 120, 124–126, 131, 134–135, 152, 154, 204, 211, 214, 221, 244–246; early, 13, 17, 35, 37, 71, 89–91, 124, 134, 225, 251, 253(fig.)–261(fig.), 263(fig.), 271–272; late, 13, 16, 18–19, 36, 66, 75, 88, 99, 124, 134–135, 152–153, 218, 225, 253(fig.), 257, 260–261(fig.), 263(fig.)–273; pre-Formative (*see* Archaic period). *See also individual phase names*

Fort Bliss, xxi, 28–30, 58, 64–76, 97, 100, 105(fig.), 118, 123, 226(fig.)

Fort Sumner, 159, 166

Fourier Transform Infrared Spectroscopy (FTIR). *See* Paleobotanical analysis

Fox Place, 16, 36, 282

Franklin Mountains, 48(fig.), 66, 117–118, 163, 214, 236

Fresnal phase, 66–70, 72–73

Fresnal Shelter, 11, 73, 80(fig.), 88–89, 93, 126(fig.), 129

Fresno projectile points, 181

Fusselman Canyon, 114(fig.), 118

Galisteo Basin, 100

Gallina culture, 276

Jornada, 5, 62; comparisons and relationships among subdivisions of, 10, 17–18, 20, 26–39, 205–210, 216–217, 222, 249, 274–286; definition of concept, 5–10, 24, 26–27, 37, 177, 179, 204, 207–210, 274; Eastern Extension, 5, 9–10, 13, 16, 18, 21, 24, 137–140, 150–154, 158–173, 226, 249–275, 278–279; environment of, 8–10; highlands (*see* Sierra Blanca/Capitan/Sacramento Highlands); lowlands, 27, 77, 86–93 (*see also* individual area names); migration from Western, 177–178, 180, 192–194; progress in research, xvii; subdivision, 6, 8–10, 12–19, 26–27 (*see also individual subdivision names*); Western, 8, 12–15, 19–23, 25n2, 43–63, 64–76, 97–123, 154, 224–248, 266, 270 (*see also* Tularosa Basin); Southern, 10, 11, 13, 18, 22, 24, 37–38, 78–79, 204–223 (*see also* Chihuahua). *See also* Rock-art style
Jornada Brown, 12, 138–143, 150, 153, 163–164, 168, 279, 284, 286
Jornada Red, 165, 168–169
Juárez, 207. *See also* El Paso
Juniper seeds, 49, 68, 70–72. *See also* Environment

Katsina religion, 179
Kelley, J. Charles, 177–181, 203, 208, 221
Kelley, Jane H., viii, 12–13, 25–26, 223, 277–281
King Ranch, 36
Kiva. *See* Ceremonial structure
Kopenbarger site, 185, 188

LA 159879, 80(fig.), 87
LA 163794, 47
LA 164814, 48
LA 169230, 101–102, 105(fig.), 109–113, 121
LA 37155, 52
LA 37156, 48(fig.)
LA 91759, 11
LA 95071, 101–102, 104(fig.), 105(fig.), 109–113, 121
La Junta del Rios, 22, 110, 177–203, 208
La Junta phase, 180–181, 183–185
La Quemada site, 240
Labor, 14, 53–54, 83, 102, 126, 233–237, 241, 245–246, 258
Lagomorphs, 11, 17, 213
Laguna Gatuna. *See* Laguna Plata

Laguna Patos site, 218–219
Laguna Plata, 254(fig.), 260, 262–264, 266–267, 269; site, 266–267, 269
Laguna Tonto, 262
Laguna Toston, 262
Lake Lucero, xxi, 108, 117
Land tenure, 8, 13, 61, 178, 192, 198–199, 202, 245, 247
Language, 197, 276
Las Cruces, New Mexico, 8, 10, 60, 86, 110
Lehmer, Donald J., 5–10, 12, 22, 26, 34, 37–38, 177, 180, 204–205, 207–210, 222, 274, 277–278
Lincoln Black-on-red, 12, 164–165, 241, 282
Lincoln County porphyry belt, 151, 163–172
Lincoln phase, xix, 12–13, 15–16, 31, 36, 143, 278(fig.)–286. *See also* Pueblos
Lipid residue analysis, 140–141, 143, 147, 154–157, 232
Lithic raw materials, 7, 43, 54–57, 184, 195, 202, 210, 210; limestone for earth ovens, 233–237; primary versus secondary, 128–136; sources, 124–137 (*see also* Obsidian)
Little Ice Age, 253(fig.), 265–270
Llano Estacado, 159, 167, 250, 252
Loma Alta site, 181, 182(fig.), 185, 188, 191, 196, 198–200
Loma de Moctezuma, 206(fig.), 213–215, 218–219, 221–222
Loma Paloma site, 189, 182(fig.)
Loma Seca site, 182, 184, 195, 198
Looting, 116, 258, 272
Los Tules site, 37
Lower Stanton Ruin, 126(fig.), 129
Lowlands. *See* Tularosa Basin, Western Jornada
Lubbock, Texas, 158, 159(fig.)

Macrobotanical. *See* Paleobotanical analysis
Madera Quemada pueblo, 15, 111, 184–185, 195
Maguey. *See* Cacti and succulents
Maize. *See* Agriculture
Majolica ceramics, 181
Manos, 147, 195, 197, 202
Maroon Cliffs, 138, 144, 154(fig.), 259–260, 262–265, 267, 269; site, 265, 269
Maya, 153
McAfee Canyon, 234–235
McGregor Range. *See* Fort Bliss

McKenzie Brown, 166
Medieval Warm Period, 255, 259–265,
267–268
Melons. *See* Agriculture
Merchant site, xviii, 16, 18, 152–153, 169–170,
172, 260, 267, 269, 272
Mescal. *See* Alcoholic beverages; Cacti and
succulents
Mescalero: Escarpment, 259, 262, 264, 267;
Plain, 10, 138, 159, 250, 252–256, 259–264, 267,
269. *See also* Apache
Mesilla Bolson (Bolsón), 110, 111, 118, 206, 216
Mesilla phase, xxv, 44–45, 57, 66, 69–73, 147,
232, 241–242; Chihuahuan manifestation
of, 208–211, 215–216, 218, 221; definition and
characterization, 12–13, 17, 37; early agricul-
ture, 87 (*see also* Agriculture); insubstantial
sites, 51, 54
Mesoamerica, 19, 24, 93, 207–208, 220, 223n1,
237
Mesquite: as food, 45, 47, 49, 67–71, 85, 143–144,
148, 172, 191, 268; as fuel, 68, 71–74
Metates, 147, 195
Microbotanical. *See* Paleobotanical
Midden: trash, 46, 80, 82, 85, 87, 147, 160, 212,
255, 265–66. *See also* Earth ovens
Migration, 22, 31, 43, 63, 173, 177–178, 192–194,
201–202, 259, 271
Millington site, 180–184, 190, 192, 194–202
Mimbres, 12, 204, 210, 271; comparison of
the Jornada with, 20, 77, 79, 82–83, 86, 99;
Corrugated, 168–169; interaction with, 20,
118, 207, 215; pottery, 57–63, 165–166, 168–169,
171, 265, 110, 165, 168–169, 171, 215, 265. *See
also* Black Mountain phase
Mobility, 51, 55, 58, 71, 79, 90, 124–136,138,
151–154, 192, 203n1, 215, 222, 252; Browman's
model, 127; logistical, 22, 79, 127, 134–136,
225, 241, 243, 245, 268; reduction in, 23, 32,
38, 89, 92, 124, 195, 197, 257, 259, 264–265,
268; residential, 17, 83, 91, 120, 127, 133–136,
158–160, 171–172, 259; seasonal, 14, 22, 81,
85–86, 89–91, 127, 152, 171–172, 191, 201–202,
212, 225; variation in, 37, 160. *See also*
Hunter-gatherer; Migration; Sedentism
Mogollon, 7, 19, 31, 35, 87. *See also* Jornada
Mojave Desert, 99, 102
Monahans, Texas, 167
Monument Spring site, 267

Morning glory, 49, 51
Mountain mahogany, 71–74, 91–92
Mountain Slope, 91, 225, 250, 252–253, 255, 257,
259–260, 264–266, 268
Multicomponent occupations, 101, 153, 160,
178, 198–199, 202, 212–213, 233, 242, 265–266,
280

Navajo, 153
Neolithic, 124–125, 135, 150–151
New Mexico Route 90 sites, 79–80, 82–83, 85,
88–91
Non-domesticated resources. *See* Wild
resources
Non-site survey. *See* Transect recording units
(TRUs)
North Hills site, 46(fig.), 48(fig.)

O'odham, 116
Oak. *See* Acorns
Obsidian, 195; sources, 7, 43, 54–57, 210
Ochoa Indented Corrugated, 22, 165, 168–172
Ochoa phase, 13, 16; villages, 16
Ocotillo, 72(fig.)
Ojasen site, 46(fig.), 48(fig.), 50
Ojinaga, Chihuahua, 180, 182, 185, 187, 189, 194,
198
Ojo Caliente de Santo site Domingo,
206(fig.), 215
Old Coe Lake, 15, 107–108, 110–111, 114(fig.)
Optimal-foraging theory, 229, 256–257
Organ Mountains, 10, 15, 34, 54, 66, 87, 107,
117–118, 236
Otero Mesa, 10, 34, 52–53(fig.), 115
Overgrazing, 102

Pajarito Plateau, 99–100
Paleobotanical analysis: Fourier Transform
Infrared Spectroscopy (FTIR), 140–141,
143–144, 147–148, 154, 156–157, 232–233;
macrobotanical, 43–51, 62–76, 81–85, 87,
125, 140, 144, 147, 152, 232–233, 257, 268–269;
phytolith, 82, 140, 145–150, 152, 154, 232, 269;
pollen, 47, 82, 87, 140, 144–147, 149, 152, 232,
259, 269; starch, 87, 140, 145–148, 152; ubiquity, 17, 44–49, 62–63, 67–75, 80–89, 125, 149,
232, 240, 251. *See also* Agriculture; Cacti
and succulents; Wild resources; *individual
resource names*

Rio Bonito, 85, 279, 281
Rio Bravo. *See* Rio Grande
Rio Casas Grandes. *See* Casas Grandes
Rio Conchos, 180–181, 184–186, 194, 208
Rio del Carmen, 211
Rio Grande, 8, 31, 37, 54, 57, 59–60, 86–87,
90–93, 166, 168, 270; Classic period, 270; La
Junta area, 177, 181, 185–189, 193–194; Rio
Bravo, 204–205, 207–208, 216
Rio Hondo, 10, 12, 78–80, 82–93, 126(fig.), 128,
131, 135, 160–161, 257, 279
Rio Peñasco, 10, 92, 266, 268, 279. *See also*
Peñasco Bend site
Rio Ruidoso, 83, 85, 279
Rio Santa Mária, 206(fig.), 211, 213
Rio Vista site, 60
Risk, 66, 75, 193, 229. *See also* Agriculture, crop
failure
Ritual, 16, 21, 51, 100–101, 106–110, 114–117, 120,
179, 197, 202, 225, 238–239, 245–246, 283;
altars, 180, 182, 197, 202; burning, 15; objects,
116–117, 223, 283. *See also* Ceremonial;
Pilgrimages; Sacred
Robinson site (Robinson Pueblo), 15, 143
Rock art, xxiii, 101, 109, 116–118, 179, 195, 197,
202, 205, 210, 220–221, 276; Jornada style,
195, 220, 223n1
Rockshelters, 11, 17, 78, 80, 224. *See also indi-*
vidual site names
Rocky Arroyo, 16, 36–37, 282
Roomblocks. *See* Pueblo
Roswell Brown, 166
Roswell, New Mexico, 8–10, 16, 18, 36–37, 161,
166, 250, 268–269, 279, 282
Roswell Oasis, xix, 10, 16, 24, 35–37, 160, 278,
282. *See also* Henderson site

Sacramento Mountains, 10, 34, 43, 47–53, 57,
66, 88–91, 93, 110–111, 116, 225–226(fig.),
231–241, 243–244, 247–248, 274. *See also*
Sierra Blanca/Capitan/Sacramento
Highlands
Sacramento Pueblo, 239, 241
Sacramento River, 234–235
Sacred, 61, 108–109, 114–117, 119, 197. *See also*
Ceremonial; Pilgrimage; Shrines
Salado Polychrome, 217
Salinas de la Unión, 206(fig.), 215
Salinas pueblos, 159(fig.), 164, 241–242, 271

Salt, 100, 107–108, 110, 115, 117, 216, 219; Zuñi
pilgrimages, 100, 107–108, 117. *See also*
Gypsum
Saltbush/greasewood: as fuel, 71–74; seeds, 49
San Andreas Mountains, 34, 236
San Andreas phase, 12–13
San Francisco de la Junta, 182(fig.), 186–187,
194, 198
Sand dunes, 66, 102, 104(fig.), 109, 138, 154,
211, 214; Samalayuca dunefield, 206(fig.),
207, 211
Santa Clara valley, 208
Sayles, Edwin B., 204–205, 207–208, 222
Seasonality, 33–34, 37–38, 78, 83, 90, 256,
264–265
Sedentism, 13–14, 18, 71, 74, 83, 100, 124–125, 135,
150–152, 160, 265. *See also* Mobility; Village
formation
Semisubterranean structures. *See* Pit
structures
Settlement: clusters, 99, 101, 109, 111–115, 118,
120, 178–179, 192, 194; diversity through
time and space, 14–19, 33, 36, 51–53, 73, 93,
106, 120, 250–251, 256, 265, 268, 272–273;
pattern, 11, 14, 28, 51–53, 90, 122, 136, 177–178,
191, 201–202, 232, 255, 265, 268
Shell, 110, 181, 183, 212, 218–220, 258; beads, 218,
258; freshwater, 23, 277, 279–286; marine,
110, 216–219, 240, 279, 285; pendants, 218,
279–280, 282–286. *See also* Shellfish
Shellfish, 37, 83
Shrines, 100–101, 108–109, 114–116, 120. *See*
also Atalayas; Pilgrimage; Sacred
Shumla projectile points, 210
Sierra Blanca Mountains, 10, 34–35, 143,
163, 171, 272–285. *See also* Sierra Blanca/
Capitan/Sacramento Highlands
Sierra Blanca/Capitan/Sacramento
Highlands, 19, 124–136, 158, 236–237, 257,
272–285; archaeological sequence in, 13(fig.),
15; ceramic produced in, 161, 163–168,
170–172; contacts with surrounding regions,
151, 152–154; contrasts with other regions, 17,
34–36, 77–93, 250; definition of, 9(fig.)–10,
30(fig.); sites in the, 124–136, 143. *See*
also individual mountain names; Lincoln
County porphyry belt
Sierra Candelaria, 207
Slate, 110

Slaughter Canyon, New Mexico, 231
Smuggler's Pass, 114(fig.), 118
Snails, 143
Social networks/Social interaction, 60–61, 65, 75, 97–123, 154, 178, 192, 221, 245–247, 250, 256, 273
Social organization, 33–34, 38, 59, 119–120, 178, 194, 197–198, 232, 237–238, 245–247, 256, 264; bands, 61, 256; boundaries, 59–62, 74, 92, 119, 154, 178, 214, 246–237, 256–258, 274–281; descent groups, 61, 258; status, 59, 109, 245–247; tribes, 48–53. *See also* Households; Social networks; Village formation
Sociopolitical evolution, 59, 109, 245–247, 250–251, 256, 273
Sonoran Desert, 7, 99, 101–102, 108, 115, 119
Sotol. *See* Cacti and succulents
South Pecos Brown, 166
Southern Jornada. *See* Jornada, southern
Spanish. *See* Contact period
Spring River, 279
Springs, 87, 100, 107, 109, 144, 172, 207, 256, 262, 264, 266
Squash. *See* Agriculture
Stone boiling, 155, 185. *See also* Earth ovens
Storage, 34, 55(fig.), 71, 80, 111, 191, 202, 229; pits, 12, 17, 51, 73, 81–88, 125–126, 149, 191, 212, 251. *See also* Caches
Stress, 59, 65, 74, 243–247. *See also* Competition; Drought; Violence
Subsistence patterns, 7–19, 43, 44–55, 64–76, 251, 276; diversity, 64–66, 71, 73–75, 268, 271, 275. *See also* Agriculture; Hunting; Paleobotanical analysis; *individual food resource names*
Subterranean structures. *See* Pit structures
Suma, 224, 245–246
Sunflower, 68–69, 71–72, 87
Sunset Archaic site, 12, 84–85
Survey, 23–24, 28, 58, 97–98, 138, 165–166, 205, 207–208, 226–228, 231, 236, 241–242, 249, 265–268, 274; transect recording units (TRUs), 21, 97–98, 101–102, 105–106, 109, 116, 118, 120–123, 234–235. *See also* Bias
Syenite, 141, 143, 163

Tansy mustard, 49, 72(fig.), 85
Tarahumara, 240, 245–247
Taylor Draw site, 165

Terrapin, 143
Territories. *See* Social organization
Tesgüino. *See* Alcoholic beverages
Texas: panhandle, 158–159, 274; trans-Pecos, 7–8, 11, 13–14, 18, 110, 118, 158, 168–169, 196, 225, 228. *See also* El Paso; Fort Bliss; Hueco Bolson
Three Rivers Black-on-White, 181, 183
Three Rivers phase, 12–13
Three Rivers Red-on-terracotta, 12, 164, 168–169, 279, 282
Tobacco. *See* Agriculture
Tornillo Shelter, 11–12, 80(fig.), 86–87
Tower Hill, 138, 145, 150, 152–154, 260, 262–263, 267
Townsend site, 35, 161
Toyah projectile points, 181, 212
Trade. *See* Exchange
Trails, 21, 97–123; Least-cost path (LCP), 106; Line-of-sight analyses, 106
Transect recording units (TRUs). *See* Survey
Tree-ring. *See* Dendroclimatology
Tribes. *See* Social organization, tribes
Tularosa Basin, 9(fig.), 51, 57–60, 92, 206–207, 214, 236; ceramic production area, 162–172, 179–180 (*see also* Ceramics); cited as component of Western Jornada, 13, 29–30(fig.), 64–76, 97–123, 180, 205–206, 274–275, 277, 282, 285–286; residents' external interaction, 152–153, 179–180, 192–196, 201–203n3; site located in, 36, 51, 87, 185 (*see also individual site names*); Tularosa Basin Lowlands, 29, 25n2, 52–53, 87, 92, 152, 154, 179, 249. *See also* Jornada, western
Tularosa Canyon, 89–91
Turquoise, 101, 110, 181, 212–213, 216–220; beads, 181; Orogrande mining district source, 218
Turquoise Ridge site, 80(fig.), 87–88, 91
Turtle/Terrapin, 143, 280, 282

Ubiquity. *See* Paleobotanical analysis, ubiquity
US Route 70 sites, 78–80, 82–93, 128, 131, 135, 161. *See also* Rio Hondo

Villa Ahumada, Chihuahua, 213
Villa Ahumada Polychrome, 181, 183, 213, 217
Villa Ahumada site, 179, 213

Village formation, 33, 124–125, 135, 178, 198–199, 201, 265–266, 272

Violence, 19, 61, 257–258, 271. *See also* Competition; Stress

Walnut, 85, 157, 232

Water, 21, 33, 143–145, 149, 155, 160, 185, 193–194, 201, 240; climate effects on availability of, 256, 259–260, 264, 266; irrigation or management of, 91, 149; precipitation, 86–87; quality, 108, 172, 264; river, 37, 92, 153, 172, 216, 225; runoff, 52, 86–87, 257; transport of, 100–101, 106–116; wells, 254. *See also* Drought; Environment; Playa lakes; Springs

Wattle and daub. *See* Architecture

Well site, 206(fig.), 211–213, 219, 222

White Sands Missile Range, xxii, 108

Wild resources, 17–18, 43, 45–52, 54, 62, 65–75, 82–83, 87–88, 171, 191, 202, 268, 278. *See also individual resource names*

Wildcat Canyon, 48, 234–235

Wood Canyon site, 82, 126(fig.), 128. *See also* New Mexico Route 90 sites

Yucca. *See* Cacti and succulents

Zuñi Salt Lake, New Mexico, 100

www.ingramcontent.com/pod-product-compliance
Lightning Source LLC
Chambersburg PA
CBHW070608030426
42337CB00020B/3713